Patrick Duncan

Patrick Duncan

SOUTH AFRICAN AND PAN-AFRICAN

C. J. DRIVER

Foreword by
Anthony Sampson

DAVID PHILIP
CAPE TOWN

JAMES CURREY
OXFORD

ISBN 978 0 85255 773 0 (James Currey paper)

Transferred to digital printing

James Currey
www.jamescurrey.com
is an imprint of Boydell & Brewer Ltd
PO Box 9, Woodbridge, Suffolk IP12 3DF, UK
and of Boydell & Brewer Inc.
668 Mt Hope Avenue, Rochester, NY 14620, USA
www.boydellandbrewer.com

David Philip Publishers
An imprint of New Africa Books (Pty) Ltd.
P.O. Box 46962
Glosderry 7702
Cape Town,
South Africa

A CIP record for this title is available
from the British Library

This publication is printed on acid-free paper

For many friends
but mostly for Randolph Vigne
because Pat wrote to you once:
'generosity, all forms of it,
time, affection, money, has
been your hallmark'.

CONTENTS

LIST OF ILLUSTRATIONS

FOREWORD by Anthony Sampson

The name of Patrick Duncan still has a special resonance twenty years after this book was published, and fifty years after he first became politically involved in South Africa. His story is all the more interesting since the peaceful revolution of 1994, because it strikes an individual, discordant note among the conventional choruses of praise and blame. In histories of the liberation struggle Duncan will always appear as a maverick, pursuing changing policies which cut across party loyalties. But his stubborn independence of mind and passionate convictions made his development all the more interesting. He was an intellectual who became a man of action, a romantic who was determined to act out his ideals, and he was always questioning and challenging the professional politicians. His colourful personality, with his integrity and originality, provides a lively sub-plot and a commentary on history which makes this book a valuable addition to the literature of South Africa's liberation.

Duncan was always impossible to pigeon-hole. When I first knew him in the early 'fifties, when I was editing *Drum* magazine in Johannesburg and he had just resigned from the British colonial service, I saw him as a generous and stimulating friend rather than as a politician. I loved to argue with him, and admired his well-stocked intellectual mind, but I was often baffled by his contradictions. He seemed sometimes to belong to an earlier tradition of aristocratic British crusaders taking up African causes; a son of the Anglo-South African Establishment. He had been private secretary to the British High Commissioner, and with his distinguished background, his charm and persuasive powers he retained influence in surprising places, including British conservative politicians and the prime minister Harold Macmillan. But he despised conservative policy towards South Africa, and was already moving towards a revolutionary position, meeting African leaders on equal terms. He could move easily between different worlds, while preserving his detachment. He was on friendly terms with prominent Afrikaners – he once took me to dinner with the young tobacco tycoon Anton Rupert – but he was appalled by the concept of *apartheid*. He became a very public supporter of the ANC, but he was outspokenly anti-communist. He was an admirer of Mahatma Gandhi and a friend of his son Manilal, but he eventually supported violence and helped to buy weapons. He was committed to a multi-racial South Africa, but he forsook the ANC for the more nationalist PAC. But his contradictions were part of his personal development and constant quest for the truth: as he weaved in and out of political parties and organisations he challenged others to define their attitudes and reasoning, and threw a new light on old dogmas. He might infuriate his former political allies and opponents, but he could still command their affection and respect, as he respected them.

The mutual respect marked his relations with Nelson Mandela who was also developing his own political thoughts and evolving his ideas through the.'fifties and 'sixties. The two men came together in 1952, when Duncan made his boldest commitment: to join the Defiance Campaign which Mandela was organising. It was a heroic gesture, to demonstrate that the ANC's protests were supported by people beyond the immediate circle of the Congress movement and its communist sympathisers, and to show that liberal whites were prepared to share black sacrifices and it earned Mandela's respect and gratitude. Duncan still had reservations about Mandela's policies, particularly his alliance with the Communists, but when Mandela was on the run in 1961 he twice visited Duncan – who was editing the fortnightly magazine *Contact* which he owned, and which had been critical of the ANC's communist links – to argue with him about his anti-communist position. After Mandela argued strongly with him, Duncan agreed that his criticisms were unjustified, and agreed that *Contact* should support the ANC's plan for a National Convention. Mandela always remembered and respected the support of a friend in need, despite his later defection to the PAC. Duncan's original identification with the Defiance Campaign retained its symbolism, but it would take over thirty years for the ANC to enjoy broader support from whites and westerners. How differently might South African history have evolved, if Duncan's defiance had been followed by many other liberal whites, as black leaders like Nelson Mandela and Yusuf Cachalia had hoped?

Duncan was always a political loner with no fixed constituency or following. His influence stemmed less from party organisations than from his radiant personality and his genius for friendship. With his warmth and generosity he had the rare gift of making other people feel better and more important than they thought they were, while his passionate arguments could often persuade sceptical critics to agree with him. But his individual development and changing ideas made it hard for others to keep up with him.

He lived in a world of ideas which ruled his life, which gave such interest to his personal odyssey, as described in this book. At a time when political life everywhere has become more circumscribed, more preoccupied with vote-counting, compromises and fixes than with ideals and issues, his life-story seems to belong to a vanished age, when intellectuals believed they could help to create an ideal new world, and worked out their own visions of the future. He sometimes reminded me of the Russian 'Romantic Exiles' of the late nineteenth century who endlessly exchanged their alternative views of the new Russia. But Duncan was always a product of Africa. He shared the commitment to the new nation of South Africa, which he inherited from his father the Governor-General, and the rest of Lord Milner's Kindergarten who had supervised the reconstruction of the war-torn country. But he saw South Africa with quite different eyes, for he was always mindful of the black majority, ever since he found friends among his father's black servants who taught him their language. Like other remarkable white contemporaries – like Bram Fischer, Trevor Huddleston or Beyers Naude – he embarked on a personal and lonely journey of discovery about his own country, and was impelled by his own experiences to work out a way to combat the horrors and injustices of *apartheid*. But unlike those three he remained outside the framework of a church or a party, and followed his conscience in directions which could be confusing, but were always dictated by his own integrity and humanity.

PREFACE by C. J. Driver
1980 *First Edition*

Patrick Duncan was an important figure in southern African politics in the crucial years between 1948 and the early 1960s when the main opposition to *apartheid* and white domination moved from peaceful protest to violent demonstration to guerilla warfare. He was the eldest son of a South African Cabinet minister who afterwards became Governor-General, and on the day of his birth one of his father's colleagues sent a telegram welcoming the birth 'of a future Prime Minister'. Yet, despite the privilege he was born to and educated in, he found the 'great aim' of his life in opposing *apartheid*, and went several times to jail for his political actions. He never held any material power in politics; yet for many years he saw himself as likely to be the first prime minister of a non-racial South Africa – and he talked as an equal to prime ministers and presidents. By the end of his life, he had given up all pretensions to holding any other than moral power and was one of the few white men who proposed violent opposition to *apartheid*. Yet it was the influence of Gandhi's satyagraha (passive resistance or 'soul-force') which informed many of his earlier political decisions and beliefs, including his founding and editing of the liberal newspaper, *Contact*. His influence on the Pan-Africanists' Anti-Pass Campaign in the Cape in 1960, when 30000 Africans marched to the centre of Cape Town to demand arrest for civil disobedience, was that of a non-violent liberal; but within three years he was trying to recruit saboteurs to send into South Africa and, within four, trying to raise money to buy arms for guerillas.

In short, his biography is, in many ways, a commentary on the political history of a sub-continent in which guerilla warfare has become endemic.

Though there is a fascination in anyone's life, at least when one can trace in detail the processes of his change and the patterns of his development, one chooses to write or to read the biography of a particular man, not of any man. The one thing of which everyone who knew Patrick Duncan is sure is that he was typical of no one but himself. A-typicality is itself part of my reason for writing his biography, for Patrick Duncan was in some ways a very odd man. Inevitably, his biography is also a political history of his times, particularly of southern Africa; but the main purpose of this biography was not to write a political history, but to write the story of a life, to explore the background, thoughts, prejudices, loves, imagination, change and development of a particular man. It is not hagiography; what one observes is something which goes beyond praise or blame. The man's dead; there's no changing him now – one may change only the way one looks at him.

To some, Patrick Duncan was simply a traitor. Others, who loved or admired him personally but who hated the way he developed politically, thought him a brave fool. Even those who accepted some of his political views could find him (in the words of one of them) a 'lovable ass'. A close political acquaintance called him 'a saint – with all the saint's usual failings'. Even in relation to his political views alone, abstracted from his personality, there is considerable conflict. Was he radical? Reactionary? A reactionary radical? A populist? A white African? A liberal? A conservative in everything but attitude to race? An imperialist? A colonial aristocrat who never really gave up his allegiance to Britain and his own class? A political maverick? Did his anti-communism really make him 'the McCarthy of South Africa', as one left-wing newspaper called him? Was he what a former colleague of his in the Colonial Service has called him – a 'damn nuisance'? Or did he contribute significantly to the independence of Lesotho? In a newspaper profile written soon after his joining the Pan-Africanist Congress in 1963 was announced, he was called 'a riddle to friends and foes alike – even, perhaps, to himself'. The profile had as headline, 'Patrick Duncan – the gentle gunman?' The query is typical. Was he a riddle, or was there some consistency which underlay all his changes and development? May it even be called development?

If to this political range one adds the complexity of reactions to his personality, one has a marsh to walk through. Was he dominated by his mother? Did her Christian Science stay a permanent part of his mind, even when he had rejected it intellectually? Was the permanently lame Patrick jealous of his brilliant younger brother, Andrew the airman? Did he spend much of his life trying to emulate or surpass his famous father? Was he a scientist manque whose intellectual development was forced into the wrong channels by his father's classical scholarship? Was he a tremendously warm and loving man? Socially hidebound by the conventions of his class? Essentially apart from other men as a result of his lameness?

The list of questions could easily be extended farther; and one needs to know that these are not the idle questions of a tentative biographer, but are positively based on the reactions to Patrick Duncan of friends, acquaintances and enemies – even members of his own family offer widely differing interpretations of his personality. Yet the more one tries to make sense of an extraordinarily various man of extraordinary passion, imagination, 'giddy traverses' and unflinching consistency, large mistakes and larger courage, the more complexity is revealed. Part of the reason for this biography is simply to make sense of Patrick Duncan's variety.

From the moment I first suggested I might write his biography, my own main motive has been to explore my hunch that, in some very important ways, Patrick Duncan fitted a role as a modern tragic hero. The line which separates the 'brave fool' from the 'tragic hero' has always been narrow. One thing, however, is certain: tragic heroes may be serious, but they aren't sad, for they seem always to have a kind of exultant gaiety, an exuberance at the possibilities of life, which makes even their deaths seem a necessary fulfilment. The theme of the tragic hero informs the whole biography – not, I hope, as Procrustes tried to fit travellers to his peculiar bed – but as one way of making sense of the life and death of a very charming and very complicated man.

C. J. DRIVER

PREFACE by C. J. Driver
First Paperback Edition 2000

I can't remember now what lonely impulse took me – aged eighteen or nineteen – to Sea Point to volunteer to help in the probably forlorn attempt by the Liberal Party to get Pat Duncan elected to the Provincial Council. I had (it seems) always been a non-racialist: during my early childhood, my grandparents had entertained black clergy and their wives to Sunday morning breakfast in the Kroonstad Rectory, and I had been taught to treat them exactly as any other visiting clergy. I had had a brief encounter with the Immoderate Left (Kipling's category) at the University of Cape Town, and had been repelled by their lack of humour and their Stalinism. I was at the meeting in Sea Point Town Hall when Patrick Duncan was asked: 'Would the Liberal Party allow black people to use the Sea Point swimming pool?' A politician would have answered: 'I don't care who uses the pool, as long as he is clean.' Pat didn't; 'Yes,' he said – and most of those who might have been persuaded to vote for him (he was the son of the first South African Governor-General, after all) went back to the United Party. However, I had found a hero: an honest politician, a patrician (Winchester, Balliol) who could have had all the comforts of white civilisation but who chose otherwise, a passionate espouser of what were never lost causes but which seemed quite chancy in those days.

In that election, I accompanied his sister-in-law, Pam Duncan, as she drove to collect old ladies too frail to walk to a polling booth, and then I fended off the United Party electoral agents who tried to suborn 'our voters' with horrid tales of the black peril. My size – that of a typical second-row forward – helped; South African politics have always been quite rough. Later, I did some writing for *Contact*, the newspaper Pat founded and edited; and, when I was in central Cape Town, I would often call at the *Contact* office to see Pat and his colleagues, and to admire the map of Africa with the steadily downward sweep of the black as colonial regimes were dismantled.

I was never a very active member of the Liberal Party except to an extent at election times; I was too involved in student politics, and indeed put my membership of the Liberal Party in abeyance when I was elected President of the National Union of South African Students in 1963. Some of the reservations I felt were the same as Pat Duncan's, though in those days I thought I was a democratic socialist or social democrat (anti-communist, of course). *Contact* was my main point of contact with him, particularly when I became, under Neville Rubin's tutelage, Editor of the very lively and occasionally even libellous newspaper of the University of Cape Town, *Varsity*. At least once I was taken to a party at the Duncans' house in Retreat, with its swimming-pool in the shape of Africa, and there I met Cynthia, gallantly coping with the invasion of her home by a crowd of people not all of whom were there for the politics.

Then Pat fled the country and – as was the way of things in the South Africa of those days – became more or less a non-person, unmentionable by name in the press, and unquotable. We heard rumours, no more: I met him briefly in New York, at the United Nations building, in 1963, where I was fund-raising for a NUSAS project in the Transkei; I was travelling on a shoe-string budget, and remember with gratitude that he insisted on buying me a meal, generous in its helpings even by American standards. After I too had gone into exile in 1964, we wrote to each other occasionally; but I had made a decision that, since I wasn't going to be allowed to make my adult life in South Africa, I would get on with what I regarded as a real life outside, rather than allowing myself to be a permanent exile. Old friends were different, of course, and in 1967 Randolph Vigne told me Pat was desperately ill in hospital in London, so we went together to see him – and found a man so passionately engaged with life and politics that dying seemed out of the question. A few months later, I found myself at his memorial service at St Martin's-in-the-Field, sharing a pew with Colin Legum; and, half an hour later, I proposed marriage to a young Englishwoman in the Embankment gardens.

Six or seven years later, after I had left Housemastering in Sevenoaks School and was Director of Sixth Form Studies in Matthew Humberstone Comprehensive School in South Humberside (Cleethorpes, to be precise), I was visiting Christopher R. Hill, an old friend from London by then teaching Politics in the University of York and running the Centre for Southern African Studies. He told me that Cynthia, after her marriage to a member of the Council of the University of York, had given all the Duncan papers to the University of York. Cynthia had asked Christopher to help her find someone to write a biography of Pat. Did I know anyone who might be interested? I had by then published four novels, and was looking for a subject for my next book. Had Christopher thought of me, I wondered. Clearly, he hadn't; but he would talk to Cynthia, he said.

And so, in 1976, I found myself with a term's sabbatical from my school – the Easter holiday and the summer holiday on each side giving me six months *in toto* – an office in the CSAS, an informal contract with my publisher of those days, a research fellowship, a grant and a research assistant. My family moved to the University with me, on the understanding that, no matter what hours I worked, there would be no complaint. For two months I read whatever the research assistant put in front of me – and for four months I wrote sometimes for sixteen hours a day: exhausting and exhilarating, one of the two spells in my adult life in which I have been able to give myself over entirely to being a writer.

Without the research assistant the book couldn't have been done at all. He supplied the scholarship I didn't have; I had a sense of the broad sweep of the times, and some knowledge of the characters, but no dates and few facts. Tom Lodge supplied lists of times, places, people – and briefing notes on the history. The papers were exhaustive: for many months of Pat's life, one could say precisely what he did each day, whom he saw, what he thought about them, what they said to each other. There was even the note Pat wrote Cynthia on their wedding morning. There were no more than one or two mysteries to be considered: the real problem was to condense the mass of information into the significant detail. Where there were doubts, there were people to consult – and they had opinions galore, because Pat's life seemed to attract amateur psychologists who wanted to explain to me what had made him tick. Alan Paton got quite upset that I didn't make use of his particular theories.

With a first draft done, we had the huge setback of my publishers not liking the book: something entirely different was required, less scholarly, more adventurous, more a novel than a 'life and times' starting perhaps with Pat's limping into Sophiatown at the head of the Defiance Campaign. We had worked too hard and too passionately to compromise; and fortunately James Currey, then at Heinemann Educational Books, was prepared to publish the book as it stood. We needed an index; I did one of names, but by then I was running a large international secondary school in Hong Kong and there was no way I had time to do a general index. Randolph Vigne – always a valiant supporter of the project – said he would do it. The maps were drawn by Tom Lodge; the photographs were chosen; and in 1980 the book came out.

That it should be thought worth re-publishing twenty years later pleases me more than I can say, partly for reasons Anthony Sampson mentions, partly because Pat Duncan was a magnificently brave man, in life and in dying. It is also fascinating to me, as a career-schoolmaster, to see what his children have done with their lives, and how they have, in their different ways, fulfilled so much his dreams of what he wanted to do: Patrick, a scientist working on ecology in France; Alexander, an agricultural economist, specialising in food production in sub-Saharan Africa; Ann, a development economist in the World Bank whose responsibilities have included South Africa and Lesotho; and Emma, a celebrated international journalist – all Pat's passions flowering in his children despite his early death.

C. J. DRIVER

ACKNOWLEDGEMENTS

I have many people to thank for help in writing this book. A primary debt is to Cynthia, Patrick Duncan's widow, now Lady Bryan, who answered many questions, some necessarily impertinent, and who allowed me access to all Patrick Duncan's and her own papers and letters, and freedom to use them as I saw fit. The Duncan children Patrick, Alex, Ann and Emma – have helped, too, as have John and Pam Duncan, Deborah Cowen (*née* Duncan), and Margaret Nedoma, Patrick Duncan's cousin. My debt to all of these will, I think, be obvious from the text.

Some two hundred people have been consulted in the course of research for this book; some are named in the text, some in footnotes, but I am grateful to all, whether they are named or not. Those I give here are only some I would like to name, but to these I have especial reason for gratitude: Randolph Vigne; Leslie and Neville Rubin; Peter Hjul; Adam Hochschild; Cyril Dunn (on whose unpublished interview with Duncan in 1955 I have drawn extensively); Albie Sachs (who is more critical of Duncan than I can agree with); Matthew Nkoana and other members of the PanAfricanist Congress; Elizabeth Feiling, especially for help with the period 1942–3; Alan Paton, Peter Brown, and other members of the now dissolved Liberal Party of South Africa; Sir Brian Marwick; the Hon. David Astor; Hans Schmoller; Professor Richard Hare; Morrice James (Lord St Bride's); and Fred Inglis, that most uncommon reader. I have deliberately gone out of my way to consult those I knew regarded Duncan as a political imbecile (though even the most critical seem to find much to admire); even when I have made judgements very different from theirs, I have not ignored them. I am grateful, too, to all who have allowed me to quote from letters they wrote to Duncan, or from personal papers.

Since many of those consulted or mentioned are still actively engaged in southern African politics, I have on occasion not named names or specified particular involvement; one serves other masters than Truth, for all that he is Hydra-headed anyway. Otherwise, I have omitted nothing which I regard as significant.

The Patrick Duncan papers now on indefinite loan to the University of York are described in the Notes at the end of the book; they include diaries, an unpublished autobiography, thousands of letters (for Duncan kept copies of almost every letter he wrote, and filed almost everything he received), press cuttings, documents, many of the records of *Contact* (the newspaper he founded and edited until 1962), speeches, articles, drafts of articles, memoranda, photographs, and more and more. A prime source of this book has been Patrick Duncan's unfinished autobiography, which he began in jail in 1960 and added notes to in 1964; it is sometimes inaccurate (small wonder, given where it was written) but never useless. Part of the point of this biography has lain in the putting together, sorting and cataloguing of these papers; there is now a detailed catalogue of them in the J. B. Morrell Library at the University of York. Documents from other libraries too have been consulted, and I am grateful for help given my research assistant by librarians of the Centre for International and Area Studies, the Institute of Commonwealth Studies, the Royal Institute of International Affairs, *The Times*, the Public Record Office, the Africa Bureau, Somerset House, the South African Institute of Race Relations, and the Maseru Diocesan Centre Archives. Thanks are due to the Jagger Library at Cape Town University, for permission to quote from the papers of Sir Patrick Duncan, now in the possession of that library, and to the librarians there for their efficient help.

Much of the work on the biography was done during a term's leave of absence from Matthew Humberstone Comprehensive School, and I am grateful to the Director of Education and the Education Committee of Humberside for allowing me a term's sabbatical, and to the Headmaster and Governors of Matthew Humberstone School for permitting me to be away from school. I thank all my colleagues on the staff who did my job for me that term.

I am grateful to the University of York, and particularly to the Board of Studies and the Director of the Centre for Southern African Studies, for appointing me to a Research Fellowship for the summer of 1976 and for constant help and encouragement in writing this biography. Christopher R. Hill, the Director of CSAS, is in many ways 'onlie begetter' of this book; my gratitude to him extends well beyond this book, however, since he has been the best of friends for many years.

My greatest debt is to Tom Lodge, my research assistant; that I have not named him as co-author is less to do with what he has contributed to this book than my insistence on taking sole responsibility for it. His industry, intelligence, imagination, patience and detailed knowledge have been such that I could not have written the book without him.

ABBREVIATIONS

ANC   African National Congress
ARM   African Resistance Movement
BAC   Basutoland African Congress
BCP   Basutoland Congress Party
BNP   Basutoland National Party
CCSA   Comite Chretien de Service en Algerie
COD   Congress of Democrats
CP   Communist Party
FLN   National Liberation Front (Algeria)
FOFATUSA   Federation of Free African Trade Unions of South Africa
FRELIMO   Mozambique Liberation Front (Frente de Libertação de Moçambique)
GRAE   Angolan Revolutionary Government in Exile (Governo Revolucionário de Angola no Exilio)
LP   Liberal Party (of South Africa)
MPAIAC   Canaries' Liberation Movement
MPLA   Popular Movement for the Liberation of Angola (Movimento Popular de Libertaçao de Angola)
NCCC   National Council of the Churches of Christ
OAS   Organisation de l'Armée Secrète (Algeria)
OAU   Organization of African Unity
OFS   Orange Free State
PAC   Pan-Africanist Congress
PIDE   International Police for the Defence of the State (Policia Internacional e de Defesa do Estado)
SA   South Africa
SACPO   South African Coloured People's Organization
SACTU   South African Congress of Trade Unions
SAIC   South African Indian Congress
SPP   Swaziland Progressive Party
SWA   South-West Africa (Namibia)
SWANU   South-West African National Union
SWAPO   South-West Africa People's Organization
UAR   United Arab Republic
UP   United Party
UPA   Union of the Populations of Angola (Uniao das Populações de Angola)

LIST OF MAPS

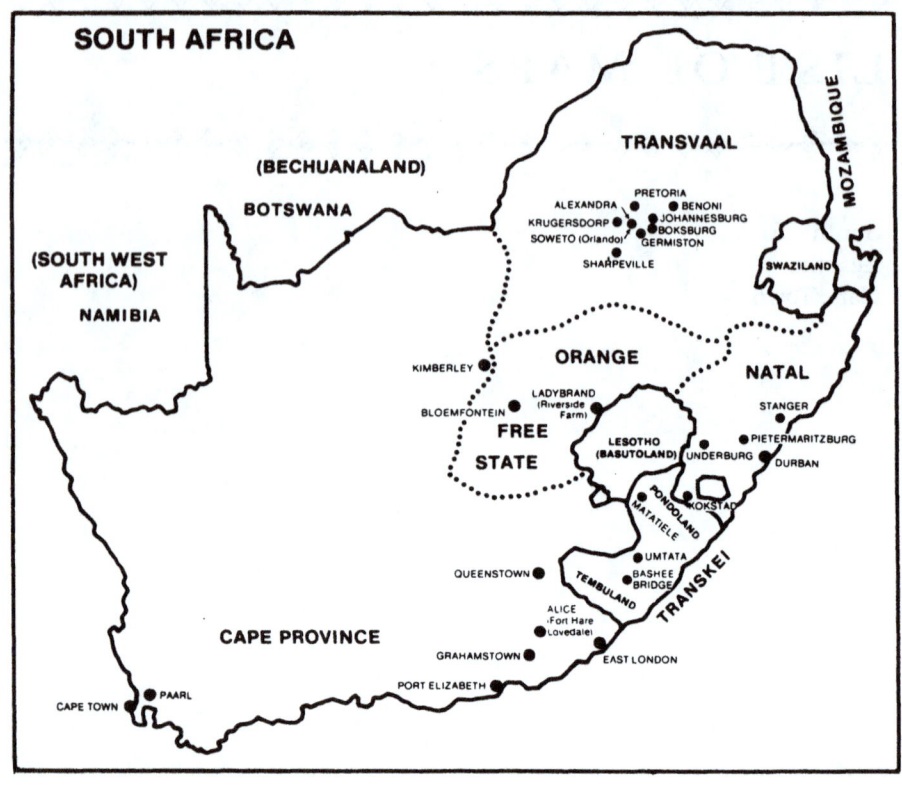

SOUTH AFRICA

(SOUTH WEST AFRICA)
NAMIBIA

(BECHUANALAND)
BOTSWANA

TRANSVAAL

MOZAMBIQUE

ALEXANDRA   PRETORIA
KRUGERSDORP   ● BENONI
● JOHANNESBURG
SOWETO (Orlando)   BOKSBURG
GERMISTON
SHARPEVILLE

SWAZILAND

KIMBERLEY
ORANGE
BLOEMFONTEIN   LADYBRAND
(Riverside
Farm)
FREE
STATE
LESOTHO
(BASUTOLAND)

NATAL
STANGER
● PIETERMARITZBURG
UNDERBURG
● DURBAN
KOKSTAD
PONDOLAND
MATATIELE
UMTATA
QUEENSTOWN   BASHEE
BRIDGE
TEMBULAND
TRANSKEI
ALICE
(Fort Hare
Lovedale)
GRAHAMSTOWN
EAST LONDON
PORT ELIZABETH
CAPE PROVINCE
CAPE TOWN   PAARL

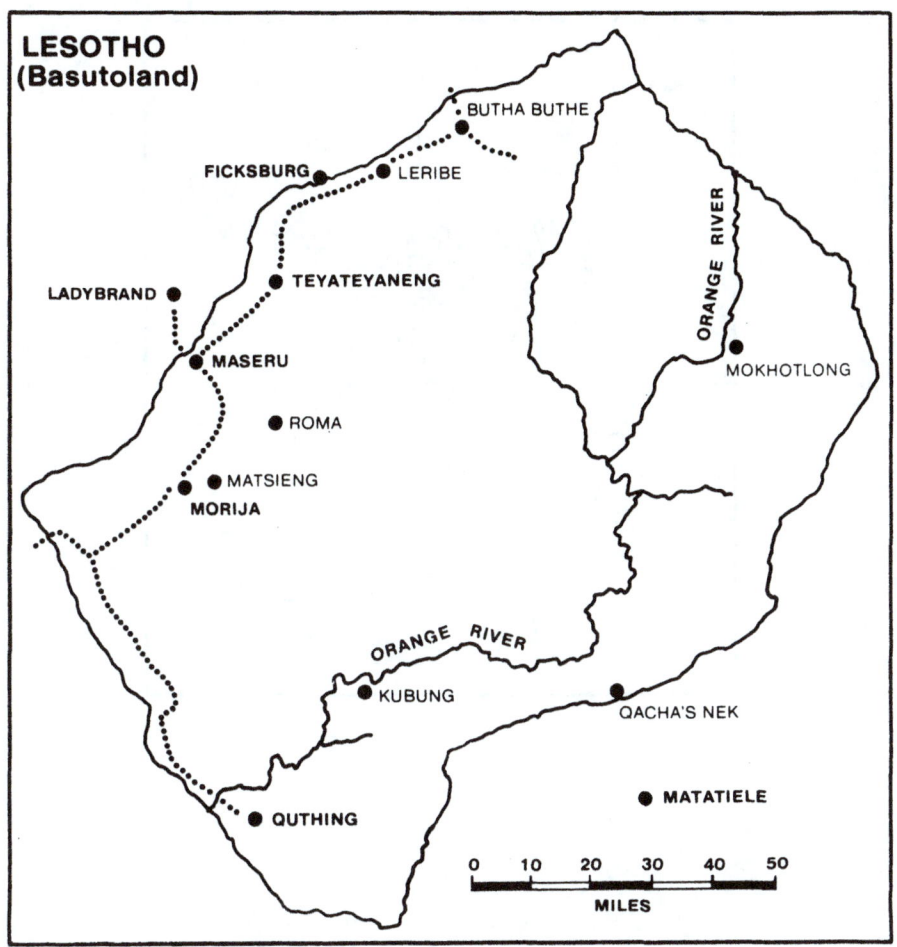

LESOTHO
(Basutoland)

BUTHA BUTHE

FICKSBURG LERIBE

ORANGE RIVER

TEYATEYANENG

LADYBRAND

MOKHOTLONG

MASERU

ROMA

MATSIENG

MORIJA

ORANGE RIVER

KUBUNG

QACHA'S NEK

MATATIELE

QUTHING

0   10   20   30   40   50
MILES

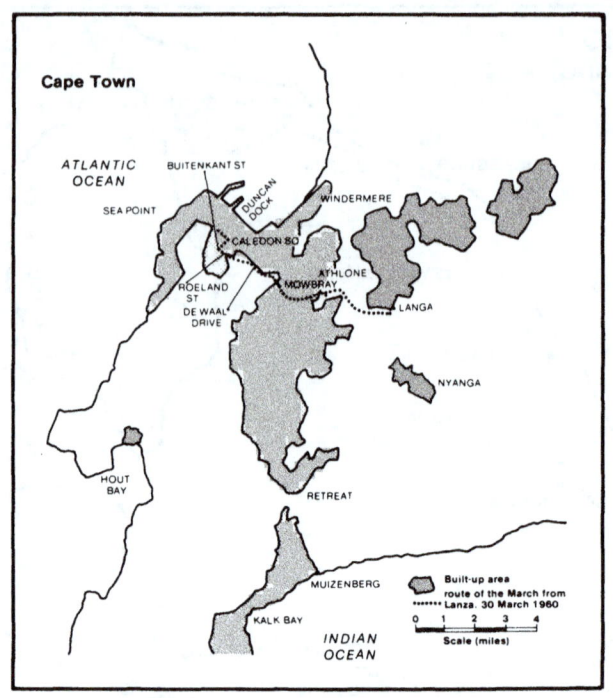

Cape Town

ATLANTIC
OCEAN

BUITENKANT ST

DUNCAN
DOCK

WINDERMERE

SEA POINT

CALEDON SQ

ATHLONE
MOWBRAY

ROELAND
ST
DE WAAL
DRIVE

LANGA

NYANGA

HOUT
BAY

RETREAT

Built-up area
route of the March from
••••••• Lanza. 30 March 1960

MUIZENBERG

0   1   2   3   4
Scale (miles)

KALK BAY

INDIAN
OCEAN

*We are not looking for a new universal meaning
of tragedy. We are looking for the structure
of tragedy in our own culture.*

Raymond Williams

*... this contradictory man, torn apart, conscious
henceforth of human and historical ambiguity, is
the essentially tragic man ....*

Albert Camus

BOOK ONE

Growing

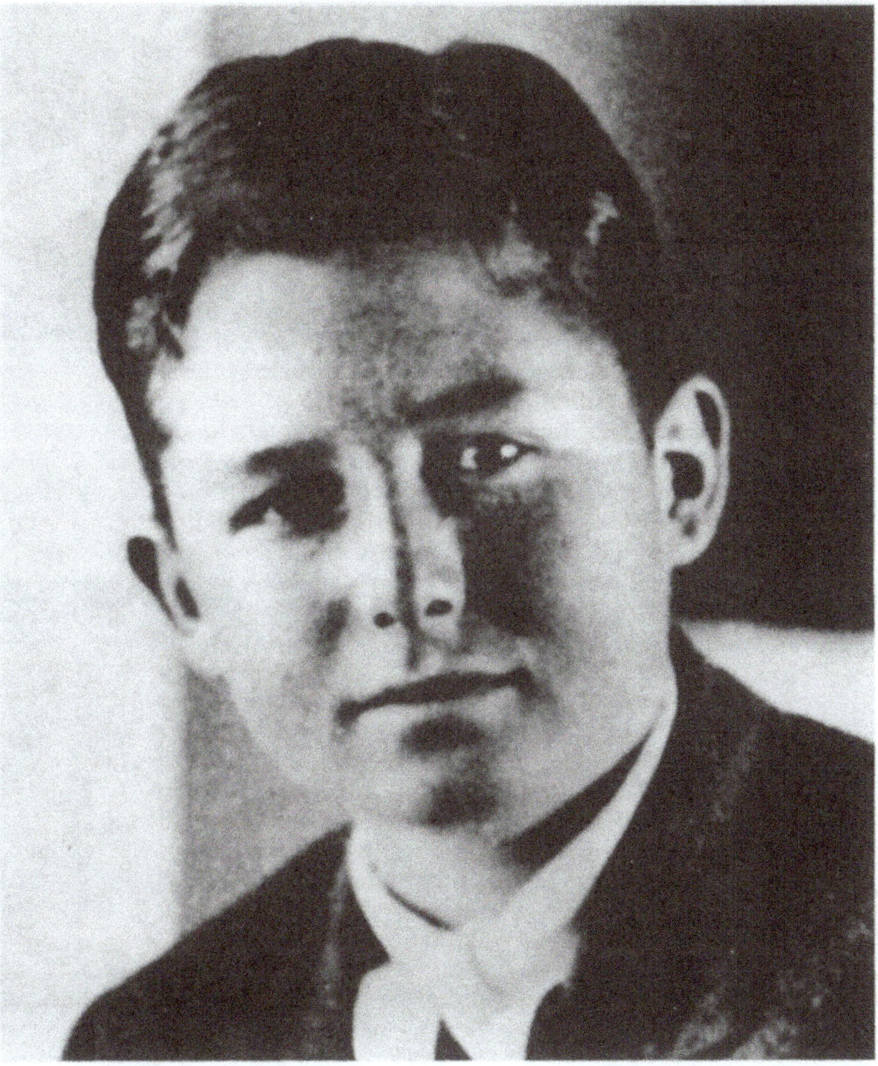

1   Pat Duncan, taken shortly before going to Winchester

2   *Drill at Arbeitslager, Konigsberg, July 1938*

3   *Pat Duncan (right) in Arbeitslager uniform, Konigsberg, July 1938*

CHAPTER 1

1918–34
'If there was no error in the world, we wouldn't need a Bible book, would we?'[1]

What most people remember first about Patrick Duncan physically is the contrast between his blue eyes – 'vivid' and 'flashing' are the most common descriptions – and his high colour; his habit of calling white South Africans 'pinks' rather than 'whites' to distinguish them from 'blacks' and 'browns' was a private joke as well as a political one. A jutting nose relieved him of any danger of being called handsome; but it was a lively and attractive face, incapable of concealing pleasure or anger. Exuberant energy made it hard for him to sit still in a chair to listen, yet he had an ability to fix his attention on whomever he listened or talked to, whether small child or prime minister; and, if he interrupted, it would be to reach behind him to find a book to look something up in – often an encyclopedia since that appealed to his kind of mind – or to say 'Gosh! Isn't it wonderful!' or 'Gosh! How marvellous!'

'Peter Pan!' said some when they heard him say 'Gosh!' or watched him climb to the top of an enormous tree with the son of a friend. There was an element of that, too, and children blessed him for it, while serious-minded adults suspected that his enthusiasm for a political idea might be equally childish. 'Energy' and 'enthusiasm' are the words which people use again and again to describe his body and his mind, and they are words he used of himself; yet he was, in one small sense, a cripple from childhood, for his right leg was badly damaged and his knee permanently immobile as a result of osteomyelitis with complications. Even years after, doctors thought it might be necessary to amputate the leg above the knee-joint. He could run only in a very slow and ungainly manner, and he walked swinging his leg out in an arc. However, when one walked with him one had to walk far faster than the usual South African stroll; as fellow South Africans would say, he walked, as he looked, like a 'typical Englishman' – a 'rooinek', a red neck, striding out in the sun and up a mountain when sensible men stayed, if they could, in the shade.

Yet he was not English; he was a South African both by birth and commitment, and his ancestry was Scottish and German. His father was the second son of a Scottish family of small farmers, who had put himself through George Watson's College, then Edinburgh University, and then

Balliol, on scholarships; and who had, after taking his law examinations at the Inner Temple, made a brilliant career in the Inland Revenue, first as private secretary to its chairman Alfred Milner, and by 1898 as its chief clerk. In 1901 he had become one of the 'kindergarten', the group of young administrators (all from Oxford) recruited by Milner, by then High Commissioner of South Africa, to help him redirect and reconstruct the former Boer Republics. Most of the 'kindergarten' moved away from South Africa; only Richard Feetham (later Chief Justice of South Africa) and Patrick Duncan senior stayed permanently, Duncan becoming, by the time of his marriage in 1916, the Unionist MP for Fordsburg in the Transvaal, and second in command of his party.

His mother was Alice Dold, one of the nine children of a German trader and farmer of Kokstad in East Griqualand. Her father, Victor Dold, had come out to South Africa to make his fortune. After gambling away on the ship all but the gold coins sewn into his belt, he had bought a wagon and eighteen oxen and set himself up as a trader in Kokstad, made some money (Patrick Duncan thought possibly by selling brandy to the Griquas, who were notoriously given to drinking it), returned to Germany to find a wife, and then went back to making a great deal of money in trading and farming. Patrick Duncan called the family 'very odd ... rent with quarrels and terribly unhappy',[2] but Victor Dold remains a shadowy figure, as do some of his nine children: one daughter, Retha, returned to Germany and became an ardent Nazi; another, Agnes, married Dr George Campbell of Durban, brother of the poet Roy; one son became a lawyer in London; one daughter became a nun; Alice, the third daughter and seventh child, married at twenty-three a forty-five-year-old MP, already one of the more important political figures in South Africa.

By all accounts the marriage of Alice Dold and Patrick Duncan was, despite the gap in age, secure and happy, though undemonstrative: they never showed any outward signs of affection for each other, even in front of their children, never touching hands, or linking arms, or kissing each other; but, then, Patrick Duncan the elder was a very undemonstrative man, a man notoriously without smalltalk, finding his greatest pleasures in talking politics, listening to serious music (a taste which his wife shared), walking or climbing, and reading philosophy and the classics – he was a first-class classical scholar, and years later his eldest son was to write with pride of asking in Blackwell's for a good translation of the *Phaedo* and being handed his father's. Most of his life had been devoted to making his mark, first in the Civil Service, then in the Colonial Service, then in law and politics. His closest confidante was Lady Selborne, wife of Milner's successor, with whom he maintained a weekly correspondence for thirty-seven years, up to a week before his death; he used to tell her everything of significance happening in South Africa, and she would advise, comment, suggest policies for the Empire and solutions for its more local problems. From this correspondence emerges one picture of the kind of man he seemed to be: serious-minded, political, devoted to Milner's concept of the Empire and to the unity of English and Afrikaners in South Africa, intelligent, scholarly, but not an amusing or outgoing man. His eldest son said of him, simply: 'he was not really interested in people; he was more interested in books'.[3] The impression one gets from his wife's diaries both confirms this and yet is more human; for instance, she wrote about the dinner at which her husband was put to sit next to Lady de Waal, 'a person who rather terrifies my poor Patrick. I feel that he must have been very dull for he afterwards told me that she had said to him "There are 47 lights in this room. I know because I have just counted." '⁴

Alice Dold was a person of very different kind. Although an intelligent woman who had been educated partly in Europe, her main ambition was to have a happy family, and she saw her main role as protecting her husband; she altered the seating arrangement at their dining-table so that he sat in the middle rather than at the head, and she could sit opposite him to help him cope with the Lady de Waals of his world. Many found her domineering and formidable, very conscious of the formalities of her position as a politician's wife, as Cabinet minister's wife and later as Governor-General's wife, perhaps even more conscious because she was so young (her husband was a Cabinet minister when she was still only twenty-eight). Those who got behind the formalities – particularly in middle age, after the death of her second son and her husband – found her warm and loving, and to them she gave the impression of having her feelings very much in control rather than of having no real feelings.

About one thing she was openly passionate, and that was Christian Science. As a young woman she had hurt her back in a riding accident and had been told that she would have to spend the rest of her life in bed. As a result of an almost miraculous self-cure she had become devoted to the precepts of Christian Science and remained so all her life: pain was a chimera, and ill health a matter for prayer and will, not for doctors and medicines.

Patrick, their first child, was born on 29 June 1918, in Moot House, Park Town, Johannesburg, the house built by Herbert Baker for members of the 'kindergarten' in Johannesburg, and the suburb the richest of rich Johannesburg. The Duncans lived half the year in Johannesburg, half in Cape Town, for Parliament sat in Cape Town and the executive branch of government functioned from Pretoria. After Patrick there came Andrew in 1920, John in 1922, and Deborah in 1926. While their mother looked after their father, nannies brought over from Scotland looked after the children – first Nanny Green and then Nanny Reid. Cook was a Miss Gasgoyne, a Roman Catholic from Northumberland and, according to Patrick, an admirable woman though virtually illiterate, whom the children called 'E-Aw' (because she had once imitated a donkey for Patrick). Alice Duncan's main influence was in religion: the children were brought up as good Christian Scientists, studying the Bible each morning with their mother, and going to Sunday school, though Patrick knew from early on that his father had no great opinion of Mrs Mary Baker Eddy, founder of Christian Science, nor of her version of religion. Even his mother noted one of his questions in her diary:

Pat: 'Daddy, do you believe that the whale swallowed Jonah?'
PD hedging: 'Oh well, everybody does, I think.'
Pat: 'Yes, but do you – because *I* don't.'⁵

Patrick says that even at six he worried about discrepancies between the 'golden rule' and the practice of the world: 'I remember sitting on the small koppie in our garden at Stone House ... in the dark and fragrant shade of the pine trees there, trying to persuade myself that "the Christian Science God is the true God".'[6] By the time he was ten he had – so he claimed in his autobiography – given up the struggle to believe. However, though he was often critical of it, Christian Science never finished its work in him, for even when he was dying he kept hold of a kind of belief.

If religious doubt started early, the childhood itself seemed idyllic. Looking back, Patrick turned again and again to Wordsworth for his images of childhood: his parents were loving and fair, they brought the children up in a succession of beautiful homes, and they allowed the children 'to do what every child has the right to do – to run wild'.[7] In his autobiography Patrick wrote (a little tantalizingly because it is so unspecific, though many of his most vivid childhood memories seem associated with smells) 'to anyone wanting to smell what patrician Johannesburg was like forty years ago I recommend a walk – not a drive, not a bicycle ride, but walk – along Rock Ridge Road in mid-morning'. Again he wrote:

> ...a delicious memory of childhood is the early morning visit to the kitchen, where E-Aw would be baking her own 'French rolls' (I never found anything as good in France when eventually I reached there), and Nanny Reid brewing herself a cup of black tea, so strong that it looked like ink. But it filled the kitchen with incense, and it tasted good, too, when we were allowed to sip it to help down the doe [sic] and shards of E-Aw's French rolls, which we were always able to steal.[8]

Again, however, he specifies no more than this; yet his autobiography hints again and again at the delighted senses: a road 'dark and cool with the shade of Austrian blackwoods', the 'trembling and sun-filtering shade'. He discovered in those years something of the same pleasure his parents took in gardens, in walking, and in the countryside. The point of reference in his memories of childhood other than Wordsworth is the Book of Genesis: his childhood had been a kind of Eden, as it is for so many white South Africans, particularly if they are of patrician birth – servants, money, fine houses, marvellous climate, good food, physical freedom. In those days, too, there was even less questioning of privilege than in South Africa now; injustice and inequality were there all right, but they were invisible to all but the most imaginative eyes. It was an odd kind of Eden, not only because one lived in pleasant and substantial houses, but also because monsters roamed freely. However, since one's parents and friends said no monsters were there, one generally accepted their truthfulness, and occasional apprehensions could be safely locked away.

Yet Patrick was not entirely happy in his Eden, partly because he saw the monsters early on, but mainly because he did not get on well with his mother, whom all her children thought of as remote from them, the last person they would choose to confide in. Years later, Patrick wrote of his mother: 'She had very definite ideas of how one ought to grow up. Ever before her was the fact that if the twig were straightened in youth it could be made straight, whereas if it were left, nothing could ever put it right. . . .'[9]

Sometimes the conflict with his mother during his early years centred on her religious views and practices; for instance, the four children were expected to gather for Bible study and prayers after breakfast each day, and by the time he was twelve or thirteen Patrick refused to attend. But most of the conflict was more trivial, and mainly the clash of two self-willed people over what in other circumstances would hardly matter: what Patrick was to wear and how formally he was to behave.

There is a rich irony, and indeed a kind of humour, in the fact that he compared his spell in jail in 1960 to the old rows with his mother which so often ended in his being sent to his room:

> Looking back I do not regret my tug of war with my mother. I am after all at this moment kept in a room by a displeased parent (the Government). I am quite resolved *never* to give in. All I can say is that I have been practising this sort of thing for forty years, and the Government has not. We shall see who gives up first![10]

If he looked back on the conflict with his mother as a first part of his political education, he also looked back on the relationship with his parents as having failed to give him an education in matters of race. Of course everyone talked politics continually in the Duncans' houses; but it was a strange kind of politics, which excluded from discussion what one sees now to have been the crucial issue and what was then known, when it was known at all, as the 'native question' or the 'native problem'. Only a handful of white people were capable of seeing what had driven the African National Congress to help organize the 1919 demonstrations against the Pass Laws, or to support the black miners' strike of February 1920, or in 1923 to pass a motion of 'no confidence' both in Smuts's government and in the Westminster government; or what had driven Gandhi to develop his techniques of passive resistance in the Transvaal and Natal. Most white people were not even aware that these things were happening at all. Patrick was troubled very early about the positions of blacks; his mother noted in her diary Patrick's asking her why 'the "Kaffirs" did not go to the "English people's" church'. When she answered 'I wonder', he replied, 'Don't say, "I wonder" – tell me'.[11]

Yet what kind of guidance could his parents have provided, in the context of the years following the First World War? Patrick Duncan senior had shown some interest in the 'native question' and had published in 1912 a pamphlet, *Suggestions for a Native Policy*, which he thought well enough of to republish in 1927.[12] While on the one hand he wanted the Africans to be 'raised to the scale of civilization', taught to use the land and allowed to own it (though only in the 'reserves'), allowed to compete for work with whites in an open market, and not prevented from learning skills and joining the professions, on the other hand he wanted to prevent social and sexual integration which was nobody's 'natural desire'. The whites would in his view retain complete political power, and their numbers be increased by massive immigration from Europe; but black Africans would not be deliberately held back by such devices as indentured labour and job reservation. Economic advance of a kind would be possible, but only in a context in which whites and blacks would be kept as far apart as possible – 'as possible' meant as far as industrial development allowed.

Later, the son was to see his father's attitude very simply, perhaps even simplistically: '... on the problem of non-racial justice, he did not spend much time, and his concentration ... [on the building of an Anglo–Afrikaner nation in terms favourable to the Empire and the English in South Africa] ... led him to "sell-out" on the latter'.[13] The supposed 'sell-out' was his father's support for the removal of African voters from the common roll in the Cape Province, the vestige of the old Cape constitution which had been largely set aside in the Act of Union. But Patrick Duncan senior did not want simply to remove African voters to a separate roll: he wished to abolish the 'native franchise' entirely. Though by 1927 he had conceded to liberal opinion in admitting that Africans could not be permanently excluded from politics, by 1933 when he agreed to support Hertzog in the interests of a joint English–Afrikaner party he had in fact returned to his views advocated in his 1912 pamphlet. Though the son was correct in his version of the father's overwhelming concern with white unity, 'sell-out' is the wrong word: the new views were consistent with those he had held since his 'kindergarten' days; liberalism was the occasional aberration, segregationism the norm.

If the father's theory and practice were to unite English and Afrikaner, to persuade the Unionist Party, the mine-owners' party, to move closer to the South African Party, the Botha-Smuts party, the son was not exempt from the usual dislike English South Africans felt for Afrikaners; and his schoolmates and he insulted and threw stones at the 'Japies' of the Afrikaans school near their own 'English' one. In part it was the new dislike that the settled English middle class felt for the Afrikaans country-people who were moving into the cities to escape poverty and unemployment, in part the heritage of the Boer War. When John Duncan was staying with the family of his godfather, General Smuts, at Doorn Kloof, he dared to describe his father to 'Aunt Isie' Smuts as 'English'. 'He is not English', said she, who had lost a son in a concentration camp in the Anglo-Boer war. 'He is Scottish – and don't you ever forget it.'[14] Yet the Duncan children seemed to some of their contemporaries even more English than most English South Africans. England was still 'home', and their main points of reference were always English, despite the fact that their father was a Scot-turned-South African and their mother only one generation away from being German. Oddly enough, Patrick was apparently not fluent in Afrikaans, though one might have expected his father to insist on it. None of the Duncan children studied it at school; and Patrick only learned the language later, and never felt completely fluent in it.

Anti-semitism was another part of his early experience of racial feeling. Patrick says his father 'was not anti-semitic, but was not fond of the Jewish community. His dislike increased as he grew older, though all his life he treasured the friendship of many Jews.'[15] The impression one gains from his father's letters is not so equivocal, and is certainly not his father's reputation among South African Jews; partly this latter derives from his use of the 1913 Immigration Act to prevent East European Jewish refugees from entering South Africa and, although Patrick remembers 'strict lectures at home against anti-semitism', he remembers, too, that one of his mother's reasons was that, 'as Yeoville, father's constituency, was largely Jewish, it might cost

him votes if we came out with anti-Jewish remarks in the wrong company'.[16]
Presumably, it would have been all right to be anti-semitic in the right
company. As Patrick half admits, his father's later views were straightfor-
wardly anti-semitic, as some of his letters show:

> There is something about the Jew which provokes the feeling of dislike ...
> unscrupulous dealing, servility, harshness ... but there are many excep-
> tions ... the distinctive physical type also seems to give an otherwise vague
> sense of antipathy something material to found upon.[17]

> ... I do not dislike Jews as such. I know some very fine ones. But there is a
> climbing type thirsting for publicity.[18]

One has, of course, to see remarks of this kind in the context of a general
anti-semitism, and that not only in South Africa. Even Hofmeyr, the great
white hope of South African liberalism, attacked the 1930 Immigration Bill
not because he was opposed in principle to limiting Jewish immigration,
but rather because the wording of the Bill was offensive to Jewish South
Africans.[19] There is a significant way, too, in which anti-semitism relates
to Patrick Duncan senior's desire for English–Afrikaner unity. He was not
simply a representative of imperial capitalism, anti-semitism and segregationism; he identified himself largely with the problems of white workers
in South Africa, and often shared their dislike of entrepreneurial capitalism.
In letters to his son he deplores the selfishness of the capitalist ethic and
refers to 'pigs scrambling round the golden trough'.[20] It is something of the
same complex combination of feelings one finds in John Buchan, or in Milner
himself. Though the father had a passion for the idea of Empire which
survived until his death, he was not a jingo: his South Africa was to be part
of a unity of equals, not simply a client state of Britain; and his political
views are not always very far from Afrikaner nationalism with its appeal
to the white working class, a hostility to Jews and, traditionally at least,
opposition to capitalism.

The son's passionate commitment to South Africa (though a South Africa
very different from his father's view of it) must be understood in this context:
whatever the realities of the culture, he felt himself to be a South African at a
much deeper level than he felt himself English and European, though
obviously he was drawn by history and culture to Britain and Europe. He was
not an Englishman stranded in an ex-colony. In many ways, this (and the
complex contradictions between feeling and fact which it implies) was to
determine the whole course of his life.

Patrick's first school was the Ridge in Johannesburg, a private school run by
two former Rhodes Scholars, Guy Nicholson and Ronald Currey. While his
parents were in Johannesburg he lived at home (his father was in opposition
from 1924 to 1933, and trying to pull together his legal practice as an
advocate, which he had had to neglect while in the Cabinet), and boarded
when they were in Cape Town and he was not on holiday. Although Patrick
talked in retrospect of 'our excellent masters', and noted that Nicholson and
Currey ran the school well, he said simply: 'it was no fun after home'.[21]
However, he enjoyed the various 'crazes' – model aeroplanes, kites, marbles,

tortoise-keeping; he wrote home about cricket, Latin, the matron's kitten; he sent home occasional drawings – a cobweb, a kettle on a spirit burner; he was excited when Mrs Currey started a tuck shop, he was excited when Mr Currey found a night adder in the swimming-pool. His letters home got longer, more mature. 'Dear Mother' became 'Dear Alcie' (her pet name), and sometimes he signed himself 'Pat' and sometimes 'Patrick Baker Duncan'. He sent home reports and bits of his written work, such as 'A flamingo's story'. He told his mother that 'Miss Dunn taught us to play Base Ball and we had a lovely game'.[22]

Only once in his letters home does he show much interest in the outside world, when he writes about the Chinese war: 'Shanghai has been blown up so that is the end of a very historical town, a portion of the great Wall has been blown up too.'[23] Most of his concerns are those of any normally intelligent and perceptive boy trying hard to make his parents see the fascination of catching alive a rat ('a giant . . . the tail about a foot long and a body about nine inches')[24], or carefully explaining that a 'goaly' means 'goalkeeper'. Once he wrote apologetically to his mother, 'we go to St George's church now but I do the lesson every day so that will make up for it',[25] and once he asked his brother Andrew to tell his mother that he was trying to keep up his Bible study.

His school reports show an intelligent, curious and lively little boy; a school magazine for 1928 reports that P. Duncan came first in his class of fourteen in English and French, but only sixth in maths. 'Exceptionally able', says one report,[26] and his headmaster wrote to his mother: 'whatever Pat's ambitions are they certainly don't seem to be quite those of other boys of his age'. But Currey was sometimes 'a little worried' about Patrick, 'for there were times now and then when he seemed to lose himself in what Kipling would call a more-than-Oriental concentration on one or other of life's problems, and in these moods he would become quite oblivious of anything or anybody about him'.[27] Patrick himself, looking back on the Ridge from the vantage-place of Oxford, wrote:

> Almost from the moment I went to the Ridge (and perhaps before too) I was always frightened about something, and that something was almost always most unreasonable. I was terrified – it seems awful to put it into print – that Daddy or you were going to pass on. I remember not getting a letter for ten days or two weeks – I imagined unknown terrors. Looking back to this manifestation of the same old state of mind (there have been many others), it seems so small and ridiculous, but I assure you that at the time it is horribly real. School was no place for me at that time. . . . The result was that I hated the Ridge and I do not think that morally and spiritually the Ridge did me any good. . . .[28]

Generally, however, what one notices in the letters of the time is Patrick's ordinariness: his enthusiasm for games; his love of small animals and insects; his curiosity about stones and comets; his enjoyment of the odd, like a featherless parrot; his pleasure in reading adventure stories; his liking of limericks. The greatest excitement of all during his early years at the Ridge was being involved in a train crash, the Hex River crash, about a hundred miles from Cape Town, when Patrick and Andrew were on their way to their parents, and about which Patrick wrote his first published essay in the school magazine.

Then, when Patrick was eleven, came the first real crisis of his life. In his autobiography he gives a very short version of the events which left him permanently lame:

> When I was 12 [sic] I had a serious attack of osteomyelitis (a disease in which the marrow and bone is infected). Nowadays it responds well to antibiotics but in 1930, at Easter time, all that there was was the surgeon's knife and peroxide of hydrogen and eusol. These were the main tools of my doctors. They removed nearly all the tibia of my right leg leaving just a spindle on which they hoped a new tibia would grow. Then they left me to the nurses ... with pus pouring out of the 18" wound, sick and unable to eat, sweat pouring off me and my hair falling out. They could do no more.[29]

The actual events were more complex, and Ronald Currey certainly believes that the long-term damage was as much a result of Mrs Duncan's Christian Science and its influence on Patrick as of the original injury and the illness which resulted from it. Ronald Currey's version runs like this: Patrick was hit by a cricket ball just below the right knee. Though he was always very stoical, and would never normally complain about even a high degree of pain, the pain resulting from what should have been a bruise was excessive even for him, and eventually and reluctantly he went to the school matron. It was by then over a week after the initial injury. First the matron examined him and then a doctor was called who diagnosed osteomyelitis and advised an immediate operation. It was impossible for the school to get in touch with Patrick's parents to ask their permission and, since Currey was unwilling to take responsibility for any delay, the operation went ahead. It was obviously a severe one, but the trouble was not as bad as it was to become.

When Patrick woke up the next morning he was (still according to Ronald Currey) so impatient with being ill, so angry at being cooped up in bed, that he refused to recognize that there was anything seriously wrong – though the symptoms would presumably have been recognized by any normal, intelligent and active child in intense pain. For Currey, it was the direct result of his mother's Christian Science that Patrick was so antagonistic to medical treatment and so ready to defy the consequences. Whatever the cause, the fact is that on waking up Patrick got out of bed to walk to the other end of the room to get a glass of water. The movement set the infection off again, and now there was a much more severe operation which involved the removal of most of the tibia, this time leaving a mere spindle on which it was hoped a new tibia would grow.[30] At this stage the doctors wanted to amputate the leg at the knee. Alice Duncan would not let them.

The biographical problem is not so much who was to blame, but how deep the influence of Christian Science ran. On the one hand, Patrick claims to have abandoned the struggle to believe in it by the time he was ten; on the other, it seems that in at least part of his mind he held on to the notion that pain and illness could be cured by prayer alone – hence his not seeing the school matron when the injury first began to hurt so intensely, and the fact that, despite the pain after the first operation, he was prepared to get out of bed and cross the room for a glass of water.

Yet, if this version is accurate, would Patrick not have felt some resentment that his mother's belief and her influence on him had been in at least part responsible for what crippled him? He had been an active and physically lively child; not only did the operation leave him lame and take years to heal but also, as late as 1953, when he was nearly thirty-five, he had to undergo still more large-scale surgery to repair the leg, and even then was not entirely free from pain. In his autobiography, he says, however:

> I do not think I should have got over it without my mother's help. She had been down in Cape Town for the session; I was at boarding school in J'Burg and lay in the General Hospital, J'Burg. She visited me every day tooting cheerfully as she drove down Hospital Hill for me to look out and see her. . . . The pain was something I cannot describe. All I can say is that it was excruciatingly painful if someone walked into the room from the vibrations of the floor boards.
>
> For years after the right knee (which never bent again) used to be so painful that I could not sleep at nights, often for half the night. All that time my mother stood by me, staying awake with me as long as I needed her murmuring encouragement and comfortable words.[31]

There is no resentment apparent in this, only gratitude and love.

On the other hand, it is also true that Christian Science was a permanent influence on him, long after the days of this crisis: he never submitted to his own illnesses, his own pain, and seemed to believe he could cure himself, if not by prayer, at least by will. Even before the illness and operation, there had been a contradiction in Patrick's personality, so that the normal, easy, warm and charming child would occasionally disappear into remote moods where he could not be reached at all, where he went into some fastness of his mind which imagined parents dead. Others noted the contradiction in the child and the man: although he was a warm and gregarious man, he was also in a sense an isolated one. There was always a part of him which he kept away from others. He knew a great many people; he had many friends and was punctilious in his friendships; many people loved him, even those who found it hard to admire him unreservedly. But always there was a part of him which was not available for friendship or perhaps even for love.

Did keeping the pain, from which he was never entirely free, to himself, and being set aside from the enormous activity his energy desired, contribute to a containment of self which was both strength and barrier? One may explain the social loneliness of his later years partly in terms of a particular upbringing, or of being the son of a notably undemonstrative father; but even his brother John and his sister, who shared the same kind of society and upbringing, felt there was a loneliness in him which they almost never broke through, and both place the cause in those years of pain and his complex attitude towards Christian Science. Patrick Duncan was not a consciously self-revelatory man. Certainly he found great pleasure in isolation, in riding alone in the mountains of Basutoland, or exploring the Algerian desert. He used occasionally to run away from Cape Town during the years of hectic political activity to recuperate on the farms of friends; and in jail in 1960 he wrote: 'Sitting alone in my small 13 × 9 feet cell I am very happy. I am very happy for two main reasons: that only in prison or in a monastery can one shut out the tentacles of modern living with its incessant interruptions: and that I am absolutely sure I am right to be here.'[32]

He would never discuss his lameness or its cause and, although in his autobiography he had to mention it, he skimmed over it as quickly as he could. He would never allow it to affect what he could do – Cynthia remembers that only once in his marriage did he ever express a regret, which was that he could not play polo. Most of the time he seemed intent on demonstrating that he could do everything anyone else could do. He always wore long trousers and hated bathing in public, for the scars and deformation were very ugly indeed. In one of his letters from Winchester he called the leg 'the curse of my life'.[33]

Patrick was six months in hospital, and spent much of the time embroidering a sampler, which he kept all his life. 'Face where the danger lies PD';[34] then he went back to Stone House and learned to walk again with an iron caliper on his leg, and crutches. He was still desperately weak and, though swimming in neighbours' pools helped him, his parents soon decided that all the family except the father should go to Switzerland to allow him to convalesce. Most of 1931 was spent in Lausanne where they took a chalet and the three boys went to school, Patrick and Andrew to the École Nouvelle. Patrick and Andrew had to work very hard to cope both with the academic standards and with the fact that they were being taught everything in French. Their mother helped them by learning French, too, and used to recite irregular verbs with them. They were also helped by Deborah's French-speaking governess, Genet Magnin, who later accompanied the family back to South Africa. (She was to stay with the Duncans as governess until 1935 when she went to teach at the South African Roedean; later she married Bailey Bekker, the politician who was to break away from the United Party to form the short-lived Conservative Party.)

The year 1931 was by all accounts and despite the leg a happy one, though Patrick only gradually learned how to cope without crutches and was still in considerable pain, often awake most of the night; the leg had still not healed properly. He enjoyed the study of French literature, and of course had plenty of time to get on with his reading; but it was very difficult for him to be in enforced inactivity while his younger brothers could take full advantage of the Swiss mountains, particularly since the brothers did not always seem to understand what Patrick was suffering.

Patrick's most vivid memories of 1931 were, however, more to do with England than with Switzerland, for on their way to Lausanne the family stayed briefly with Lady Selborne at Blackmoor House. She was then in her seventies, a formidable though kindly lady. She was of course a particular friend of Patrick's father, with whom she had corresponded already for nearly thirty years. Most of the family were awed by Lady Selborne and the army of servants in Blackmoor House. The only one not awed was John, then just turned eight:

> At lunch one day he said to Lady Selborne in his most carrying tones: 'Lady Selborne, are you a Christian Scientist?' 'No, John, I am afraid I ai'n't.' By this time the butler, as well as everyone else, was listening, for

though every morning all the servants attended morning prayers I do not think any of them had heard this awe-inspiring woman catechized. John continued: 'Lady Selborne, WHY aren't you a Christian Scientist?' She was equal to the moment, and gave a superbly conservative answer: 'Well, John, the Church of England's done me very well for over seventy years, and I expect it'll see me out all right.'[35]

In 1932 the family went back to Johannesburg. Patrick had first a tutor and then went for a term as a day boy to St John's to bring him up to standard before going to Cape Town to board at the Diocesan College for Boys, usually called Bishop's. Still ill and weak, with a year in a civilized Swiss school behind him, with intellectual interests both by upbringing and as a result of his enforced inactivity, he was unlikely to find a South African private boarding school a comfortable place. If childhood had been Paradise, the leg and operation a private Purgatory, Bishop's was Hell. Of course some staff and a few of his fellows were kind to him, but mainly he was intolerably bullied; he was small, he was clever, he liked speaking French, he had little self-confidence, he was late in reaching puberty, and above all else he could not play games. Some masters, even some pupils, might rebel against the games-playing ethos; the official policy of the school might be to promote and value many-sidedness; but to almost all pupils, many 'old boys', and many staff the ultimate success, the accolade, the only side of many-sidedness which really mattered was a First XV blazer. After all, games such as rugby were 'character-building'; so, if you couldn't or wouldn't make yourself good at games, you had failed to build your character, you were soft, and were weak – no wonder your voice took so long to break.

One of the few at the school Patrick remembered with affection was the headmaster, Hubert Kidd, who taught him Greek and who, in six months of force-fed extra work – all of which Patrick accepted and was grateful for – brought him up to the standard of his classmates who had been studying it for two years. Indeed, the one thing at Bishop's at which he was successful was his work, and Kidd wrote to Patrick's father in 1934: 'he is quick to learn and intelligent; and he has a good language sense, and what is rare among the boys here, classical upbringing'.[36] But the school remained a personal Hell. Though Patrick apparently did not know, his father was trying to get him into an English school (he consulted Ronald Currey about Repton, and Hubert Kidd about Uppingham), partly because he wanted his son to try for a classical scholarship to Balliol, partly because he and his wife realized Patrick's misery, and partly, as he told Lady Selborne, 'in the hope that it will make him less the eccentric'.[37] Eventually, through the good offices of Lord Selborne, who was on the governing body, Patrick was offered a place at Winchester, although he was by then sixteen and exceptionally old for entry. He accepted the offer with alacrity and never once regretted it, though it meant going far away from home. In a sense his childhood had ended when he was eleven.

CHAPTER 2

September 1934–41
'This is a civilized country'[1]

Patrick Duncan's time at Winchester was extraordinarily happy. Although, after the bullying at Bishop's, he inevitably had misgivings about his new school, he soon found that Winchester was what he called 'a civilized country':[2] his peer-group accepted him naturally and kindly, and he was not despised for being lame and unable to play games. Initially he felt a little ridiculous in the uniform (on weekdays suits with straw hats, variously beribboned to show status, and on Sundays formal morning dress, tails and top hat), thought the school 'full of the worst (in some cases) foolish traditions and rules',[3] found the jargon odd (a 'tother' for a prep school, 'thoke' for holiday, Founder's Day 'hatch thoke', and so on), and being 'in Sweat' (the condition of being a new 'man') a little undignified for a sixteen-year-old, but he soon enough fell in love with the place, its tolerance of eccentricity and high regard for intelligence. Even its discomforts became in retrospect pleasurable: the cold tubs in the morning, the bitter east winds, the bad food (for in those days the housemaster was paid so much per pupil, and bought pupils' food out of the lump sum, thus encouraging frugality in the matter of meals, even in the kindest of housemasters).

He made new friends, some of whom stayed friends for the rest of his life: Jeremy Pemberton, Henry Kitchener (heir to Lord Kitchener of Khartoum), Derrick and Jim Bailey, the sons of Sir Abe Bailey, the South African financier, and others. He was in Sunnyside, a boarding-house run by Malcolm Robertson, 'the Bobber', and his sister Sheila, and 'the Bobber' was a humane and concerned housemaster. House Tutor was Eric James, later Headmaster of Manchester Grammar School and, as Lord James of Rusholme, Vice-Chancellor of York University. His teachers included Francis King, of Rugby and Balliol; Walter Oakeshott, later Warden of Lincoln College, Oxford; and C. H. O'D. Alexander, later British chess champion.

Academically, he did not do well, except to an extent in modern languages and in the sciences, though he was in the non-specialist division for science; his knowledge of classics, though good by South African standards, was feeble by Wykehamist. Walter Oakeshott gave him private tuition in Latin but, at the end of his first half-term, he was '19th of 19' in his division, though his housemaster commented that he had 'a good mind' and seemed happy. Then his leg went wrong again – there was so little flesh left over the shin-bone that the slightest knock would cause re-infection, and the veins so damaged that the return-flow of the blood was disrupted – and he was sent to his doctor-uncle, Robert Duncan, in Kew Gardens, for most of the rest of the term. But by July 1935 he was '7th of 19' in his division, and got his Remove into the Sixth.

Once there, he went back to being '17th of 17'. His main teacher of the time wrote, with schoolmasterly severity, 'I believe he has far greater capacity for classical scholarship than he himself will allow',[4] and a term later, even more severely, 'he likes to do things in a different way from others'.[5] But in sciences, French and Spanish he did well, in July 1935 coming '1st of 18' in chemistry. He began to study Russian and even Afrikaans. He was even talking of a science degree at one stage, but 'the Bobber' reported to the Duncans that Eric James had dissuaded him.

Some of the comments of his teachers, especially Francis King and 'the Bobber', seem extraordinarily perceptive in the light of his later development. Francis King talked of 'his rather restless desire to do everything at once', and wrote in a final report: 'I hope he will outgrow his present tendency to dilettantism, for he has many qualities which have made me value him as a member of the division and as a friend'.[6] Malcolm Robertson, in his chatty and lengthy reports and letters to the Duncans, notes that Patrick is 'volatile in his changes of ideas and interests',[7] and that 'his cocksureness and crudities of judgement have been stimulating (as well as his sound knowledge of and vivid interest in many things)'.[8] 'Cocksureness' is an interesting reflection of the way in which Patrick had apparently recovered from Bishop's. One of 'the Bobber's' most interesting comments is this:

> ... at present he talks of farming, or Labour propaganda, or anything which comes into his head. He delights in being – or more often posing – as a rebel or critic.... I think his consciousness of his physical limitations makes him determined to do tiring things at times – also to take an original line mentally, whenever possible![9]

But, as well as being reaction to the lameness, his rebellion was also against white South Africa, which he felt had treated him so unjustly at Bishop's: he began to realize some of the flaws in South African society, and when the Italians began preparing for the Abyssinian war, he became a passionate adherent of the Emperor of Abyssinia. He joined Miss Pankhurst's society which was rallying support for Haile Selassie; he tried to get leave from his Housemaster and, when he refused, from the Headmaster to go to London to see the Emperor; he drew a war-map of Abyssinia collated from all other maps he could find; he read old books on Abyssinian history. In October 1935 he wrote home:

> So far the Italians have been too Devilishly efficient. I am absolutely convinced that all resistance in Abyssinia will be broken and the Emperor killed before many weeks. If I could only supply the poor devils with 250,000 machine guns – one for each Italian soldier's death. The only way for them to counter war is by war.[10]

From his enthusiasm for the Abyssinian cause he was led to anti-fascism. He read and distributed the *Daily Worker*, went to listen to Cripps in the town hall, read books and pamphlets from the Left Book Club, wanted to fight in the Spanish Civil War, and generally proclaimed himself at the least a socialist. In a mock-election in November 1935 he stood as a communist, and came second in the polls, though warned his parents, 'Now don't take this seriously', because none of the pupils did.[11]

It is hard to tell how serious Duncan's brief period as a socialist was; he said to Cyril Dunn in 1955: 'I went up to Oxford hoping to be very active Left Wing, but I went to one meeting and that was enough to put me off. I just didn't like the other Communists and I didn't go again, probably on snobbish grounds. Oxford was then very snobbish....'[12] His socialism does not seem to have been a very deep-seated conviction; but his feelings about the Abyssinian war ran much deeper: for instance, reacting to an article in *Round Table*, he wrote to his parents, 'I don't like to hear that Italy *must* get Abyssinia in the end. I must be narrow-minded, but I *loathe* the word opening-up when applied to a country. It reeks of commercial enterprise, sacrificing all that is good in the old civilization, without giving any adequate replacement. Exploitation.'[13] This for once sounds like his own mature voice, and points forward to what he was to think and feel later about Basutoland.

Yet what one has most sense of from Patrick's letters at the time is the huge political muddle in his mind. Even the extent to which his feelings for the Emperor and Abyssinia were what he later called a 'rebuff'[14] to white South Africa was not particularly clear at the time: he continued to feel himself a South African in exile, not an Englishman back in his true home, and he demonstrated little loathing for the politics of white South Africa. Partly of course he was like any adolescent, sometimes reacting against, sometimes accepting, his father's views; but there was little consistency. If on the one hand he called himself 'anti-fascist' and 'pro-Abyssinian', on the other he wrote: 'I do wish Britain would accept Hitler's often reported offers of friendship and leave stingy frantic France for herself'.[15] When his mother wrote to him about how impressed a Mr Fourie was with Nazi Germany, he replied:

I should be [impressed] too, but any country which every few months has to be bolstered up with some terrific national emotion, where starvation is so close (although the most moving patriotism and self-denial is there too) any country which goes back to racialism, rule of might, torture and whose self-confessed aim is *War*, and conquest of Russia, to me is utterly loathsome.[16]

He objected equally strongly to a letter from his 'Uncle' Hermann Speiser, a German diplomat who had married Retha Dold, with its 'three pages of pure Nazism'.[17] Yet he wrote to his father about South Africa: 'When the gold goes there won't be enough in the country to keep these Groisy [sic] Jews going. Let's hope they take the tip and depart.'[18] Again, although (or perhaps because) he was getting letters from his father justifying his voting for the removal of Africans in the Cape from the common voters' roll, Patrick wrote to him about the Africans in South Africa:

To expect two races to live in the same country, guided by the same interests (as we and the Bantu will be, when gold is gone) and keep apart, is ludicrous. It is impossible to keep such a great nation eternally under. They will every year become more educated.... You say 'The white races will never accept a position where the Bantu will have superior voting power'. They will jolly well have to, one day, as I think. And I think the present Union Government is taking the easy (and only) path; but it is a path which will lead to explosions, and not peaceful reform and revolutions.... If we have any sense we will allow ourselves to be absorbed into the Bantu Races, who look as if they will rule Central and South Africa one day....[19]

He ended his letter, 'So far the Bantu has given all and taken nothing,' and then added wryly, 'I am afraid all this is very confused, but you will get the drift of it'.

A few months later, however, he wrote to his father:

Why can't we send all our natives to Angola, P[ortuguese] E[ast] A[frica] and N. Rhodesia only having mines, which always benefit the natives, and no farms. Or would we crumble up with not so much and such servile native labour or must we work together in the same community, each tolerating the other, and helping the other, but not marrying each other.[20]

Do the mines benefit blacks or no? How does one get absorbed without some inter-marrying? If repression is the easy but only path for white South Africa, what other path may there be? Yes, he was confused, as he knew quite well; but yes, too, he was beginning to ask some of the questions which he was to try to answer in action in later years, because there is a drift in his letters towards the most difficult questions a white South African has to face. But he was still a white South African, and when he heard an old missionary preach he wrote home the normal white South African reaction to such people and such ideas: 'All the Church people here love more a black man whom they know not at all than one of their compatriots in say, South Wales, Newcastle or Glasgow.'[21] Of course it is scarcely a surprise that a young man, only just out of adolescence, should not have clear and developed political ideas; the point is not so much that he, the individual, was confused, but that he had to find his way within such conflicting systems of political theory and political values as he had learned at home and was learning at Winchester.

One gets the same sense of an undirected pursuit of old and new ideas and old and new passions in the development of his interests at the time, though some were to remain permanent. He had started to collect old books in 1931, when the family stayed briefly in Edinburgh; he began now to develop this interest, tying it to his interest in the Abyssinian war and in Africa generally. He began to study and collect old maps. He spent most of the time he might have been playing games instead in the library (before he left Winchester he was appointed one of the library prefects); he grew passionately interested in bookbinding and typography (an interest he shared with his friend Jeremy Pemberton). He played chess. He began photography. He grew interested enough in architecture to think seriously about it as a profession, and consulted his godfather Sir Herbert Baker about his prospects. He swam, walked and cycled, and did some shooting in term and vacation. He began to think more often about conservation and the soil, building on an interest which may be traced even farther back than his parents' enthusiasm for gardening and the countryside, since his Dold great-grandfather was the model for Muller, the German forester of Kipling's 'In the Rukh', who quotes Heine, who claims the services of Mowgli since he is 'the head of all the *rukhs* in the country of India and others across the Black Water', and who tells Gisborne that he remembers

> When dere was no rukh more big than your knee, from here to dere plough-lands, und in drought-time der cattle ate bones of dead cattle up and down. Now der trees haf come back. Dey were planted by a Freethinker, because he know just de cause dot made der effect. But der trees dey had der cult of der old gods – 'und der Christian Gods howl loudly'. Dey could not live in der rukh, Gisborne.[22]

Above all else at Winchester, it was the sheer physical presence of the past which caught his adolescent imagination: the ceremony of 'illumina' where, at the end of the winter term, 'a thousand candles were put into holes in the great walls round meads, and the school song "Domum, domum, dulce domum" was sung';[23] the warden's garden; the cloisters; the hexameter-slogan painted inside the seventeenth-century building in the meads which read: 'Aut disce, aut discede. Manet sors tertia: caedi' ('Either learn or leave. There does remain a third fate: to be flogged.')[24]

All in all, Winchester gave him back the sense of belonging somewhere which he had lost at least from the time of his illness onwards. On his way to Balliol in 1937 he wrote a long letter to his mother in which he looked back over his schooldays; it is an odd and even mysterious letter:

> Then I went to hospital, and when I came out it was only your help that saved me from despair, and the twisted outlook that might so easily have come, and that in fact did begin to show its head in shame at my scarred limb. At Bishop's the chaps were not too sensitive, and often passed remarks about my size and general age. I was convinced that I should never grow, that I was not as others, and this was torture ... and that is how I went to Winchester, hating myself. Something gave me the idea that because my chin was not as developed as others, I was hopelessly damned. I despised myself, and because I did not make many friends at Bishop's, I thought I was a hopeless case. The worst badge of all was my voice, which I loathed with unbelievable remorse. To show the extent of this feeling, once at the Hyde Park Hotel you were quoting me to me, and in doing so you raised your voice – quite unconsciously, I hope, and think – and that was far worse to me than all possible personal abuse. ... I got over most of that at Winchester, for which I shall always be grateful. If I did not drain my full academic draught at St Mary's, I found there something I had waited a long time for....[25]

Holidays from Winchester were spent mainly in Kew Gardens with his uncle Robert Duncan, a widower. The household included a son John, a little older than Pat; a daughter Margaret, Pat's age; a Cockney housekeeper; and an aged and conservative great-uncle whom Pat delighted in teasing with his socialism. Pat was fond of Uncle Robert although he cultivated a rough manner and was often critical of Patrick's reports from Winchester. He was fond, too, of his cousins, though Margaret was rather terrified of her noisy and lively cousin with his extravagant views on everything under the sun and beyond.

Other holidays were spent with Winchester friends, with family friends like the Menzies Wilsons and the Holtbys, and he managed to terrify many of his friends' parents by insisting he could learn to skate despite his lameness, or by climbing a castle's walls. He had to show he was not a cripple. Sometimes he stayed with former members of the 'kindergarten' and their associates: Philip Kerr, by then Lord Lothian, the Lionel Curtises, the Hichens family, the Herbert Bakers. Most of the 'kindergarten' remained close friends and acted as an extended family to each other's children. The Herbert Bakers were exceptionally kind to him, and he spent much time with their son Henry, who had been at Winchester a few years before and who was now an up-and-coming engineer. 'Uncle Herbert', 'Aunt Florence' and their children lived in a beautiful Caroline house, Owletts, in Cobham in Kent, and Patrick was full of admiration for the skills of the father and Henry: the way Sir Herbert had converted the old Brewery at Winchester to a library, and the electric clocks which Henry had designed and built in stainless steel, enamelled with emblems of the various countries of the Commonwealth to show the time all over the Commonwealth as well as in Britain; one was in Owletts, one in Winchester.

The other person who made an enormous impression on him was Lord Lothian. He was a rather lonely old bachelor, with a retinue of servants and two enormous houses, one Blickling Hall, an Elizabethan *palazzo* in Norfolk, and the other Newbattle Abbey, near Edinburgh. On one visit to Newbattle, Lord Lothian gave Patrick the sword worn at George IV's coronation by the then Marquis; he gave him, too, much time and talk – of psychoanalysis, of bolshevism and of religion (he had been born a Catholic, and had become a Christian Scientist, so they had plenty to argue about, some of which Patrick reported to his mother).

While at Blickling in January 1935 Patrick attended one of the moots of the group, mainly ex-'kindergarten', who planned the policy of their periodical, the *Round Table*. Lord Lothian, Lady Astor, Mr and Mrs Lionel Hichens, Mr and Mrs Lionel Curtis, Dougie Malcolm, Mr John Maud (later Sir John, High Commissioner of South Africa, and later still Lord Redcliffe Maud, Master of University College, Oxford) and Mrs Maud, Robert (later Lord) Brand, John Dove, Geoffrey Dawson (editor of *The Times*) and Mrs Dawson, Bishop Furse, and Dermot Morrah, were all at the moot he attended, though when he wrote to his parents about the meeting he was not sure of exactly who everybody was. Still, 'They all seem a jolly fine crowd, and I attended their meeting, for the most part very interesting'.[26]

Two other episodes of his Winchester days are significant. The first was a trip to Wales in April 1936, organized by Francis King, a don and later housemaster of Patrick's elder son (reputed at Winchester to be a socialist), when several Winchester sixth-formers were billeted on Welsh mining families. Although Patrick had looked forward to the visit with some trepidation – he was afraid the visitors might seem patronizing – he found that he enjoyed the Welsh scenery and admired the people. He and a friend stayed with the Tom Davieses of Rhymney, and were very taken with both husband and wife; he 'treats us all as his equals (only too rare a thing in South Wales), but does not get enough to live healthily on', he told his parents.[27] Patrick went into a level, to the coal-face which the unemployed miners worked for themselves; he went ahead of the other Winchester boys, but found the darkness and foul air too much for him, so crawled out backwards. 'The big fault' of the Welsh miners was, he noted, 'social grovelling, but a new healthy socialism will blot that out'.[28] Years later, when campaigning for coloured and African support for the Liberal Party in South Africa, he would make a point of staying in the houses of those he was recruiting to his cause; it was one of his ways of trying to understand from the inside the kind of problems they faced.

Secondly, in the summer of 1936, he made another European visit, the first of a series. Starting in the company of the Robert Duncans, he visited Paris (which he found dirty), then went on with them to Nyon on Lake Geneva, then to Vevey, before leaving them to go through Provence to Marseilles, where he caught the MV *Tabien* to sail round Spain and back to England by the beginning of September. He had wanted to go into Spain itself but the Civil War was in full swing, so he had to content himself with studying Russian for an hour a day, giving the communist clenched-fist salute to a fishing boat which flew the fascist flag, and scaling the after-mast (a hundred feet of it) to survey the ship below.

Letters from Patrick Duncan senior to his eldest son during the years at Winchester and Balliol are interesting from two points of view. First, they show clearly how the father tried to steer the son on to what he thought the right lines – 'steer' rather than 'direct' or 'channel', because the letters show a concerned and usually humane man trying hard to understand and sympathize with his son, rather than an authoritarian *paterfamilias*. Certainly the letters are a useful corrective to the common view of Patrick Duncan senior as a forbidding and humourless man, though it is obvious, too, that Patrick's relationship with him was more formal and, in a sense, more intellectual than with his mother, for when Patrick wrote to them separately he wrote to father of books, ideas and politics, to mother of friends, gossip and feelings.

Though Patrick Duncan senior often argues from positions which have been so parodied that it is difficult to take them seriously now, they must be taken so if one is to appreciate the man he was, and the man his son was to become. If that is difficult, at least it is easy to feel a certain sympathy for him as he tries to influence his son, given as Patrick was to sudden tacks in mid-stream. 'I am not sure that I agree with your plans for the future,' he writes. 'Anyhow, you should not leave out Oxford. Apart from what you get from the life there, an Oxford degree opens many doors, and the long vac. gives you a chance of going abroad and learning to speak foreign languages.'[29]
Again, he writes:

> I liked your report – but don't leave your Latin in the cold. It is not as attractive a language as Greek, nor is its literature, but to be able to write good Latin prose means that you have a real grasp of style and expression which will serve you in using any language.[30]

When Patrick is thinking of being an architect, his father writes very gently to point out that it might mean no Oxford, and to suggest he talks to Herbert Baker:

> But you must think very carefully about it all round because it is a big decision and I will not stand in the way of your finding the work which suits you best. . . . . I had an idea that you were thinking of Foreign Office service not the SA service but the British.[31]

When Patrick is thinking of a career in South African journalism his father
writes:

> Journalism here does not offer a very wide scope, nor is it a short and easy
> way to fortune.... London is the place I should make for if I were looking
> for a career in journalism or indeed in anything else. It is lovely to have a
> dream castle...at the end of a vista but unless some Fairy Godmother
> lands you there on a magic carpet, or whatever form of transport they use
> the road to it is hard and sometimes dusty. My imagination is subject,
> perhaps enslaved, to a severely practical control. The wings of yours are
> not yet clipped.[32]

The other interest of the father's letters of 1934–41 is that they cover what
were in many ways the most fascinating years of his political career; they offer
a detailed insight, from a position of power and influence, of white South
African politics at a time when, to whites at least, it was very controversial.
There are also real senses in which the relationship between father and son
during these years – indirect though much of it was, since they lived mainly in
different countries – helped provide Patrick with a political perspective
which was to set him apart from traditional South African liberalism.

After his brief period (1921–4) as Minister for the Interior, Education and
Public Health in the coalition between Smuts's South African Party (SAP)
and the Unionists, from 1924–33 Patrick Duncan senior had been in opposition to Hertzog's National Party. After Smuts's government fell, the SAP
and the Unionists had joined forces and, from 1929, Duncan and Hofmeyr
were in effect the main leaders of the SAP after Smuts himself. After Britain
left the gold standard in 1932, Duncan led the opposition attack on
Hertzog, the Prime Minister, who wanted South Africa to remain on the
gold standard, partly as an assertion of her independence from Britain.
Eventually, in 1933, Hertzog was forced to concede, South Africa left the
gold standard, and his National Party split. Though Smuts himself was
tempted to join with dissident Nationalists, Duncan was largely responsible
for persuading him not to, but rather to aim for coalition with the
Hertzogites. Eventually this coalition was to become a fusion between the
SAP and the Hertzogites in the new United Party. This was of course very
much in line with Duncan's dominant aim of promoting English-Afrikaner
unity, and his certainty that this was the way forward for South Africa led
him to concede – and to persuade Smuts to concede – that the Bill to remove
black and coloured voters from the common roll in the Cape (already at the
committee stage in Parliament when the talks about fusion began) and the
Land Bill (which removed some more land-owning rights from blacks)
should not be made obstacles to the fusion. Duncan himself became
Minister of Mines in the Hertzog–Smuts Cabinet of 1933.

On the Bill to remove the black voters from the roll, Hertzog compromised
a little; the Bill became one which placed blacks on a separate roll rather than
one which removed their franchise entirely; and the Bill, despite continued
black and liberal opposition, became law in 1936. Some blacks might have
lost some of the few rights they had held; but white unity was promoted, for a
time at least. Hofmeyr, rather to Duncan's disgust – for he distrusted that
kind of liberalism – found a way of speaking and voting against the Franchise
and Land Bills without resigning from the Cabinet.

It is clear from Duncan's letters to his son that he, unlike Hofmeyr, was not simply compromising in the matter of the rights of Africans, but that he actually saw the Cape franchise as a danger; he wrote in February 1936:

> We are still in trouble with our native legislation. The Bill first introduced which took away the Cape native vote we had to withdraw as such a storm of sentiment was raised against it that we should not have got the necessary ⅔rds majority and then we should have had the whole native question as a battleground in a general election with Hertzog on the one side and Smuts on the other, and the Great United Party would have gone up in smoke. So now we go back to Hertzog's original bill of 1929 which allows the natives to elect three members to the House of Assembly. I do not like that as well as the first one but our party seems to be able to unite on it – which is the first necessity.[33]

In his next letter he bewails the 'mass of sentiment which people satisfy their souls who will not look at the facts of the situation'[34] and, a month later, reacting to one of Patrick's letters, he writes at length:

> In the far future, as you see it, we shall be like one of the West Indian islands where the white man gradually is eliminated or like a S. American state where there is no bar in sentiment against race mixture and the S. African of the future will figure in various shades of duskiness. Looked at with the cold eye of reason I admit it is difficult to look into the far future and see a way of escape from one or other of these alternatives. And yet some instinct which it is difficult to analyse makes me refuse to accept them. I have a great liking for the Bantu peoples and admire many of their qualities but I do not look forward to Bantu rule in SA. If I were told by some revelation of the future that in say 50 years' time the Bantu or his admixtures was to be the dominant power in SA politics most of my interest in the country would die. To that extent I am a racialist.[35]

That he had other misgivings, too, is clear from other letters of the time, in one of which he wondered whether 'this and succeeding Parlts are really going to give the natives a fair deal. It will mean a change of heart ... generosity is not a conspicuous Afrikaner virtue.'[36]

Four months before his death in 1943, he had reached a degree of pessimism and a realization of how flimsy was the unity he had worked so hard for: 'taking the European racial divisions', which had come to a head as a result of the war, 'with the problem of adjustment among whites and coloureds', he wrote, 'I am not an optimist as to the future of the Union'.[37]

Part of this realization undoubtedly stemmed from the role he played when South Africa and other Dominions followed Britain in declaring war on Germany. Duncan had been close to Hertzog at least since the time of the Status Bill of 1934, which confirmed South Africa's autonomy in terms of the Statute of Westminster, and which he had supported so wholeheartedly that he earned the hostility of many people in Natal, then as now the most 'English' of South Africa's provinces. In 1935 he had accompanied Hertzog to Britain, and reported to his son:

> We have had a wonderful time in England also a useful one – as far as Gen. Hertzog and I are concerned. We have got to know the British Government personally, and to understand their outlook.... General

Hertzog has gone back with a clearer conception of what the membership of the Empire means to S. Africa.[38]

Then in 1936 Duncan was appointed Governor-General, largely because Hertzog wanted a South African, not a man sent out from Britain and, if he could not have a *ware boereseun* ('a true son of the Boers'), he preferred someone who was at least a naturalized South African. Although Duncan had never felt entirely at home in the rough and tumble of politics, he disliked the thought of being made into a figurehead; however, after much private debate and pressure from his Cabinet colleagues, he accepted the post and a GCMG to make him Sir Patrick and his wife Lady Duncan.

In the matter of the declaration of war in 1939 he was, however, to be considerably more than a figurehead. On 4 September 1939 a motion proposed by Hertzog and calling for neutrality was rejected by the House of Assembly. Constitutionally the thing for the Governor-General to do was to accept a dissolution of Parliament but, after much thought, though without consulting anyone else,[39] he instead asked Smuts to form a new Cabinet. His reasons were apparently entirely domestic, though his long belief in the Empire must have influenced him, too. He explained to Lionel Hichens:

> ... I believe it is a matter of dispute ... whether a Governor-General should ever refuse his Prime Minister's request for a dissolution.... I could see no alternative. A General Election now on the neutrality issue would have been the scene of intense bitterness possibly even bloodshed.... When war broke out the house was divided and the two leaders of the government party submitted conflicting motions to the house. That of General Smuts was adopted by a substantial majority.... I therefore told Hertzog that I could not see my way to reject the decision of the house.... I am clear about the decision and if there was no precedent in the book it is time there was one....[40]

As he predicted, a result of his action was that the always shaky United Party split, and many Afrikaners withdrew their support from the Government and from the Governor-General himself. It is an obvious irony, and apparent from his reactions to Chamberlain, Munich and Churchill, that Sir Patrick had not wished to go to war with Germany; as late as January 1940 he could write to his son: 'I should wish that this war if it had come would have come not by reason of a challenge to Hitler over Poland but in defence of an attack on some vital interest of ours.'[41]

It must be said plainly that Sir Patrick was not a liberal in any sense of the word; he was an imperialist, a conservative and, at best, a paternalist in the matter of race. His eldest son did not, in other words, come from a tradition either of liberal dissent or of liberalism subdued for the sake of other ends. Sir Patrick did not believe in moral gestures; though he might despise the day-to-day shenanigans of politics and politicians, he believed that politics concerned, above all else, power and the control of power, and he despised the equivocation of a Hofmeyr. If Hofmeyr thought Duncan lacked political courage, Duncan thought Hofmeyr lacked political honesty. In 1943 he wrote to his son:

> You will know of course that there was a very serious Cabinet crisis owing to Mr Hofmeyr's inability to agree to a bill which Government has decided

to introduce dealing with the interpenetration by Asiatics of European residential quarters of Durban and other towns. Mr H having carried his opposition almost to the point of resignation found that a way was open to him of allowing the bill to be introduced and passed without his re-signation from the Cabinet – apparently by his being allowed to make a speech against the bill which would make his position clear to the public. That is where I think he is wrong, and where, through personal vanity, he has led his colleagues and the Government to the brink of disaster.

I honour him for his liberal principles and for the courage with which he opposes all attempts to subject the coloured races on the ground of colour to discriminatory legislation. The present intention of the Government about this bill was bound to bring him up against this problem in an acute form. He had to decide whether the bill was totally unacceptable to him and he should therefore oppose even to the point of resignation or whether in view of the circumstances of the country in and outside SA he should not let larger considerations prevail and waive for the time his liberal principles . . . what I object to is that all that should be done in public so that people could see what a stand he had made for his principles. That is what I call political vanity.[42]

It is in this attitude that Sir Patrick provided such a significant part of his eldest son's political education, for when Patrick himself became actively involved in politics he was always interested in power, not simply in maintaining principles and integrity. He came from a very different back-ground from that of the traditional Cape liberals; and some of his later difficulties with the Liberal Party may be traced directly to some of the objections his father had to Hofmeyr. It is perhaps the most important legacy given by Sir Patrick to the son who was to stand for so much that his father would have found objectionable.

After Winchester, Balliol seemed a little anti-climactic, and in several of his first letters home Patrick confessed he was finding the change difficult. Although in one of his last reports to the Duncans, Malcolm Robertson had said, 'I think he could achieve a First if he could concentrate for once!',[43] it was exactly this concentration on any one thing which he could not achieve. He started by reading Modern Greats (philosophy, politics and economics, now usually called 'PPE'), though from the first he hankered a little after Modern Languages. However, it was apparently regarded as rather an 'inferior school' at Balliol and, if Duncan himself was uncertain about his aim, his father was not: he wanted his son to achieve the same kind of success he had done, and his severe advice was that Patrick should read a great deal, get to know a few of the better dons, and have 'a small clique' of worthwhile friends. To this Patrick replied:

I think that you were right, and I wish that I could find such a collection of 'Pharisees' that would take me in, but I have not yet got that air of effortless superiority, or even the consciousness of it, that would make admittance possible. I know a huge number of people, all over the University, and no one of them well. . . . I should be very glad to get into a clique. . . .[44]

But of course he was not his father, and Balliol in the 1930s was a very different place from what it had been in the late 1880s. Above all else, it was political: among Duncan's contemporaries were Edward Heath, Denis Healey, Roy Jenkins, Julian Amery, Maurice Macmillan, Niall MacDermott, Philip Kaiser (the American economist and diplomat, and Kennedy's ambassador to Senegal and Mauritania), W. W. Rostow (the economist and the author of *The Stages of Growth*), and Eliud Mathu (the first African in the Kenyan legislature). Duncan had gone up to Oxford expecting to be very political, and had planned to join the Labour Club; but he found he did not like its members. At the end of his first term, he wrote home: 'While still of the left, I do not think Oxford is the place for violent discussion.... Not that I shan't read Marx and be convinced by him: the thing is that the Labour Club is too hysterical and I don't like it....'[45] But it was an odd version of Marxism he planned to be convinced by, since he went on: 'I feel actually that true segregation will only become possible in a Communist S. Africa.... One only has to look at the USSR to see how successful their native policy has been.'

Soon after, however, he wrote to his parents that he was collecting money for the International Students' Service, the main purpose being to help Austrian Jews. He wrote, too, that after hearing someone use the expression 'Dirty little jewboy', 'I blushed inwardly at what these people have to put up with'.[46] Three months later he wrote: 'I have no racial feelings towards Jews but I think we must insist that they are absorbed and cease living as a people within a people.'[47]

His energies were mainly devoted to his social life. There were some thirty-five South Africans at Oxford, several of them at Balliol and at Trinity next door, and Duncan helped found the Oxford South African Club, which met at Rhodes House to hear visiting speakers and to drink mulled claret. At the suggestion of John Martin, Chairman of the Argus Group of South African newspapers, he and some friends produced two numbers of a news-sheet on South Africa, until his father advised him to abandon it. He was elected, through the good offices of Julian Amery, to the Gridiron Club, a dining club, which he enjoyed a great deal. He joined the Officers' Training Corps mainly for the sake of the cheap riding, and rode regularly. (Despite his stiff knee, he was a competent horseman, though he had to ride with a long stirrup on one side and couldn't grip properly; he once rode, much to his parents' displeasure, in a steeplechase, a 'grind', though he came off at the second fence.) He made many friends, some South African, some English, some American, some German, though none – except Kurt von Wilmowsky, grandson of the great armament-maker Krupp – apparently as close as his Winchester friends. He gave small lunch-parties in his rooms in college, went to sherry-parties, walked in the Parks, called on friends, dined at the 'Grid', and generally found pleasant ways to get through his allowance of £400 a year, though he often felt guilty about how much he spent. He continued his interest in music, especially Bach, in old books, and in printing and typography; he bought a typewriter and typed his essays, and some of his letters, and searched everywhere in Oxford for decent writing-paper but ended in getting a supply from London.

He began to be more serious about girl-friends, and he wrote home about some: Mary Turvey, whom he had met on board ship coming back from South Africa; Kitty MacLain; Nina Brodiansky, a White Russian whom he used to see in London; and Rosemary Menzies Wilson, whom he had known and written to for years (the Menzies Wilsons had lived in the Transvaal, and they and the Duncans had holidayed together) but with whom he fell briefly in love at Oxford, and of whom he wrote to his mother in April 1938:

> I have absolutely fallen for [Rosemary]. It was awful. Every moment I was away from her I was miserable, and many moments that I was with her I was too, for she is not happy.... I was torn in two. It won't last long, this appalling feeling. But it is quite frightful while it lasts. I don't suppose it is anything more than a momentary spark, but while it lasted it was good.[48]

During his time in South Africa in 1937, Duncan had read with gusto the *Decameron* (in Italian, to make it a little more respectable) and had written to his Winchester friend, Jeremy Pemberton, about it, and about a romantic passion he had developed for a lady several years his senior and already safely engaged to someone else. In March 1938 he wrote to Pemberton again, this time bewailing the class prejudices which had prevented him from talking to a maid in one of the houses he spent the vacation in: 'the loveliest girl ... so intelligent and absolutely ravishing'.[49] In short, at least one of his interests at the time was exactly what one might have expected.

Work mattered little. Duncan went to one lecture only in his first term, and his tutor, the economist Maurice Allen, 'soon realized that my essays were simply boilings down from the Encyclopaedia Britannica'.[50] After two terms Allen told him exactly where he stood, and in July 1938 he reported to his mother that 'one term or two of Modern Greats has been enough to tell me that I shall never be an economist',[51] and that he had resolved to change Schools to Modern Languages. In October he started French language and literature with a new tutor, a Miss Shipworth. Although he often wrote to his father about the books he was reading, often they were not what he should have been reading, though he stuck to philosophy more than to economics; but conversation took priority over books. Even the French was not a great success, though, thanks to a final term or two of cramming, he managed to get a Second, though not a good one. Academically, he felt he had little to be proud of.

Indeed, as he wrote home, 'I personally feel conscious of the enormous influence of Oxford in the vacs, rather than in term',[52] and there were ways in which at least one of his vactions was to exercise a much more profound influence on his development than his three years at Balliol. Certainly he made the most of his vacations, not only keeping up with his relatives, his Winchester friends, and the 'kindergarten', but also travelling abroad. Over the Christmas vacation of 1937–8 he visited the Canaries with an Oxford friend, and kept a diary, full of intellectual inconsistencies, though nearly always interesting.[53] He walked immensely, did a mule-back trip across one of the islands, made some local acquaintances, talked Spanish politics to anyone who was not afraid to, cursed unpleasant muleteers who tried to cheat him, noted that 'colour and class are con-comitant on the islands', reported a funny conversation with an awful Englishwoman and a very moving one with an eighty-year-old English exile, Bilbrough, the son of a rich family who had squandered all his money and who lived now in isolation, not least because he was completely deaf, and who acted as local printer to the islands.

Bilbrough gave the young men coffee 'in filthy cups', and for two hours they tried to talk to him. But, generally, Duncan's reactions were an odd mixture of undergraduate snobbery and a delight in spartan simplicity after what he felt were the fleshpots of Oxford: 'Oxford teaches one to *need* luxury,'[54] he wrote home after going for a two-day walk in the Canaries with no food except oranges.

In the Easter vacation of 1938 he went with three Oxford friends on a tour by car of Italy – Florence, San Marino, Ravenna, Padua, Venice, Milan, Lake Garda, Verona, Bergamo and so on, and then back home via Switzerland, France and Belgium (where he took great delight in speaking Afrikaans to Flemings and finding they understood him completely). Near the end of the Italian tour he reported to his mother, 'I like being among aryans in a dago land';[55] yet in the same letter he managed to convey a 'spot of time' perfectly:

I have done something so perfect today that I must tell you before the memory fades. It was at Ravenna ... in the pine forest. We had just seen a Roman church built in 400 AD covered with the loveliest mosaics, in blue and gold, in green and yellow and red. We bought a cheap lunch and drove out to the Pineta. It lies on the low [sound? sand?] between Ravenna and the sea. It is a Spanish growth of the Mediterranean pines, thick lawn grass carpeting the ground. I left the others in the car and went and lay down in a sheltered [illegible] ... I must have crushed some thyme, because the whole air was sweet....

The most important of the tours was to Germany in the summer of 1938. Duncan had organized the tour carefully, through his mother's German relations, through family friends called the Arnolds, through Kurt von Wilmowsky of Balliol, and through Helmuth von Moltke (executed by Hitler in 1945) and his wife Freya. Helmuth's mother was one of the Rose-Innes family (her father had been Chief Justice of the Union), and Alice Duncan had stayed with the Moltkes when she was at school in Germany, so there were many connections between the Moltkes and the Duncans: Helmuth's father, Chief of Staff of the German Army from 1906 to 1914, had been a Christian Scientist, Helmuth had been a Rhodes Scholar and a protégé of Lionel Curtis of the 'kindergarten', and he and Freya had visited South Africa in 1934, when they had met the Duncans and Patrick, and again in 1937. Through Hermann Speiser, Duncan had arranged to work in an *Arbeitslager*, a work-camp, for three weeks; he was to stay with his Dold relations beforehand, and the Moltkes, Wilmowskys and Arnolds afterwards.

Looking back he saw his three weeks in the Reichsarbeitsdienst (the state work-camp service) as 'one of the turning points in my life':

I smelt for the first time the evil stench of totalitarianism. I wore the swastika badge, the jackboots, and the uniform of the Reichsarbeitsdienst. I worked like a trojan for 'the New Germany'. Although I could hardly speak German I spent most of those three weeks arguing with the nice young Germans who were in the camp. They were friendly, yet most determined to let their young visitor from Süd Afrika see the true light. And I was just as determined to let them see the beastliness of Hitler. I kept a detailed diary, and today, with so much artificial after thought anti-nazism in the world I am proud to turn back to that old diary and see that I did all in my power to stop the most evil government in the World's history.[56]

Some of Duncan's German diaries still exist, though later he crossed out the names of anti-Nazis he met and later still destroyed some of the diaries. He wrote a report, too, on the Reichsarbeitsdienst for Con O'Neill, then Third Secretary of the British Embassy in Berlin, which the Ambassador sent to the Foreign Office, and the Foreign Office on to the Ministry of Labour, the Board of Education and the War Office, which republished extracts in a confidential 'Monthly summary' for serving officers.

The comments he made at the time do in general bear out the claims he was to make later about his reactions. Some things about the work-camp he went to (near Köningsberg, at Taw near the Lithuanian border, where the *arbeitsmänner* were raising the level of a dyke to prevent winter flooding) he admired: its cleanliness, the physical strength of the young men, the hard work done. But, although he himself enjoyed using his body in hard labour for five and a half hours a day, mainly shifting earth, he loathed the mindlessness and regimentation of the camp. As he reported to Jeremy Pemberton, the camp was 'fine for body – hell for mind';[57] and in his report to the Embassy he confessed that at times he actually thought of running away. He particularly loathed the wireless which blared out waltzes, marches and propaganda fifteen hours a day. In his draft report he said:

Each day there is talk lasting an hour on political subjects. I read one lecture on the USSR. It is prepared by material from HQ, and is wildly incorrect, apart from a natural bias. To this political atmosphere all minds lean willingly. The result was that the men were like so many gramophone records.[58]

He argued when he could, though his German was not really adequate (for his mother spoke no German at home, except to his father to keep secrets from the children), but after a week of this decided it was fruitless, and talked no more politics; instead, he took occasional advantage of his privileged position to duck particularly unpleasant work, to stay in bed for the early-morning flag-parade and political talk, or to go off on his own to watch birds and butterflies.

The final comment in his draft report was: 'I enjoyed the work; but [deleted] I have learnt to hate compulsion [deleted] but I have changed my mind [deleted] But I believe ... that such a system could not be transferred to the British Empire, even were it desirable.'[59] In the actual report to the embassy he was stronger: 'I would finish by saying that in a land where all is compulsion, the compulsion with the RAD is one of the best, and as they say themselves, it is practical socialism. But to me personally that is not a point in favour.'[60] He knows, in other words, that there is something objectionable; but for his positive values he is thrown back to a system of values more his father's than his own. It is an odd comment on his conclusion to this report, too, that when he was back in England he wrote to Germany to find out more about the *Arbeitsdienst*, because he thought a similar system could be started from English public schools. A letter to his father after leaving the camp shows, too, that his reactions at the time were not as tidy as he was to make out later:

This country is a great mixed kettle of fish. It has a lot of good in it. The new architecture for instance is I think marvellous. There never were any serious slums – those there are the Govt however has made no attempt to clear. The autobahnen are an example to the world, perhaps even to N. America. Most incredibly, unemployment is abolished and the economic system is working full-speed. The security this gives to the worker can be imagined. Prices are fixed, so that middlemen can never speculate antisocially. The birthrate has been successfully stimulated.... The debit side in my mind is longer and more serious than the credit. As an old worker said to me in Berlin: – I had not spoken to him about politics and he suddenly said: 'Ich möchte nicht in D.sein'. I asked him if he didn't love his country. He only answered: 'you see all that is lovely: you don't know what we see' so I asked him what his wages were before and after. Before 1933 he got 50–60 RM but now RM 32.50 pfg in a week. He then drew an expressive finger across his throat. All the working class with few exceptions, as far as I can see, are of the opinion that they through lower wages, are paying for i. unemployment's death, ii. schönheit, iii. army.

Actual starvation is only prevented in many cases by winterhilfswerk as workers on the Reichsautobahn live in barracks and get 19 marks a week to feed self and family.

The secret police have immense power. It is generally agreed (except in Arbeitslager) that they have supra-legal powers.[61]

In the same letter he says, 'I am terrified. I know a war has got to come...,' but he says, too, in that letter: 'The only hope for jews is to drop their religion and amalgamate; and in S. Africa to drop their anti-German and anti-Dutch and definite communistic tendencies.'

Seeing Helmuth von Moltke in Berlin, and meeting Con O'Neill (who was to resign from the Diplomatic Service after Munich, so opposed was he to the Nazis) and Trott, another of the 'Kreisau circle' later executed by Hitler, all helped to sort out his impressions. Freya von Moltke recalls the time thus:

Helmuth had fetched Patrick from the train in Berlin.... He had taken him into his office, put him into a chair and explained what National Socialism was, meant, did, and warned him – since he obviously felt he needed the warning – not to have himself taken in by some things that might seem good to Patrick.[62]

Duncan's reaction to this is recorded in his German diaries:

The result of course is that I am completely devoted to him. I admire him as I admire few other people in the world. If I thought I could help him in any way I would certainly do it for I believe he is taking great risks.[63]

But still his devotion appears to have been mainly to the man, and he did not entirely comprehend his ideas, though he begins to see the struggle in Germany from the point of view of the kind of opposition to Hitler advocated by Trott and Moltke – that is, largely pacifist, intellectual and aristocratic, though the Kreisau circle did include some trade unionists. Prittie in *Germans against Hitler*[64] calls its membership 'mostly conservatives and land-holders', and its policy 'a synthesis of conservatism and socialism'. The latter is not at all a bad statement of Patrick Duncan's later political position. It is after the talks with Moltke, O'Neill and Trott that Duncan notes in his diary a meeting with an army officer, whose name is crossed out, who 'credits the story of Buchenwald Concentration Camp' and 'who also sees the fight as not between collective communism and collective fascism but between both and INDIVIDUALISM, my creed, my gospel, for which I am going to fight'.[65] It was one of the two most important single political ideas of his life, and was to direct much of his thinking for the next twenty years.

Of course his German visit was not all politics; he had a very pleasant stay with the Wilmowsky family at the Schloss Marienthal, where the opposition to Hitler was that of the aristocratic rich to the 'collectivism of the fat, bald ex-shopkeeping Parteileiters',[66] and with his Aunt Retha (who shocked him by saying that when she looked into the eyes of the Führer she felt she was looking into the eyes of God). He caused a minor crisis at Kreisau by deciding, on the spur of the moment, to cross the border into Czechoslovakia and to spend a night there (his first attempt to find a room nearly landed him in a brothel, but he realized in time and found more respectable lodgings). He went to see *Tristan und Isolde* at Bayreuth and hated it, partly because Wagner was not his beloved Bach, partly because the actress playing Isolde was old and fat. He read, especially at Kreisau, and especially about Frederick the Great, whom he elevated to the status of personal hero. He met a number of girls and fell briefly for Gerda Arnold, *nouvelle et merveilleuse:* 'I ashamedly longed to be alone with her. She is one of the most marvellous things on this earth, and was definitely showing a green light.'[67] That was until he met the other daughter of the family, Marina, who was equally pretty.

Back in England, in early September, he wrote to his mother: 'It is only now I have left Germany that I feel how much I love it, and what a good time I had there. I owe the Germans a great debt of gratitude which it will be hard to pay. Thank you for making your friends my friends.'[68]

After the summer of 1938, his brother Andrew joined him at Balliol, and Patrick did all he could to steer Andrew to social success and happiness, and wrote home regularly to say how much he enjoyed having him there to share the pleasures of Oxford. When Sir Abe Bailey gave Patrick £15 and Andrew £10, Andrew bought a gramophone and Patrick more records, and the brothers took great pleasure in listening to music. Almost all Patrick's letters home refer to something they have been listening to, and he sent favourite records as presents to his mother. Patrick continued in the Officers' Training Corps, and Andrew joined the Flying Corps. Social life flourished, and Patrick went on seeing much of Kurt von Wilmowsky and something of Hilgard Muller, a Rhodes Scholar who was later to become Foreign Minister of South Africa. He was elected Treasurer of the Bryce Club. Andrew and he spent weekends with various members of the 'kindergarten', and lunched with them when they came to Oxford. He was working slightly more now he had changed Schools, but found he preferred philology to literature.

One of the most interesting views of Patrick Duncan at the time is that of Philip Kaiser, an American Rhodes Scholar a year senior to him at Balliol, and President of the JCR in 1938–9. In Kaiser's mind, Wilmowsky and Duncan are closely associated, the first an ardent German nationalist, not a National Socialist but unwilling to accept much criticism of the Reich, and the latter always ambivalent about German politics and reluctant to join in any serious political discussion. Kaiser found Duncan in other ways very pleasant: hospitable, approachable, friendly, and easy and interesting to talk to, with a degree of social self-confidence unlike that of the average English undergraduate. Indeed, he fitted much more easily into an American than an English social mode, and always got on well with Americans, sharing their optimism and openness; and the main tension Kaiser (a Jew) found in his relationship with Duncan was simply in the matter of Duncan's Germanophilia, and in his friendship with Wilmowsky. Though Kaiser remembers that Kurt loathed Goebbels with great passion, he remembers, too, that Kurt felt Hitler had a certain mystique and even greatness. His predominant memory of Duncan at the time is of political confusion and intellectual bewilderment, sitting oddly with lively charm and social confidence.

Richard Hare, also a Balliol contemporary (and later a Fellow of Balliol before becoming Professor of Moral Philosophy at Corpus Christi), remembers something of the same conflict, though he puts it down to a different cause:

> He was not a comfortable sort of person. I think I was struck even when at Oxford by the tension (which to some extent affected all of us, but him more than most) between love of the good things of life (music, books) and a desire to play our part in a world that was likely to fall to pieces, which would preclude our enjoying them. Oxford at that time (as now) was ... full of incompatible ideals, often embraced simultaneously by the same person.[69]

One sees his conflict in two instances, one minor, one major. First, in late 1938 Patrick Duncan turned down the opportunity to be Treasurer of the Anglo-German Society, because he thought it pro-Nazi and because 'you simply can't tell people you think their Government is hell'.[70] Second was Munich. Later Duncan was to record his reaction to the Munich Agreement thus:

> When Munich came, I threw myself into Lindsay's anti-Chamberlain bye-election in Oxford City, when he was defeated by Hailsham (then Quintin Hogg). I invented one of the slogans they used: 'Hitler wants Hogg. We want Lindsay'. I went blithely into working-class areas of Oxford, thinking that, being of the 'proletariat' they must be Labour. I soon learnt (*a*) that these beefy and profane women were among the toughest conservatives in the land, and (*b*) that their idea of fun was *not* to be canvassed by a teen-ager student.[71]

Yet his letters of the time give a very different impression. Four days before the Munich Agreement, he writes home, 'I still believe war is inevitable between us and Germany,' and adds, 'I am alone in this belief', which is an odd comment unless he is referring only to his immediate circle. A week after the signing of the Agreement on 30 September 1938, he writes: 'To think that a week ago we all expected to be at war with Germany within a day or two! It all seems like a bad dream now....'[72] Of course this was a common enough reaction at the time, but it hardly squares with his remark in 1955 that he had 'felt rather strongly that Munich was a mistake'.[73] Later that October he wrote to his father:

> Politically I agree with what you say about Czechoslovakia. We must make no attempt to interfere with Germany. But such a policy just has to swallow

the hard nut (!) that we will in future take a *very* second place in Europe. We may have to look forward to a Pax Germanica in Europe.... Perhaps in a German empire is to be found eternal peace and that to oppose such a situation would merely be narrow nationalism. I really feel that at the moment, but *daren't* say so alone.... Lindsay was beaten fifteen minutes ago by 12 000 to 15 000.[74]

There are two possibilities: either he was attributing to himself at the time of Munich the kind of feelings he thought he should have had (not an unknown phenomenon), or else he was taking an easy line with his father, who much preferred Chamberlain to Churchill, not least because Churchill had been one of Milner's fiercest critics during his time in South Africa. What is certain is that Patrick remained friends with Kurt. On the night before the election, Patrick, Kurt and others went off to the cinema, which is hardly a sign of commitment to the anti-Munich cause.

In November Duncan dined with Helmuth von Moltke in London, and wrote to his mother of his fears for him in the Reich, because of his work as a lawyer for German Jews. 'He is simply one of the greatest people I know,' he wrote:

The only reason he gives me for his hate of Hitler is that it is a proletarian regime making a clean break with European traditions.... I wish I could be so certain of any views.... I like him immensely, that is all I can say. That is all I can say about most things, I like or I do not like. How uncritical and blind.[75]

In the Easter vacation of 1939, he worked in the editorial department of *The Times,* thanks to a request by his father to Geoffrey Dawson, the Editor; once again, his attitude to Germany produced problems, and he told his father that someone in the editorial office called him 'a Nazi dupe'. His letter went on:

the government does not realize the sort of spirit in Germany ... the thing to have done would have been to have let Germany expand wherever she wants. Keep quiet and friendly.... If she really wanted war then we could accept the challenge and appear as the Slavs' and the Romans' and the Scandinavians' liberators....[76]

Later he wrote to his father: 'One is looked upon as a Nazi Spy if one has one good word to say for Hitler.'[77] England in 1939 was not a comfortable place for a Germanophile, even one who hero-worshipped Moltke and, some of the time at least, disliked National Socialism.

In the summer vacation of 1939, Patrick, Andrew, and Kurt von Wilmowsky went out to South Africa. Patrick and Kurt went ahead to spend a fortnight with German friends of Kurt in the Canaries, and then Andrew joined them. They went in *Durban Castle* as far as Lobito Bay in Angola, spent a few days there, then went by train to Elisabethville in the Congo. After a day there, they caught a train to Northern Rhodesia, then went on to the Victoria Falls, then to Bulawayo, where they caught a plane to Johannesburg, and then a train to Durban. After a very pleasant holiday in Durban, the three young men joined Sir Patrick Duncan's entourage for an official tour of the Transkei. They travelled in the White Train, specially built for governors-general and royalty, and were fêted and dined. While Patrick enjoyed some parts of the vice-regal magnificence, there was considerable tension between his parents and himself, though Andrew – always more diplomatic and easy-going – avoided it. Patrick became very impatient with the protocol of the tour, and particularly with his mother's insistence on the proper forms of behaviour; he wished to be more informal with the people they met than his mother thought the Governor-General's eldest son should be, and there were fierce arguments. The twig was even less malleable at twenty-one than it had been in early childhood.

One minor incident on the tour was to have a considerable effect on Duncan, still uncertain as he was about a career. A young policeman on escort duty, whom Duncan made friends with, said to him on parting: 'Goodbye. I hope that you will take a job in the civil service here, and that you will go far in it.'[78] This remark was later to encourage him to apply for a post in the Colonial Service, and to ask for a posting to Basutoland.

The declaration of war on Germany by Britain, and South Africa's declaration shortly afterwards, affected the three young men in very different ways. Andrew, who had taken a pilot's licence with the Oxford Flying Corps, decided to stay in South Africa and to join the South African Air Force. Patrick received a letter from the OTC in Oxford to return at once and did so, catching a boat in early October 1939 and, after many scares about submarines, arriving back in England about 14 or 15 October. Kurt von Wilmowsky was of course trapped by his German nationality. Sir Patrick offered to look after him for the rest of the war so that he could escape the unpleasantness of internment – there were many Germans in South Africa who were interned, some throughout the war. Kurt felt he could not accept this, refused Sir Patrick's offer, left South Africa illegally and tried to get to the German community in South-West Africa. He was arrested in South-West Africa and almost immediately shipped back to internment in England. Once again, he was offered refuge, since the Master of Balliol offered to take responsibility for him so that he could continue his studies and take a degree. Apparently the British authorities were willing; but Kurt was not. He felt he could not desert his nationality, and from what Duncan says in letters of the time it is also clear that Kurt was more a Nazi then than he had been before the war. All the same, Duncan did what he could for Kurt in the internment camp in Sutton Courtenay, sending him books, clothes, food-parcels, looking after some of his belongings and his money, and the two wrote to each other regularly. In July 1940 Kurt and many other internees were being transferred by troop-ship to another camp in Canada when their ship was torpedoed. Kurt was among those drowned.

For years after the war, Duncan tried to return to the Wilmowsky family in Germany both the money and the belongings Kurt had left in his safekeeping; the correspondence with lawyers in England, South Africa and Germany, and with Kurt's family, goes all the way through to 1953. Duncan tried to send tea and coffee to Germany in 1946 to pay the Wilmowskys for the camera which Kurt had in fact given to him at their last meeting; permission was, however, refused. He worked hard to get Kurt's money which had been left banked in England back to the family; and, in the end, when Kurt's younger brother came out to farm in South-West Africa in the

1950s, Patrick gave him Kurt's camera, even though he had already sent £60 for it to Kurt's father.

Duncan's first letter home from England reported that he had arrived in a 'changed England';[79] but he soon caught the dominant mood of the period, though as he knew Germany at closer quarters than many English people did he was full of foreboding of what would succeed the 'phoney war'. Soon after his arrival, he appeared before the recruiting board. At the medical examination, he was pronounced very fit, but because of his lameness he was classified as unfit for active service (although he told his parents that he could have passed if he had wanted to).[80] So he went back to his books, and continued with the OTC as an NCO training new recruits.

Although many of his contemporaries had already joined up, there were enough people left in Oxford to make life interesting. He became President of the Bryce Club, and enjoyed organizing its dinners. He spent much time talking to Eliud Mathu, and found him a most interesting man – it was virtually the first time he had had the opportunity to talk to an African as an equal. He read a little more systematically in preparation for Final Schools. He debated evolution with a Jesuit, and thought he won. He gave a talk on South African politics to the South African Society. He ordered some 'superb new writing paper as a sort of insult to the war which will soon drive such things out of existence, the things that make life in England so much more pleasant than life elsewhere'.[81] He looked after his brother John when he came in the New Year to join the Royal Navy. Patrick had tried hard to persuade his parents not to let John come over for this purpose. In December he had written home: 'What is the point of John's life being wasted in a futile struggle. We all here know that it is a futile struggle . . . the less we have to do with this war the better.'[82] 'We' is presumably 'South Africans', and it is clear from this just how ambiguous Duncan's feelings about the war still were, though in May 1940 he was to make an unsuccessful attempt to dissociate Balliol from the Union's vote for peace.

Despite what the young policeman had said to him on the Transkeian tour, he was still thinking of trying for the Diplomatic Service, which seems to have been his father's wish; but in November he told his father that Diplomatic exams had been closed for the duration of the war. He wondered if he should try for the Colonial Service in Bechuanaland or Basutoland, and a couple of months afterwards applied, though initially he seemed to want to stay in England for the rest of the war, to do what he could. In June he took Final Schools, and got his Second. There was some talk of his taking a post in Intelligence – Lionel Hichens suggested it – and he met a mysterious man, presumably from the War Office, on the station at Bletchley, though nothing came of it. A group of undergraduates including himself went to Sir Alfred Zimmern, Professor of International Relations at Oxford, and an active internationalist both before and after the war (he was Secretary-General of the constituent conference of UNESCO in 1945), for advice on their idea of starting an underground anti-German movement in preparation for the invasion. 'There is going to be no invasion,' Zimmern told them and advised them to go back to whatever they were doing.[83]

From mid-June until July he worked in a forestry camp in Shropshire, enjoying once again the hard physical work. He spent ten days visiting his father's family in Scotland, then went back to Oxford where he learned that the Colonial Office had offered him a vacancy in Basutoland, if he could pass a medical. Although there were some last-minute doubts about his fitness – the board questioned whether he could ride with his bad leg, since Colonial Officers in Basutoland had to be able to ride well to do their work efficiently – he passed, and began to look for a passage out to South Africa. In the meantime, he stayed briefly with the Hichens family – he was there when the family learned that Lionel Hichens had been killed in an air-raid – and then moved to Robert Duncan in Kew. As he told his father, he was drawn to London and the blitz 'by my fear of fear', [84] and he stayed there from September to December 1940, working first as a member of the London Labour Reserve, mainly clearing bomb-sites, and then in the East End, helping a friend, Hugh Rowntree Clifford, whose father ran the Baptist West Ham Central Mission, and acting as an air-raid warden.

Three times he had to give up his berth in ships bound for South Africa to those with higher priorities than he had, but eventually sailed in a Dutch ship from Liverpool on 29 December 1940. The ship was bombed with incendiaries just before leaving, but not damaged; it set off a magnetic or acoustic mine soon after leaving Liverpool; and, in mid-Atlantic, it was fired on and chased by a ship, and only just escaped by doubling back under cover of a rain squall. The captain did not wait to find out the pursuer's nationality, and Duncan thought it advisable to throw some of his German diaries overboard. The passengers fortunately did not know that the cargo consisted of seven thousand tons of depth-charge explosives bound for Cape Town. Even so, the strain of the voyage was such that two of the eleven passengers committed suicide during the voyage, and a third, whom Duncan had made particular friends with on board, killed himself soon after they landed, in late January 1941.

Duncan stayed only briefly with his parents in Cape Town, though he enjoyed being back a great deal. His father gave him a car, and his mother gave him a beautiful saddle. He bought some of the clothes and equipment he would need in his new work, and by 5 February 1941 was in Maseru.

BOOK TWO

Changing

4 *Wedding reception at High Commission House, Wynberg, Cape. General Smuts is in the bottom left hand corner of the photograph*

5   *Tom Fraser, Jean Fraser, Cynthia Duncan and Pat Duncan at Pitso in Maseru, 1951. The men are wearing Colonial Service uniform*

6   *Riverside Farm, near Maseru*

CHAPTER 3

1941–5
'Time's Short Enough...'[1]

Basutoland was – indeed, is – a peculiar country. First, it is one of the few countries of modern Africa which was created by its own people rather than by the makers of imperial maps; though its people were not originally all of one tribe, they were shaped by geography, outside forces, and internal diplomacy, into one of the more cohesive nation-states of Africa. Although only created in the early nineteenth century by the canny rule of Moshoeshoe, they are – and feel themselves to be – a single people, the Basotho, and for once tribe and country coincide and cohere. Of course there were conflicts: between the aims of the colonial administrators, the traders, the missionaries and the chiefs (major and minor); between the chiefs and the people; between those who parcelled out the land and those who worked it; between the rich and the poor. However, overriding all these antithetical forces, there remained a strong feeling of nationhood.

Secondly, the smallness and poverty of the country are more complex than the usual simplicities of these terms. It is a small country (roughly the size of Belgium) and with a relatively small population: the 1946 census gave 553 827 Basotho as being in the country, and 70 778 working outside; the white population was very small too, no more than 2000 in 1941. On the one hand, the country is made to seem even smaller by the concentration of the population in the narrow strip of lowlands to the west, the concentration of whites in Maseru, and the absence at any time of half the young Basotho men and many young women working in South Africa – in the mines, in industry, on farms, in private houses. On the other hand, the very concentration of the population in the west makes the three-fifths of the country which is foothills and mountains, to the north-east, east and south, rising as they do from the 6000 feet of the lowlands to over 11 000 feet in the Maluti and Drakensberg, seem even more desolate and vast. Travel in those regions has always been difficult, except on foot or on horseback, or more recently by Land-Rover or light plane. The mountains are cut by deep valleys and fast-running rivers, for most of the major rivers of South Africa rise there. The Orange flows from the far east of the country, through the south and out to the west, having gathered the waters of most of the other Basotho rivers. The Caledon flows down from the north and along the northern and western borders, before joining the Orange. The Tugela and Elands rivers rise in the eastern mountains, the Drakensberg, and flow east and south into Natal. The mountains and rivers protect the country, but also impoverish it; the mountains are cold and often bare, and the rivers wash away the topsoil from mountainsides, foothills, valleys and lowlands alike.

Thirdly, it is a country entirely bounded by South Africa – the Cape Province to the south, the Orange Free State to the west and north, and Natal to the east. Moshoeshoe forged the original tribes into a nation; established and fought for his frontiers (though his best land was stolen by the Boers); gave his people a single language, a new religion (for he invited the missionaries into his country and they helped make the Basotho among the most literate people of Africa), a unified army, and a legal system which consolidated the old laws of custom and chieftaincy; but he could not create wealth for his country. So, for all the historical independence of Basutoland and the post-colonial independence of recent years, it is still dependent on South Africa in crucial ways. People and scenery are its assets; even agriculture is hampered by overcrowding in the lowlands, by poor soil, by dangerous erosion. Though there are some diamonds in the mountains, and perhaps other mineral resources yet to be discovered, Basutoland depends economically on South Africa, which employs so many of its people and controls much of even the local economy. Yet it is a country anxious to maintain the independence Moshoeshoe created, first against Chaka and his impis, then against the Boers, then against the Cape, then against the British. Though Basotho politicians argue about how best to achieve this, none actually wishes to become part of South Africa. The independence may not be particularly real, but it is better than being a fifth province or a new Bantustan.

It was largely the independence of Basutoland from South Africa which first attracted Duncan to working there, rather than in South Africa where he would have been expected 'to enforce a native policy evolved by a parliament of fanatical anti-natives'.[2] Yet of course he himself was no more independent in his first job than are most young men; his first two months were spent in Maseru, working in the Secretariat, and he was, like some of his fellow junior officers, somewhat disillusioned. A few days after his arrival he wrote to his mother thus:

> Work here is slack. Secretariat works $5\frac{1}{2}$ hours a day. I work hard in the 5, but the other ADCs don't. They have nothing to do.... Basutoland, Mother, is heavily overstaffed.... There's *no* hope of promotion here –. There's not enough work to do for those who have been promoted. Tom Fraser was right in saying the country could almost be run on one DC and native clerks.[3]

He told his parents he regretted not having pushed harder to get into the Foreign Office because of the menial nature of his present job, and a week later told his father that he would prefer to join up. (After all, one of his brothers was doing brilliantly in the South African Air Force, and the other was in the Royal Navy, though shortly to transfer to the South African Navy.) Sir Patrick tried hard to make his eldest son see that drudgery was an inevitable part of a first post in any kind of public service, though he also made it clear that he did not regard Patrick's present work as a life's work, and Patrick seemed to accept this, for a time at least. So, although the drudgery continued – keeping accounts, filling in forms, paying wages – he searched for other interests, and soon found enough to make the job seem more worthwhile.

At the end of March 1941 he was transferred to Leribe, on the northern border of Basutoland near Ficksburg in the Orange Free State, as a temporary Assistant District Commissioner. Here he was dealing with people, not ledgers. Although he was a lowly member of the Colonial hierarchy (for he was not even a District Officer), he had much to learn and something to do, for the District Commissioner's office administered and supervised the 'native' side of the legal and administrative system (the Basutoland system was one of 'dual rule', the traditional chiefs running their wards under the generally benevolent guidance of a Colonial Officer), supervised the collection of taxes, acted as a Court of Appeal from the 'native' courts, and did all the usual trivia of a Colonial office – report-writing, paying pensions and wages, aiding the poor. It helped, too, to discover that his father was still remembered for the work he had done as Legal Adviser and Judge of the High Courts in the High Commission Territories while in legal practice in the Transvaal, when he came to Basutoland to hear appeals from the local courts. But Duncan was still not over-impressed with the Service; he soon found himself in conflict with his District Officer, and felt, too, that indirect rule included connivance at petty injustice – especially abuse of the system whereby local chiefs could fine tribesmen, which he regarded as evidence of the collective force of the tribe being used to contain individualism. He found, too, the attitudes of his superiors in the Service mainly complacent; he was ambitious, and impatient with the slow ways of hierarchies.

One of his early near-brushes with authority concerned old Thomas Mofolo, author of one of the early African novels, *Chaka*. Mofolo wrote to the Secretariat in Maseru from Matatiele, a small town over the border in the Cape Province, where he was living in poverty and misery, having lost the farm in the buying of which he had infringed the Land Act of 1913, which made it illegal for an African to buy land unless it was contiguous to other land owned by Africans, or unless in a 'native area'. Duncan telephoned the Magistrate of Matatiele about the case, but was warned by a brother-officer against interfering in what was a South African matter (though Mofolo was a Mosotho). Then he himself sent money to Mofolo, arranged for Mofolo to be helped by the District Commissioner of Teyateyaneng in Basutoland, to which the old writer had moved, and wrote to his mother for help. For the next few years, Lady Duncan paid Mofolo a monthly pension of £3. He never told Mofolo who paid the pension.

> When . . . I was posted to Leribe I boiled inside when I saw the terrible way that chiefs and administrators were neglecting their flock, the people. . . . Still I carried on, and had no thought of giving up. I *had* to. I had led a pretty dilettantish life up till then. To throw Basutoland up would be a confession of failure, so I argued.[4]

Or, at any rate, so Sir Patrick argued, because despite what he wrote later Duncan himself was often tempted to throw it up, for instance to enter the South African Defence Force or to go full-time into soil conservation. Sir Patrick wrote:

Lord Harlech came especially to me to say that he was very disappointed to hear of your attempts to get away on military service and hoped I would use all my influence to dissuade you. The only job that will be available for you will be something at some base some office work of some sort or another and he said that what you are doing now bringing you directly in touch with the needs and ambitions of the land will be an experience of much greater value ... he was looking to you as one of the men who would be looked to by the C[olonial] O[ffice] to carry out the long overdue changes. ...

Lord Harlech was then High Commissioner to the territories of Basutoland, Swaziland and Bechuanaland; he himself wrote a long letter to Patrick Duncan in December 1943 to advise him not to give up the Colonial Service in favour of soil conservation, which – to be done properly – required training in agriculture.

There were consolations in the drudgery and disappointment. He began violin lessons in Ficksburg, though his various postings meant that he would never get continuous enough teaching. He bought a dog, a ridgeback which he called Tray. He read widely, continuing his old Winchester and Balliol interests and extending his African ones. He rode a great deal, both in the course of his work and for pleasure (though he was thrown badly in April 1941 and broke his lame leg). He began to keep bees. He wrote many letters to family and to friends in England. He entertained and was entertained; not only was he charming and sociable, but also his father was Governor-General of the Union, and a governor-general's son was a good catch in Maseru. Sometimes, indeed, Duncan felt a little too much in demand; there were more young women in Maseru than young men, so many of the latter being on active service, and in one of the letters to his mother he called it 'a real blot on our civilization – that girls should have to go out and husband hunt. ...'[5]

Maseru was the social centre of the lives of most of the Europeans in the territory, even those who lived several days' ride away; and like most of the young officers Duncan used to return there regularly from his post in Leribe – and of course when his leg was broken he had to. In Maseru one of his early friends was Elizabeth Feiling, an Oxford don's daughter, who had been sent to South Africa to recover from tuberculosis. Elizabeth Feiling remembers that when she first went to Maseru in January 1942 she had been advised, seriously, to take long white gloves and to call on all the Heads of Administrative Departments; she did not take the advice but, when calling on the wife of the Government Secretary and being asked, somewhat uncivilly, whether her name was German, she remembers a young man, with a leg in plaster, who was lying on a sofa in the shadows at the side of the room, saying, 'Well, in England it is a good Tory name!' The two semi-invalids immediately found much in common. Elizabeth had heard about the Duncans from London friends, had met Sir Patrick and Lady Duncan in Pretoria, and had heard a great deal about Patrick himself. They both knew Oxford and Balliol well, since her father, the historian Keith Feiling, was a don at Christ Church and Fellow of All Souls. They both had brothers called Andrew. Both were given to somewhat unconventional behaviour, and had the patrician's scorn of euphemisms. Both had German ancestry. For the next two years they saw each other a great deal, rode together, were invited out together (they were known locally as 'the Babes in the Wood'), read and discussed the same books, and argued about religion. Elizabeth Feiling herself was a deeply religious person, and after leaving Maseru went to work on a mission-station in the Transkei; Duncan, on his arrival in Basutoland, seems to have decided that it was in some way necessary to be an Anglican, and was confirmed as such in November 1941, though he did so more as a gesture of conviction that the state needed religion than out of religious conviction itself. If anything, he was a pantheist rather than a Christian, but he did read a great deal of theology and spiritual explorations at that time: Pascal, Jan Hus, Bunyan and so on. Like a number of his fellow-officers, he was deeply suspicious of the role of Catholic missionaries in Basutoland, and a number of his letters home are virulently anti-Catholic. He and Elizabeth Feiling found much to argue about in this, though they hardly ever talked politics, at least of the local or South African variety.

Duncan was always very attractive to women of all ages, though he was never a womanizer. His lameness made some women wish to mother him, and there is little doubt that he enjoyed being mothered, though he also hated people pitying his lameness. Once again, this explains something of the complexity of his feelings towards his own mother, who had tried so hard to 'bend the twig' and whom Duncan felt did not always love him as much as his straighter second brother. There was in him, then and later, something of the *puer aeternus*, of Peter Pan, apparent not only in his zest for adventure and his curiosity, but also in his relationships, with women especially. Elizabeth Feiling recalls that this part of his personality jarred on her at times, and made her feel uneasy, though of course it was just this which generated the affection of others. In Maseru in the early 1940s he was known as 'Mad Pat', not because he was a fast-living drunken young man (he was in many ways puritanical), but because he seemed always to be at the centre of the social life of the white community, even though he loathed dancing. The young in Maseru led very sociable lives, eating dinners, going on picnics, playing bridge, swimming, riding and, once a month, going to see the film which came to the local cinema. In 1941, in Maseru, Duncan met a Johannesburg girl called Erica Berry and, although it seems not to have been published, they were engaged from February 1942. Erica, who was a friend of Duncan's younger sister Deborah, used to stay often in Leribe and Maseru, and in April 1942 and a couple of times afterwards Duncan went to stay with the Berrys in Johannesburg. Quite when the engagement was broken – or even whether it was broken at all but rather was simply forgotten – isn't clear, though it seems to have been some time near the end of 1944.

Maseru in 1942-3 was in many ways almost Edwardian. For all the pressures of the war and its miseries – according to Elizabeth Feiling, ten of the eleven young men from Basutoland who joined the RAF were killed, and several others risked being cashiered for deserting their posts in the Basutoland Service to join up – life for white people in Basutoland was very pleasant, if a little unusual in its social setting. There was of course misery to be found close enough to home – for Duncan in the injustice created by dual rule, in the corruptness of the chiefs, and in what he felt was the complacency of the Service, though he greatly admired Arden Clarke, who took over as Resident Commissioner (the most senior position in the Basutoland colonial

administration) in June 1942; for Elizabeth Feiling, working in the Health
Department, in the fact that many of the Basotho were infected with venereal
disease (always one of the side-effects of massive migratory labour), in
rampant malnutrition, and in the perpetual threat of pellagra, bubonic plague
and typhus. Looming over all else was the knowledge of the war in Europe
and North Africa. But the life of white Basutoland was perhaps even more
pleasant than the life of white South Africa, since the whites were more
homogeneous. The married Colonial Officers lived and entertained in their
pleasant houses, usually built of unburned brick or the local sandstone which
weathers to a golden brown, and they were usually served by a retinue of
Basotho housemen, maids, nursemaids, cooks, gardeners, stable-boys and
chauffeurs. The traders were often the children and grandchildren of the
earliest whites to arrive in Basutoland – Ellenberger and Casalis, for instance
– and knew the country and the people, as well as living as comfortably as the
administrators. A few of the missionaries – of whom there were close on seven
hundred in the Territory – were intelligent and educated men. The junior
officers of the Service included a small group of pleasant and lively young
bachelors, Tom Fraser being a particular friend of Duncan, who could be
relied on to enjoy parties and make others enjoy them.

For Duncan, miseries other than the occasional drudgery of his job began
to obtrude on the social gaiety. First, on 31 May 1942, his brother Andrew
went missing somewhere in the Libyan desert. Neither his plane nor his body
was ever found, nor was he ever officially posted as having been killed. The
family waited for months, as hope gradually disappeared. Elizabeth Feiling
recalls that at the time Patrick Duncan seemed more distressed at his
mother's grief for Andrew than at his brother's death; but in some of his
letters home in 1942 one senses both grief (though in the manner of his class
and the time it was understated) and anger at the wastage of a promising life.
Certainly, one of the effects on him was a renewal of attempts to join up; he
even wrote to General Smuts himself in an effort to be accepted. But the
Basutoland Service would not release him, though he went as far as to think
of resignation, until he was advised that he would still be prevented from
going on active service.

Shortly before Andrew was reported missing, Sir Patrick informed his
children that he had cancer, and after nearly two years of agony he died in
July 1943. Although he had tried to resign from the governor-generalship,
Smuts advised that the resignation should not be accepted, and the message
from the King to Lady Duncan paid due tribute to his having died in office.
In his diary Duncan wrote:

> Thursday 7th October 43. I have not written in this diary since Father
> died. He died at 3.45 in the afternoon of Saturday 17th July 1943. A very
> great man. May his example live in my life. May my death have some of the
> beauty of his. . . .[6]

But in the autobiography he notes that the last illness tried his father's 'stoic
patience to the limit',[7] and in the interview with Cyril Dunn he said that his
father's 'intolerable pain ... towards the end ... damaged his relationship
with Mother: he became irritable with her, accused her of neglecting him'.[8]

At the state funeral in Pretoria, Smuts spoke of Sir Patrick's forty-two years of service to South Africa, in which he 'preserved that air of sober sympathetic detachment which made him sympathize with opposed sections and made him a sane, healing and inspiring influence in our national life....'⁹ He called Sir Patrick the 'finest product' of Milner's 'kindergarten', and said: 'If he was not of the stuff which makes popular leaders, he had in him the stuff which leads the leaders....'¹⁰ Duncan's own judgement of his father was this:

> What has made our country great is the great transfusion of European ways of life that took place during the nineteenth century. Father was the highest type of British civil servant. The standards of him, and of those who with him reconstructed the country after the Boer War, have deeply influenced for good the standards of the Union's civil service, and it is here that I look for his true monument....¹¹

Sir Patrick was cremated and his ashes placed in a plinth at the Duncan Dock of Cape Town harbour, which had been named after him a few months before his death. But, instead of the public and filial eulogies and the state monuments, or the judgements that may, with justice, be made about his failing to see the great issues of South Africa because of his concentration on reconciling the 'opposed sections' of the white population, one may care to remember most of all one sentence written by an old man, dying in great pain, to Hilda Grenfell, whom he had loved as a young man: 'Andrew the airman lies somewhere in the Libyan desert.'¹²

Six weeks after his father's death, Lady Duncan came to stay with Duncan in Maseru. In October he wrote in his diary: 'Mother has come to stay. She arrived at the end of August.... It is lovely having her to stay.'¹³ But in fact it was not lovely: she was still the dominating mother, and without Andrew and her husband to care for she focused all her terrible maternal energy on Patrick. In the autobiography, Duncan tells more of the truth: 'She stayed a year with me. It was a difficult year for both of us. She still tried to bend the twig, but the twig resolutely refused to be influenced, and we had several differences.'¹⁴ Their differences at this stage were not political since, although Duncan was beginning to be concerned about the treatment of the Basotho, he was still not questioning the system in itself, but rather was asking for more humanity in the system. He showed little interest at the time in the political problems of South African blacks, and his letters show little evidence of his later political feelings. Though it is not clear which period of the relationship he is referring to, Duncan told Cyril Dunn in 1955 that:

> My mother was very conscious of her class; she practically carried Debrett about with her as a guide. So I made a point of ignoring Debretts.
> Mother was always fed up with the way I talked to taxi drivers and such. She was fed up about it and there may have been bitter motives on my part. For instance I took Sesuto lessons in the bedroom of one of the servants at Government House.¹⁵

The last sentence presumably dates the episode to his time in the Colonial Service, that is, to between February 1941 and his father's death; but perhaps the most fascinating part of the statement is 'there may have been bitter motives on my part'. Why 'bitter'? Is he referring to her social attitudes, or to his lameness? Elizabeth Feiling remembers clearly that Patrick told her his mother was in some way responsible for what had happened after the initial injury, and that he blamed her religion for his lameness, though he also admired his mother's courage and often expressed his gratitude to his parents for sending him to Winchester.

Part of the conflict may have been to do with his engagement to Erica Berry, since Lady Duncan does not seem to have approved of this, or to do with his developing friendship with Elizabeth Feiling, though there seems to have been understanding and admiration on both sides between Lady Duncan and Elizabeth Feiling. Most probably, however, it was mainly the conflict between two people temperamentally very close. Lady Duncan at that time, grieving as she was for her favourite son and her husband, was a formidable and magnificent woman. Her impending arrival had been a matter of great excitement to social Maseru, nor had her presence been a disappointment. Although not beautiful, she was handsome and dignified, indeed vice-regal in her bearing and manner, the very picture of an aristocrat in her social self-confidence and with her emphatic and rather loud voice. She was also, even in mourning, capable of being great fun. Elizabeth Feiling remembers her mimicking various South African characters, including Barney Barnato, and dinner-parties at Patrick's house were often very amusing, though another friend remembers Lady Duncan reciting Browning at interminable length after dinner one night; there was of course no question of anyone's leaving the table until she had finished.[16] But she did not hold with her son's youthful informality, nor the somewhat casual habits of his household, and he resented her interference as much as he had ever done. Fortunately, early in 1944, she bought a farm near Westminster in the Orange Free State which she named Fortrie after the Duncans' Banffshire home, and son and mother were able to reconcile themselves to each other's similarities and differences. Duncan wrote:

> In the end she asked me to let byegones be byegones, and we made it up. She never tried to direct my life again, and for the rest of her life we were on the best of terms, and I was able to enjoy, in the fullest sense, the beauty and nobility of her loving character.[17]

It is interesting that, even in 1960, when he was writing the autobiography, he found it necessary to mention that the victory was his: 'she asked me to let byegones be byegones' – not, one notes, 'we agreed to let . . .'. The battle may have been over, but it was certainly not forgotten.

According to Duncan, one of his mother's objections to him at this time was to his passionate concern with soil conservation, which more than anything else reconciled him to the drudgery of some of his work in the Basutoland Service, and which he thought for a time might be the purpose he was searching for. It was certainly one of the oldest interests he had: as a schoolboy he had written to his father about the wild flowers on Table Mountain, and his father had passed the letter on to Deneys Reitz, author of *Commando* and then Minister of Agriculture, who had in turn shown it to Smuts to reinforce arguments for more careful conservation. His earliest letters from Basutoland show that he reacted almost immediately to the problem there: he was deeply impressed by the work of Russell Thornton, the Director of Agriculture, whom Duncan called 'a gift from heaven, for he has energy and farsightedness and a persistence which melts even soil erosion'.[18] Though he was, as always, to put an individual stamp on his concern, it was in fact very much part of the aim of the whole Basutoland Service to combat erosion and improve farming: Gideon Pott, Duncan's immediate superior at Teyateyaneng in 1947, used to tell all his assistants that he spent half his talks at *pitsos* – the tribal gatherings called by chiefs or Colonial Officers to explain new developments or to argue old problems – on agriculture, and that ne wished them to do the same; and Agricultural Officers from all over Africa were brought to see what was being done in Basutoland.

The extent and effect of the erosion were painfully obvious: the earliest missionaries had called Basutoland a country of great trees and of thick grass; but, owing to bad farming, the felling of the trees to supply the diamond mines of Kimberley with timber, and heavy rainfall on denuded soil, by the 1940s the lowlands were deeply eroded, the mountains bare, the agricultural production far too low to support the population. When it rained, the rivers ran yellow with silt from plains, foothills and mountains. Though the administrators thought they were being very active in combating erosion, Duncan, being Duncan, thought that not enough was being done, except by Russell Thornton and the agricultural officers of the Service, with whom he spent as much time as he could spare from his usual duties, discovering the nature of the problem and learning possible solutions – contour ploughing, regrassing and reforesting, building small dams, and so on.

Duncan's contribution to the struggle against erosion was a little pamphlet, *The Enemy*, published under the pseudonym of 'Melanchthon' ('Black Earth' in Greek, since 'Dun-can' means the same in Scots) by the Morija printing works in 1943.

The pamphlet is in two chapters, 'The brick wall' and 'The way over'. The 'brick wall' is what has been erected in the conflict between civilization with its material needs and desires, and nature with its limited capacity to survive the rapacity of human civilization. After a brief account of the development of the planet and the arrival of life 'as a by-product of the great processes of nature . . . a small new-comer, and very humble', Duncan goes on to describe the rise of civilization which 'has given us our souls, and much of what is lovely in our lives', but which has also driven us to take more from the earth than it is capable of giving. 'White civilization', in particular, has exported rapacity:

> Everywhere it goes it teaches man to increase his needs, and it forms large groups of men who do not live on the land, and produce no food. They live by dangling their city-products in front of the farmer, who in his efforts to become rich in these goods, increases his production of food.

If this process is not checked, southern Africa, too, will end up as a desert as unproductive as Mesopotamia; and there is little time left.

The second chapter suggests some of the solutions: noting the kind of effect that war has had on the spiritual health of Britain, he argues that 'When Germany and Japan are beaten we must not cease to fight', but that the new

enemy must be the forces which are destroying the planet. Ruthlessness may
well be needed:

> Armies will have to be maintained to compel the un-co-operative popu-
> lations to respect the common weal. The Russians compelled the
> Ukrainian and Cossack peasants to co-operate in collective farms. It is
> possible that the collective will be the most suitable unit in the fight, but
> any method that can be found must be used. . . .

(These are extraordinary sentiments in view of both some of his earlier beliefs
and his later ones, when Russian collectivization became a symbol of all he
loathed, as German collective work-camps had been. Once again, one may
see how little Patrick Duncan's attitudes were those of traditional liberalism;
compulsion for the greater good might be a necessity.)

Though the actual suggestions for the struggle are a little vague, the
conclusion is stirring stuff:

> We have enunciated 'Full Employment' as being one of the aims of
> peace. . . . [It] must not be . . . pointless activity for the sake of activity. It
> must be directed to Utopia. In this great aim there are many methods of
> attack. One of them is the development of a form of Agriculture that will
> not destroy the soil. And this must be the first. If it is not, there may be no
> others.[19]

It would have been surprising if the pamphlet had had much effect,
especially since only two hundred and fifty were printed. Thirty years later,
when the old concerns of the Tennessee Valley Authority and the better sides
of the Colonial Service had been taken up and popularized by writers like
Rachel Carson, and when pollution, ecology and conservation were words
which everyone knew, the pamphlet might have been taken more seriously,
though some of it – its avowal of the virtues of war, its preparedness for
ruthlessness – would no doubt have seemed as shocking as its dominant
concern has become fashionable. Duncan gave away a number of copies to
those he thought might be interested, and others were bought by the Director
of Agriculture, by other Agricultural Officers and by missionaries for
distribution. In his autobiography he comments thus:

> I stand by all I said in the pamphlet, but of course no one reacted to it.
> Then, as the years went by I began to see that as far as South Africa is
> concerned no really constructive work will be done until we have got rid of
> our race-obsession; that it is the first task, no matter how urgent the saving
> of the soil may be. I think that that is true, though soil erosion remains a
> national emergency.[20]

But, as the pamphlet itself argues, this is a *non sequitur*, except perhaps in
purely personal terms: a totalitarian government might well be able to
conserve the soil as well as, if not better than, a democratic one. In personal
terms, what matters is that, for all his own arguments about the urgency of
the problem, and though he toyed with the idea of going to the Tennessee
Valley to learn better how to rejuvenate the soil, conservation was not
sufficiently immediate to engage his imagination, to provide what he called in
the autobiography a 'great aim'[21] for the conduct of his own life. It was only
near the end of his life, when he was living in exile in Algeria and had forgone
his personal political ambitions, that he was to return to this passionate

concern, and to see it within an even larger context of the relationship of humanity to the planet.

It was during negotiations for printing *The Enemy* at the Morija printing works, run by the Paris Evangelical Society, that Duncan met Hans Schmoller, a young Jewish refugee from Nazi Germany who worked there as a printer. Their mutual interest in typography, old books and Bach drew them together, and they became lifelong friends. After Duncan's death, Schmoller (by then one of the directors of Penguin Books) wrote a generous addendum to the 'official' obituary in *The Times:* 'his gift for friendship was remarkable', he said.[22]

Schmoller had come as a refugee to Basutoland in the late 1930s, but had been interned in 1940, after the fall of France, along with most other Germans in southern Africa and the High Commission Territories – this despite his anti-Nazi sympathies. (At the tribunal he was asked whether it was true that his parents were still alive in Germany and, when he said that was so, was told internment was in his own interests and to protect him from Nazi blackmail.) After a pleasant week in Maseru prison, where he was an honoured guest, he was sent to a huge camp full of Nazis, where he and other anti-Nazis were immediately in danger of their lives. An appeal to the authorities was successful, and he spent the next two years in 'anti-Nazi' internment camps. In March 1942 the principal of the Teacher Training College in Morija at last managed to persuade the authorities to release him back to Morija.

For Schmoller, their friendship was essentially non-political; Duncan and he shared some interests which had little to do with Africa or politics, and Schmoller regarded Duncan as very un-typical of the usual colonial servant, much warmer and more spontaneous than most, neither anti-German nor anti-Jewish, impatient with bureaucracy, and free from cant. But, whether or not Schmoller realized it at the time, their friendship did have a political dimension: Duncan was reminded of what he had learned in Germany in 1938, and was given still more concrete reason for loathing Nazism; Hans Schmoller knew more than most of the 'final solution', and was to lose his whole family to the camps. After one conversation with Schmoller, and after reading a report in the *Economist,* Duncan wrote to his mother about the extermination of the Jews:

> Extermination. I simply can't get it out of my head. How do people bring themselves to load human beings into cattle trucks, and take them to human abattoirs? Who burns the mountains of corpses? Who could deafen his ears to the screams? Who could use the bayonet, in cold blood, or the rifle, or the noose, on thousands and thousands of men and women innocent of any crime? The answer apparently is 'Nazis'.[23]

It was relatively early for someone not Jewish to realize and feel fully what the 'final solution' meant; and it was an important stage in the growth of his political mind.

Another friendship was with the Cassidy family, though this was almost entirely non-political. Mrs Cassidy was a second-generation South African married to an English engineer; they befriended Duncan on his arrival in

Maseru, and their house was always open to him. Sharing the same kind of easy manners, they were to remain among his closest friends in Basutoland, even when Duncan's later political choices lost him many friends there. Their son Michael recalls Duncan as being 'the perfect adult for a small boy'.[24] Michael was the small boy with whom he climbed, dangerously, to the top of an enormous tree. Duncan used to take him riding, and Michael remembers that, when once his pony ran away with him and Duncan had to overtake him to head the pony off and grab its reins, the occasion was not one for alarm or fear, but for glee and excitement – 'Gosh! Wasn't that exciting?' Duncan bought him a bow and arrow, and taught him how to use it. Duncan gave him a ridgeback puppy. Duncan knew something about everything a small boy could possibly be interested in – birds, butterflies, wild animals, stones, fossils, stars – and when he did not know he would go to great trouble to find out. Everything done with him was an adventure; age, responsibilities, good sense were not allowed to interfere. Michael Cassidy remembers that one day when he was bicycling back from school he heard a car hooting behind him. Looking round, he saw it was Duncan driving. Knowing what a maniacal driver Duncan was, he left the road and went down the steep grass embankment to safety. Duncan simply turned the wheel and followed him to the bottom of the embankment, taking the car where no car could go; and when the car stuck there it was a huge joke. Young women to whom Duncan proposed marriage (for all his earlier scorn of husband-hunters, he proposed quite often in those years) might see this lack of sense as childishness; but to a small boy it was magnificent, and Michael used to walk with a stiff knee in imitation of his hero's lameness (though Michael remembers, too, that discussion of the leg was one of the few taboos in their friendship).

Another of the friends of those years (and later) was Dr Basil Whitworth, who still thinks of Duncan as 'one of the most outstanding and kindest people I have known': 'He was often bubbling over with some new enthusiasm – e.g. an agricultural development, or natural foods, or an environmental subject – on which he would talk with great vigour and apparently detailed knowledge.'[25] He recalls that when Duncan heard that their daughter had had her collection of first-day stamp covers accidentally burned he quietly went round all his acquaintances and friends in Basutoland, got together another collection, and presented it to her. One understands why children adored him: his generosity, his unfussiness, his enthusiasm for everything great or small, his honesty.

One understands, too, that to his superiors in the Colonial Service the childishness of 'Mad Pat' did not always recommend itself. In April 1943 he wrote ruefully to his parents; 'Melanchthon realizes that his vice is over-statement and over-enthusiasm'.[26] Gideon Pott, his District Officer in Teyateyaneng, recalls 'having told Patrick that he was an administrator and not a missionary';[27] yet it was exactly this administrative slog which Duncan loathed, and which he was sure was responsible for what eventually turned into a duodenal ulcer that continued, undiagnosed, until 1959, when he had a major operation following its perforation.

However, it is clear, from letters of the time and from the diary which he kept intermittently from May 1943 onwards, that his work for the Service was not altogether frustrating. After his short stay in Leribe and the episode of the broken leg in April 1941, he was posted back to Maseru and the Secretariat, where he leavened the office-work by beginning to learn Sesotho. In December 1942 he passed his 'Basuto Statute Law' exam. He moved from the bachelors' quarters to a house of his own. He began to apply to his garden some of the techniques he had learned from the Agricultural Officers, and waxed very enthusiastic about compost-heaps and vegetables. Most of 1943 and 1944 he stayed in Maseru (his mother was with him from August 1943 to February 1944), but in September 1944 he was sent as relief District Commissioner to Qacha's Nek, on the pass through the Drakensberg mountains to East Griqualand and Matatiele in the south. Near the end of the year he was posted as District Officer at Mokhotlong, a station in the eastern mountains, accessible only by light plane or on horseback. This was real work, and the life was spartan enough to make him feel worthwhile again, in just the same way that two-day walks in the Canaries or a period in a German work-camp had made him realize how he despised the 'flesh-pots' of Balliol: 'I am writing this', he told Pemberton in January 1945,

> in a most lonely spot up in the Drakensberg. It's not on the maps, the position is 29° 18′ S − 29° 5′ E. We are two days' ride − 65 miles − from roadhead . . . and everything is incredibly remote. We have however great compensations − trout fishing − solitude − grand scenery and above all fascinating, satisfying work.[28]

The most interesting work involved attendance at *pitsos;* many of them in 1944 concerned the need for soil conservation and local propaganda for the National Treasury, which Charles Arden Clarke, the Resident Commissioner, had proposed in 1942, since he felt that attempts to introduce greater democracy to the territory would be significant only if the Basotho could exercise financial responsibility. However, the proposals had met with great opposition, since they weakened the old authoritarian status of the chiefs and also increased taxation. Duncan's chief asset in this work was his growing command of Sesotho; he was one of the few Colonial Officers who bothered to learn the language. Although he passed his Grade 1 exam in Sesotho in mid-1943, it was in Mokhotlong that he first perfected his use of the language systematically, taking advanced lessons with a Mosotho in his office. Though he found much to be critical of in the administrative side of the Service, he loved his work in the field, the long journeys on horseback to remote *pitsos* in the mountains, the spartan conditions of being 'on tour' through 'his' territory, the interminable court-cases (for the Basotho regard litigation often as a kind of social game played to relieve the monotony of their normal lives, and delight in argument). In this way, he could deal with the people face to face, without the interposition of rigid administrative structures, and he could work without an interpreter, so understanding without mediation the problems the people had.

In September 1944 he recorded in his diary, 'This work is the most fascinating I have ever chosen,'[29] and when in early 1945 he was told that he was being transferred to the High Commissioner's office in Cape Town he was not at all pleased. If he were allowed to stay in the district, he felt he could actually achieve something. He wrote in his diary after getting the news of the transfer:

A great idea is turning over in my mind – of asking for this district for some years so as to restore its lost grass. This is the one district of hope – administrative action is almost enough to restore fertility. In the lowlands great works and mints of C[olonial] D[evelopment] F[und] money will be needed.[30]

To his mother he wrote:

What really worries me is that I feel I could do a job of work in a district. That at the moment I'm doing one, that at last I'm beginning to understand and love the Basuto and their language.[31]

But Cape Town it had to be, and in the end he accepted the transfer with good grace. It was to produce at least one great change in his life.

CHAPTER 4

1945–8
'If all my choices had been as wise....'

Patrick Duncan's first job in the High Commission Office was as an assistant secretary on the administrative side (the 'administrative side' was the 'Governor's Office' of the three High Commission Territories; the 'representative side' represented the United Kingdom in the Union). At first he worked very hard and often very late, reading papers and documents and absorbing as much as he could, but soon found time for friends and a social life very different from the isolation of Mokhotlong. He went to the Thursday-night concerts in the City Hall; he found an old music shop which sold him sheet-music, mainly of J. S. Bach; he went out with various young women; and he met some interesting political figures, including Piet Cillié, then Foreign Editor of *Die Burger*, probably the best of the Afrikaans newspapers, and of whom he was to see a great deal in his later political days in Cape Town, and of course the High Commissioner himself, Sir Evelyn Baring, and Lady Mary Baring (formerly Lady Mary Grey, a granddaughter of Lady Selborne).

At the end of May 1945 the Office moved to Pretoria – the bulk of the High Commission had to follow the South African government in its twice-yearly move – and Duncan went to live with the Junods, a famous Swiss missionary family and old friends of the Duncans. The father was a prison reformer as well as a missionary, the mother worked in the Bureau of Information, the eldest daughter at a clinic run by the University of Witwatersrand, the second daughter for the Springbok Legion, a left-wing ex-servicemen's organization, and the son and third daughter were still at school. Duncan was treated as a son of the family. Mr Junod was often away from home, and in his absence Duncan was a useful and pleasant companion for Mrs Junod and her children. Moreover, the Junods were gifted musicians who played enough instruments to consitute a small chamber orchestra and who had a vast collection of records, to which Duncan added his J. S. Bach. He even started piano lessons, never having been able to work continuously enough at learning the fiddle to be very proficient, though later he and his wife Cynthia used occasionally to play duets on the violin and piano; he had a very good ear and knew much music by heart, so could entertain himself by 'listening' to it in his head when he was travelling. In Teyateyaneng he used to get very excited about a cock which crowed the theme of a Borodin concerto.

Strangely enough for the 'Mad Pat' of Maseru, he went through a time of considerable shyness in Pretoria. Recording in his diary the kindness of one Mrs Pocock, who gave him lunch every day, he wrote: 'I was fighting a great shyness and her kind thoughtfulness did as much as anything to help me to outgrow it.'[1] It may have been something to do with his return to white South Africa – it was, after all, the first occasion he had lived close to it for any length of time since the miserable years at Bishop's – compounded by having lived in the isolation of Mokhotlong; or it may once again have been a symptom of that part of him which needed to retreat from the world, to disappear into himself as he had needed to do in his days at the Ridge, even before the characteristic was aggravated by his repeated experiences of pain. In the political days in Cape Town he would often take a period of deliberate retreat on friends' farms – for instance, at Miss Murray's farm at Elgin – and would sleep, read and walk. He was a warm and friendly man, but it was in part at least an effort of will which made him so; those who knew him well could often see, not *through* the immediate impression of charm and warmth *to* something else (since that way of putting it would falsify his personality), but a kind of shadow of his personality, not only vulnerable but specifically wounded.

During his time in Pretoria, Duncan got to know better his young sister Deborah, then at the University of Witwatersrand. He saw something, too, of his brother John's fiancée, Pam Read. John was by then running his mother's farm, having been demobbed from the South African Navy, to which he had transferred from the Royal Navy after being interned in Algeria in 1942 when his ship was sunk in the Mediterranean. Patrick Duncan went often to Fortrie, sometimes taking Deborah and Pam with him – it was only a three-hundred-mile drive on good roads – and now that his mother had abandoned her attempts to 'straighten the bent twig' they enjoyed each other's company.

Early in 1946 the High Commission Office moved back to Cape Town. In April Duncan became Private Secretary to the High Commissioner, and in May he moved to live in High Commission House, along with Morrice James, who, after a time before the war in the Dominions Office, had joined the Royal Navy as a rating and had come out at the end as a colonel in the Marines. James and Duncan became immediate friends; they shared political views, a passion for music, and a rather raucous and under-graduatish sense of fun and humour. Lady Mary Baring was away in England from May 1946 until early 1947, and Morrice James and Duncan saw a great deal of Baring; together they often climbed Table Mountain and, although Baring was a shy, often moody and somewhat difficult man, both James and Duncan enjoyed his company. Particularly outstanding was a visit to Sterkfontein Caves in the Transvaal, where Morrice James and Duncan went for a swim in the dark underground lake. They carried their heavy carbide lamps with them, but the water put them out. They panicked, but were guided back to shore by Baring: 'there, like Charon, stood this magnificent figure, lighting us to what looked like the shore of the dead'.[2]

Duncan describes Baring at length in his diary of the time:

He is a very earnest Wykehamist with an a brain who by perseverance compels it to work on the a plane. He is an unstable character – cycloid someone has called it – subject to violent fluctuations. When the mood descends life is difficult for all who are near him. He is earnest and careful to take pains to do his job in every way except entertaining. . . . [3]

Describing his months living at High Commission House, he continues:

He was shy and I was shyer, and meals were a penance. He could not have been more *giving* towards me. Yet a confidence was lacking, a warm hearted ability to enthuse those under him. I owe the Barings an immense debt. I would follow her anywhere; but he is a difficult master for a P[rivate] S[ecretary] and I was his PS. [4]

The autobiography is less critical, and defends Baring's role as Governor of Kenya during the Mau-Mau rebellion; but Duncan also confesses that he was 'not a very good Private Secretary'. [5] For instance, he forgot to pack the High Commissioner's sword on a visit to Swaziland during the royal tour of South Africa in 1947, and had to scurry round Swaziland officials to borrow one. However, being Private Secretary did allow him to see something of southern Africa (both he and Morrice James had to accompany Baring and other officials on their regular tours of the Union and the High Commission Territories) and gave him an opportunity, too, to meet a good many white South African politicians – Ministers, their Private Secretaries, and old General Smuts himself, since Smuts and Baring were intimates.

Duncan had of course known Smuts all his life; the Duncan boys called him 'Oom Jannie' and, though Sir Patrick and Smuts had not been particular friends – Smuts was an autocrat with his Cabinet, which Sir Patrick resented, and anyway he had little respect for what he felt was Smuts's amateur philosophy of 'holism' – the two families had seen a good deal of each other. The Duncan boys occasionally holidayed on the Smutses' farms: Doornkloof near Irene, and Rooikop near Rust de Winter dam in the northern Transvaal. Patrick Duncan in his autobiography recalls several discussions with Smuts; on the future of Afrikaans (he says Smuts told him it would die out in a few generations), on communism (Smuts told Duncan in 1937 that it was a spent force), conservation and so on. A particular memory was of driving to Rooikop in an open Buick:

Whenever we would pass people – Afrikaners – at the side of the road, resting or outspanned, Oom Jannie would stop, and strike up a conversation. I shall never forget his prodigious memory for people and names, and the delight that his conversations caused. He always had this human side in him, though often the cares and hurry of the autocrat's life prevented him from showing it.

But Duncan recognized, too, that Smuts's long reign was coming to an end, and that Smuts realized full well the limitations of what he had done in South Africa. His version of Smuts is less that of a world-renowned statesman than of a tired old man facing a very uncertain future and harsher historical judgements than the acclaim accorded him in his lifetime.

The most significant event of these years for Duncan was his meeting with and marriage to Cynthia Ashley Cooper. The Duncan parents had met the

Ashley Coopers before the war, when Patrick Ashley Cooper had gone out to South Africa on a business trip. Patrick Ashley Cooper had been responsible for resuscitating the Hudson's Bay Company after its decline in the early twentieth century, and had in the process become one of the most prominent businessmen in England. Among other things he was a director of the Bank of England. All three Duncan boys had stayed with the Ashley Coopers while they were in England, and both Andrew and John had met Cynthia, though when Patrick stayed with the Ashley Coopers in late September 1938 Cynthia had been away. (As a girl Cynthia and her sister had always thought of Patrick as a 'strong silent man striding over the veld', though they were not quite sure what 'veld' was.) During the war Cynthia had worked in a convalescent home for Canadian officers, then in a military hospital in Aldershot, and then moved to Sir Archibald McIndoe's plastic surgery unit in East Grinstead, where she had worked as a nurse for two and a half years. The injuries dealt with there were appalling, sometimes impossible to repair – airmen who had crashed, soldiers who had been burned in tanks in the western desert, civilians (including women and children) who had been injured in bombing raids – though it was also, by all accounts, an inspired and magnificent hospital, which McIndoe deliberately made as pleasant and unregimented as possible, since so many of the patients had to return again and again. After the war Cynthia had been invited by the John Martins (he was Managing Director of the Argus group of newspapers and also a director of the Bank of England) to visit South Africa.

Patrick and Cynthia met first while Cynthia was staying with Lady Duncan at Fortrie, and again in Pretoria when Patrick invited her to a small dinner given by Baring for the conductor Dr Sargent (later Sir Malcolm). From Duncan's diary one guesses it was at this dinner and the concert afterwards that he realized he was in love with Cynthia. (They sat immediately behind Jan Hofmeyr and his mother, and during one of the dramatic silences in the Pathétique Symphony 'Ouma Hoffie' said in a loud whisper to her beloved son, 'Hoe laat is dit, Jantjie?' 'What's the time, Jantjie?') Certainly, he had been due for three months' leave in England with Baring – was in fact booked to leave by ship in a week's time – but cancelled his passage and took his leave at Fortrie, so he could see more of Cynthia. However, after driving his mother the five hundred miles down to Grahamstown so that she could give away prizes at a girls' school, the old problem with his lame leg cropped up again and he had to rush back to Maseru hospital, where he spent three weeks being treated with penicillin, and could only write letters to Cynthia and wait anxiously for hers.

When his leave was over, Duncan and Morrice James took a small seaside house in Milnerton, in Cape Town; they swam each morning before going to the office and enjoyed the scenery and social life of the Cape. Cynthia was there, too, staying with various friends, and they saw a great deal of her. Another companion of that time was Nicholas Monsarrat, later to become a bestselling novelist, and at this time working for the Information Office and – according to Duncan – a hot left-winger who argued hard against some of their views of South Africa. Duncan was apparently 'Mad Pat' again, recovered on the surface at least from the shyness he had felt in his first year in the High Commission Office, and he and his friends enjoyed some light-hearted and occasionally irresponsible pranks. There were still of course official duties, particularly during the royal family's visit to South Africa in early 1947. Duncan had to accompany Baring on several parts of the royal tour. He got permission for Cynthia to join the High Commissioner's flight from Maseru to Cape Town via Bloemfontein (Cynthia was then staying again at Fortrie), and she joined Duncan and James in their Milnerton house – Cynthia named the three of them the 'Milnerton Kindergarten'. Later that month, Duncan went with Baring to Swaziland, where he caught tick-bite fever. While he was recovering from the fever in a Pretoria hospital, he proposed by letter to Cynthia, and she accepted, first by letter, then on the telephone. They were both very happy, and Patrick wrote Cynthia sonnets in praise of her beauty (just praise, but bad poems) as well as daily love-letters.

Together again in Cape Town, they decided to marry as soon as possible, partly because Morrice James, whom they wanted to be best man, was about to go back to England. The royal visit was to end on 24 April, the royal ball in honour of Princess Elizabeth's 21st birthday was on 21 April (Patrick took Cynthia and, despite his usual dislike of dancing, enjoyed partnering her, and the elegant ceremony of the ball), and on 25 April they were married in the chapel at Bishop's. Cynthia's parents were not able to get out to South Africa in time for the wedding, so Cynthia was given away by Major Piet van der Byl (an important figure in the United Party, an MP and Minister of Native Affairs, and father of the Foreign Minister of rebel Rhodesia). At the reception at High Commission House afterwards, the toast was proposed by General Smuts, and then they went on honeymoon, first to the Van der Byls' farm near Caledon, then to Meadowbank on the coast above Durban, the beautiful holiday home of Lady Duncan's sister, Agnes Campbell.

'A diary is no place to describe these things,' Duncan wrote;[6] but a biographer cannot avoid writing about his subject's marriage, for all the difficulties of doing so when one partner is still very much alive. The public man cannot be separated from the private, though Duncan tried as best he could to protect his family from at least some of the consequences of his political choices. According to Duncan himself, Cynthia was deeply influential in his political development and, without her support and agreement, he could scarcely have taken some of the risks he did. Cynthia Ashley Cooper (now Lady Bryan) is, in her own way, as complex a person as Patrick Duncan was, though her complexities are of a different kind. In some ways she is an instinctive Tory, very much the daughter of a self-made man; yet she is also capable of considerable radicalism, and impatience with cant and pomposity. It is very important in her husband's biography that she has never had any racialist feelings. While not in the remotest sense an egalitarian, she has a thoroughly English sense of fairness and justice; for instance, when she lived in Basutoland, she refused to allow shopkeepers to serve her before Basotho who had been queuing in front of her and, trivial though it may seem, it impressed the Basotho at the time enough for them to remember it twenty years later. Her dislike of the colour-bar in South Africa stems largely from this kind of morality: how unfair, how unjust, that an ignorant, ill-educated, badly mannered white person should be thought superior to a black person in every way more worthwhile! Cynthia has, too, the social confidence of her class, an insistence on talking to everyone in the same tone of voice, and on expecting similar standards of conduct from everyone. Though this may mean harsh judgements, she does not patronize or condescend. Slim, dark, fine-featured, certainly very attractive, active, a fine horsewoman without being at all 'horsey', she has, too, a tough resolution underlying the social graces; one cannot imagine her dissolving in tears, resorting to hysteria, throwing a tantrum, reclining on a sofa. She is fiercely protective of those she loves, almost exclusively loyal; personal commitment, once given, would not easily be withdrawn. She does not share Patrick Duncan's easy charm, and can be very disdainful of those she dislikes, without any compunction about showing what she feels; yet is also capable of being both witty and tender. All the same, one would not like to make an enemy of her, and it is probably fair to say that more people admire her than like her; yet she was (and is) much loved. In a sense she was the stronger character in her marriage to Patrick Duncan; it was not that Patrick was weak, but that Cynthia was the steadying influence, the emotional bedrock. One acquaintance calls her 'the calm at the centre of Patrick's hurricane'.[7] It is an accurate image, yet in no sense is she placid, easy-going, relaxed; for a start, no one of that kind would have been likely to have married Patrick Duncan. In many things, she was his ideal complement; while she did not share all his intensities (for instance, although she enjoys music, she never felt the same passionate commitment to J. S. Bach as he did), she admired his energy, his fearlessness, his wide-ranging mind, and she provided him with the emotional security he so desperately needed, the secure domestic base from which he could sally forth, and she is as brave as he was, though never as foolish as he could be at times.

Of course, as in almost all marriages, there were tensions and difficulties. Fortunately, Lady Duncan thoroughly approved, so much so that it has been said she 'arranged' the marriage. (She may of course have thought she had done so, and very possibly she encouraged it; but, given Duncan's stubborn resistance to his mother's interference, and Cynthia's own character, an 'arranged' marriage is scarcely credible.) Agnes Campbell, too, was very happy with Patrick's choice of a wife, and she and Cynthia became close friends; indeed, Cynthia describes Agnes Campbell as her substitute-mother in South Africa. But other members of the Duncan family were not as close to Cynthia, and thought she was too much a restraining influence on Patrick, in the emotional as well as in the practical sense. There were also the classic intersibling difficulties over money and inheritances, and as usual it was the outsider not the actual sibling who got blamed. On Cynthia's side, too, though her mother (Kathleen) and Patrick became close friends, her father – from all accounts as formidable a person in his way as Lady Duncan was – at times thought his son-in-law flighty, both in politics and finance and, though he gave useful advice about personal finances, made sure that most of the money he gave his daughter was in trust for specific purposes, such as the education of her children. (In fairness, one should perhaps add that Sir Patrick Ashley Cooper was such a canny man in money matters that he might well have protected his daughter's money even if she had married King Midas himself.) Later, Duncan and his father-in-law became quite close, and Ashley Cooper certainly disapproved of racialism, and approved his son-in-law's opposition to the Nationalists. Some of Patrick's South African friends (though by no means all) found Cynthia's upper-class Englishness too formal for them, and preferred Patrick's more open and casual manner, or thought Cynthia imposed her social *mores* on him. Some of Cynthia's English friends (though again by no means all) thought Patrick wild and dangerous, especially in things political; thought, too, that it must be difficult for Cynthia to be married to a man with so much of the *puer aeternus* in him, and blamed him for subjecting her to the dangers of his political life. The truth of the matter probably includes both sides: Cynthia is not as easy-going socially as Patrick was, though he, too, wished to hold on to certain formalities of social behaviour. Patrick was not at all an easy man to be married to, for all his charm and courtesy; he was given to pursuing his ideas and feelings to their logical conclusions, and men of that kind are never very comfortable. He was psychologically a complex and sometimes moody man. But it is also clear that Cynthia loved him for these qualities; some find perfection boring, and prefer human beings. It needs saying, too, that they shared decisions. Contemporaries of Duncan sometimes found it strange that he always insisted on talking to Cynthia before making decisions. Some thought of this as weakness of some kind, as if a true strong man made 'his woman' do what he wanted; some regarded it as admirable that decisions which affected both were shared by both. One has to understand, too, that Cynthia shared her husband's politics. She became a member of the same political party that he did at the same time that he did and resigned from it when he did. She would no more think of making peace with the government which banned her former husband than she would of trading with the devil. Just how important she was to Duncan's political development will become apparent in due course.

It must be said, all the same, that the money given to Cynthia by her father after her marriage was very important, especially when Duncan resigned from the Colonial Service. Sir Patrick Duncan had not been a wealthy man – he was too scrupulous to make money out of his political position, too busy in politics to make much as a lawyer, and as Minister of Mines he had been one of the few men of his class not to benefit from the boom in gold shares in the recovery from the depression of the 1930s – and he had left everything to his wife. When she died in 1948 she left the farm to John, £8000 to Patrick, and a little less to her daughter. As a matter of policy, after 1952 Patrick Duncan put what he owned in his wife's name and, though he was no fool in financial matters (for instance, increasing Cynthia's trust funds by some successful advice on which shares to buy), he tended to leave day-to-day finances in Cynthia's capable hands. Even though Cynthia's money was largely tied up in trust funds for fairly specific purposes, it did provide both of them with some security – for instance, in the matter of educating their children.

Altogether, it seems to have been a good marriage. Patrick was deeply in love with Cynthia, and she with him. When they were away from each other (and Duncan's work, both in Basutoland and afterwards, took him away from home a great deal) he wrote to her almost every day, often late at night before going to sleep, or early in the morning before setting off; and when Cynthia went on holiday she, too, would write almost every day. When they quarrelled, they did so as a matter of policy in private; and their quarrels were the usual ones of those happily married. Patrick cured Cynthia of unpunctuality by simply going off on a long trip and leaving her behind because she wasn't ready when they had agreed they would leave. Both were adults when they married (Patrick was twenty-eight, Cynthia twenty-seven), and both had learned independence; and, though they needed to adapt to each other's lives and habits, they were mature enough to do so without feeling threatened. They were to need these qualities in their marriage, for again and again they were to take decisions which made it necessary for them to change the course of their lives: when he resigned from the Colonial Service; when he became National Organizer of the Liberal Party of South Africa; when they moved to Cape Town for him to become Editor of *Contact*; when he fled from South Africa after his banning; when he went to Algeria to represent the Pan-Africanist Congress; when he decided to stay there after being sacked as the PAC representative, even though he had to work away from their home in Algiers. The marriage was put under strains which many would not have survived; yet the strains strengthened rather than weakened it. Years later, when he knew quite well he was dying, he wrote to Alan Paton: 'Tomorrow we shall have been married 20 years. If all my choices had been as wise, I should have no regrets. As it is I have very few.'[8]

The years that followed their wedding were years of great domestic happiness. Morrice James had returned to England in May 1947, so Duncan and Cynthia lived three weeks in the house in Milnerton, before moving up to Pretoria, where – after a few weeks at the Country Club – they moved into a small house near Rissik Station. Then, in late 1947, Duncan was posted back to Basutoland, to be Assistant District Officer at Teyateyaneng which, although only thirty miles north-west of Maseru, was very isolated; the only white people there were the keepers of the three stores, the District Officer, Gideon Pott, and his family, a policeman and a doctor. A little later came Cyprian Thorpe, an Anglican missionary, with whom they became close and lifelong friends.

One might have expected Cynthia to find the change from the life she had lived during the war and in South Africa afterwards a little difficult; but from the start she loved Basutoland generally and Teyateyaneng in particular, housekeeping, gardening, riding, walking, visiting friends in Maseru and family at Fortrie. When their first baby was due, Kathleen Ashley Cooper came out from England to help. In February 1948 Patrick was born, and he was of course as extraordinary and beautiful as only a first child can be. When Cynthia went on a short holiday in May 1949, leaving her son in the care of her husband and their English nanny, Duncan wrote to her: 'Your son is unbelievably well, good looking and good. I feel very proud of him.'[9]

The only personal sadness of those years (1947–8) was Lady Duncan's death. In May 1947 she had gone with Deborah on an extended visit to England. In August, after suffering months of increasing pain, she eventually acknowledged it and allowed herself to be examined in hospital; when the surgeons operated, they found she was in such an advanced stage of cancer that they could do nothing except sew the wound up again. Lady Duncan was anxious to return home, but a sea-voyage was out of the question. Duncan turned to

General Smuts for help, and Smuts sent a Dakota of the South African Air Force to London to collect Lady Duncan and fly her back. General and Mrs Smuts met her when the plane stopped briefly in Pretoria, and she was then flown on to Bloemfontein, from which John Duncan and a farmer-neighbour collected her and drove her back to Fortrie – 'desperately weary and changed', Patrick Duncan noted in his diary.[10] He was with her often in her last months, and there was none of the old resentment between them. He was with her when she died on 12 April 1948, aged only fifty-five, and he wrote in his diary afterwards: 'She was true to her own philosophy, and her courage and her smile rarely left her.'[11] She had been able to see and hold her second grandson Patrick (her first was John and Pam's son, called Andrew after the airman) a few weeks before her death, which was a joy to her and a comfort to her children. One rumour after her death had it that in her last illness she had her Christian Science books burned; but there is no direct evidence that her religious views wavered. Her only deviation seems to have been that, although the precepts of Christian Science disapprove of alcohol, she found she enjoyed a glass or two of sherry in the evenings; it is hardly a burning of the books, and her example was to become important to Duncan sooner than he might have expected.

The momentous public event of 1948 was the victory of the Afrikaner Nationalists in the May general election. Malan's National Party took seventy seats, Havenga's Afrikaner Party nine, and their combined forces in the House of Assembly were more than enough to outweigh Smuts's United Party with sixty-five seats and its ally the Labour Party with six, even though, thanks to a delimitation of constituencies which favoured rural seats, the Nationalists and Afrikaner Party together polled one hundred thousand votes fewer than the United Party and Labour Party. Some had foreseen the change, and had realized that the pressure of liberals inside the United Party was alienating some supporters, that Havenga's Cape moderation would attract the old Hertzogites who had before been unwilling to back the hard-liners (what South Africans call bitter-enders, *bittereinders*), that Smuts's impatience with local issues in preference for the great international ones upset the parochial, that besides Smuts and Hofmeyr there was no depth of talent in the United Party; but, foreseen or not, the way was left open for Malan and the reunified Afrikaner Nationalists. Most South Africans, white and black, were shattered by the change.[12]

It is easy enough, with hindsight, to realize why it happened and why the triumph of Afrikanerdom represented not so much any real change in the direction in which South Africa had been travelling (at least since the time of Union, when the chances of a liberal franchise outside the Cape had been abandoned in favour of settling with the racially intransigent Boer Republics) but simply a speeding-up of the journey. If segregation and oppression had been the practice (and in some things, like the Immorality and Land Acts, the policy) until 1948, they were now the total policy, and the main aspect of that policy was to consolidate the practice invariably. The reaction of whites outside the Nationalist camp was mainly more to do with what they thought their own interests – the protection of their economic power, the preservation of their language and their connection with Britain – than with any fears of still greater dispossession and oppression of blacks. The death of Hofmeyr in December 1948 gave liberals even less to hope for in the moderating of racialism, and the death of Smuts in 1952 made white non-Nationalists even less capable of seeing how the world had changed. They wanted the old ways back again, but without the new ideology; and what opposition they did provide to Afrikaner Nationalism was 'often ineffective, shortsighted and unwise',[13] though whether having Hofmeyr and Smuts alive to lead them would have made any real difference is doubtful. After all, it was generally agreed that Hofmeyr's attitude to African education and Smuts's desire to make the recommendations of the Fagan Commission (whereby the permanent presence of Africans in towns would be accepted) part of United Party policy had lost them as many votes as Havenga's moderation and Malan's refusal to accede to the anti-democratic policies of the Nazi Ossewabrandwag had attracted. (It is worth noting, in parenthesis to this last point, that B. J. Vorster, until recently Prime Minister of South Africa, was actually rejected as a candidate for the National Party in 1948 because of his war-time support for the Ossewabrandwag.) The failure of the War Veterans' Torch Commando in 1952–3 to counteract Afrikaner Nationalism was to demonstrate exactly the same confusion in the opposition: Did opposition go as far as allowing coloured ex-servicemen to be members? Could opposition resort to extra-parliamentary tactics? What kind?

Patrick Duncan seems to have shared the dismay of most South Africans at the result of the 1948 election, though he told Cyril Dunn in 1955 that 'I had been betting that they would get in and I thought they would never be put out again through the ordinary constitutional channels ...', and letters to his mother confirm this – for instance when he wrote in June 1947 that the political outlook was 'very gloomy. The Malan–Havenga pact looks serious and Havenga has a huge reputation amongst English-speakers and Jews....'[14]

It seems clear, however, that until the Nationalist victory of 1948 he had had no thought of throwing up his career in the Colonial Service – for all his dissatisfaction with it – in order to devote himself to South African affairs. In 1947 he was briefly in touch with Professor L. J. Du Plessis, an economist at Potchefstroom University, who described himself to Duncan as a 'Nationalist, and a republican, and a Calvinist',[15] without adding that he was also a member of the Broederbond, the secret society which aimed to forward the power of 'pure' Afrikaners in every area of South African life. Thinking that a remark in a letter from Du Plessis implied that he should enter politics, he wrote in August: 'I have no intention of entering politics.'[16] But by August 1948 he was able to write to Cynthia, 'I am so worried about politics. I feel that if I ever am going into them I had better act while there is still a parliament,'[17] and in December 1948 he made a special visit to Natal to talk to Edgar Brookes, a white senator elected by Africans to represent them in the second house of the South African Parliament. Thanking Brookes for his courteous reception, Duncan wrote: 'We now feel quietly certain that we must join in the fight if possible and we are on the look-out for ways and means of doing it. One of them would perhaps be [deleted: I think the thing to do is] to try for Parliament as soon as possible....'[18] Brookes took the Duncans' visit very seriously; in 1949 he put forward Duncan as a potential principal of the University College of Fort Hare (then for all southern

African and expatriate 'blacks', though its students were mainly African); and in May of that year he suggested that Duncan approach General Smuts to offer himself as a potential MP in the United Party interest, though Duncan did nothing about this, probably because he was already convinced of the necessity of extra-parliamentary opposition. Certainly, by August 1949 Duncan was capable of writing to Brookes in much more radical terms:

> I see no hope of a reversal of the constant trend to oppression which South Africa has shown at the cross-roads since the great gift of the franchise in 1853. No hope, that is, in parliament, based on a white franchise. But there is no ground at all for despair if once we can get a non-racial franchise. It worked for over 60 years to the satisfaction of the Cape and I do not see why it should not work in the framework of the Union. But to get it! Could not civil disobedience, pass burning, strikes, and passive resistance do it? Despair will breed discipline, and oppression unity. Surely history shows than when men really need a great leader, somehow he usually manages to be about?[19]

Did he see himself as that 'great leader'? Possibly; but the extraordinary thing which the letter shows is the rapidity with which he had moved from a notion of parliamentary opposition to a position not far from that of the African National Congress and its allies at the time, a position in which effective opposition is equated with 'civil disobedience, pass burning, strikes, and passive resistance'. Nor was it simply an intellectual position he had reached; in less than three years he was to resign from the Colonial Service and to join in exactly the kind of civil disobedience he had advocated – the Defiance Campaign of 1952, in which many blacks and some whites wilfully broke the law in order to court punishment in the interests of justice. He had travelled a long way in a very short time.

What had changed him?

It is inevitable, though dangerous, to assume that a man in the process of changing his mind should do so in a logical and rational progression, or that there is some climactic moment in the process in which he recognizes what has happened; one has the various public and private pronouncements he makes, and one takes them more or less in normal chronology. Yet one knows from experience that the process is much more complex: two steps forward, one back, two sideways, one diagonally. At the end one looks back and says, 'Oh, I have come from A to X via, B, C, D, E and so on,' yet the probability is that one came from E, returned to A, leaped forward to M, retreated to K, jumped to X, retired to P. The pattern is one thing, the process another, and the process is much harder, perhaps even impossible, to reconstruct. Yet one has to assume the process to make sense of it, to pattern it. Patrick Duncan was an intelligent and reasonable man, but also an imaginative one, and the imagination works more obliquely and rapidly than rational intelligence.

The change was in part simply a reaction to external events, to the various measures enacted by the Nationalist government in office: the Prohibition of Mixed Marriages Act and various amendments to the Immorality Act (first introduced in 1927); the Group Areas Act; and, above all else, the preliminary talk of the Separate Representation of Voters Act, the terms of which were published as a Bill in February 1951, but which had been in the air since 1948. The Act would do much the same to coloured voters in taking them off the common roll with whites as Hertzog's 1936 Act had done to African voters in the Cape, but with one vital difference: in 1936 Hertzog, a constitutionalist, had sought for and obtained a two-thirds majority of both Houses of Parliament, voting separately, as the South African Act of Union laid down. Now the Nationalists (though not initially Havenga and the Afrikaner Party, who were 'Hertzogites' in their attitude to the Constitution at least) were prepared to bend the rules to get *apartheid* of voters, by a simple majority, or by both Houses voting together, or by anything which would work to their ends. For many, this was the ultimate threat, not so much because of what it did to coloured voters (after all, the United Party had done the same to African voters before the war) but because it threatened what they called 'parliamentary democracy', and the Constitution of the Union. Duncan explained his feelings very carefully to Cynthia in August 1948:

> Yesterday I had no thoughts for anything except the news that Malan is to abolish the Native reps and take the coloureds off the common roll. It is a cynical and immoral act. The representation given to the natives in 1936 was considered by Gen. Hertzog an amendment to the Constitution and he voted it in by a 2/3 majority of both houses. The right of the coloureds in the Cape to vote on the common roll is entrenched in the SA act. To propose now to abolish both by a simple vote is a flagrant piece of uncon- stitutionalism and shows that my fears that the extremist Broederbond tail would wag the dog in this Govt were all too justified.[20]

The rest of the letter makes the reasoning plain: the concern is not so much for the Africans and coloured voters who are losing their minimal voting rights, but for white South Africans:

> Things are darned serious and we're nearer a Peron dictatorship than we think.
>   The next piece of constitution-killing will be that the existing loading of 15% in rural areas will be increased to 25% at the expense of the towns. After that what? Probably British subjects who have not naturalized as Union Nationals under the new Commonwealth citizenships acts will *not* get the vote. Then the Nats ought to feel safe about the next election.

In short, in late 1948 it is the disappearance of the old quasi-democratic forms which worries him more than the rights of Africans and coloureds. But by 1949 a very different attitude is apparent, though he is still by no means the radical he was to become:

> All government is a necessary evil: it is when a government becomes unnecessarily evil, like Hitler, Stalin or Malan, that one is *compelled* to take sides against it. I want a bourgeois democractic South Africa with a non- racial franchise, such as worked very satisfactorily in the Cape for 70 years. Even when that has been obtained S. Africa will be an unhappy country, but the amount of unnecessary evil will have been reduced.[21]

'Hitler, Stalin or Malan...'!

Just how far he had moved during the years in Basutoland is even more apparent if one compares the attitude apparent in this letter with earlier letters. For instance, in 1943 his mother had made him a member of the South African Institute of Race Relations. Thanking her, he wrote that he would read the Institute's publications with 'interest and a critical eye':

> I do *not* approve of putting into the mind of the South African Native the idea that he must fight for democracy. *That* way leads to Congress-Babu-government, which is inevitably followed by Akbar-rule. Those chattering monkeys that we are turning out from our high schools will never be fit to govern their own people who disown them. They have no *culture* in the German sense – no racial body of beliefs, behaviour, morals, customs without which a man is only half a man. They parrot learn what these left wingers have to teach them about strikes, about votes, about equality before the law. *How* can a man who herds cattle in the Maluti, and who does not know that such a place as Russia exists, or America? How can he vote for a national Parliament? I see that one of the publications of this 'Institute of Race Relations' is How you can Increase your Wages. In fact teaching the African how to strike. The only government that Africans will ever (in the next 1000 years) have is autocracy. And the only clean Government they will have is a White government.... These ones that talk of the Atlantic Charter for the Eskimos. Don't they realize that it is only one or two peoples in the world that can run democracy. Even the French can't do it.[22]

More than thirty years later the letter still makes one wince; the anti-Indian sentiments are an extraordinary reflection on the changes which were to make him think of Gandhi as the greatest political and spiritual leader of modern times. Even the more moderate letters are often conventionally racialist: 'The Colour bar does not count much for me. I should not like to live with natives but I enjoy meeting them over tea.'[23] He was, as one might expect, a relatively humane employer to his servants, if very paternalist in his attitude: 'I told him my usual conditions – high pay, no notice to be given on either side, lots of work.... In Solomon's case too I shall keep him at it all day – and after all an idle man is not really a happy man.'[24] But even in this he was capable of a certain amount of insight; four months later, on the same subject, he wrote again:

> Why is it that the natives are such a rotten lot when they live near us? I needn't give the answer; it's too obvious. But it seems that short-term policies of good treatment are no good. The whole black–white relationship is rotten, rotten, and can only lead to personal and national friction.[25]

His attitude to the colonial administration was equally inconsistent. For instance, soon after his arrival in Basutoland he wrote, in defence of paternalism, that 'we really are here to protect the individual against the chiefs in so far as they are tyrannous, to maintain the authority of the chiefs in so far as people are rebellious, to raise and redeem an ignorant and poor nation, to bring our light to their darkness'.[26] Yet he was capable of seeing the discontent of the Basotho under the colonial administration, and noted that there was 'deep feeling among even our loyalest black friends that they are without rights and without liberty'.[27]

If there is any one consistent strand which runs through all the letters from Basutoland, it is a concern with individual justice. In 1942 he had told his father about a Mosotho policeman he had caught embezzling £10:

I felt so incredibly mean – me with my comfort, my position, my car, my warmth & money – bringing this poor devil to book. After all, there's no getting away from the fact that we have taken the larger helping in SA and we do hang on to it enviously, jealously, carefully. And what right have I, one of these greedy rich children, to demand any standards from the robbed poor children. We may talk about our holy duties to the blacks – but are we unprejudiced judges? And yet I agree that if the whites were to walk out there would be chaos. In so far as we can approach the ideal I feel we should openly give the blacks equal opportunity. After all the usual argument is 'You can't give the blacks skilled work because they can't do it' and this is nonsense. If they can't, then there's no need to stop them.

I feel that the present way is leading to real trouble – so there's a social as well as a divine argument.[28]

He objected to the way the officers in the Service used prison labour to provide themselves with free firewood; he called the system by which the chiefs were empowered to fine tribesmen iniquitous; he told his mother that 'the days of sahibs' were over, and that whites would have to learn to live more simply; and, in short, whenever he was brought face to face with an individual problem, an individual injustice, he reacted to it – but, for the time being at least, he seemed incapable of generalizing from particular experiences to a more general attitude.

Patrick Duncan's own assessment placed much of the blame for his loss of a democratic principle which he thought he had grasped in England on his time in the Service. In his autobiography he wrote: 'As the years went on in the service I found that my feeling for democracy got weaker, and I became more assimilated to the atmosphere of the service.'[29] Yet it is clear that his retrospective view oversimplifies the process; he was not particularly a democrat when he joined the Basutoland Service, and his comments during the period 1941–5 reveal clearly that his assimilation 'to the atmosphere of the service' was only a partial one, that some of his attitudes were much more those of a typical white South African, but equally that some were more far-sighted and humane.

It is during his time in the High Commission Office that he was most susceptible to an ethos he did not intellectually approve of. How else does one make sense of the contrast between his feelings for Hans Schmoller, his horror at what was happening in the concentration-camps,[30] his reaction to the first films of the liberated camps ('It is beyond all description horrible. The blinding impression is of human life dragged down into primeval filth where morals just don't exist.... Yet I think all should see that picture simply because something new has come into the world ...'[31]), his hatred of individual injustice and some of his other attitudes of that period? For instance, in the same letter as he reacts to the first films of the extermination-camps, he writes that he sees

the big problem of the future as the population problem. If the population of India is going to increase at the rate of 5 000 000 each year where is it going to end? They starve. Already when they starve owing to immense numbers it seems to be England's fault for not sending the Roast Beef and potatoes. England logically ought to be allowed to massacre 5 000 000 babies....[32]

Is this gallows humour? Or is he perhaps reacting to the concentration-camps by taking note of the information but finding it so unthinkable that it is – has to be – immediately put aside as somehow not part of human experience at all? A clue is in a letter a week later to his mother about his sister's reaction to the same films: 'I agree with what Deb said about the Concentration Camp pictures except that I am not ashamed of having German Blood in me.'[33] The release of the full information about the camps in 1945 was shattering to most people, especially those with European connections or traditions; to Germanophiles it was doubly shattering, and to those of German origin often psychically unbearable. It was documented and documentary, so it had to be true; yet it could not be true, unless one accepted possibilities about one's own humanity which very few were able to accept. To his mother he wrote:

> Ever since the Nazi system has crumbled I have felt deepest sympathy with Germany. I have thought of all my friends there and wished them well. A German book or magazine, a German conversation in the street has made me feel an affinity renewed. The good people there have suffered and will suffer and it angers me to hear loose talk about all the Germans who should be sterilized etc. Even with war criminal trials I am for letting bygones be bygones up to a point of course. A short sharp vengeance for the top Nazis and otherwise a warm tenderness for the ordinary people who will otherwise suffer unspeakable things in the coming winter. I would not have brought up all this if the feeling in me had not been so strong.[34]

'Up to a point of course' one agrees with a charitable view of this kind. However, it is not charity which is at issue, but rather a particular kind of coming to terms with Nazism, one which allowed him both to disavow Nazism and not to hate the part of himself which loved Germany and was originally of Germany. It is exactly the same kind of conflict one observes in his attitude to South Africa: Patrick Duncan was a white South African, and his father's son; to see through the racial myth in which he had been nurtured required an act of imagination, not simply an act of reason.

Patrick Duncan's own version of how he learned to see through racialism places the credit on Cynthia:

> Cynthia, quite unwittingly, did this for me, and after knowing her for only a short time I found myself deeply influenced by her simple English, or I should say European, way of looking at race. That it was quite simply of no importance.
> I have shown earlier how my ideas and my mind had been formed by Europe. Now that I had married Europe the process completed itself.[35]

The images of 'Europe' in this passage are very interesting, and confirm the earlier analysis: he needed the emotional as well as intellectual sponsorship of what he chose as his image of Europe (obviously a partial image, one comprising Winchester, Balliol, the better traditions of upper-class life in England and Germany, J. S. Bach, courteous manners, hard-working and God-fearing Welsh miners, and *The Times*) before he could see through the racial myth. So, when he turns to describe the actual event in his autobiography, he once again uses language of a particular significance:

At about the beginning of 1947 the first of four remarkable events happened to me, events of such clarity that looking back on them they seem to have the power of visions.

I suddenly realized that the racial feelings of White South Africa were a gigantic illusion, that race had no important meaning, and that in what mattered all men were equal. I have never understood this before, not with all the deepest layers of my being. Now I did. It was like being cured of a disease, or as if for the first time one could see clearly. So much that had puzzled me fell into place and made meaningful patterns.

I suppose that something like a conversion happened to me. I cannot remember where it happened but I can remember that it did happen, at about that time.[36]

One will need to look at the other three 'visions' at a later stage, as well as at a vision which does not need the qualification of quotation marks. But this moment of Patrick Duncan's life is of crucial significance, since out of this so much else of the next twenty years was to grow.

It is impossible to say why the 'vision' should have happened when it did, or even exactly when it happened. One may see easily enough that it represented a pulling into order of a great many disparate strands of his thinking up till then, and a sloughing off of some of the earlier racial feelings. The high regard for individualism, the loathing of political or social bullying, the passion for individual justice, all come together at this point, and from 1947 onwards the occasional racialist remarks of the earlier letters disappear: there is no more anti-semitism, no more anti-black comments, no more jingoism about the British. Quite simply, he has become a non-racialist. It may of course not have been enough to be a non-racialist (indeed, Patrick Duncan himself was to move to this view); but, although many accusations were made against him in the political years that followed – that he was obsessively anti-communist, that he was politically naïve, that he was politically ruthless – the one accusation which was not made, even when it might have been easy or convenient for his political opponents to do so, was that he was in any way a racialist. Ezekiel Mphahlele, the writer and scholar, who got to know Duncan well from 1954 onwards, and who worked as a correspondence secretary for the Africa Books business which the Duncans bought in 1952, makes exactly this point: 'I hated liberals and their Party (as I still do) but there was something genuinely felt and unpatronizing about Patrick. He looked like a man who has a vision that is born of his intensely individual calibre and sensibility....'[37]

One may see the process more clearly if one notes the kind of imagery which he used to describe this 'vision': 'like being cured of a disease', 'as if for the first time one could see clearly', 'something like a conversion happened to me'. This 'vision' (and at least one of the later visions) is very similar to the kind of experiences of conversion or healing recorded by Christian Scientists. If it is true that, despite his intellectual rejection of the doctrine of Christian Science, it remained a considerable force in his emotional life, one may see why Patrick Duncan attributes so much of his non-racialism to his wife's unwitting influence. It was not so much what Cynthia did or believed which mattered to him. What mattered was that falling in love with her – 'marrying Europe' is his image – completed a process of healing which had been begun by Winchester and Balliol; 'my ideas and my mind had been formed by

Europe', he wrote. It was not so much that Cynthia gave him new ideas or attitudes; she enabled him to put 'into place' the past confusions and inconsistencies which mark his political thinking up to 1947, to make 'meaningful patterns' of 'so much that had puzzled me'.

As always, the problem with this kind of psychological history is that it assumes the primacy of the individual and subjective mind, and tends to underestimate the material and objective circumstances. It needs saying, first and clearly, that Duncan was not the first South African to become a non-racialist and indeed that many South Africans (communists and liberals, black and white) had travelled to the same destination by very different roads; some seem never to have been racialists at all, and some reach non-racialism by more rational routes than the visionary or imaginative. Secondly, his discovery that race does not matter only takes on significance in terms of the kind of life Duncan was to lead from 1947 onwards; this was no temporary conversion followed by a convenient back-sliding to the old ways. Thirdly, it is important that the 'vision' through the racial myth seems to have happened before the advent of the Nationalists in May 1948; Duncan's political career was not simply a reaction to Afrikaner Nationalism, but grew from roots deeper in his own imagination.

The reading of Gandhi, especially of *Satyagraha in South Africa*, came after his 'vision' through the racial myth and shortly after the election victory of the Afrikaner Nationalists, and it was the combination of his realization of non-racialism with a study of Gandhi which led him to abandon his initial notion of working from within the United Party and to decide that the only possibility of change existed in extra-parliamentary opposition. In his autobiography he calls this 'my second sudden experience', not a 'vision', though this time he places the experience exactly, on the lawn near their small house in Teyateyaneng:

> Suddenly I realized that there would never be any constitutional way out of the cul-de-sac into which this Nationalist victory had led our country, and that there were only two choices: violence or non-violence.
> I realized with utter clarity that the greatest service anyone could render to this country would be to increase the awareness of South Africa's peoples in Gandhian methods.[38]

Certainly, this is clear evidence that Duncan had reached, by a parallel route but entirely independently, the same kind of conclusions which the Programme of Action adopted by the African National Congress in Bloemfontein in December 1949 set down, largely as a result of the pressure of the Youth League of the ANC: that to bring about change it would be necessary to use boycotts, strikes, civil disobedience – in short, all the usual techniques of non-violent opposition, though not necessarily from Gandhian motives of 'soul-force'.

It is often assumed, by South Africans and others, that to be a non-racialist and prepared to use extra-parliamentary techniques of opposition in some ways implies socialism; it is a view fostered by the South African government for its own ends, of course. But it was certainly not true of Patrick Duncan, in 1947 or later. He had, it is true, voted Labour in the British general election of 1945 (his joint citizenship of South Africa and Britain and being in the Basutoland Service entitled him to vote); in 1955 he told Cyril Dunn, 'I'm very glad I did [vote Labour]', though he said he would not do so again, since 'they mismanaged England hopelessly'. This was really the last twitch of socialism in him, at least until the mid-1960s. Seeing Freya von Moltke again in 1947 when she brought her children out to South Africa to visit the Rose-Innes side of their family helped to confirm his views. Just as Moltke had opposed National Socialism from a position which was liberal rather than socialist, traditionalist rather than left-wing, individualist rather than collectivist – but opposed it all the same, enough to die for his opposition – so Duncan was to oppose Afrikaner Nationalism from a set of values very unlike those of some other South African liberals. Duncan had written to Freya in England after the war, and was the first to greet her and her two children when the boat docked in Cape Town. Although she did not at first recognize him, she wrote to him soon afterwards to say 'why it meant so much to me, that it should have been you, who was the first yesterday.'

> Since Helmuth died and even before I felt very strongly, that we were a team throughout the world, a strong community, who belonged together in aims and outlook and unity in strife, Helmuth and his friends at first, but quite a number of other people, other friends outside Germany also. This team still exists and the men who have died in it and for its aims are still very much in it. When I got your letter in England . . . . it very much struck me, that you also should be one of them, were one of them.[39]

Patrick Duncan's opposition to what he was beginning to see as a new version of Nazism was strengthened by the bond he felt with Helmuth von Moltke, and he was to renew his connection with Freya von Moltke in the 1960s. It is almost political orthodoxy in our times to assume that socialists are the truest and fiercest opponents of political injustice, that conservatives are, if not proponents of injustice, at least prone to accept it more passively. But Patrick Duncan was not a socialist, ideologically or otherwise; to pretend otherwise, to argue that he was a crypto-socialist for instance, would be to falsify him. Whether his political conservatism made him a less than fierce opponent of Afrikaner Nationalism and *apartheid* than he might otherwise have been must remain a question for later chapters.

CHAPTER 5

1948–52
'Surely God can use even a bent tool'

Although Patrick Duncan was happy in Teyateyaneng, got on well with superiors and brother-officers, and enjoyed meeting and talking to the Basotho, he was very restless, not only because of his increasing conviction that his role lay in South Africa, but also because he felt he was being underused in the routine work of a District Officer. He was a man who had to work hard in order to be happy. Brian Marwick (from 1949 to 1952 First Assistant Secretary and from 1952 to 1955 Government Secretary and Deputy Resident Commissioner) was one of those who knew that, to keep Duncan in the Service, he would have to be found jobs more in keeping with his talents and temperament. Marwick made a first move by getting Duncan seconded on a refresher course, one of the 'second Devonshire' courses, whereby young Colonial Officers were sent to Oxford, Cambridge, or London for two terms to study some subject of their choice. Mainly, those seconded chose subjects likely to help them in their work: law, anthropology, agriculture. Marwick was a little nonplussed when Duncan said he wanted to study Marxism, but did nothing to discourage him, despite its apparent irrelevance at the time to the affairs of Basutoland. Duncan asked, too, to study at the London School of Economics rather than at Oxford or Cambridge, which he felt were 'too far away from things and people of interest to Africa',[1] and the man in charge of the courses arranged for Harold Laski, the erudite, eloquent, liberal socialist, to be Duncan's tutor.

Duncan explained his choice of Marxism as a study thus: 'if the Communist Revolution was going to succeed they would have to tackle Africa and I wanted to know what it was about'.[2] It seems clear from this and from the autobiography that his purpose was neither simple intellectual curiosity, nor an attempt to be persuaded by Marxism (as he had said he would be at Balliol), but more an attempt to arm himself with an opponent's weapons. He knew why he loathed Nazism; he had an increasingly clear idea of why he loathed Afrikaner Nationalism; he had now to find a more intellectual base for the loathing of communism which had developed since his flirtation with socialism at Winchester. His diary records his and a brother-officer's reactions to a communist rally in Cape Town on May Day 1946:

.... after dinner to the grand May Day meeting of the Communist Party in the City hall. Only half the seats were full and of those three quarters were rather sloppy looking coloureds and natives. A succession of bad speakers drew rounds of rather half hearted applause especially when 'white people' like Sam Kahn and Snitcher spoke of 'unspeakable bestiality of Smuts's conduct and of the White race in South Africa'. A self-satisfied gentleman named Moses Kotane spoke of the 'continuation of the fight to crush the fascist beast in South Africa' etc. etc. After a surprising interlude when a nice looking girl called, I think, Rebecca Plop sang a song about a nightingale the chairman threatened us with some working class records. Hamish and I ran out ... satisfied that these people are not to be feared. They are men of contemptible mental powers.[3]

By 1949 he seems to have decided that 'these people' were more to be feared than he had originally thought, though even after his first term at the LSE he could write:

I do not take seriously the threat of Communism to any country as long as the Red Army is not on its borders. That is not to say I do not fear Communism in the world. But if the Red Army is on the borders of South Africa the world will be lost anyway and will be past praying for. Until then I am confident that no Communist movements will ever succeed in South Africa.[4]

In February 1950 he wrote to Cynthia of going with some LSE communists 'to hear Harry Pollitt the traitor broadcast': 'I walked out when he started on the my country wrong Russia right stunt.'[5]

Obviously, his attitudes were in part the result of the cold war, then at its most intense after the communist take-overs in Eastern Europe; but they represent, too, deeper feelings about liberty and the role of the state. He did not go to the LSE to learn about Marxism, but to learn more about what was wrong with it.

Duncan flew to England in early October 1949, and Patrick junior, the nanny, and Cynthia – pregnant with her second child – followed by boat. Duncan stayed with Sir Patrick Ashley Cooper in the Ashley Coopers' flat in London, and Sir Patrick and he breakfasted together each morning. Occasionally Cynthia would join them during the week or for weekends, leaving young Patrick in the care of a new nanny, Miss Maxim, who was later to assume very considerable importance in their lives. More often, however, Duncan would go for the weekends to Hexton Manor near Hitchin to join his family. In October he auditioned for the Bach Choir in Westminster Cathedral, and was sad to fail. He saw something of James Gray, Editor of South Africa, who introduced him to various political figures and civil servants. He renewed his acquaintance with Lord Hailey, a former governor of the Punjab and the United Provinces, and an authority on African and Asian affairs. In November Alexander was born, whom Patrick named Ramoholi ('father of mists') in honour of the season. In November he saw Smuts on a visit to London. He visited Oxford to see his sister Deborah, who was taking a second degree there, and to see Jim Bailey, then working on his thesis, later published by Blackwell under the title National Ambitions – the thesis, a theory of civilization which refuted the grandiose versions of

Spengler, Marx *et al.*, appealed greatly to Duncan. Of Deborah, whom he found extravagant, he wrote to Cynthia: 'She has in fact my faults, and I am annoyed at anyone who has my faults!'[6]

Mainly, however, his social life was in abeyance, for intellectually his two terms at the LSE were as satisfying as his time at Oxford had been wasteful. In his autobiography, Duncan claimed that all he did outside his reading and writing was 'a bit of anti-*apartheid* stuff . . . addressing some very elegant young ladies at a finishing school on the tragedy of South Africa', talking to his fellow-officers on the course, and going to listen to Alan Paton speaking at the South African Mission headquarters.[7] In fact, he did considerably more than this, though his being a serving officer in the Basutoland Service meant that he had to act with caution or risk his post.

Most of his time, however, was devoted to reading, both in the LSE library in Houghton Street and in the British Museum, to attending Professor Keith Hancock's seminar on colonial subjects, and to writing a weekly essay for Laski on such subjects as 'How Marxist was Marx?' and 'The twilight of the godless'. The latter, an argument that history had passed Marxism by and a demonstration of the illogicality of some of its central precepts, he sent as an article to the *Economist*. It was rejected, but the submission renewed his acquaintance from Oxford days with Alastair Buchan, then Assistant Editor, and soon afterwards the *Economist* asked him to review R. N. C. Hunt's *The Theory and Practice of Communism*, which he did with great pleasure, ending his review with the hope that Carew Hunt's book would 'bring nearer the day when it will require the same order of courage to confess oneself a Marxist as it does now to support the flat-earth theory'.[8]

His reading started with Marx and the Marxists – including Engels, whom he admired considerably more than his collaborator, calling him 'a kindly and brilliant man, more like Leonardo in the universality of his mind than any other figure I can think of of [sic] the nineteenth century', and Trotsky, for whom he felt the kind of warm regard that liberal intellectuals seem to reserve for his brilliance and wit, and perhaps for his failures, too. Marx he called 'simply . . . satanic', because he reduced all humanity 'to the status of will-less puppets', and Stalin 'a cruel and totally immoral tyrant, of the quality of the Borgias'. Duncan was never a man for half-hearted judgements, though he had the grace to say 'Lenin I know less of'.[9]

From Marxism he moved on to sociology and race, and in the second term to African and South African affairs, using Brazil as a point of reference. Books which made particular impressions were Jomo Kenyatta's *Facing Mount Kenya* and Monica Wilson's *Reaction to Conquest*, Eddie Roux's account of black political history, *Time Longer than Rope*, and I. D. Mac-Crone's *Race Attitudes in South Africa*.

Laski himself Duncan found an attractive man and a generous and kindly teacher; Laski's unexpected death in March 1950 was a great sadness to him. A month after his death, Duncan wrote a memoir of Laski for his own records and, in July 1951, hearing that Kingsley Martin was writing a biography of Laski, he sent him a copy, which Martin apparently found useful, though he warned Duncan that not all Laski's reminiscences had been entirely truthful.

The memoir includes a detailed account of Duncan's second tutorial with

Laski, a record he made the day after. Instead of reading his essay, Duncan had asked Laski questions: about apparent contradictions in the theory of Marxism, which somehow led to a discussion of the relative merits of Milner, whom Laski admired very greatly, and Churchill, against whom Laski felt some bitterness for attacks made on him in 1945; about South African problems and possible solutions; and so on. One part throws some light on Duncan's own political thinking at the time. Laski had said that 'white men of good will ought to stand up with their opposite members among the blacks and dare Malan to do his worst...'. 'I said that I agreed, but that without power – without a party behind them – these men of good will would not be able to do much more than just stand up.'[10]

Perhaps Laski's own remark, carefully remembered, was part of the cause of Duncan's later decision to join the Defiance Campaign in 1952; but, more importantly, it is clear that Duncan was thinking, in 1949, about power, not just about principle. The major lesson taught him by his father had been remembered: what was the point of making a moral stand if you had no power to give your action a point? Without power, principle became a moral luxury, a self-satisfaction and no more.

Laski's teaching was to reinforce this view, as a letter Duncan wrote in January 1950 shows. Not only are the ideas influenced by Laski's, but the language, too, shows that Laski had made an impression:

> England has in the last ten years been changing the attitude of the upper classes to the lower classes. [Partly by appealing to the upper classes to modify their behaviour] but mainly by changing the earning capacity ... by taxation, by a thousand acts which have tended to raise the one nearer the other. In the same way we in South Africa must not cease for a moment to press on the consciences of the Whites to change their attitudes, but we must also work to bring such pressure to bear on them that these attitudes will be ... more humane.... The non-European is exploited today not because the White happens to have the wrong attitude, but because he is powerless. And in history powerless groups live uncomfortably.[11]

As he was leaving the tutorial, Duncan recalls, he asked one last question: could Laski help him visit the 'colonial areas' of the Soviet Union? It is typical of Duncan that he should have wanted to reinforce his study of Marxism by actually visiting, not just the Soviet Union, but the 'colonial areas' of the Soviet Union, to see communist theory at work; and it is typical of Laski that he tried to help arrange such a visit, though in the end it came to nothing. One understands completely why Duncan should have regarded him as the greatest teacher he had ever met, for all his disapproval of some of Laski's ideas: as always, he had a capacity for admiration which could surpass intellectual disagreement. After Laski's death, Duncan corresponded for years with Laski's widow Freda, and was deeply moved by a letter and a cable of support when he went to jail in 1953.

It was through Laski, too, that Patrick Duncan made one of his more significant political acts of 1949–50: at Laski's suggestion he wrote a brief memo on ways in which the British government might contribute to the downfall of the Afrikaner Nationalist government, which Laski promised to put before Attlee, the Prime Minister. Whether the memo[12] was ever discussed is not known. Given the pressure of the impending general election, it seems unlikely. But the point of the memo is not so much its effect, or even lack of it, but what it shows about Duncan's political thinking at the time. There are two particularly important aspects: first, unlike many analyses of South Africa at the time, this does not pretend that the advent of Malan's government in 1948 represented a turn-about in Union policy; rather, it was an intensification of a process visible at least a century before. Secondly, the memo suggests a course of action: the stopping of gold sales.

> The Union is due in the next 12 months to get £140m from this source, and knows that its whole economy depends on this source, on, in fact, the USA. The USA disapproves strongly of the Union's policies, and would cease to do anything to support the Union the moment that it was clear that the UK also disapproved. The Nationalists are more completely in the power of the UK than any other group in the world today. This is a fact which must be ever-present in the mind of anyone considering what ought to be British policy in South Africa.

In the context of 1949 it was a radical proposal and, if it had become known in South Africa that Duncan had suggested such an action, he would no doubt have taken over from Michael Scott, the Anglican clergyman who had appeared before the United Nations in 1949 to plead the cause of the Africans of South-West Africa, as *bête noire* of white South Africa.

Duncan always admired Scott a great deal. He had known Mary Benson, who was then acting as Scott's secretary in London, since childhood and in 1950 went to see Scott, though exactly what they talked about Scott himself cannot recall. But, given Scott's concern with South-West Africa, it seems likely that another of Duncan's political actions in 1949–50 arose partly from the discussion, though Duncan was also reacting to what he felt was the considerable threat of the Nationalist government's emulating Hitler's *Anschluss* by simply taking over the three High Commission Territories, particularly the most vulnerable, Basutoland. The Territories were, and are, significant parts of the Nationalist scheme of *apartheid;* to put the case baldly, they would make excellent 'bantustans'.

The pressure from South Africa for the incorporation of the Territories goes back well into the nineteenth century, and even Selborne's relatively enlightened Memorandum of 1907 on the unification of South Africa assumes that the Territories will be included. Although the Act of Union of 1909 included a specific section to safeguard the Territories, a schedule to the Act sets out detailed provision for their transfer. Negotiations about transfer or incorporation went on throughout the period 1913 to 1948, successive South African governments asking for transfer, successive British governments hedging, particularly on the question of their pledges to the populations of the Territories not to transfer them against their wishes, pledges which Hertzog in 1935 seemed prepared to honour. But the advent of the Nationalist government in 1948 meant renewed demands for immediate transfer of control, and in 1950, after the Commonwealth Prime Ministers' Conference of late 1949, Dr Malan was widely reported to have told the British government that 'the people of South Africa were becoming impatient'.[13] Given the Nationalists' propensity for dispensing with the Constitution of the Union, and – even more seriously – the fact that Smuts, too, thought it was time for transfer, many people, like Scott and Duncan, felt that an *Anschluss* was imminent.

Even before this, in October 1949, Duncan had seen members of the Fabian Colonial Bureau about the threat of transfer, and Scott and he had been in touch with the Anti-Slavery Society. Among Duncan's papers is a minute of a meeting between Patrick Gordon-Walker, MP, then Parliamentary Under-Secretary for Commonwealth Relations, and a deputation from the Anti-Slavery Society, the Fabian Colonial Bureau, and the Quakers' Committee on Slavery; obviously, as a serving officer in Basutoland, he could not have joined the deputation, but it would seem that he helped brief it, since he was sent the minute. After Malan's threatening remarks, Duncan wrote a long memo to Buchan of the *Economist*, suggesting how the British government might tackle the problem of transfer.[14]

Once again, it is an extraordinary document, showing how far Duncan had moved since the early 1940s and since his 'vision' of non-racialism. Even if one loathed the 'caste society' of the Union, Duncan argued, one had to face the facts of the total dependence in real terms of particularly Basutoland and Swaziland on the Union. One might have to face the possibility, too, that the British government would be forced to cede at least these territories to the Union. But, rather than a 'sham settlement' which would 'sacrifice the helpless populations [of the Territories] on the altar of Commonwealth bonhomie', Duncan suggests one which would give the Territories what amounts to independence before transfer or cession. Although Duncan does not use the word 'independence', it is clear he is applying to the Territories some of the ideas he had taken from Gandhi and the Indian independence movement: 'The principle controlling the transfer must be "africanization before efficiency." The HCT are, and must remain, first of all simply places where the African can feel a man, can feel at home....' The specific conditions he suggests are:

a. Africanized organs of administration, police etc. with no more than a European resident.
b. Representation in the Union parliament.
c. Local African languages given official status.
d. 10-year handing-over period, with the aim of completing the process of Africanization before the final transfer.

He adds: 'Efficiency, at present, does not enter into it.'

The alternative to this kind of conditional transfer would be, he thinks, 'unconditional cession', after which the Territories would be:

just three more dreary 'native reserves' under the control of the Native Affairs Dept, their inhabitants stripped of all rights, driven by hunger from a white-controlled reserve to the 'white man's towns', and hounded out of them to work on the white man's farms, stripped sometimes of any legal right to exist anywhere, in any reserve, town, or farm.

Bechuanaland, in his argument, could be used as a particular bargaining-point, since it was more independent of the Union and economically more viable as a Territory than Swaziland or Basutoland. Another bargaining-point would be the 'positive' side of the theory of *apartheid*, which could have little reality without the transfer of the Territories. The British government could, in other words, help force the Nationalists to take their own theory seriously, and the transfer of the 'Africanized' Territories to the Union would be a kind of leaven in the Union, ensuring better rights for all black people, not just those in the Territories.

As a scheme, it is not particularly credible, but the memo contains important ideas: 'Africanization', a greater independence for the Territories, the notion of the Territories as a kind of political and racial leaven in the Union, and, once again, the insistence on *Realpolitik*. All these ideas were to be developed in the next few years, and when he returned to Basutoland in 1962 he still believed passionately that it was one of the main assets in the struggle of black South Africa for freedom and independence.

In January 1950 Patrick Duncan heard a rumour from one of his brother-officers that, on his return, he was to be posted as a Judicial Commissioner and, soon afterwards, Marwick confirmed the posting. It was an intelligent move, because not only did it give Duncan greater independence within the Service – his job would be to act as a court of appeal from local courts, both in Maseru and on tour – but it would also make greater use both of his capacity to learn quickly (he would have a lot of Sotho and other law to learn) and of his command of Sesotho; moreover, his father had done almost exactly the same job in the 1920s, and this appealed considerably to his sense of family.

In May he and Cynthia left the children in the care of Nanny Maxim and their grandparents at Hexton Manor, and drove through France and to Switzerland, camping on the way and staying with friends near Dijon. In June the family sailed for South Africa, and then went by train to their new house in Maseru.

Patrick Duncan enjoyed his new job as Judicial Commissioner as much as he had expected to, though it was hard work; he knew little about Sotho law and – except for the sketchy *Laws of Lerotholi*, Moshoeshoe's codification of and additions to customary law – there were no books. Nor were there case-histories or precedents, except some in the High Court archives and several thousand unfiled in the Judicial Commissioner's Office. Though his predecessor, Gordon Driver, had been an energetic and popular Commissioner (so popular that Duncan was known as 'the new Teraefara', 'the new Driver'), he was not a scholar, and relied on his common sense and general legal knowledge rather than on particular precedent. Duncan began immediately to accumulate judgements and cases for what was to become his book on *Sotho Law and Customs* (eventually published by Oxford University Press in 1960) and got in touch with Julius Lewin, a brilliant young Professor of African Law at the University of the Witwatersrand, and a former student, too, of Laski, originally to consult him about points of law, though soon they became political confidantes and allies.

By tradition the Judicial Commissioner was entitled to a Mosotho Assessor, and by good fortune Duncan got as Principal Assessor Chief Leabua Jonathan, afterwards Prime Minister of independent Lesotho; they quickly made friends, and each held the other in high esteem. The two men constituted a court of appeal, sometimes sitting in Maseru, but more often travelling into the interior, by plane or on horseback, either to constitute a court in some outlying area, or to inspect the scene of a dispute, for instance over land. Often they went to places where the people had never seen a motor-car, or train, or even bicycle, though they were used to light planes; they stayed in the 'places' of local chiefs, or on mission-stations, or simply camped.

Often the journeys by air were tricky operations: Duncan remembered one in particular, when he and a Treasury officer flew with their pilot from Mokhotlong, in the Drakensberg mountains. Delayed by the District Commissioner, with whom they had stayed, and who wished to send mail with them, they took off later than planned, in their small single-engined plane. They flew west, but ran into dense cloud and an electric storm. The pilot turned south, but there was cloud there, too. He turned back – and then realized he was lost. He brought the plane down, looking for a landing of any kind. Spotting a building, he managed to land on a footpath, narrowly avoiding a herd of grazing cattle. The place, they learned, was Mohlanapeng, in the Maluti mountains; they were taken in by the local teacher, who put them up in the empty mission-house, saw that they were fed, and next morning turned his school children out to clear a runway – one which pointed steeply downhill, straight at a ravine.[15]

With such excitements, it was small wonder that Duncan looked back on his eighteen months as Judicial Commissioner as his best time in the Service. The Basotho are a litigious people (often a symptom of land shortage), and the melting-pot of legal systems in Basutoland – Sotho customary law, British equity, the Roman–Dutch law of South Africa – gave them considerable opportunity for practice:

> We heard many cases. Some were matter for tears, as human cruelty lay exposed. Some were matter for acute interest, as Sotho history and culture opened themselves to our view. And some were cause of gigantic laughter. Many of these cases had been brought by people purely to amuse themselves. This sort of case amused both parties, the audience, and, not least the court. Litigation was cheap; there was no television or football; and life tended to be dull. Most cases, however, were routine disputes, often over land or chieftainship affairs.[16]

One of his letters to Cynthia in early 1951 gives an account of a fairly typical day on tour:

> Today I rode nearly 6 hours and thought much about you and our boys. . . . I have heard only *two* cases so far as all the others needed Mathen as prosecutor and he is only due on tomorrow's plane. This is in a way luck as one of the cases needed an inspection of a land and a boundary and we rode out today to do it.
>   We rode up the Mokhotlong river and among flowering mints and gladioli (red) we finished the hearing of the case. Then Leabua and I discussed judgement over an excellent picnic lunch. . . . Then (with no hurry as we had time in hand) we called the parties and I delivered judgement in Sesuto extempore – it was a long one. By this time 40 or 50 men had collected round – their horses were grazing on a nearby meadow strip – and they formed the body of the court.
>   Then we saddled up . . . and the crowd waited and rode with us as a cavalcade towards home. The sense of friendship and welcome was

overwhelming and I thoroughly enjoyed the day. I had no hat, alas, and to-night I am a blend between tomato & beetroot. . . . Apart from this nothing much has happened. . . .[17]

So taken with his new job was he that, when Edgar Brookes wrote to him suggesting that, if he were still thinking of a return to the Union and greater involvement in its affairs, he might apply for a vacancy in the University of Natal, he refused. The post was as 'Housefather' to the students of the new 'Non-European Section' of the University; the post offered not only interesting and constructive work in itself but also what Duncan called 'a certain freedom of political action which is naturally ruled out while I am here'.[18] He offered two reasons for refusal: first, that his work as Judicial Commissioner was both interesting and responsible and, secondly, that Basutoland was a crucial place in the opposition to *apartheid*.

The reasoning behind this second view was made plain in a short memo he sent to Lord Hailey in London in December 1950; although it is called 'Native administration in Basutoland', it is in effect an argument for thinking of Basutoland as an integral part of South Africa's political future. His argument is that the 'apartheid-state has too many real forces working against it to survive ... is a chimera, bred in the deserts by an unnatural union between the spirits of Calvin and of Hitler', and that 'a hero will arise who will destroy it'; destruction will not happen 'without suffering and disorgani-zation', of course, and he seems to suggest a form of partition – 'We may expect something like a more severe Palestine.' In this, he argues: 'Our task surely is to help the Basuto first to survive the breakdown as a group and then to play their part in the South Africa of the late 20th and of the 21st centuries uncontaminated by today's infectious hatreds.'

When he gets on to more concrete terms his argument is weak: for 'the People as a whole', compulsory education; for 'the Educated class', a place in government and in the economic life of South Africa; for the chiefs a real place in day-to-day administration – education and Africanization, in short. But, again, the real point is in his seeing Basutoland as a kind of historical Achilles' heel of South Africa, a non-*apartheid*-state in the middle of the *apartheid*-state.

In August 1951 Duncan left his family behind while he made a quiet trip to England, flying via Bechuanaland and Lisbon, apparently because he did not wish his superiors to know he was going. Even now, it is a slightly mysterious business; some of those he saw in London – Basil Davidson, the Africanist and journalist, and David Astor, editor of the *Observer* – are not sure what the trip was about. He stayed briefly with the Ashley Coopers at Hexton Manor, visited the Festival of Britain, and called on a few other friends. He saw Lord Hailey to tell him 'how unhappy the HCT were';[19] he saw Victor Gollancz the publisher, perhaps about his publishing a cheap edition of Gandhi's *Satyagraha in South Africa*, since Duncan later tried to persuade Penguin and Gollancz to publish one jointly;[20] he saw Krishna Menon, the Indian High Commissioner who, as he told Cynthia, 'immediately under-stood what I was at', but dissuaded him from his 'original plan'.[21]

What 'original plan'? Even Cynthia cannot now recall exactly what the purpose of the trip was, though she knows it had to do with the relationship of

Basutoland and South Africa. The best information is a brief postscript to a letter nine months later to Schmoller:

> I hope never again to do anything confidential or secret. When I went to England in 1951 I did so for such reasons and realized how wrong it is. My aim then was to collect money for a national fund for the Basuto (*a*) to educate them, (*b*) to defend them at home and abroad when the anschluss comes, as come it will soon. As a civil servant it was a wrong thing to do, although the action was correct and based on a correct analysis. I have confessed since then and feel somewhat better about it.[22]

But even this hardly makes all clear. As far as one knows, no Basotho were privy to his plan, and whom he confessed to is not known. Presumably he saw Menon because he thought Indian support in the event of an *Anschluss* particularly important (the Indian delegation to the United Nations was the most vociferous in its opposition to *apartheid*); but the exact details of the plan remain a mystery.

As it transpired, his analysis was wrong; the South African government has so far used subtler means of controlling Basutoland (and Lesotho) than an *Anschluss*. But even the 'national fund' seems an odd notion; did Duncan really think in 1952 that the British government would accept an *Anschluss* so passively that private citizens would have to raise the funds to defend the Basotho? All one may be sure of is that Duncan's plan would have been non-violent, and very probably Gandhian, since he was even more immersed in Gandhi in 1951 than he had been in 1948.

One moment of the trip to England – nothing to do with its purpose – is worth recording. He wrote to Cynthia, from 'above Bechuanaland' at '23.15 Thursday 16 August 1951':

> My darling, Before I go to sleep I must write as I want to catch the post at Leopoldville and I must record the other worldly beauty and novelty of it all. We are at 17 000 feet. Below us lies limitless Kalahari, pale silver in the bright moonlight. Far over to the left lie the lights of, I guess, Francistown. Further to the left and slightly higher, hangs Southwestern horizon by a continuation of our swift flight and the earth's rotation. Above us floats a full moon and behind us in constant alternation our tail light winks red-white-red-white-red-white. Sirius is rising over the Eastern, starboard, wingtip. Outside, our world of the Clippership and the stars seem curiously united.
> Inside, all is futuristic beauty, cleanliness and comfort.

He was always able to give himself over completely to the experience of a moment, to a purely sensual delight in the immediate. Driving himself forward, in search of some 'great aim', he still had time to observe, and to enjoy being alive; it is exactly the same quality Michael Cassidy had seen from his child's view of the man, a capacity for delight and wonderment. It is out of this capacity that some of the complex contrast of process and pattern derives: it is not simply the biographer who searches for pattern, but the man himself; he wishes to make sense of his life, to 'do something real', yet the immediate keeps breaking in, turning the pattern back into a process which is much more disorderly, much more immediate.

The 'secret' trip to England gives a clue to Duncan's attitude to the

Basutoland Service at this time, for all his enjoyment of his particular work. There was, apparently, considerable dissatisfaction among younger officers about general conditions in the Service, which they felt was backward-looking and too hierarchical, and a number of very talented officers either resigned from the Service or asked for transfers elsewhere.[23] Duncan's position was more complicated than dissatisfaction with the Service; he was less and less satisfied with the whole colonial set-up in Basutoland. Leonard Thompson, the historian, who had known Duncan a little at Oxford and who stayed with the Duncans in 1951 while working on the correspondence between Sir Patrick Duncan and Lady Selborne, recalls Duncan's 'revulsion from late British colonial society in Basutoland' over the matter of the Maseru Club. Both Basotho and whites had contributed to a local war-memorial fund; both Basotho and whites had died on active service; but the bulk of the money was used to create the Maseru Club, which was in those days only for use by whites. Duncan was 'utterly overwhelmed by the injustice of the arrangement'.[24]

Neither in his autobiography nor in his letter of resignation does Duncan mention dissatisfaction with the Service as contributing to his decision to resign; he concentrates rather on his positive reasons, although he does see a conflict of interest between his South African-ness and his service to Britain:

> I was devoured with interest in the South African situation. Yet I was serving the British Parliament. Somehow that couldn't go on. My deepest loyalty lay not to Britain, much as Britain had meant to me, but to a non-racial South Africa. I couldn't stay on, as if I were a Briton camping for a period in South Africa.[25]

He was still reading anything and everything by or about Gandhi he could lay his hands on; he had talked about Gandhi and Gandhism to his Basotho friends and acquaintances, and their response – and the fact that the South African Congress movements, African as well as Indian, were planning to use Gandhian techniques – convinced him that Gandhism would work in South Africa. After all, Gandhi had begun to use his particular form of passive resistance in South Africa (ironically, against the British administration in the Transvaal of which Sir Patrick Duncan had then been acting Lieutenant-Governor). Of course *satyagraha* ('soul-force') depended on opponents who could respond to that moral force but, in 1952, Duncan believed that some Nationalists (not all) were decent enough men to recognize justice when it confronted them. His own father had worked closely with and believed in Afrikaners – Botha, Smuts, Hertzog, Havenga – and the old kind might still have more power than the new semi-Nazis like Verwoerd and Vorster. And had not the Africans of South Africa demonstrated for generations that they preferred non-violence to violence? That they used petitions, passive resistance, strikes, non-co-operation, rather than violence, for all that they had cause enough to use violence?

> The trouble was that Gandhi was a saint, and I was far from it. Surely the path that seemed good for South Africa was too high for me. This puzzled me for many months. Then I had another of my sudden 'visions'.... Suddenly the idea came to me: 'Surely God can use even a bent tool.' It seemed to me that what was wanted was for God to have some sort of tool

with which to demolish the bad house. No doubt he would have preferred a straight one. But it was possible that there were no straight ones. In that case he might be glad to have an imperfect one.[26]

This was the third of his 'sudden experiences', his 'visions', though he disclaims the visionary idea: 'I did not see a blinding light, as St Paul did. I did not fall down unconscious as do many *izangoma,* and many Christian converts. Nevertheless these things happened as I have related them, in the places I have described. And they have changed my life.'[27]

It is an extraordinary moment in one's reading of the autobiography, partly because of the image of the 'bent tool', partly because Duncan's sense of personal destiny is so completely revealed in this passage. His mother had tried so hard 'to straighten the bent twig'; thanks to his crippled leg he was in a sense literally a 'bent twig'; now at last he could be useful in some great aim. One finds coming together in this moment, this 'vision' or act of imagination, all the circumstances both of his subjective history and of the objective conditions within his country:

> That led up to the final experience; and this time it was at the desk in our old house in Maseru where I had a south-facing study. I was looking out towards Qoaling (the mountain), when the certitude stole on me that my destiny was to give everything I could, everything I have, all my time, and all my strength, to the one cause: ending the colour bar.

Did he see himself as a man of destiny? Apparently he did. Just as he had told Edgar Brookes in 1949 that 'history shows that when men really need a great leader, somehow he usually manages to be about',[28] so he had told Lord Hailey that 'as with earlier monsters, a hero will arise who will destroy' the *apartheid*-state.[29] Part of his objection to Marx was that Marxism denied the efficacy of political individualism, which was Duncan's creed. Until well into the 1950s he was sure that he would be the first prime minister of a non-racial South Africa; his father had after all been Governor-General, and had not old General Botha sent a telegram when he was born to welcome a future prime minister? His brother's godfather had been a prime minister, and he himself had been close to him. He had been at school and university with men who wished to lead their countries, and with one at least, Edward Heath, whom he had known a little at Balliol, who was actually to be a prime minister. It is not at all inconceivable that, in a different country or at a different time, he could have been a prime minister himself. He might be a 'bent tool', not a saint, but it might not matter. Destiny might have chosen him, and at last all the events of his life might have come together: his birth; his childhood; his crippled leg; his unhappiness at Bishop's; Winchester, Balliol and the LSE (had not Laski told him of all the great men he had known?); the Basutoland experience; a wife easily capable of being a prime minister's wife....

It would be very easy to stand back from all this and either deride it or be gently dismissive. He was not to be prime minister of anywhere. He was not even to be the leader of a political party. He was to be sacked by the executive of the Pan-Africanist Congress in exile. He was to die in exile, representing no one but himself, only fifteen years later. But, in 1952, he did see himself in a heroic mould:

Only one thing remained to be done. I had read much about South African history, and knew that the crisis, which was now certain, would be dangerous. To get involved might mean discomfort or death. It would not be possible to turn back once one had launched out. Was I prepared to face everything? There were things worse perhaps than death. Everything?

In the end I decided that I was ready.[30]

It is characteristic of South African history at least since 1948 that each new crisis had been seen by at least some South Africans as *the* crisis, the point of no return or the point of change: the election of the Nationalists; the death of Hofmeyr; the Torch Commando; the death of Smuts; the Defiance Campaign; the Treason Trial; the bus boycotts; the Anti-Pass Campaign; Sharpeville and Langa; the banning of the Congresses; *Umkonto we Sizwe*; the Republic; the Bashee Bridge murders; this or that resolution of the United Nations General Assembly; the Terrorism Act of 1963; the dissolution of the Liberal Party; the split between *verligtes* and *verkramptes* in the Nationalist Party; leaving the Commonwealth; the election of Progressive Party MPs; the death of Malan; the assassination of Verwoerd; the promised 'independence' of the Bantustans; the strikes in Natal and elsewhere; the riots of 1976; the revelation of corruption in the Nationalist Party; a guerilla war in Rhodesia – what one selects from the list depends on where one stands, and the list is by no means complete: but for each crisis there are people who claim it as the beginning of the end. Liberals, lacking certainties about the dialectic of history, are particularly prone to this, and Patrick Duncan was no exception, not because he was altogether a liberal but because he had the kind of mind which needed crises: it is another aspect of his delight in the immediate. It was to take him years, and much disappointment, to learn to see the course of history as less rapid than he hoped for.

So, in 1950, it was to be an *Anschluss* on the Territories; so, in 1952, it was to be the Defiance Campaign; so, in 1953, he was to write to Basil Davidson, 'Something tells me that the whole issue of the HCT is reaching its last phase ...'.[31] It was in part out of this that he produced his pamphlet, *Three Centuries of Wrong*:

> *For the Van Riebeeck Tercentenary 6th April, 1952*
> *And for the centenary of the Cape Constitution of 3rd April 1852 which gave equality to all races and which lasted 68 years.*[32]

The title refers to Smuts's pamphlet on the oppression of the Afrikaners, *A Century of Wrong*. Since he was still in the Service, he used his old pseudonym of 'Melanchthon'.

The tercentenary celebrations of 1952 were both a South African attempt to match the Festival of Britain celebrations of the previous year and a glorification of the white settlers of South Africa, particularly the Dutch (which meant, too, a celebration of the fact that at last South Africa was ruled by a 'pure' Afrikaner party). The Congress movements, for their part, planned protest and a campaign of civil disobedience. Duncan's title, sub-titles and the occasions for publication make the purposes of the pamphlet plain: it is an essay attacking the entrenchment of racialism, mourning the loss of the old Cape liberalism (though Duncan was seldom uncritical of its limitations), and an appeal for a change of heart and mind in white South Africa. White South Africa is 'pessimistic, destructive, and confused', he wrote, despite being 'the most powerful state in all Africa'. Why? Because of a 'deep conviction that the present caste-state cannot last'.

> If we know that change is inevitable, then we must choose the best time to have it. In South Africa we have a simple choice: early and safe or late with hate. If we relegate our problems to our children, we shall face a fresh 'Boer War' that will poison relations between White South Africans and non-White South Africans not for two generations, but finally.... That fresh Boer War might begin today.... That is why to-day, Van Riebeeck day, 1952, is the point of no return for our country.

The pamphlet, 'not the place for detailed blueprints', sets out no programme of action, for instance ducking the issue of the suffrage, but claims only one essential: 'there must cease to be discrimination built on race alone'.

One left-wing newspaper found much to praise in the pamphlet; a few friends who knew the pseudonym congratulated Duncan; most of South Africa neither read nor heard of it. Another point of no return had been passed.

However, Duncan himself was busy writing and printing a letter of resignation from the Service. He consulted Brian Marwick, who tried to persuade him that more might be achieved in a more limited area and less in the larger, but who recognized that Duncan was determined on his new direction. He gave the Service six months' notice of his leaving, and in May 1952 sent out a printed letter to his friends, giving his reasons for resignation: he was sorry to be leaving the Basutoland Service, his very interesting job, and his friends, black and white, but as a South African he had to choose his own country. White supremacy 'had reached its last phase' and, unless Nationalism was replaced by 'a Liberal State', it would 'dissolve in violence, and be replaced by a tyranny more hideous even than that aimed at by the present government'. There were two ways of change: violence or non-violence. Although the situations of India and South Africa were very different, Gandhism must be made the way of change, for the alternative was too horrible to contemplate:

> We are leaving so I can go into politics. By this I do not mean that I wish to go into Parliament. Even if I wished I do not flatter myself that any constituency would want me. In any case I do not wish it. Our Parliament today is a White parliament, and can do no more than the White group itself can do.... My politics will be extra-parliamentary acts not forbidden by the constitution, and, as far as lies in my power, they will be just.[33]

'Just', but presumably not legal. The letter ends with an expression of hope that Sir Patrick would have approved of his action, and a promise 'that I shall never do anything that he would be ashamed of'. The decision was made: what he believed to be his destiny had been accepted.

It was not made easily; Cynthia was very unhappy to be leaving Maseru and Basutoland, even though they were only moving across the river to a small farm, called Riverside because it was on the banks of the Caledon, but on the Orange Free State side. She was worried, too, that he was leaving the security of the Service for a much less certain future. It is not comfortable being married to a man of vision, however much you approve of what he believes in. Fortunately there were few financial worries; Cynthia bought the farm, and Patrick used some of his inheritance to buy a book business, dealing mainly in Africana, from the widow of one Fred Rose. Almost immediately he put the business in Cynthia's name, partly to protect her and the children if he got into political trouble, partly on Gandhian principle. But once a decision was made no regrets were permitted; you had made a choice, you had to stick to it. Even when he was dying, fifteen years later, and she broke down and cried at his bedside in the Westminster Hospital in London, he said to her, 'Please don't cry – we know I may die...'.[34]

BOOK THREE

South Africa

7   *Pat Duncan and Manilal Gandhi leading the ANC procession into Germiston in 1952*

8   *At the Lewins' before the march into Germiston, 1952. From left to right: Eleano Lewin, Pat Duncan, Alan Paton, Dorothy Paton, Manilal Gandhi and Julius Lewin*

9   *Pat Duncan, Patrick Duncan and Chief Leabua Jonathan, 1955*

10 Cynthia Duncan

11 Pat and Cynthia Duncan in the sea
at Meadowbank, Cape, October 1955

12 Pat Duncan and son Patrick feeding swan at Hexton

13 *Pat Duncan with Alan Paton (centre), 1956*

14 *The South African delegation meets Dr Nkrumah during the All Africa Peoples' Conference, Accra, 1958. From left to right: Pat Duncan, Ezekiel Mphahlele, Dr Nkrumah, Rev. Michael Scott, Cynthia Duncan and Jordan Ngubane*

CHAPTER 6

1952–5
'Chasing two hares'[1]

Taking the decision to enter South African politics was not the same as finding a role. It was true that Duncan now had various solid bases in his politics: he opposed *apartheid* and desired non-racialism; he thought that the choice was simply non-violence or violence, and that the choice of either lay entirely in the hands of the opposition, so opted for Gandhian methods, even though *satyagraha* meant treating the Nationalists as honourable men; he loathed Marxism and socialism, and distrusted communists; he believed in votes for all, not in a qualified franchise (a lesson Gandhi and the Basotho had taught him); he thought that democracy was a principle, and the efficiency of a state merely desirable, not necessary; and he knew that power was an essential ingredient in political success. But, though he was a man with many friends and some admirers, he was of no party. His intellectual independence worked against his knowledge of *Realpolitik*.

Moreover, the opposition to the gathering strength of Afrikaner Nationalism in the late 1940s and early 1950s was in confusion. Appeals for unity proliferated; there was so much disunity, and yet such clear need for unity. On the side of the whites, the War Veterans' Torch Commando, founded in April 1951, gathered together white ex-servicemen and their supporters into what at one stage looked like a genuine anti-fascist mass movement (it had nearly a quarter of a million members by late 1952); but above all else it avoided the racial question, actually stating as policy the desire that the racial question be 'taken out of politics'. The United Party, practically leaderless after the death of Hofmeyr in 1948 and Smuts in 1952, seemed if anything to be moving closer to the Nationalists in its attempt to win the impending general election of 1953. The Labour Party hardly existed. The Torch Commando tried to put some iron into the soul of the United Party, and with it and the Labour Party formed a United Democratic Front for the election, though its members were still divided about the political role of the Commando; the Natalians, for instance, preferred secession to united fronts, and were eventually to break away to form a short-lived Union Federal Party.

On the other side of the opposition, the Communist Party had dissolved itself in 1950 to pre-empt the passing of the Suppression of Communism Act; but former members of the party and 'statutory' communists (that is, non- or ex-communists defined by the government as communists) were still hounded by police, press, and a 'liquidator' appointed by the government to wind up the affairs of the party. Many former Communist Party members continued to work through trade unions or the Congress movement, some retired from the action or discovered 'ideological differences', some began regrouping as an underground party. The African National Congress was in conflict with itself over such matters at the influence of communists, and tactics and leadership: younger Africanists from Lembede's Youth League agitated against the older leaders; the 'National-minded Bloc' rejected all forms of inter-racial co-operation; the right wing urged the use of what institutions were still available to them; the far left argued for 'non-collaboration' in all things; and nobody was quite sure which was right-wing and which left. When Albert Luthuli was elected President in place of Moroka in December 1952, Anthony Sampson, then Editor of Jim Bailey's African magazine *Drum*, and in a unique position to know these things, told Duncan that it represented 'a swing to the right in Congress. It is said that Luthuli is much less likely to be browbeaten by Reds in the background than was Moroka.'[2] Yet Luthuli was in fact a much more militant and radical figure than Moroka, and his election more a sign of increasing impatience in the Congress with the old ways of discussion, appeal and petition than any battle with communists. In the two Indian Congresses of the Transvaal and Natal, which together comprised the South African Indian Congress, much the same conflict happened, too, much the same confusion. The Trotskyite factions, the Non-European Unity Movement, Tabata's All-African Convention, urged 'non-collaboration' to the extent that they regarded any action as collaboration with the enemy. Anyway, Duncan could join neither the ANC nor the Indian Congress movements, since they represented racial groups of which he was not a member, though he did apply several times for membership of the ANC. On 3 December 1953 he told Nelson Mandela that he had written to the local branch of the ANC 'applying for membership': 'I have thought a lot about this, and am quite clear that I would like to join. To me it is a logical consequence of joining the campaign last year. In this way I shall be bound by Congress decisions, and shall find a place in the struggle for our liberation.'[3] There is no reply to this letter among his papers, though he does actually seem to have had his application accepted by the ANC branch in Ladybrand. Unfortunately only the second page of the letter from Philip Motseta, the Chairman, survives, so it cannot be dated, though other evidence places the incident in late 1953 or early 1954; Motseta wrote: 'We shall treat you like any other black man or African.... You are to pay 2/6 yearly and that is all I shall send you a membership card for 1954....'[4] He mentioned his acceptance as a member in a letter to Luthuli in March 1954, though whether this membership was ever official is unknown, and seems unlikely.

When the Congress of Democrats was formed in 1953 as a home for white supporters of the Congress Alliance, he would not join that either, since many members were formerly of the Communist Party. He told Cecil Williams after a meeting with him and Jack Hodgson that he thought they were 'fundamentally on the right lines', but that there were 'certain difficulties which make it difficult for many S. Africans particularly if they are (in overseas language) right-wing or centre, to join you . . .'.[5] He explained to Chief Luthuli that at a meeting with Piet Beyleveld, Chairman of COD, he had said 'in the opinion of the country the COD was communist or communist-dominated, and that as a Christian I could not join'.[6] But how seriously he took the offer of membership, and how seriously COD took it, is clear from an exchange of letters with Eddie Roux, a botanist at the University of the Witwatersrand and an ex-communist. Duncan wrote:

> Beyleveld ... suggested that I join ... COD, and since then I have been thinking very seriously of doing so. My trouble of course is that I can't afford – and do not wish – to join a set that are just the CP revised, and rumour has it that the ... COD is just this. But I knew you were on the committee, and felt that if there were other members like you on it I would like to apply (I gather there might be some difficulty in getting in, but I would apply despite this).[7]

Roux replied in his usual gnomic and witty way ('Win' is Mrs Roux):

> The line you suggest ... would ... strengthen my own hand with my associates (who are almost exclusively commercial travellers), and your acceptance would be a test of their sincerity. I don't think we can quibble with the published prospectus of the company. They are serious business-men and prepared to work. It is difficult to elaborate in view of possible scrutiny but Win presents a minority report saying that cash on delivery is not suited to your business which depends on the integrity of its name.[8]

In the event, Duncan accepted Mrs Roux's advice, and did not apply.

And how could he possibly join his father's old party, the United Party, all-white and increasingly reactionary in its desperate effort to grab back votes from the National Party? Even when the Liberal Party was formed after the general election of 1953, which saw the Nationalists returned with even more seats though still no total majority of votes, he would not join, because – although it was close to much of his thinking – it did not seem enough concerned with establishing itself as an actual power in the land. Moreover, the Liberal Party had initially as its policy a qualified franchise, not the universal adult franchise he both believed in and saw as a necessary requirement of large-scale black support.

What, then, of a new party designed to meet all his requirements? It was an idea he considered for several years, though he never got enough support to take any real action. As early as August 1952 he suggested the need for a new party, an 'All People's Party',[9] which would bring together all the elements in the opposition – Congressmen, liberals, anti-racialist conservatives, even communists and fellow-travellers. By 1954 he was talking of a 'Christian-Democratic group' which could have the same relationship with the ANC as the COD had, and which would 'strengthen the non-racial idea in the churches, and ... strengthen the Christian idea in the liberation move-ment',[10] and in June 1954 he wrote to a friend that he had actually started such a group with two black Anglican priests, John Skomolo and Michael Mohaleroe.[11] He tried out similar ideas on others of like mind; but there was no great enthusiasm for the scheme, and after 1955 the Christian-Democratic group is not heard of again, though the 'All People's Party' remained a long-term political dream.

In 1951–4 he was in fact closer to the Natal Indian Congress than any other organization. He was particularly close to the Mahatma's second son, Manilal Gandhi, who had worked in South Africa and India with his father and who had returned to South Africa to run the settlement, the *ashram*, at Phoenix near Durban which his father had founded, and to promite his father's ideas, mainly through his newspaper *Indian Opinion*. Manilal Gandhi had, virtually single-handed, run his own passive resistance campaign in South Africa, sitting on benches marked 'For Europeans Only', using the white section of the Durban library, going into the Free State despite its regulations restricting the presence of Indians, and serving several jail sentences in the process, despite the fact that he was getting old and was often ill. Many people found Manilal a pale shadow of his father; but Duncan, who understood what it was to be the son of a famous father, and admiring the Mahatma above all men, found himself much in sympathy with Manilal. When, in December 1951, Manilal went to the ANC Conference in Bloemfontein called to consider the techniques the ANC and its allies would adopt unless the Nationalist government withdrew its most repressive legislation, Duncan had gone quietly (for he was still Judicial Commissioner) to meet him at the railway station at Modderpoort, to talk passive resistance and *satyagraha*.

The plan of action drawn up by the ANC and representatives of the Indian Congress movement and the Franchise Action Council (mainly a Cape group) set out a series of measures against various laws and statutes, including the Separate Representation of Voters' Act, the Group Areas Act, the Suppression of Communism Act, and the Bantu Authorities Act. The culmination of the action was to be a Defiance Campaign, to start on 26 June 1952, 'Freedom Day', when volunteers would flout those laws with the specific intention of being arrested and jailed. The government pre-empted the starting-date by banning various ANC and trade union leaders, and expelling Sam Kahn, the Communist MP, from Parliament, and Fred Carneson, Communist MPC, from the Provincial Council; several of the banned leaders, including Moses Kotane, the Communist and Congress executive member, immediately defied the bans, addressed meetings, were arrested and jailed. Their stubborn fortitude gives part of the context in which Duncan's own participation in the Defiance Campaign needs to be seen.

Duncan in fact disliked the term 'defiance'; for him, it should be an exercise in Gandhian *satyagraha*. (Duncan's own translation of this difficult concept was 'truth-firmness'; a better seems to be 'soul-force', since that gives more the sense of an active force, a 'working-upon' that which the 'soul' wishes to change.) If other South Africans saw the son of a former governor-general go to jail in a good cause, would they not be moved to hasten peaceful change, to withdraw South Africa from the brink he saw her approaching? In May 1952 he went to stay with Father Trevor Huddleston in Rosettenville, at the Priory of the Community of the Resurrection, mainly to see if there was anything he could do to help in Huddleston's campaign to prevent the destruction of Sophiatown, the so-called 'Western Areas Removal' scheme, in which blacks would be moved from their homes and land and dumped in a not-yet-built township at Meadowlands, but also to get in touch with ANC people in the Transvaal about joining the Defiance Campaign. In late May he saw Moroka, then still President of the ANC, and talked to him about his own possible role as well as asking him about the plans of the ANC in opposing the 'Western Areas Removal' scheme. Nothing was decided at his meeting with Moroka, but the discussions with Huddleston – and Huddleston's own example – added to his conviction that it was a duty to join the Defiance Campaign.

Of course deciding exactly how to 'defy' was not simple; his resignation from the Service only became effective in November 1952 and until then he was bound to be loyal to its regulations. Nor was he entirely sure that the spirit of the Defiance Campaign was sufficiently Gandhian, partly since Manilal Gandhi, with his strenuously ascetic views of *satyagraha,* was not happy about Duncan's joining the Campaign and thought that a role less to the forefront might be more useful in the long term, and partly since the Campaign seemed as much aimed at embarrassing the government (locally and internationally) as at loving the rulers into the truth. Duncan was worried, too, about the possible effects on the United Party of the Defiance Campaign; for all his dissatisfaction with the UP he was realist enough to know that 'soul-force' would have more chance with it than with the Nationalists. He wrote to Julius Lewin in September:

> Please help me...with advice. You know I want to assist the Civil Disobedience campaign actively. Almost certainly I should be used as a stick to beat the UP with. I don't want to lose the UP a single vote [in the general election of March 1953]. *But* I don't want to delay showing solidarity with these brave men one day longer than necessary.... What do you counsel?[12]

He exchanged letters with De Villiers Graaff, later to be leader of the UP. Graaff asked him to avoid any action likely to embarrass the UP until after the election, and Duncan replied that he promised not to do anything before the election 'that I do not feel compelled to do'.[13] His reply was in no way ironic, as the attitude he was to take towards the UP during 1953 makes clear.

Other events complicated the decision still further. In late August, driving too fast (he often did) on the wrong side of the road (he sometimes did) over the brow of a hill, he crashed into another car (also going fast, but on the proper side of the road). Fortunately, the man whose car he crashed into wasn't hurt, but Duncan had broken his lame leg badly. He was carried off to hospital, where he gave Dr Basil Whitworth detailed instructions, with a diagram, of exactly the angle at which the leg should be set to give him the most mobility. He tried, too, to persuade Whitworth to set the bone without giving him an anaesthetic, and Whitworth had to use all his authority, and the rights of an old friend, to insist that an anaesthetic was necessary. Duncan, however, got his own way when he refused to eat the white patients' diet, and demanded exactly the same diet as given to Basotho patients. He was three months in hospital, in plaster up to his waist, and came out just in time to help with the move from Maseru to Riverside Farm.

While he was in hospital, in October, serious rioting broke out in Port Elizabeth and various other towns. Despite denials of responsibility by Congress, Duncan was convinced the troubles arose from the Defiance Campaign, and all his old worries about the lack of preparedness for true *satyagraha* resurfaced. He wrote to Christopher Gell and Julius Lewin to say he would no longer support the Campaign, and must look for another role.

Christopher Gell is one of the most remarkable characters in this story. After doing brilliantly at Wellington and Cambridge, and then in the Indian Civil Service, he had in 1945 caught poliomyelitis, which crippled him so badly that he was virtually immobile, physically so frail that he had to spend all but a few hours a day in an iron lung. Emigrating from England to South Africa for the climate (his wife was South African), and appalled by what he found there, he turned himself into a considerable influence in South African radical politics, and set up a 'behind-the-news' digest, the *Africa X-Ray Digest*. Gell wrote, too, for Manilal Gandhi's *Indian Opinion*, and in August 1952 Duncan got in touch with him, to tell him of his resignation from the Service and of his admiration for Gell's articles. Gell replied: 'Writing is about all that is open to me. And so few people (white people) read! But that, too, is good for our conceit.'[14] Initially Gell and Duncan were close. As Gell pointed out, there was much similarity in their backgrounds – physical disability, English public schools, and service as Colonial Officers – though later Gell was to feel that Duncan made many unwise choices, and was to become very critical of him.

Now, at least, he replied gently to what he felt was Duncan's over-reaction to the riots in Port Elizabeth: riots, he said, 'are liable to happen any time, any place ... pacific efforts ... need not be jettisoned at the first explosion...'[15] Lewin, who with Anthony Sampson was largely responsible for arranging Duncan's actual participation in the Defiance Campaign, told him much the same. Sampson saw Yusuf Cachalia, Secretary of the Transvaal Indian Congress and Joint-Secretary with Walter Sisulu of the Defiance Campaign, and found great enthusiasm for Duncan's participation. So, with Gell's and Lewin's reassurances, with disavowals from the ANC of responsibility for the riots, and with the welcome of the Congress movement, Duncan was persuaded to go ahead, and he encouraged Sampson to arrange for him to 'defy' as soon as he was out of plaster and able to walk again.

On 31 October the family moved to Riverside, Duncan arriving in an ambulance and still walking on crutches. Riverside was a large house and a small farm, a little way upstream from the bridge joining the Orange Free State and Basutoland. The single-storied and rambling house, with pink walls and thatched roofs, faced out across the Caledon river towards Maseru; in front of the house were a pleasant flower-garden, rockeries and a swimming-pool, to one side a cottage which they used to rent out, and behind servants' quarters and a large vegetable-garden. The farm itself was mainly hillside, and most of the farming centred on a small herd of milk-cows, though the Duncans grew mealies and potatoes, too; they chose it mainly for its physical position, for the house and the pleasantness of the farm, rather than for its profitability – more, in short, a place for a gentleman and his family to retire to than for a political activist to set up as base-camp. But politics was not the Duncans' only concern: they had the stock from Fred Rose to sort, classify and price, catalogues to prepare and send out, book-sales and auctions to attend, the farm, gardens and house to run, and servants and the four farm-hands to supervise. Perforce, most of Duncan's energy had to go on the book-business. His interest in agriculture was more theoretical than practical, and he tended to leave the farm and gardens to Cynthia and their farm-hands; the farm was too small to make much money and what profit there was came mainly from the milk-round which the previous owner had set up in Maseru. Cyril Dunn has described Duncan's farming as 'walking around his fields talking politics and occasionally swiping the head off a thistle with his stick' and the farm as 'chiefly a place for the Duncan boys to gallop around on Basuto ponies, with small Basuto boys similarly mounted',[16] though both descriptions are a little unfair, since Duncan did plant trees and make sure erosion was countered. Still, he was more a bookseller than a farmer, and fortunately Africa Books did fairly well. He worked very hard to build up the business – often eighteen hours a day, once right through the night – and soon established a reputation among bibliophiles in South Africa and abroad for efficiency, concern and reasonable prices. He employed various assistants – June Stutley, wife of an official in the Basutoland Agriculture Department; a little later, Doris Paterson, an energetic globe-trotting Scotswoman; and, from 1954 as a part-time secretary, Ezekiel Mphahlele, who had been sacked by the Bantu Education Department for his political views and activities. Duncan was away a great deal, and much of the burden of running the business fell on his assistants and on Cynthia. When one considers how much else he did while they lived at Riverside, it is remarkable that Africa Books ever made a profit at all. For a time the Duncans considered a profit-sharing scheme with their farm-hands on the lines that a farmer-friend, Jean van Riet, used very successfully on his Free State farm; but Riverside Farm made so little profit that there was not much point in sharing it.

Three weeks after their arrival on the farm, Anthony Sampson sent Duncan a telegram to say that the SAIC, through Cachalia, had settled on a date for his participation in the Campaign. A week later, on 28 November, the *Star* carried the first public announcement of Duncan's joining the Defiance Campaign; *The Times* carried the story next day, and the *Observer* the day after. 'Sir Patrick Duncan's son joins defiance body', the *Star* reported:

> In a statement he says: 'We are approaching the greatest crisis in our history. It is no longer in the power of White South Africa to impose on non-White South Africa discriminations based purely on colour....
>
> 'All that is in the power of White South Africa is to choose whether the change will come with or without violence. If White South Africa turns today to naked force to preserve the present caste system it will be held responsible by history for the race war that will probably destroy our country.'...

A few days later a group of four whites in Cape Town announced their intention of joining the Campaign; they included Albie Sachs, son of the old trade unionist Solly Sachs. On 6 December three other whites in Johannesburg said they would join Duncan: Bettie du Toit, a trade unionist, Percy Cohen, a dentist, and Freda Troup (later Levson), a writer. Soon afterwards four other Johannesburg whites announced that they would join, too.

It was an important moment for the Campaign, ensuring massive publicity in South Africa and abroad, and making the Defiance Campaign more representative of the whole South African population, and harder for the

Nationalists to dismiss as merely the lunatic behaviour of black people under the influence of communist agitators. Though the Africanists might object to white participation as a dilution of purely African grievances, the Joint-Secretaries of the Campaign, Cachalia and Sisulu, issued a statement which said: 'Mr Duncan has shown great foresight in taking this brave stand.... We hope that this will have wide repercussions among Europeans in South Africa and arouse maximum consciousness for right and justice.' The participation of Duncan and others would, they went on, 'help ... avert race antagonisms...'.[17]

Up to that point the main force of the Campaign had been in the hands of Africans and Indians, though some Coloured people were to join in the Cape Town defiance on 8 December. In June a group led by Nana Sita, an old disciple of the Mahatma, had been arrested in Boksburg location, some for not having passes, some for entering the location without the necessary permit. In Port Elizabeth thirty volunteers went into the railway station using the 'Europeans only' entrance. By the end of July some eight hundred people had been arrested, by the end of August 3198, by 6 October 5264, and by 22 October 6880. By the end of the year, the total was to reach 8065, close to the Joint Planning Council's aim of ten thousand volunteers. But the participation of whites, and especially of Patrick Duncan (if only because he was his father's son) gave the Campaign new impetus; white South Africans, up to then, had tended to see the defiers generically, not individually – as Indians or Africans, not as Cachalia, Singh, Moroka or Conco. Indians and Africans were collectives, the defiers a collective, individually invisible; Duncan, Troup, *et al.*, were visible, had biographies, and could be interviewed for white newspapers.

On 28 November the government, which had until then blamed the Campaign variously on the Mau-Mau, on communists, on the Torch Commando, and on the United Party, introduced a new seriousness into acts of defiance; the Governor-General and the Minister of Native Affairs (Verwoerd) issued a proclamation under the Native Administration Act to make it an offence for anyone to incite an African to break any law, and for anyone to hold a meeting of Africans. The maximum penalty was to be a fine of £300 or three years in prison. It was the first stage on the way to the Public Safety Act and the Criminal Law Amendment Act of 1953, and to the draconian measures against 'terrorism' in the 1960s. Although legal opinion in Johannesburg held that the proclamation might well be *ultra vires,* some of the defiers were apparently shaken by its severity, though in the event none pulled out. However, it did in fact signal the approaching end of the Defiance Campaign; the rulers had not been persuaded by love and truth – they had merely grown harsher.

Patrick and Cynthia Duncan drove up to Johannesburg on the Saturday before the latest phase of the Campaign, and found themselves honoured guests (though one member of the ANC told Duncan at a party that he was an 'imperialist spy'[18]). The Lewins put them up in their Parkwood house, Cachalia and his wife entertained them in their Fordsburg flat, and Dr Yusef Dadoo, President of the TIC, came to talk to them in Parkwood. Lewin and Sampson organized a press conference, to which came most of the journalists representing the overseas press, and at which Duncan said he had 'thought defiance' for four years, and that he looked forward 'to the growth of the African National Congress and the South African Indian Congress as a great, responsible non-European movement'. He denied communist influence in the Campaign, though he said that of course there were communists among the defiers.

> But surely the fact that they have had to adapt themselves to passive resistance shows that they are not calling the tune.
> If I thought this organization was communist, I would not be prepared to co-operate with it.[19]

On the 8th – the day set for the defiance – the Lewins gave a small lunch-party for the Duncans, Alan and Dorrie Paton, and Manilal Gandhi, who happened to be in Johannesburg but who had not yet joined the actual Defiance Campaign. During the lunch, and at the urging of Duncan, Manilal decided that he would join in that very afternoon, a decision which delighted Duncan.

After lunch Duncan and Gandhi joined the other defiers outside Germiston location; there were about forty of them – thirty-eight were arrested altogether, twelve Africans, nineteen Indians, seven whites – but there was a large crowd of other Africans, too, none of whom was afterwards arrested, and several carloads of armed police and security police in plain clothes. Many of the defiers were students, some from Fort Hare, some from the University of the Witwatersrand; the Africans included the writer Alfred Hutchinson and Peter Molotsi, who reappears in this story years later.

Duncan was asked to lead the procession into the location, which he did, going at a great pace on his crutches, to which he had tied the Congress colours of green, yellow and black; the other defiers followed, the crowd milling round them in great excitement. They marched round and round the location, singing Congress songs; but no one was arrested. So Duncan stopped the procession, called for something to stand on, and got up on a bench to make a speech. In both Sotho and English, he called for equality, non-violence, and action in a spirit of peace and love. The crowd responded, the women giving the traditional ululation, and Duncan ended his speech with the Congress cry, 'Mayibuye, Afrika' ('Come back, Africa'). Since the police still showed no sign of arresting them, Duncan got off the bench and began to lead the defiers to the gate of the location. Bettie du Toit turned to the nearest policeman to say: 'Aren't you *ever* going to arrest us?' He replied: 'Okay, go and get in that car.'[20] The fourteen journalists present, several respresenting the overseas press, thought they had been arrested, too, though it transpired that they were only being warned for not having permits to be in a location.

Those arrested were taken to Germiston police station and were held the statutory forty-eight hours before being charged, Duncan in a cell with three other white defiers. On the first night the police beat up some young Africans in the yard outside the cells, apparently to alarm the defiers. On the 10th, the thirty-eight arrested appeared in the Germiston Magistrate's Court charged with contravening the new proclamation, with entering the location without permits, and – in the case of the African men – with not having passes. The prosecution asked for a remand, and the defence asked for bail which, after some argument, was set at £50 each for the whites, and £20 each for the Africans and Indians, with an additional condition that none enter the Germiston location. The magistrate said, in fixing bail, 'We are dealing here with a race, in my opinion, primitive, easily led, who will, under emotion, act as under calmer reflection they would not otherwise do,'[21] and set the trial for January 1953.

In the event, the seven whites and Gandhi were brought to trial separately; and the other thirty accused had their trial adjourned to February, and the main charge dropped, so they received only light sentences.

The Congress leaders felt that the legal validity of the new proclamation should be tested in the courts, which made it necessary for the defiers to plead not guilty. Both Gandhi and Duncan felt strongly that they should plead guilty, accept the verdict of the court, and go to jail – indeed, all the defiers had agreed to go to jail rather than pay fines – but accepted the majority decision to plead not guilty. The Joint Action Council engaged lawyers for them – George Lowen appearing for Duncan, Bettie du Toit and Gandhi – and they settled down to a long trial. In his press-cuttings book on the Defiance Campaign, Duncan wrote a marginal comment on the report of their trial: 'A setback and a lesson – Never let lawyers control a political case. George [Lowen] is a great lawyer and has a great heart. We should have pleaded guilty and not appealed. Manilal was right.' The case dragged on to 5 February, the police witnesses claiming that a riot had nearly started, that Africans had tried to overturn a police car, that cars had been bumped and banged after the arrests, that the women's ululation was a war cry, George Lowen and the other lawyers for the defence claiming not only that the proclamation was *ultra vires* but that the police witnesses were totally unreliable. The defiers were found guilty, made statements before being sentenced (Gandhi said, 'If the court considers that I have committed a serious offence, then I ask that the severest sentence be imposed upon me', for he was a true *satyagrahi*[22]), and were sentenced: Duncan, the 'ringleader', got a hundred days with compulsory labour, or a fine of £100; Gandhi fifty days with compulsory labour or £50; Bettie du Toit, Freda Troup, Selama Stamelmann, Percy Cohen, the same as Gandhi, but half suspended for three years; and Syd Shall and Margaret Holt, both students, twenty days or £20.[23] George Lowen immediately gave notice of appeal, and once more the eight were released on bail pending appeal. Immediately after being sentenced, all – including Gandhi – went to have lunch at the Carlton Grill in the centre of Johannesburg; 'no one raised an eyebrow', Duncan wrote in his diary, enjoying the joke of eight convicts breaking the colour-bar in Johannesburg's smartest restaurant.

Eventually, all eight were to withdraw their appeals and most served their sentences or part of them. Manilal Gandhi served his full fifty days less remission. Bettie du Toit went to jail with Freda Troup for their full twenty-five days less remission. Duncan himself did not withdraw his appeal until June 1953, and he was then in hospital in Basutoland, recovering from a massive operation on his bad leg. His decision to drop the appeal was announced in Johannesburg by Trevor Huddleston at a protest meeting against the 'Western Areas Removal' scheme, and he read out a message from

Duncan which called the scheme 'without parallel in history' for its cruelty; 'a farmer would not treat his animals so'.²⁴ At the end of October Duncan went to prison, first briefly in Germiston, then in Boksburg, but he was in no condition to serve a hundred days, and after a fortnight paid the rest of his fine and was released. He was bitterly ashamed of this, for all that he found his fortnight of sharing two cells with a floating population of between seven and fifteen criminals loathsome. Life inside became a little easier when his fellow-prisoners discovered he had been a magistrate, and he set up an unofficial legal advice centre; but then there was trouble between Duncan and a young gangster, to whom the other prisoners deferred, and after Duncan had complained to a warder about being kept awake at night the young gangster told the prison superintendent that Duncan had been preaching communism. The prisoners were reallocated in different cells.

On Duncan's release, he issued a statement denouncing the treatment of black prisoners, and soon afterwards wrote an article for the *Observer* on his fortnight in jail, which was republished in Israel, Sweden and India. When asked by the *Observer* to supplement it with reasons for his not serving the full sentence, he cabled:

> Reasons inability serve whole sentence stop Livelihood farm and books stop. Earning capacity seriously affected during last year by healing thighbone December, pedicle tissue graft May diagnosis chronic osteo-myelitis November which neutralized four months added crushing expenses. Non-whites our group except Gandhi served two weeks I felt bound to do same but could do no more.²⁵

Looking back on his part in the Defiance Campaign, Duncan was to feel that he had made many mistakes. First, he thought having a lawyer in a political case was a mistake. Secondly, they should have pleaded guilty: they had deliberately broken a law by way of protesting against it, they had planned to go to jail, and they should have gone at once. Thirdly, he should have been physically able to complete the sentence. Fourthly, they should not have appealed: 'we were still chasing two hares, as the Basuto say', he told Cyril Dunn in 1955. On the credit side, he did feel considerable pride in having joined the Campaign, and in having helped make the Campaign 'non-racial'.

There was little public criticism of Duncan for not having served the full sentence. Before going to jail, he had told a reporter from the *Bantu World* that he would be unlikely to serve more than ten days of his sentence and he took to jail with him a certificate from his doctors to say he needed daily injections of penicillin to help the healing of his leg.²⁶ When Dadoo, Cachalia and Mandela came to wish Duncan, Bettie du Toit and Freda Troup good luck in the jail terms, Cachalia offered to pay the fine on behalf of the Joint Action Council, and there was a crowd of Congress supporters waiting to greet him on his release from Boksburg, though the police in the end released him at Germiston railway station to avoid the crowd. Still, he managed to meet up with the Congress supporters and his sister. A few people felt he had failed in not serving out his full time, but most did not, thinking rather that he had done most of what he set out to do. He himself agreed with the few who criticized him, though he knew better than most how real his reasons were.

For some, like Christopher Gell and Julius Lewin, Duncan's participation in the Defiance Campaign was the finest moment of his political career. In lending the prestige of his family name to the Campaign, and sacrificing the regard of his own kind and class, he for once managed, in their terms, to submit his own individuality to the discipline of a larger movement. In others, his participation aroused considerable antipathy; till then he had been regarded as merely eccentric in his views – now he was positively mad. Some of his former colleagues in Basutoland could barely bring themselves to talk to him, and Cynthia, too, was cold-shouldered, and had to listen to criticism of her husband from English friends who felt he was going too far too fast. Too gregarious and warm a man to take rejection easily, Duncan was glad to have new friends to turn to. He wrote to Lewin in January 1953: 'Thank you for your cheering and sustaining letter. It is unpleasant to be regarded as a traitor to one's class or race or whatever it is called. As you so rightly see the compensations for this rejection far outweigh it.'[27]

Whatever the criticism and self-criticism, Duncan's action in leading the defiers into Germiston on his crutches caught the popular imagination of Africans in a way that no other of his actions did, and he is remembered by ordinary Africans in South Africa now for that rather than for anything else: in the imagination of the older generations of black South Africa he is not Duncan the Governor-General's son, nor Duncan the Liberal, nor Duncan of *Contact*, nor Duncan the white PAC member, but Duncan who joined the Defiance Campaign on crutches.[28]

The months between the trial and his two weeks in prison had been very full: he and Cynthia were still trying to settle into Riverside; Africa Books took up a great deal of time; the farm had to be farmed and the gardens gardened, and even with servants to help there was much to do. He had to keep alive his newly made links with the Congress movements (in December 1952, after the Germiston Defiance Campaign, he had been invited to the ANC Conference in Johannesburg and, introduced to the Conference by Moroka, the outgoing President, he had been greeted with shouts of 'Mayibuye, Afrika!' and his short speech, on the South Africa he looked forward to, had been greeted tumultuously[29]). He began to do a great deal of occasional journalism, for *Indian Opinion*, for the liberal *Forum*, for the Bloemfontein *Friend*, and for English and American periodicals (for instance, his long article on 'Satyagraha in South Africa' for the *Round Table*, which offers one of the most complete accounts of the 1952 Defiance Campaign), and worked on a longish pamphlet, *The Road through the Wilderness*, which he published in May 1953. In March he went to talk to one of the 'Shoe Parties' organized by Huddleston in Rosettenville, and took as his subject 'Changed relationships of a modern world'; at the same time he talked more to Huddleston about the 'Western Areas Removal' scheme and how best to oppose it. In May Cynthia and the children went to England to stay with the Ashley Coopers at Hexton Manor, and the day after they left he went into hospital in Johannesburg for a complex set of operations on his bad leg, which involved scraping away from the bone the detritus which was causing continual suppuration and ulceration to the old wound, grafting a pad of flesh from the good leg over on to the old wound to give it a little more protection, and grafting skin taken from his thigh to his shin-bone to replace the pad of flesh. For weeks his legs had to be strapped together, to allow the graft of flesh from good leg to bad to 'take', and it was both exceedingly painful and very undignified. He worked when he could on *Sotho Law and Customs*, for the publication of which he had been promised a grant from the Basutoland Service, and received a string of visitors, both Johannesburgers and from overseas. In late June the doctors allowed him to be transferred to Maseru hospital – too soon, as it happened – so it was not until July that he could go back to Riverside. Even when he went to prison in late October the leg was by no means properly healed.

The Road through the Wilderness, which he published in mid-1953, offers an interesting account of his political attitudes at the time, though he was to change his mind about some of what he wrote almost by the time he had published it. It is also one of the most closely argued political arguments he ever advanced, and in some things original.

The pamphlet is addressed to English South Africans. Duncan is quite clear about the aim of the Nationalists towards them: they are to remain a 'ruled, subordinate minority', and will learn what the majority of South Africans have long since learned – what it is to be without political power in their own country. Yet, although the Nationalists had many forces working for them, they had greater forces working against them: the power of God; world civilization; the love of liberty; economic forces; and world opinion (he makes an odd distinction between world 'civilization' and world opinion). They have weaknesses, too: growing industrialism worked against Calvinism; the predictable economic success of the *volk* would loosen the bonds which gave them political unity; the 'kraaling-off of the *volk*' would drive some of its best brains to seek intellectual refuge abroad; the English minority would not easily be assimilated to Afrikanerdom; the power of the Dutch Reformed Church, like that of all institutional Christianity, was in decline; and – greatest weakness of all – the doctrines of *apartheid* were self-contradictory.

The conclusions which Duncan draws from these arguments are, first, that English South Africans will remain subjugated to the Nationalists; secondly, that the Nationalists will remain in power as long as political power remains in the hands of whites; and, thirdly, that eventually 'emancipation will come through a combination of the political power of the African people and the conscience of the Whites'.

Facing these 'facts', and urging that since South Africa was as much 'our' (i.e. English South Africans') country as anyone's, Duncan argues, first, that the United Party should receive support in its rearguard action against Nationalism, even though it will almost certainly remain in permanent opposition. Secondly, though the new Liberal Party has much to recommend it in principle, it cannot be seen as an alternative to the United Party; like the new Federal Party which had its main strength in Natal and as its main policy the idea of a looser connection between the provinces of South Africa, the founders of the Liberal Party were 'without an adequate appreciation of the part that political power plays in politics'. If the Liberal Party were to limit itself to statements of principle and non-parliamentary politics, it might be useful; but in parliamentary opposition the United Party is much worthier of support. Thirdly, to advocate revolution is both wrong and inexpedient, wrong because a civil war is too appalling to contemplate and inexpedient because it is always 'inexpedient for an unarmed man to threaten a man with a sten gun'.

If in the short term the United Party offers the best hope of stirring the conscience of the whites, in the long term the evocation of the latent political power of the Africans will depend on the formation of an 'All People's Party', which will need to reject both 'international Communism' and 'Pan-African Nationalism' and work for a unified South Africa. Since it seems too soon for the establishment of such a party, Duncan argues for two more immediate actions, the first the calling together of a 'federal body' of 'all organizations in South Africa which in any way are against the colour-bar', and the second a setting-up of a group of whites who will live non-racially, identifying themselves with those deprived of political and other rights and working for non-racialism – as an example he cites some of the Civil Rights groups of the American South.

While none of the measures he suggests will remove 'all our tensions', they will at least reduce them to 'manageable proportions, and ... enable us to continue to build in reasonable security ... SOUTH AFRICA FOR THE SOUTH AFRICANS for then we shall all of us, Africans, Indians, and Whites, be South Africans'.

Much of the argument of the pamphlet reveals his preoccupations at the time – his acknowledgement that the UP would be in permanent opposition, his search for an all-embracing political party, his distrust of the Liberal Party, his desire for a small group of whites to set an example of non-racialism – but it is an odd comment, too, on his relationship with the Congress movement in 1953 that he does not even mention it in the pamphlet, though he was applying for membership at the time. Much in the pamphlet points forward to later developments in his political thinking, too – on revolution, on the permanence or impermanence of white settlement in South Africa – but the most fascinating aspect of it is the way he conjoins the evoking of 'African power' and 'White conscience' as a single force.

Duncan was not a political philosopher nor even a political theorist. His mind was more of the 'here-and-now' kind, reacting to events rather than reflecting on tendencies; it is the same quality which make him delight in newness and 'adventures', the same quality that so appealed to young Michael Cassidy. The fallacies in his argument, his tendency to confuse what he wanted to happen with what he expected to happen, his muddling of 'ought' and 'is', are easy enough to demonstrate; but if one is not looking for a coherent philosophy, but rather for an understanding of the problems he faced in choosing a political role, then the conjunction of 'African power' and 'White conscience' explains a great deal else of the confusion in his political thinking, then and later. He could see no contradiction between the two and his disavowal of revolution; and there is a sense in which, if one does disavow revolution for being 'wrong' or 'inexpedient', or both together, successful appeal to 'White conscience' is essential. Unless one were to suppose that the blacks would remain permanently subjugated, and if one disapproved of revolution, then one had to aim for a change in whites' hearts which would cause them to give way as blacks advanced. If one stopped believing in the possibility of a change of heart, then one had to believe in revolution – not in its efficacy or desirability, but in its inevitability. Duncan could not do this, at least in 1953.

It would be easy enough to justify the argument if one were to call him, say, a political moralist rather than a politician, in the sense that George Orwell was a political moralist: for a revolution to be real, it would have to involve a change of heart. Yet Duncan was too much concerned with the politics of power to be described as mainly a political moralist. He knew that the force which could actually change the course of events in South Africa was 'African power'. Yet to accept 'African power' as the only major force meant accepting the inevitability of revolution. In other words, he needed to believe in the conjunction of the two forces, 'African power' and 'White conscience', and so he could not choose a single role. If he joined the Congress movement, it would be to set an example to the whites. If he joined the Liberals, it would be in the hope of making them an agent of 'African power'. (He was not of course alone in this; anyone who could not share the certainties of the Marxist dialectic was in much the same position, whether he were white or black, and even among Marxists there was often uncertainty about the role of whites in the liberation movement. It is easy to say that one cannot serve both God and Mammon, but not everyone is sure which to serve.)

One finds in this an explanation of much which is confused and confusing in his political thinking until well into the 1960s. How else was it possible for him to urge English South Africans to remain loyal to the United Party, while he himself tried to join the ANC? How else could he write to Cynthia in 1953 that the Liberal Party members 'have forgotten that politics is of the heart, not of the head. Their true function is to write books and pamphlets not to try to get people to vote',[30] and yet join the same party himself in less than two years' time? How else could he desire an 'All People's Party' in 1953 and, less than two years afterwards, not support the Congress of the People, even though he was personally invited to attend? Because communists were part of it? Were they not part of 'All People'? And how else to reconcile these two remarks, the first made in 1952 during the Defiance Campaign, the second in a letter?

> There is only one internal power that can challenge successfully the colour bar backed by embattled Afrikaner nationalism. That is the working class largely African....[31]

> Although I admire many of the leaders of the ANC and like them, although I respect deeply what they did in the late campaign, and although I think their present leader [Luthuli] is one of the greatest S. Africans, I do not want them to succeed. For after all is said they are still a sectional movement....[32]

It would be easy to accuse him simply of hypocrisy, or to do what *Advance* did in its review of his pamphlet, to accuse him of wanting to use the power of the African people to rescue English South Africans from the trap of racial chauvinism;[33] but he was more complicated than that. In both examples his own resolution was to propose the formation of a party which would contain both power and conscience – in the first he rejected communism and pan-African nationalism and argued for a 'South African Party open to all Races

in a programme of emancipation', in the second for 'emancipation ...
through a non-sectional movement, non-sectional from the foundation up,
and vowed to non-violence'.

In just the same way he would argue in one breath for white people to
continue to support the United Party, and in the next try to join the ANC
himself. In crude terms, he was allying himself as 'a white with a conscience'
to African power. Similarly, when later he joined the Liberal Party, then the
party of white conscience, he did so in the hope that it would attract African
power. Given his commitment to peaceful change, and his political realism, it
was necessary for him to contain the contradiction in his own actions and
thinking; if he had been a more hypocritical man, it would have been much
easier to opt for one side or the other of the contradiction. If in the Defiance
Campaign he had been 'chasing two hares', in his search for the conjunction
of African power and white conscience he had to ride two horses, even though
they did not always travel together.

An aspect of his concern for non-violent change within South Africa was
his hope for international intervention. As early as 1950, when he attended
Paton's talk at the South Africa Mission in London, he had argued for
intervention, expecting 'that like slavery *apartheid* would be stopped by
world-wide action'.[34] In 1953, following the example set by Michael Scott, he
submitted a memorandum to the United Nations Special Commission on
Apartheid and then published the full text in *Indian Opinion*.[35]

'Before 1948,' the memo says, 'under the influence of economic laws, the
various groups were drifting slowly together. The rate of drift was not nearly
fast enough ... but ... too fast for the Nationalist party.'[36] It goes on to
examine the possibility of partition as a solution and argues that, for it to be
justly done, the non-whites would have to get four-fifths of the country, the
whites one-fifth; yet, since that would 'involve vast movements of populations, and could only be achieved by the use of military force', which only
the whites possessed, it was 'not likely to be done with justice'. Rather than
partition it would be *apartheid,* unlikely in practice and unjust in theory.
'What is more likely is a further entrenching of the power of the white group,
a growing oppression of the non-whites, and a progressive robbing of their
rights.' The conclusion of that process would be 'race war', affecting not just
South Africa but the world. 'The question which must soon be decided by
the world is this: how long can a cancer, so small in actual extent, yet so
enormous in potential threat, be allowed to exist in the body of the world-
community? South Africa has proved itself to be unfitted for self-
government, and the world organization ... should ... draw logical conclusion from this fact.' They were brave words in South Africa in 1953.
Duncan continued to believe in and appeal for world intervention in South
Africa, in October 1953, for instance, writing an article for the *New Republic*
calling on the United States of America and Britain to back United Nations'
intervention in South Africa;[37] if appealing to the 'White conscience' failed,
if the latent power of the blacks could not bring about peaceful change,
there remained a third possibility – that the United Nations would intervene.
The fourth possibility was the great unthinkable: revolution.

Duncan's next action in search of a political role was to arouse more anger and resentment among white liberals, particularly those of the old Cape tradition, than almost any other.

In 1953 there were still seven (white) representatives of the black people in the two Houses of Parliament, three in the Assembly, four in the Senate – this representation was what Hertzog's 'compromise' of 1936 had retained of the old franchise arrangements of the Cape, as modified by the Act of Union. The three in the Assembly represented the Cape Province (Cape Eastern, Transkei, and Cape Western); Mrs Margaret Ballinger had held the Cape Eastern seat since its inception in 1938. The Transkei was held by another liberal, and Cape Western by a communist. The four Senators were elected by a cumbersome procedure of indirect voting in four huge constituencies, two in the Cape, one in Natal, and one in the Transvaal and Orange Free State; the last had been held since 1948 by William Ballinger, husband of Margaret Ballinger.

In mid-1953 Duncan decided he wanted to stand in the next election for the Senator to represent the Africans of the Transvaal/Orange Free State, even though it would mean opposing William Ballinger. The Ballingers had been keen for him to stand for another seat, but when they found out he meant to challenge William they were hurt and angry. However, Duncan was adamant, and announced his candidature to the press on the day of his release from Boksburg jail. Publicly, he expressed no criticism of Ballinger; privately, he told Philip Motseta, Chairman of the Ladybrand branch of the ANC, that Ballinger's 'five years' resistance to apartheid' did not 'add up to more than a tickey-worth'.[38] (A tickey is the old South African threepenny bit.) Other reasons were that he wished to further the work he had started in the Defiance Campaign; to represent an area which was largely Sotho-speaking; to further the aims of the ANC and to make clear where he thought the Liberal Party failed. 'Ballinger . . . conceives the primary task as being to change the attitude of a large number of whites. I do not disparage this idea. . . . But I remain absolutely convinced that the major battle is in the heart of the black man, not the white. . . .'[39] In his election circulars, he went further and attacked the Liberal Party for its attitude to the franchise. How could blacks vote for the candidate of a party which would keep the franchise a privilege of the educated? 'Liberals wish to give concessions to Africans, but . . . they want to maintain the supremacy of the whites.'[40]

Duncan's decision to stand created a problem in his relationship with the ANC, too, since it was considerably divided about whether to make use of the vestigial institutions of democracy, or whether to boycott them entirely. In the matter of the Natives' Representative Council, which Moroka had called a 'toy telephone', since 'we have been speaking into an apparatus which cannot transmit sound and at the end of which there is nobody to receive the message',[41] the ANC had decided eventually on complete 'non-collaboration', but in the matter of elections for 'Natives' Representatives' there was indecision. When, for instance, Brian Bunting stood in the by-election for the Cape Western seat after Sam Kahn's expulsion from Parliament for being a communist, calls for boycott were ignored, and Bunting was elected by a large majority. Duncan had some Congress support: Philip Motseta helped him considerably in his campaign; and Zeph Mothopeng, an ANC man then teaching in a Basutoland school, helped him revise and translate into Sotho his election statements and newsletters. In July 1953 he went to talk to Luthuli about the possibility of ANC support, and reported to Cynthia afterwards that the ANC would either not enter Senate elections or would support him. In November he wrote to Mandela in Johannesburg asking for support in his candidature, and in December was invited to be a guest speaker at the ANC Conference in Queenstown; other speakers included Piet Beyleveld of COD and Yusef Cachalia of the SAIC. Duncan was introduced by Professor Z. K. Matthews, Vice-President of the ANC, as a candidate for the Senate. Given the divisions about whether to boycott all institutions or not, and the fact that the divisions were by no means between left and right, Duncan did not think it wise to ask for specific support. However, in his circulars, he made his allegiance to the Congress movement plain, and actually said in one, 'I became a member of the African National Congress'.[42]

Another problem was created by the candidature of R. G. P. Pretorius, a farmer from Duiwelskloof; if Duncan split the anti-*apartheid* vote with Ballinger, Pretorius might well get in. This was another argument against Duncan's candidature, and many liberals, including Huddleston and Gell, appealed to him to withdraw. Duncan was determined not to.

In the event, the decision was forced on him by ill health. Just before the election campaign began, he had a duodenal haemorrhage. When his doctor X-rayed him, there were two ulcers, one at least perforated. Told to go to bed and diet, Duncan went to bed, but did not diet. 'The thing cured itself,' he wrote afterwards.[43] But he realized that he had been pushing himself beyond his physical limit, and resolved to withdraw from the election. His statement of withdrawal, issued at the end of July 1954, urged that African voters in the Transvaal and Free State support Ballinger, though his relationship with the Ballingers was never to be entirely happy again.

The oddest aspect of his mind during these years is the religious one. Intellectually he had rejected Christian Science:

> About Mary Baker Eddy – as the Duke of Wellington said: 'Sir, if you will believe that, you will believe anything.' What does it matter if the pin in my bottom is only the prompting of my mortal mind? Why should I take all the trouble to persuade myself that it is not there when it is much simpler to pull it out?[44]

That is plain enough – good commonsensical stuff, from a man who claimed to have rejected Christian Science in his teens. Yet he always did his best to pretend that pain was of no significance (witness his attempt to make Basil Whitworth set his broken leg without an anaesthetic) and he seemed to think the mind cured illness (witness his treatment of a perforated duodenal ulcer). For his brother John (not a Christian Scientist) and for Cynthia there was and is no doubt: Christian Science remained close to the centre of his emotions, whatever his intellectual attitude may have been.

In an odd way, his attitude to Christianity was almost the reverse of this: he was attracted to a peculiarly Anglican version of Christianity, though it never took deep spiritual hold of him. Anti-religious at school and university, he had been confirmed as an Anglican when he went to Basutoland, yet not out of any passionate conviction, but rather as a recognition of a particular social role: Basutoland was a deeply religious country, and the various sects of missionaries had enormous hold over the people; Colonial Officers went to church, not necessarily because they were Christian, but because Colonial Officers went to church. Mrs Cassidy, herself a devout Christian, remembers Duncan as much more a pantheist than a Christian in his early days in Basutoland: he worshipped the God in Nature, not the God beyond it. He called himself Christian because he had been born a Christian, not because of particularly Christian beliefs, and he went to church on Sundays (sometimes) because one *did* go to church on Sundays. Moreover, he had many friends among the clergy, particularly the Anglicans, and especially Cyprian Thorpe when they lived in Teyateyaneng; Christianity was a matter of custom and form as much as a matter of profound commitment.

In short, he was an occasional churchgoer rather than a devout churchman. He had no real grasp of theology: when he wrote in 1954 that 'Satyagraha is Christianity in action',[45] that is exactly what he meant. In his mind, Christianity was an ethical system and, while of course it may be true that *satyagraha* is a form of 'Christianity in action', it would be just as true to call it 'Hinduism in action'. Christianity in action is a great deal more than *satyagraha*, even if one treats *satyagraha* as a universal religious ethic. A letter to Christopher Gell makes the matter plain:

> Christianity has got to grow up now, and to accept in its fullest sense the fact of the many roads, and the full implications of tolerance. In that ... the strength of the Church of England lies. It combines traditions – necessary to transmit the body of the church down the generations – with tolerance – necessary to provide a home for the 20th century minds.[46]

In short, Christianity without religion and a Church without doctrine.

What interested Duncan in Christianity, what made him urge the formation of a Christian Democratic Party, was its political possibilities. A long letter to a clergyman-friend about the 'formidable advantages' such a party would enjoy makes this clear: the country is covered by a 'network' of missions and churches, an 'unrivalled system of bases' to reach rural and urban people; Christianity was very strong in the rural areas, where 'Emancipation still suggests "Moses" rather than "Marx" to the thinking, reading part of the population'; a Christian party would get 'overseas support'; above all, 'Christianity really does unite the white and non-white groups more surely than any other thing, more even than the economic system'. Its only disadvantage might be that the name 'would scare off some Jews and Indians who otherwise might be good members', but 'every attempt ought to be made to bring them in and to welcome non-Christians'.[47] Some of the limitations of Duncan's attitudes to religion are clear from this; he saw Christianity primarily as a moral and social force which he could approve of, not really as a religion at all. Of course it is an attitude common, not only among Anglican laity, but among certain of its clergy, too. The Church was broad enough to accommodate almost all views, including a vaguely defined theism or even agnosticism.

Yet that does less than justice to Duncan, because he does seem sometimes to have believed in some kind of God – not necessarily a Christian God, loving and personal, but a Divine Will, a source of natural justice, a judge of the most supreme court – and he believed in prayer, again not necessarily as a direct communication with God, but as a communication with oneself, a form of meditation. Before the Defiance Campaign he wrote several letters which mention the power of prayer. To Oscar Bull, a clergyman who helped edit the Christian newspaper *South African Outlook,* he wrote: 'Much prayer – that of Manilal Gandhi – who is quite simply a saint – brought the idea [of *satyagraha*] back to South Africa and much African prayer is helping to maintain the spirituality and gentleness of the Campaign.'[48]

He wrote to the Anglican Archbishop Clayton about his plan to join the Defiance Campaign: 'I am desperately in need of guidance and have been praying for it,' he said, and asked for support from the Anglicans for the Defiance Campaign.[49] Clayton's reply was gentle, but inconclusive:

> probably I shan't myself agree with everything you do. . . . Liberalism is of its very nature rather fissiparous. But I shall always remember that you are on the side of the angels. . . . I should like to send you my blessing. May you . . . [be] guided by the Spirit of wisdom and courage.[50]

In the same letter to Clayton, Duncan wrote, too, 'it is possible by political action to be an agent of divine will',[51] and in *The Road through the Wilderness* he claimed for his side 'the first great reservoir of power . . . the power of God'.

> Working through human history, exercising a polarizing influence on human wills, constant even if not always immediately victorious, the divine providence is working in South Africa today. . . . This force, the greatest in the universe, may to-day seem far away and weak. . . . But over the years it works away without ceasing, and over the years will exercise an incalculable influence over the wills, hearts and minds of even our greediest whites . . . like the air we breathe this polarization towards the absolute is always with us. It can be felt strongly when different groups are brought together in charity, for instance in the Christian church.[52]

Of course, he was writing the pamphlet for all English South Africans, not just for Christians, and he may have been aiming at an inoffensive statement of the divine; but, on the basis of that, one could call him a theist, though certainly not a Christian in any more than a cultural sense.

Separating his views from his friendships present another problem: of the men he most admired for their political courage, three were Anglican clergymen – Michael Scott, Trevor Huddleston, and Arthur Blaxall, the saintly old priest who had devoted his life to the service of the blind, and who was to be jailed in his seventies for working for the banned Congresses. He saw the role of these friends, both within the Anglican Church and on behalf of a non-racial South Africa, as a kind of quintessential Christianity; since their political attitudes were the result of their Christian belief, he tended to see a necessary coincidence between the two.

His experiences as Registrar of the Diocese of Basutoland helped disillusion him with the Anglican Church in South Africa – and in his vision of Christianity the institutional side could not be discarded as easily as some radical Christians have done, since 'social' Christianity was a significant part of its potential force in politics, not a stumbling-block to 'true' Christian radicalism. The Diocese of Basutoland had been set up as separate from Bloemfontein in 1950, and shortly afterwards Duncan was asked to act as Registrar; it was not an onerous post, involving mainly legal advice to the Bishop (John Maund) and other clergymen in their clerical duties. In 1952 there were fifteen priests in Basutoland serving fifty thousand Anglicans, twenty-two thousand of whom were communicants; so it was not a large diocese, though it had considerable problems: of finance; of being a relative latecomer compared to the major missionary movements, the Paris Evangelical Society and the Catholics; of serving many very isolated parishes; and most of all of racial inequality, both between the parishioners and between the clergy. Some congregations were mixed but, since worship was conducted either in English or in Sesotho, most were not. Some parishioners thought this policy rather than custom. At the Synod in 1952 Bishop Maund found it necessary to remind his audience of the rule Archbishop Clayton had laid down at a Provincial Synod: 'no confirmed member of the Church, whatever his race, may be excluded from any Anglican congregation'.[53]

On the spiritual equality of all its members, the Church was unequivocal. On the issue of discriminatory stipends for black and white priests, Duncan was sure that it was not. At the second Diocesan Synod, in Maseru in December 1954, he moved: 'That the Bishop be respectfully asked to unify the list of stipends and allowances for all clergy irrespective of race as soon as the necessary funds can be raised.'

He spoke fervently for his motion, arguing that 'in these dark days in South Africa the Church of God is the one sure anchor that still holds', and that it was time the 'problem of differential allowances' was faced.[54] It was a matter of principle, although, because it was a poor diocese, he had included the words 'as soon'; he calculated that it would cost £2250 a year to raise the stipends of black priests to the level of white priests. The Synod had already been deeply divided on several matters to do with race, and this last proposal caused a furore. Two members tried to move the deletion of the last phrase. Some spoke against it, one, Father Dove, arguing that 'the fact of the equal worth of all men before God does not necessarily imply that all should receive the same salaries',[55] though *Mohlabani* reported him differently, and Duncan wrote to *Mohlabani*[56] confirming its version. When it came to the vote the motion was passed, with several abstentions and two votes against. In a small diocese that was a serious division.

Duncan told Blaxall afterwards that he had few regrets at having insisted on raising the matter, though he thought he had lost several friends as a result. He had discussed the motion beforehand with Bishop Maund, who wished it neither to be put nor passed, not because he was against the equality of the clergy, but because he thought it dangerous that black priests should become, relative to their parishioners, rich men, and knew only too well that if stipends for white priests were lower than they already were he would get none to serve in his diocese. In the event, a few months later, he decided to replace Duncan as Registrar, and asked Gordon Driver – the 'Teraefera', who had gone back to being Judicial Commissioner when Duncan resigned – to take over. Bishop Maund gave many reasons, except the one Duncan was sure was true, that he had embarrassed the Diocese by asking for equal stipends for its clergy. On his copy of the speech he made in favour of his motion on equal pay, Duncan has written, simply, 'the speech that got me the sack'.

It was a considerable disillusionment; committed more to the institution than to the creed, he had found the institution wanting in what he regarded as fundamental. After 1955 one hears no more of the political role of the churches in the liberation struggle. Though he remained on good terms with his clerical friends, by the 1960s he seems to have been more or less an agnostic, though in the last months before his death he was to experience another of his 'visions', and the only one specifically religious.

Duncan's involvement in the affairs of Basutoland during the years he lived at Riverside ran considerably deeper than his concern with the Anglican diocese; he and his brother-in-law Denis Cowen, the constitutional lawyer, whom Deborah married in December 1955, were the most important non-Basotho influences on the country's political development, outside a handful of Colonial Officers in senior positions. He was an adviser to and confidant of Ntsu Mokhehle, founder of the Basutoland African Congress (BAC), and helped write the BAC's first manifesto.[57] He was adviser to and confidant of Chief Leabua Jonathan, and was responsible for suggesting to Chief Jonathan that he set up the Basutoland National Party (BNP); the earliest draft of its constitution is in Duncan's handwriting. He helped members of the National Council form opinions of various reports about the country's political development. He wrote about Basutoland for many periodicals, in South Africa, Basutoland and abroad. He wrote the first detailed account of its case-law. He and Cynthia kept open house for a stream of Basotho and overseas visitors to Basutoland – teachers, clergymen, chiefs, politicians, Colonial Officers, journalists, writers, and a host of others; moreover, it was an open house which was non-racial at a time when Basutoland was still nearly as 'segregated' as South Africa itself. To some visitors from overseas, the Duncan household might seem still very colonial in its customs, but some British visitors – and many South Africans – found it an idyllic refuge. Both Patrick and Cynthia spoke Sesotho fluently, and their two sons so much so that they could not be distinguished from Basotho children by their voices, and the Duncans' fluency helped them to avoid what so many blacks find despicable in some white liberals, the double standard, a patronizing condescension to blacks which they do not have to members of their own class and race. So, when a Mosotho chief at a party at Riverside got very drunk and made unpleasant advances to Cynthia, Duncan lost his temper, exploded at the chief, asked him to leave his house, and in short behaved exactly as he would have done to anyone drunk and unpleasant – the chief's blackness did not enter his mind, at any rate as far as an onlooker could tell (and the onlooker who told this story happens to be black himself). His standards of personal conduct might have been formal and a little old-fashioned, but he applied them equally to everyone. It helped of course that he admired the Basotho both nationally and culturally, for their courage, their psychological independence, their linguistic skills, their social conservatism, their wit and good humour in the face of poverty, discrimination and colonial high-handedness. It helped, too, that he had demonstrated his non-racialism in practice, by joining the Defiance Campaign and going to jail, but his position among the Basotho was not just that of a friendly white man, an 'honoured guest'; he was more than that, he was Patrick Duncan – in short, to the Colonial authorities, a 'damned nuisance' or, to the Basotho, almost a Mosotho himself. Any discussion of his role in Basutoland in those years needs to be in that larger context: it is not enough to analyse his specific acts, or the people and policies he influenced; his primary influence was his presence and his behaviour, not what he did or said or wrote on this or that occasion.

Duncan's close association with Mokhehle dates from 1952, when he was in hospital in Maseru recovering from the car crash; Mokhehle used to visit him almost every day, and they talked over Basutoland and African politics. Only 34 in 1952, Mokhehle had had the first part of his political education with the ANC Youth League and at the University College of Fort Hare, from which he was expelled for political activity in 1942, though he was readmitted in 1944. In 1950, with a Master's degree in zoology and an education diploma, he had returned to teach in Basutoland, and had immediately become involved in politics. Personally a most attractive man – and indeed physically very striking, though he calls himself 'ugly'[58] – and both intelligent and passionate in his politics, he seemed to Duncan almost predestined to be a leader (and indeed he would have been Prime Minister in 1970 if it had not been for the State of Emergency declared in the middle of the general election which his Congress Party seemed to be winning).

Early in 1953, after a visit by Walter Sisulu of the ANC to Mokhehle and others, the BAC was founded. Duncan told Ashton in 1965, 'when he [Mokhehle] held the first meeting he asked me to attend, but I refused on the ground that I had moved out of Basutoland and should do nothing publicly in their politics'.[59] 'Nothing public' seems to have been flexibly interpreted, and did not include helping to correct Mokhehle's first draft of a manifesto for the BAC. Duncan's comments and deletions range from verbal emendations to 'Nonsense' written in the margin, but are mainly corrections to comments on the history and administration of Basutoland, rather than to policy, which was discussed under three headings:

A. We oppose Incorporation of Basutoland into the Union...
B. We want self-government in Basutoland by the Basotho now...
C. Discrimination must quit Basutoland....

Duncan also noted that various clauses about South Africa – for instance, 'We oppose the Union of South Africa because it is a fascist state and not a democracy' – were 'no business of BAC', because he knew how tricky the relationship was always going to be.

In 1954, the British High Commissioner appointed a committee, under the chairmanship of Sir Henry Moore, a retired Colonial Governor, to examine the structure of 'Native Administration' in Basutoland and to make recommendations about it – that is, in effect, to look at the system of dual administration by the District Commissioners and the chiefs and to try to close the gap. The Moore Report made four main recommendations: first, that the Paramount Chief and the Resident Commissioner form a 'supreme council' or 'permanent advisory committee' (based in Maseru, the colonial capital, not Matsieng, the Paramount Chief's 'place' and centre of the 'Native' side of the Administration); secondly, that various powers be decentralized to District level; thirdly, that the District Commissioners be given more control over the chiefs in their Districts; fourthly, that the allocating of land to tribesmen be removed from the chiefs to new 'land-boards' in the Districts.

The Moore Report was opposed by Basotho of all shades of opinion; in February 1955 the District Councils one after the other voted against its recommendations and in March 1955, at the insistence of the Resident Commissioner, who refused to accept outright rejection of the Report by the National Council, but asked that recommendations be voted upon one after the other, they were again rejected, one after the other, by huge majorities until, having got to the 38th paragraph (out of 148) in eight days, the Council was dismissed by the Resident Commissioner, who accused the members of irresponsibility. The Resident Commissioner was convinced that Duncan and his ally, Ntsu Mokhehle, were behind the rejection of the Report, and had, in fact, shortly before the National Council, warned the senior chiefs, 'the sons of Moshesh', to beware of Duncan. The chiefs apparently thought this a huge joke, for they had their own good reasons for opposing the Report.

In two articles in the *Friend* in January, Duncan summarized both the Moore Report and the major objections to it among the Basotho; he was speaking not for himself only, but for the Basotho. Although it was generally accepted that the chieftainship did need overhauling – too many chieftain-ships were sinecures, too many chiefs were drunks or lazy, and the institution of chieftainship had been tainted by the 'ritual' or 'medicine' murders of the 1940s – and accepted, too, that dual administration was ineffectual, the Moore Committee had fudged the main issue, which was to give the Basotho legislative powers. After all, the National Council, since its inception in 1903, had had *de facto* rights in the making of customary law, which the Moore Report would now remove, though in hearing evidence the Committee had said that any business to do with a legislative council was outside its terms of reference. The chiefs saw much of their most important power being whittled away, both to District Commissioners and to the new 'land-boards'. The Paramount Chief Regent was apparently convinced that her powers were being undermined, and she and her advisers were angered at the suggestion that they move from Matsieng to Maseru, not the colonial administrators to Matsieng. There were also deep suspicions that the Report was paving the way for incorporation of the Territory in the Union, rather than for self-government.

Cyril Dunn said at the time that the National Councillors were so opposed to the Moore Report that, if they had been asked to vote on the date which headed the Report, they would have rejected it, too; and, meeting after its official dissolution, the Council wrote to the Resident Commissioner, the High Commissioner, and the Secretary of State for the Colonies, demanding the resignation of the Resident Commissioner, the Government Secretary (Brian Marwick, who had served on the Moore Committee) and various others. The BAC, meeting soon afterwards, went so far as to burn the Moore Report publicly.

It is in the way of these things that the unpopularity of the Moore Report helped both to unite the country – there were few reports that could have brought together on the same side Paramount Chief Regent, 'the Sons of Moshesh', the elected members of the National Council, and the BAC – and to promote the independence movement; rejection of the Moore Report was a clear stage on the way to the independence of 1970.

After 1955, Mokhehle and Duncan drifted apart. Duncan told Ashton in 1965: 'I think he found my views too conservative and too favourable to the Chiefs'.[60] However, when he wrote a 'Who's who among Basutoland leaders' in 1958, his portrait of Mokhehle was generous:

> He is a man of devastating simplicity and frankness; capable of personal humility and national intransigence. The Congress which he leads is responsible more than any other body for the present development [towards independence]. The last few years have shown that not only has he the fire necessary to energise a situation; he has also the understanding, patience and the endurance without which statesmanship is mere wishful thinking.[61]

But for all his admiration of Mokhehle, Duncan found what he thought an element of instability or demagoguery in the man; for instance, in 1958, when Mokhehle had written in *New Age* what Duncan thought an overblown reaction to a small incident involving some schoolchildren, he said: 'Mokhehle should have taken the trouble to get good information.'[62] However, in 1962 he told his sister that 'Mokhehle remains the outstanding popular leader';[63] and he and Mokhehle were close during Duncan's exile in Basutoland (1962–3). Moreover, Duncan at no stage seems to have joined in the smear campaign against Mokhehle, which branded him a communist, when in fact he was a revolutionary socialist who disclaimed violence. 'I abhor violence', Mokhehle is quoted as saying in *Who's Who in Africa*. 'But because I get excited when I talk and because I am ugly I seem violent to others.'[64] Sadly enough, passion and honesty are not qualities always prized in politicians, even by passionate and honest men themselves.

As Duncan pointed out, his own brand of conservatism was closer to Chief Leabua Jonathan's than it was to Mokhehle's radicalism. Moreover, he felt that any political party which wished to unify the Basotho would have to be a plainly Christian party and, according to Leabua Jonathan himself, Duncan was responsible for suggesting the merging of the BNP and a planned Christian Democratic Party. Leabua Jonathan is a devout Catholic, Mokhehle apparently anti-religious; the BAC was often anti-missionary and anti-Catholic, and the Catholics were virulently anti-BAC and anti-Mokhehle.

However, the major point of difference between Duncan and Mokhehle was to do with the institution of chieftainship, and it was largely this which led to Duncan's shift of commitment (until 1962 anyway) from Mokhehle to Leabua Jonathan, from the BAC to the BNP.

When Duncan arrived in Basutoland in 1941, the institution of chieftainship was in disarray. First, the Paramountcy was in dispute, following the early death of Chief Seeiso in 1940. Should the Paramountcy pass to his brother Chief Bereng Griffith, or should it be held in regency by the Paramount's widow Amelia Mantsebo Seeiso for the infant Constantine Bereng Seeiso? The dispute dragged on for years, dividing the other chiefs and indeed the nation, until finally succession was settled on Constantine Bereng Seeiso (now King Moshoeshoe II), with his father's wife holding the Regency until 1960. Secondly, chieftainship was often unenlightened. However, the chiefs could not be sacked by the people as was sometimes possible in Bechuanaland. Moreover, as Duncan found early on and to his disgust, the chiefs often abused their powers of fining the people for their own selfish ends. Thirdly, there were simply too many chiefs and headmen, partly as a result of traditional nepotism by successive Paramounts. Attempts to reduce numbers were part-cause of the 1947–8 'ritual' or 'medicine' murders (where bits of the victims' bodies are used for magic), since some chiefs wanted 'strong medicine' to protect themselves from loss of power and position.

Despite all this, Duncan learned considerable respect for the institution; chieftainship was not entirely autocratic, as he was to see in *pitsos,* the tribal meetings where all men had speaking-rights and considerable freedom of speech. Furthermore, the system of land-tenure depended on the chiefs and, though a better system of holding land might improve agriculture, it would also be a blow to the traditional notion that no one in Basutoland *owns* land but is merely lent it for as long as he uses it sensibly. The system of land-holding was at the heart of the social system: destroy the power of the chiefs, and one might be destroying the whole nature of the society. Better to remove incidental injustices and keep the old system. Admiring the British system of government as he did, Duncan saw prospects, too, that the Paramount Chief could become a constitutional monarch on British lines (which is roughly, after much to-and-froing, what did happen, at least after the King's temporary exile in 1970). In his memo on 'Native administration' sent to Lord Hailey in 1950, Duncan wrote:

> We must accept that for the next fifty years at least the chieftainship is going to be a reality to the great mass of the people. The chieftainship must therefore be drawn more fully into day-to-day administration and not be a mere buyer of policies worked out in its absence and pressed upon it by high-pressure salesmanship. We must remember that the chieftainship already forms a civil service reaching from the highest in the land right into the intimate life of the village. We must remember that it is not inordinately less efficient than might be expected, and we must therefore press on to the Native Administration every function that we believe them capable of, and a few more for good measure. Thereby we might reduce the expense, duplication, friction and chaos implicit in having a double civil service with no defined limits to authority and with little liaison.

In short, in the matter of chieftainship, he was essentially a conservative, in the strictest sense of the word: though he thought it needed modernization, to weaken or abolish it might damage a culture and society he believed in.

Duncan's personal relationship with Chief Leabua Jonathan was even closer than his with Ntsu Mokhehle. Leabua Jonathan, a great-grandson of Moshoeshoe I, had left school after Standard VI, and had then worked on the Rand mines before becoming an administrator for a senior chief. From 1950–2, he had been Assessor to Duncan as Judicial Commissioner. Leabua Jonathan remembers with gratitude how Duncan lent him books and documents about the history of Basutoland, and it is obviously with this in mind that Duncan, in *Contact* in 1958, described Leabua Jonathan as a 'wide reader'. Leabua Jonathan recalls that Duncan taught him the proverb 'One should learn to swim by swimming', and says, simply, 'we shared the same views, but it was through his influence more than anyone else's that I took an active part in politics...'.[65]

Duncan could very properly be called the first begetter of the Basutoland National Party, which was to win thirty-one of the sixty seats in the first election for a self-governing Basutoland, despite the earlier successes of Mokhehle's Congress Party, and which is still (in 1977) in power. He told Ashton in 1965:

> Leabua's National Party was my idea, and the name was my idea. We thought of it in about 1955 or so in my car on the way back from Matsieng (where Chief Jonathan was then one of the Paramount's advisors) to Maseru. The idea was that a party was needed as strongly national as the BAC, but without the BAC's socialistic and anti-chief and anti-religious lines....[66]

Chief Leabua Jonathan himself is quite open in giving credit to Duncan for the start of the BNP; yet even so it is something of a surprise to realize just how closely he worked with Leabua Jonathan from 1953 onwards, though by 1959, when the BNP was formally founded, Duncan was in fact living in Cape Town. He put the idea of a 'Chieftainship Committee' to Leabua Jonathan in 1956, as a pressure-group for reform of the institution. He outlined the first draft of a manifesto for a Christian Democratic Party (his old South African idea writ small for Basutoland), which explained the meanings of 'Christian', 'Democratic', 'Party', and suggested seven points for its programme: 'boitsoaro' (self-government) under the protection of England; no annexation to South Africa, but good relations; no colour-bar; constant technical development of Basutoland, with 'encouragement to be given to foreign capital, with sure guarantees on both sides'; agricultural development; 'justice to all groups in education'; fight against communism, especially through social and economic reforms.[67] With Leabua Jonathan, he worked out who on the National and District Councils would be sympathetic. With other sympathizers, the first draft of the manifesto was worked on, expanded, then cut.[68] By December a manifesto for a Basutoland National Party had been drafted, in terms mainly more vague than the original seven points, for instance on foreign capital and religion ('Christian' in the first draft is described thus: 'principles of social life and government based on the gospel and on the Pope's encyclical letters'; in the latter, 'The party stands for the maintenance of freedom of worship and religion'), but stronger on chieftainship:

> The unity of the nation depends on the chieftainship, and the people revere the descendant of Moshesh as their father. The Party will support the chieftainship; but the chieftainship must accept modernization. It must look forward to a democratic future, not back to an authoritarian past.

A meeting on 22 December at Riverside discussed 'Reports on past 11 days', 'Organization', 'Key persons to contact', 'Launching', 'Publicity', though in January 1958 Duncan wrote Chief Jonathan a note: 'I am afraid the calf does not seem to be doing too well.'[69] Soon enough, however, the meetings and a great deal of work in canvassing support began to produce results, and the draft manifesto, 'as amended 10 January, 1958', was thought firm enough to be cyclostyled on Duncan's machine at Riverside.

Duncan's direct involvement in the affairs of the BNP obviously lessened after he moved to Cape Town in 1958, but his relationship with Chief Leabua Jonathan remained close enough for the latter to ask him to go to his tailor in London in 1958 to order him a new suit, in any 'smart cloth you may fancy'.[70] More importantly, Chief Leabua Jonathan was among those who welcomed Duncan back to Basutoland most warmly after his banning in South Africa in 1962.

Duncan continued to have high regard for Chief Leabua Jonathan to the end of his life. One incident was, as we shall see, to cause him a great deal of political trouble; even so, in 1965, he told Ashton:

> He is a gifted patriot and a strong speaker ... he has a natural gift for parliamentary eloquence, and some historical learning. He attracted the more conservative nationalists by his dignified and clear message, and by his fearlessness. I admire Leabua's personality.

By 1965 admiration for 'personality' seemed to exclude admiration for politics, since he adds: 'I am sorry that he has bowed so deeply in Verwoerd's direction.'[71]

The relationship with Mokhehle, Leabua Jonathan, the BAC, and BNP by no means exhausts either Duncan's significant relationship with the Basotho or with Basotho politics in the period up to 1962 and his return to Basutoland. His editorship of *Contact* from 1958–62 was to bring him in close touch with many Basotho, and particularly with Bennett Makalo Khaketla, intellectually the most outstanding man in Basotho politics of the period. The son of a peasant family, he was largely self-educated; after teaching in South Africa, he returned to teach in Maseru in 1946, then had another spell teaching in South Africa, and in 1955 became editor of *Mohlabani* ('The Warrior'), and deputy of Mokhehle in the BAC until his disaffection in 1960 and his foundation of the Freedom Party in 1961 (later to merge with the Marematlou Party as the Marematlou Freedom Party). Duncan thought very highly of him, at least until 1959, and for a time they worked together closely; Khaketla was a writer and an expert on Southern Sotho, and Duncan approached him in September 1952 to translate Gandhi's *Satyagraha in South Africa* into Sotho, which Khaketla was keen to do, since he admired Gandhi, was strongly in favour of the Defiance Campaign, and was one of the Basotho who most encouraged Duncan in his resignation:

> Your decision to resign your present post with all its golden future (for with youth and ability on your side, were you not destined to become RC [Resident Commissioner] or Governor?) is indication of your determination to see that right triumphs over wrong.[72]

Later he told Duncan he was returning to teach in Maseru and this Duncan welcomed since 'things are beginning to happen politically here'.[73] They continued to keep in close touch, partly through Mokhehle (though relations between Mokhehle and Khaketla worsened in the late 1950s), partly through their work in the Anglican diocese, for Khaketla was a devout Anglican.

The first issue of *Mohlabani*, written by Zeke Mphahlele, Zeph Mothopeng, Mokhehle and Khaketla, was printed on the duplicating machine at Riverside (though Duncan did not know its contents at the time). *Mohlabani* attacked inequalities in the Colonial and Civil Services, discrimination in Basutoland, and the phoney altruism of the Colonial Service. Duncan admired *Mohlabani* for its hard-hitting line, wrote regularly for it, later advertised *Contact* in it, and used to rely on Khaketla for inside news of Basutoland. Khaketla was one of the four Basotho leaders singled out in *Contact* in 1958 as especially influential. However, in 1959 Khaketla attacked Duncan, first in *Mohlabani* for his influence on and political preference for Chief Leabua Jonathan and later in *New Age;* the latter Duncan could not forgive, and their relationship came to an end.

The years after Duncan's release from jail in 1953, and until he left Riverside in 1958, were among the happiest of his life. If he was not yet sure of his role in South African politics, he had a role in Basotho politics; and, though he earned much anger from former colleagues, he found new allies and friends among the Basotho. He was proud of his sons, though he was beginning to worry about their education, not only in schools. He told Dunn:

> We won't let them shout at the servants, but when other white boys come here *they* shout at them and of course our boys want to conform, to be one with the gang. The longer we delay sending Pat to a prep school here the worse it will be for him. But there's a prep school here in Clocolan [a local small town] and they have a school bus with a white driver and before they set off they fill up with stones to throw at the Basotho youngsters en route.

It is not surprising that he should have worried; Patrick, aged twelve and sitting a scholarship exam, was asked to write an essay on 'What role does colour play in your life', so wrote an essay analysing the negative effect going to a white school had on his friendships with Basotho children. He was criticized by his teacher for having missed the point of the title. But at least it was something for them to have Basotho friends at all, to be able to speak Sesotho perfectly, and to have space to run wild. Pat was known as 'Mojalefa' ('heir') and Alex's name, 'Ramoholi' ('father of mists'), given to him in London in 1949, had stuck. In June 1954, the third child, and first daughter, Ann, was born. On the farm, Duncan planted trees and grass, and wrote proudly to Cynthia of taking a crop of 1000 pounds of potatoes, working side by side with the farmhands and as always enjoying hard physical work. He took great pleasure in starting a small controversy in the *Potchefstroom Herald*[74] about the origins of the town's name (the *Potchefstroom Herald* called him 'Patrick Duncan of Riverside Farm', not 'Duncan the Defier'). He joined the Natal Society for the Preservation of Wild Life and National Resorts, and was able to tell the readers of its newsletter about a rare species of eagle, the lammergeier, which the Basotho call 'Ntsu', and which he had seen in the Maluti mountains. He visited Lovedale College to inspect for them the Africana in their library. He took Cynthia on holiday to Madagascar, managing to combine both pleasure and politics, for the island was on its way to independence. Both he and Cynthia enjoyed its freedom from the colour-bar, and Duncan described it as 'the most Afro-Asian land of all, with Polynesian and Melanesian roots laid bare for all to see'.[75]

But under the impression one has of happiness, domestic contentment, productive work, useful influence in Basotho politics, and pleasant holidays, one notes sudden anger and senses even despair, though usually both were held in control. He felt that the Congress Alliance was being taken on a wrong road by its communist members, and in particular was to be disillusioned by the role of the ANC in withstanding the 'Western Area Removals.' If the Congress was going in the wrong direction, which group would organize the latent African power he believed in? Were there any signs that the conscience of the whites had been touched? On the contrary: the signs were exactly the opposite. In particular he was deeply hurt by the refusal of a passport, on nonsensical grounds, to a sixteen-year-old African, Stephen Ramasodi, who had been given a scholarship to Kent School in Connecticut; it seemed to him cruelty of an intolerable kind to a youngster without any defences against the adult world. He still believed – had to believe – that there could be a non-violent way to end racial tyranny; but his statements of the alternative grew more pressing as each year passed. In 1952 he wrote:

> We must not give up hope ... though we ought to be battening down our hatches. We've had the hurricane warning, what with the Durban riots [the riots of 1948 when Africans attacked the Indian community] and now the Mau Mau. I feel that the latter might quite suddenly become a continent-wide movement. If it did then I think one should be almost tempted to despair.[76]

In 1953 he wrote to Cynthia: 'There is no comfortable way out – through which good sound conservatives (among the whites) can lead us. Our future will be settled by the demonic side of our population. We cannot now avoid a fever of destructiveness. I would like to channel this on to a wicked system, not people.'[77] In 1955 he told an African friend that he believed 'a philosophy of force is forming, especially among the younger generation of blacks'.[78]

It was a theme in his thinking which was not to find its full expression until the 1960s, but it is a theme all the same: a solution to the racial problem *had* to be found, or else. . . . Any technique which did not involve violence but which might work had to be tried; so, in July 1955, he and Trevor Huddleston sent a joint letter to *The Times* urging 'that in future both committees [of the Olympic and the Empire Games] make it a condition of South African participation that the teams be chosen without regard to race'.[79] It was one of the earliest proposals of this version of boycott, and the United Nations Commission on Apartheid raised the matter in October. When Dennis Brutus set up his non-racial South African Sports Federation in 1958 it was natural for him to ask Duncan to be Patron. Acts of this kind made Duncan, along with people like Huddleston and Michael Scott, loathed and feared by white South Africans; yet, if someone did not use these means soon, South Africa was headed for ghastly violence which he believed would save nobody, white or black.

In late September 1955 the security police carried out a number of raids on various organizations (including the TIC, the ANC, and the COD) and individuals. Patrick Duncan was one of them. They took a pile of documents away, without exception very innocent; but they showed Duncan their warrant, which was issued for the purpose of allowing them to seek evidence of treason or sedition. As soon as the security police had left Riverside, Duncan sat down to write an open letter to the Minister of Justice (whom he preferred to call 'Minister of Police'). He himself was the more complete patriot, he said, since his loyalty was to all the people of the country, not just a section, and he suggested how the Minister might serve his country better.[80] The anger in the open letter goes beyond any appeal to conscience. Duncan was beginning to learn from all this: he had had his brief experience of jail, and now was learning the kind of intimidation most blacks faced daily.

CHAPTER 7

1955–8
'Always a bad combiner ...'

The crucial decision of the second half of Duncan's years at Riverside was his joining the Liberal Party. It was a conscious and complex one, made for closely defined objectives and on various personal conditions, and both objectives and conditions (they combine in peculiar ways) explain more than the decision itself: they explain the peculiar role he was to play within the Liberal Party, the uneasiness he often felt in it, the kind of allies which he gathered to himself, and even in part his later resignation from the party and his joining the Africanists.

The first part of his decision to join derived from his attitude to the United Party. In December 1953, after his release from Boksburg jail, he wrote: 'Up till ... 1948 ... it was possible, though not intelligent, to believe that the white group ... might reverse the century-old trend away from the equality of the non-racial Cape constitution of 1853. After 1948 it was no longer possible.'[1] Yet it is also clear that, until 1953 and for a time after the publication of *The Road through the Wilderness*, he retained a loyalty to the United Party; after all, his father had been one of the main movers of the 'fusion campaign' which brought together the Hertzogites and the Smutsites into that very party. Moreover, there were – even after 1953 – liberals within the United Party, who stayed there first in the hope of bringing it back to the path Hofmeyr might have led it on and, secondly, since they thought it had some chance at least of defeating the National Party in elections. Duncan thought they were wrong, at least in their second hope; but he thought, too, that the United Party would provide some kind of parliamentary opposition.

For many white liberals, the combination of the Defiance Campaign (which they might not approve of, but which showed them clearly how those they wished to be liberal towards were thinking), the backing the United Party gave the Nationalist government in its reaction to the Campaign, particularly in the Public Safety Act and Criminal Law Amendment Act, and the defeat of the United Democratic Front in the general election of 1953 was enough to break the loyalty they felt to the United Party. Hence the formation of the Liberal Party in 1953, as a party initially for white liberals of the old Cape non-racial but gradualist tradition, though it soon began to attract other liberals of a more radical kind. Duncan, who already knew that the only real hope of getting rid of the Nationalists and in moving away from racial tyranny lay in the power of black South Africa, did not, however, follow the Liberal Party in its rejection of the United Party, not only because he still felt that liberals would have more influence as a leaven within the UP, but more because he thought the Liberal Party was not open enough to the power and leadership of blacks. So, in October 1953, he wrote to Gell: 'As I see it, the ideal for the UP is to come to represent the decent side of white SA on the colour issue – damning the consequences. It stands 100 times as good a chance of doing this as the Liberals because it will carry over the [party] machine.'[2] Yet, at the same time, he made it clear that he stood to the left of the Liberal Party, not to the right; he told Legum in November 1953:

> ... the Liberals do not envisage the evoking of the latent African political power as desirable or possible. Although I could hardly quarrel with the Liberal programme, I do differ entirely from them over this. Until this power is in some way realized and expressed, Liberal programmes remain so much pious dreams.[3]

He told Legum, too, that the Liberal Party had 'a bad name ... among Africans', above all else because it had as policy the notion of a qualified franchise and, though this accorded with the old Cape franchise done away with in 1936, Duncan knew that universal suffrage was both necessary to attract mass black support and desirable in itself: one had to learn how to swim by swimming, as he had told Leabua Jonathan.

His views on the United Party were, however, inconsistent, not only with his views on other political parties and movements, but also with themselves: for instance, in May 1953, when he was writing *The Road through the Wilderness*, he told Gell, who had written criticizing his view of the UP:

> Of course I agree with you – the UP has practically no hope of getting back. I agree – it is unlikely that UP strength will stay at 800 000 [its vote in the general election] whatever happens. I agree, the UP isn't liberal at all. I agree, Race Relations will continue to deteriorate under the Nats. I disagree about its [the UP's] finding its soul – it hasn't one ... its function ... [is] to hold together what it has which is a good machine and good traditions for as long as possible. If it starts looking for a liberal soul it will inevitably lose to the ruthless Nats for as we agree race relations are deteriorating. In deteriorating race relations the white South Africans will look to their guns, not to mildly Liberal abolitions of pass laws etc....[4]

By 1955 he had given up all hope in the United Party and he wrote to Lewin what amounted to a retraction of that part of *The Road through the Wilderness* which advocated support of the UP. As far as he could see, there were the 'real Nats' and the '"tame" Nats', alias the UP, which supported the Nationalist government in all crucial matters.[5] So that removed one of his objections to the Liberal Party. There remained a major objection: if to evoke the political power of the blacks was vital, should he not concentrate his energies on working with the Congress movement?

There were two impediments, the first political, the second more practical. He would not join the COD because it seemed to him dominated by communists and fellow-travellers; anyway, it was limited to whites, and he did not wish to work in a whites-only organization, whatever the theoretical justification for doing so. Yet he did feel committed to the Congress movement, in part because of the Defiance Campaign, and in part, too, because he had admired its leaders ever since meeting them in 1952. At the same time, he was not at all happy at the direction the Congress movement had seemed to be taking since the Defiance Campaign; even at the ANC Conference at Queenstown in December 1953, he had felt that communist influence was increasing:

> the whole atmosphere of the conference was dominated by the Party line. That is to say that the USA and the UK were lined up as the bogeymen, the USSR etc. as liberators from colonialism. The support that the USA has given to the Union at UNO, together with the financial tie-up over uranium etc., lent much weight to those views. For much of the time during this conference I was on the platform, but during the most rabid moments I left the platform and went to sit in the body of the hall.[6]

In the same letter, he says of the Congress of the People, 'combined rally' of the ANC and the other Congresses, 'the CP are planning it.... This may be something quite impressive.' Earlier in the year, he had been less sure; he wrote to Gell: 'What do you think of the Congress of the People? I am not at all sure I like the look of it.'[7] He went on to quote from a pamphlet by Arthur Wauters, *Le Communisme et la decolonisation*: 'Le parti ouvrier peut très bien utiliser, sous certaines conditions, d'autre partis et fractions de partis, mais il ne doit se subordonner lui-même à aucun parti....'[8] Duncan was convinced that this was what the communists were doing: the formation of a popular front on the lines of those of the 1930s, which the communists would then use for their own political ends. Certainly, it is now known that the reconstitution of the Communist Party began in 1953 and the first national conference of the underground party was held in 1953. Yet it is true, too, that nearly all the communists active in the Congress movement from 1953 onwards had been communists beforehand and, while they un-doubtedly approved of the Congress of the People, to give them all the credit for it would seem (now, at least) a mistake. One cannot make a simple equation of 'Communist Party = Congress of the People'. Moreover, the Freedom Charter, a minimum programme adopted at the Congress of the People, which laid down common objectives for all the Congresses, may hardly be called 'communist'; at the most it is socialist, and even then not thoroughly so. Even when some of its authors were put on trial for treason, the prosecution was unable to prove it a communist programme. The communists themselves regard it as no more than an interim programme.

One needs, at this point, to define Duncan's attitudes to communism and communists more closely, for all the difficulties of doing so. His ideological opposition to Marxism had been well established by the time of his stay at the LSE in 1949–50; he thought Marx had contradicted himself, he thought that Marxism was intellectually and spiritually defunct, and he thought, too, that communism did not work – if the Soviet Union was anything to go by, communism had failed. He had read Trotsky's *Life of Stalin* and, though perhaps he was quite glad anyway to see the Revolution subverted, was convinced this was what Stalin had done. It is this attitude which persuaded him initially that communism was not a real threat in South Africa. After all, the communists had in 1952 submitted themselves to passive resistance, which in its purest form of *satyagraha* was a denial of materialism and hence of Marxism.

From 1952 onwards, although he still makes the occasional remark about the death of communism, he does so less and less; rather, he begins to find its influence more pervasive, especially in the Congress movement. At the same time, he was anxious to give communists their due; their effectiveness and growing power were for reasons other than the purely Marxist. First, the communists were genuinely non-racial; Duncan called it a 'great fact ... that the CP since 1924 has consistently followed a non-racial line, and that it has lost immensely in support, both among white and black, through doing so'.[9] It is only apparently a *non sequitur*, for his argument was that most political movements in South Africa had been nationalist at least, and often racialist. Secondly, the communists succeeded because of their 'consistent hard work and far-sightedness'; he cited as example the success of the weekly newspaper *Advance*, 'competently produced ... [with] local news and much overseas news.... I hear they sell about 35 000 a week, which if true is a formidable circulation for this country.'[10] (Anyone who worked in anti-*apartheid* politics in South Africa will accept this point, whatever his or her politics: again and again, communists proved themselves both in efficiency and industry, and in being able to think more than one step ahead, if only because they had a coherent intellectual framework on which to plan.) Thirdly, the equation of 'communism' with everything the whites did not like – black nationalism, anti-racialism, passive resistance, liberation – had made 'communism' thus defined seem attractive to those deprived of their rights. Fourthly, whatever the situation inside communist countries, their international policies were much more attractive to the blacks than those of the West, which so often seemed to be supporting the *status quo* in South Africa; and when black South Africans visited communist countries they were received as honoured guests, not dangerous agitators.

His acknowledgement of why communists were being so successful in the Congress movement is significant; even if it is entirely without ideology in the Marxist sense, that, too, has a certain significance in an understanding of his mind, because one cannot typify Duncan's attitude to communism as being just like that of the South African government and its supporters. Of course he was not a communist in any way; but when the *Golden City Post* published a short biography of him with an article of his on Basutoland in 1955[11] and called him 'anti-communist' Duncan replied that it was 'not ac-curate', since he supported holding out 'the hand of friendship' to communist countries.[12] Similarly, after Khruschev's attack on Stalin and Stalinism at the Twentieth Congress in February 1956 Duncan reacted in two ways. The first was to say what amounted to 'I told you so' – Stalin's brand of communism had been utterly corrupt, utterly ruthless, and he had been saying so for years:

> It is the second most diabolical regime in the century – Hitler's was the worst. Communism uses the same methods as Hitler to achieve a better object: the raising of the standard of living.... Stalin's regime was so bad that his successors have been forced utterly to reject it.[13]

The other reaction was shown in a letter to Lewin in May 1956 about the newspapers of the Congress movement:

> Now that the USSR is obviously reforming why can't New Age and FT [*Fighting Talk*] drop the bitter anti-US and UK line. I would be in with them boots and all if they would do this. I admire their racial line very much indeed. The thawing of the Cold War is the most heartening thing since 1945.[14]

It is clear from this again that he was no ideologue or even ideologist; though it was possible for 'the party line' to change radically (as, for instance, on the relations of Nazi Germany and the Soviet Union), it was hardly likely to abandon its version of reality so far as to begin apologizing for imperialism.

There is another element in his attitude to communism which both complicates one's images of his mind and which may offer, too, an explanation of contradictions. Several times at this point in his life he suggests that South Africa has a choice of three routes:

(a) Marxist class hatred of the whites
(b) Hitlerite race hatred of the whites
(c) Gandhism: a desire for emancipation exempt from hatred.[15]

In the light of his praise for the non-racialism of the communists in South Africa, the equation of communism and racialism is an extraordinary one. The explanation lies back in his own experience of Nazi Germany and in what Helmuth von Moltke taught him: the real battle in the world was not between fascism and communism, but between individualism and collectivism. Seeing the battle thus, he was able to see nationalism, fascism, nazism and communism all within that single force, collectivism, while he himself stood on the other side, individualism. The reason he could equate communism and racialism while at the same time admiring the non-racialism of the Communist Party was, in fact, not contradictory. Because communism was a collectivist philosophy, it would lead to a collectivist state. Such a state in South Africa would mean the treatment of the population in class-groups. Therefore, the majority-group, the African group, would rule. But he loathed thinking in group terms, for out of such came the oppression of the individual. It was not that he thought communism a greater immediate threat than Hitlerism or nationalism, but that he saw them as stemming from the same kind of world-view, which threatened his own: the longer Afrikaner Nationalism survived, the more chance of communism. Therefore, for people to suppose that in attacking the communists he was taking the side of the government was, to Duncan himself, patently absurd.

This extreme individualism was a theme which ran throughout his thinking, well into the 1960s. In 1965, for instance, he was to write to George Sachs: 'The twentieth century is in fact Marx's century, with Hitler as one of his greatest followers.'[16] It is of course absurd to call Hitler a 'follower' of Marx; yet if one redraws the map of Duncan's mind to concentrate less on the standard modern dichotomy socialism/capitalism, and more on the dichotomy individualism/collectivism, one has at least a working explanation, and one which goes a long way in resolving some of the apparent contradictions in his thinking and behaviour in politics.

A second, much less theoretical reason for his growing disillusion with the Congress movement was its failure to organize resistance to the removal of the people of Sophiatown, Martindale and Newclare to Meadowlands and Diepkloof, the 'Western Area Removals' scheme. The ostensible reason for uprooting the twenty thousand families of the three townships was 'slum-clearance'; the actual reason was that the Western Areas were one of the few urban areas where blacks could buy and hold land and property. Close to the centre of Johannesburg, they represented, too, a barrier in the way of physical *apartheid*; if the Western Areas were cleared of Africans, white Johannesburg would be able to expand comfortably. So the people of the Western Areas were to be removed to Meadowlands and Diepkloof, in the South-Western complex of townships (now called Soweto) farther from Johannesburg, easier to isolate in the event of disturbance, and where they would not have rights to buy and hold property or land; and, finally, the people were to be removed from their 'slums' (homes, schools, shops, churches, meeting-halls, cinemas) not to a newly built township, but to what was still mainly open veld, with sewerage, standpipes and roads, but no buildings.

Duncan had become involved in the Western Areas as early as May 1952, when he stayed with the Community of the Resurrection in Sophiatown. When, in June 1953, he dropped his appeal against his sentence for defiance, he told the *Star* that if what was being done to black South Africans in the Western Areas were done to white Johannesburgers they would regard it as a 'hallucination':

> I would like to ask what the Minister thinks of the rights of property under the moral law – what he is going to do about the poor, the old, the widows, the sick, and the people who, after working a lifetime, have earned the security of their own homes.
>
> What are they going to do out in the open veld at Meadowlands? Perhaps the Minister will refer the matter to one of his committees. Perhaps he may not even do this, for he may say that they are only Natives and it is well known to the Government that Natives do not need shelter against frost and rain, just as their school-children do not need food because of the long hours that they sleep.[17]

Huddleston read this statement out at a protest meeting on 29 June called jointly by the ANC and SAIC and attended by two thousand delegates; four Indian Congress leaders were arrested at the meeting, Yusuf Cachalia actually from the platform as he got up to speak, and Huddleston only prevented the arrest of Mandela and Sisulu, two of the speakers, by saying he would demand arrest himself.

On his release from Boksburg jail, Duncan again stayed in the priory of the Community of the Resurrection, and talked to Huddleston, Alan Paton and others, particularly about the resistance which the ANC and the SAIC had planned. In July 1954 he wrote to Alan Paton offering his services in a resistance group to oppose the removals:

> Trevor Huddleston has let me know about your inspired plan for resistance in the Western Areas, and that you had thought of me as one of the group.... I'm with you – I have talked it over with Cynthia. I would like to make two conditions ... (1) that the ANC agrees and (2) that no one pleads 'not guilty' thereafter.[18]

By 1954, defiance of a law could mean five years' jail, heavy fines, and up to twelve lashes.

On 8 February 1955, Duncan, speaking at the opening of an exhibition of photographs to show how little a 'slum clearance' scheme the removals were, offered 'to any one who does not wish to move voluntarily to stand shoulder to shoulder by him, when the might of the Government comes to take his home from him. I wish to place the onus on the shoulders of the Minister to move both the owner and myself.'[19]

On 9 February the removals – or what the Black–White Western Areas Commission, under the chairmanship of Huddleston, called 'legalized theft' – began, with the help of armed police and troops. ANC volunteers helped families ordered to move to find other places to stay in the area, and the *Montreal Star* reported an unnamed ANC spokesman as saying 'the Congress plans to call a "kneel down" prayer day protest strike soon', and that 'Secret plans are reported to have been worked out of other passive resistance along the pattern set by ... Gandhi in India'.[20] But there was no real resistance; the new penalties against defiance, the presence of armed police and troops, the tactics of the authorities in removing first those who were inadequately housed, and the lack of proper organization by the ANC produced passivity without resistance. Duncan wrote to an African friend on 11 February:

> I am afraid that without Luthuli's leadership the ANC in the Transvaal is cutting a sorry figure. [Luthuli had been banned and restricted to his home in Natal shortly before the anti-removals campaign and was critically ill in hospital.] On Monday ... a representative of the ANC ... told me that the ANC had the 100% support of the population in its determination to resist passively and not to move. On Wednesday the move took place, and not one person followed the ANC line. How we need Gandhi's realism and humility – and truth. I did all I could. I had a shrewd idea that this would be no organized resistance, so I offered publicly to stand with any householder who had made up his mind not to go, in his front door, and to place the onus on the police to get me as well as him out of the way. That may still lead to something. I realized that it might be a sentence of five years, but it was the least I could do.[21]

He meant what he wrote about the jail-sentence, for he and Cynthia had discussed the matter beforehand, and as always he needed her approval before he acted publicly. But his gesture led to no act of resistance.

In the matter of Bantu Education, Dr Verwoerd's scheme for keeping 'the non-European non-European', introduced in April 1955, he felt much the same about the ANC's role in resistance. The initial boycott of schools soon petered out, and the main effect of the resistance was the sacking of militant teachers. No doubt Duncan's judgement of the ANC was harsh – with its leaders harried, banned or jailed, with little money, and with new and savage laws to face, the ANC was in real difficulties. Though Duncan kept close personal links with some Congress leaders, especially Luthuli himself, all the same he felt Congress had failed the people of Sophiatown, Newclare and Martindale, and indeed of all South Africa.

For those who knew South Africa in those years, one of the most haunting of all the African protest songs is the one which goes, simply:

Meadowlands, Meadowlands, Meadowlands,
Meadowlands, Meadowlands. . . .

No comment other than the name was needed. The government, on the other hand, declared Sophiatown, Martindale and Newclare 'white' under the Group Areas Act and renamed the area 'Triomf' – Triumph.

The Liberal Party had itself removed one of the objections Duncan had to it by moving away from qualified franchise to universal franchise at its 1954 Conference, although Duncan felt its policy on the franchise was still equivocal. His last major objection remained: that the Liberal Party thought of itself as a parliamentary party, as essentially a white party, instead of looking outside Parliament for the power to bring about change, which meant looking to black South Africa. But it would not be enough for white Liberals to say to blacks, 'Look, if you will join us, we shall lead you to freedom'; exactly that kind of condescension made many Africans loathe and indeed fear white liberals, and Duncan – like some in the Liberal Party – wanted not simply a non-racial movement but a movement with enough black leaders to ensure that the membership was really non-racial. He told Dunn in June 1955:

> If I join any movement now it must be in a subordinate place under someone who's black, because I'm not a dictator and because I don't think anything else could satisfy the Africans that it wasn't white leadership dressed up. Unless the Liberal Party does produce some Black leaders I don't want to join them.

In March 1955, after an exchange of letters between himself and Jordan Ngubane (a journalist and farmer, close friend of Manilal Gandhi and Luthuli, very anti-communist for both personal and ideological reasons, and a founding member of the ANC Youth League), Duncan told Paton that Ngubane was thinking of joining the Liberal Party (a number of ANC members in Natal were also members of the LP), and in April 1955 Ngubane did join. This was a significant influence on Duncan's own decision, for he admired Ngubane greatly and, moreover, if anti-communists in the ANC would join the LP, it might help to make it genuinely non-racial, not a white party with academic ideas of non-racialism. He did, however, make one other important qualification to Paton of his commitment to black leadership: 'I don't think I ever said that I wanted to identify myself with "Whatever action the non-Europeans might want to take. . . ." I fear I could not pledge that sort of support to any organization I know of.'[22]

Having almost taken the decision to join, he happened to be in Cape Town for Africa Books. While he was there, he met and talked to Leslie Rubin, the Senator who represented Africans of the Cape Province, and Oscar Wollheim, a social worker and one of the better-known Liberals in the Cape tradition, both of them founder members of the Liberal Party. Both told Duncan that his version of the Liberal Party was not theirs, and he nearly changed his mind back again. It was largely Alan Paton and Jordan Ngubane who persuaded him not to, since they shared many of his views of the future of the Liberal Party. However, Duncan still held back. He had asked Paton in March if there was a Liberal Party branch in the Orange Free State: 'If not would you permit me to make the opening move to set one up? My position is that I would only wish to join if some suitable African assumed the leadership. I know the right man – Dr Aaron Lebona ... perhaps ... a bit conservative but that would be no fault in the OFS.'[23] Paton, knowing that Duncan had disagreed with two very prominent members of the party in the Cape, no doubt remembering past problems, and very probably foreseeing others, told Duncan that he would need to discuss the question of his joining with Mrs Ballinger, but soon afterwards wrote to Duncan to say that she would be delighted to have him in the LP. So, wrote Paton, would he and Peter Brown, a farmer from near Pietermaritzburg, and then Secretary of the LP.

There was one last duty to be completed before joining. Duncan drove from Riverside to Natal to see Luthuli, who was still in hospital recovering from high blood pressure and a suspected cerebral haemorrhage. Not only did he have enormous personal respect for Luthuli – 'one of the few really big men in this country ... a king-sized man'[24] – but he felt loyalty to the Congress movement. He told Luthuli what he planned to do; Luthuli said he was sorry Duncan would not 'join our congress', but wished him well.[25]

In October 1955 he and Cynthia went to the Provincial Congress of the Liberal Party in Natal. Writing in the Liberal Party newsletter, Duncan said of the meeting: 'It was a momentous occasion. . . . All races were represented, and during the whole proceedings ... I saw no signs that those present gave thought to their racial group. All were South Africans, and all considered the others in the fullest sense South Africans too.'[26] Both he and Cynthia joined the Liberal Party during the course of the meeting.

It was not an unconditional commitment. For instance, Duncan made it clear that he would work for an unequivocal statement that the Liberal Party stood for universal adult suffrage, with no 'ifs' and 'buts'. That is, he was joining the Liberal Party to make it as close as possible to his old idea of an 'All People's Party', a mass-movement to smash the colour-bar in South Africa. Certainly other Liberal Party members saw his joining as an accession to the left of the party: Jock Isacovitz, leading Transvaal Liberal and one of the first Liberals to be banned, wrote to him just before he joined:

> I would be very happy if you join the LP. It might do something to counter developments ... which have been causing me some concern. . . . The basic difficulty in the LP is that the national leadership is fairly far to the right compared with the general membership of the Party. . . . You should be able to play some part towards this.[27]

Todd Matshikiza, the composer, was to tell Duncan in 1956: 'When we heard of your new post we knew you would move the Liberal Party from its present garden-party attitudes.'[28]

There are problems in any discussion involving the word 'liberal'; like 'romantic', it has come to mean so many things that it may have ceased to serve any useful function as a verbal sign. In South Africa whites often use 'liberal' to mean 'non-racial', and some joined the Liberal Party only because they and it were non-racial. Since communists, too, were non-racial, 'communist' and 'liberal' became synonymous, though not to communists, liberals or Liberals. There were, for instance, some in the Congress of Democrats who called themselves 'liberal', though never 'liberals': that is, on the white left, the adjective 'liberal' was less pejorative than the substantive 'liberal' or the designation 'liberal'. There were some who joined the Liberal Party who would, in most other societies, have called themselves 'socialists', some who would have called themselves 'conservatives'. The extent of one's 'liberalism' in the Liberal Party could be defined sometimes in terms of the extent to which one was prepared to go in opposing racialism and the government; thus Patrick Duncan was 'very liberal', a 'left-wing liberal'. Sometimes one's left-wing-ness in the Liberal Party could be defined in terms of one's commitment to socialism; thus Patrick Duncan was 'not very liberal' or a 'right-wing liberal'. Sometimes 'liberal' was defined in relation to the Congress movement. Brian Bunting wrote in 1958: 'There is no ideological unity in the Liberal Party, there are only Liberals and Liberals. One wing of the Liberal Party can almost be described as reactionary; but another wing is moving ever closer to the Congress point-of-view, and already works closely with the Congresses in some centres.'[29] In those terms, Duncan was 'very liberal' in his desire to co-operate with the Congresses, but 'reactionary' in his attitude to communism. Yet another complication is that, whereas many whites were 'liberal' or 'liberalist' or even 'liberalistic' in a perjorative sense of 'non-racial' (also 'impolitic', 'impractical', 'dangerous' and 'wicked'), many blacks (not only in southern Africa) used 'liberal' in a perjorative sense of 'half-hearted', 'condescending', or, occasionally, as a synonym of 'bourgeois', or – more particularly – 'not in favour of complete equality of white and black'.

Yet, for all the problems of the term and for all the lack of 'ideological unity' of the Liberal Party, there were ways in which most of the members of the Liberal Party were liberals, in more English and positive senses of the word. They were reformists, rather than revolutionaries (some Liberal Party members became revolutionaries after 1960 but, when discovered, were expelled from the party). Most if not all would have accepted the adjective 'liberal' in front of their substantive nomenclature: 'liberal socialist', 'liberal capitalist', 'liberal conservative', and so on. Many, though not all, were gradualists; that is, they thought social change disrupted fewer lives if it did not occur without warning and preparation. Most disliked thinking of people in groups, and preferred to think of them as individuals; while by no means all were egalitarian, nearly all preferred moral and political judgements based on individual worth rather than on race or class. Most had some notion of democracy, if not all were democrats. Many thought there was a connection between morality and politics.

One needs to complicate the problem still further by saying that in South Africa white liberals, white socialists, and whites communists tended to live rather similar kinds of lives, though their backgrounds were often very different. They tended to be intellectuals – that is, they cared about ideas, books, and the arts. Because they were in opposition to the government and (at least) to the most easily visible parts of the social system, and because they were in a small minority within their own class and race, they were generally non-conformist and tended to be anti-authoritarian; even those who accepted the authority of a creed or ideology tended to be critical within that creed or ideology. They tended to look outwards from South Africa, to have links abroad; many were able to choose to leave South Africa, temporarily or permanently, and were able to lead satisfactory lives elsewhere (it has always been much more difficult for black exiles to find this kind of home abroad). It is worth noting that one is discussing no more than a few thousand people; the Liberal Party never had more than five thousand members (and of these only a proportion were white), COD about five hundred.[30] That is, for all their ideological differences, they had sociological links, though not only because there were so few of them, and in that sociological sense there is a certain 'liberality' linking them.

Within non-South African senses of the word, Duncan was in some ways not a liberal at all, even after he joined the Liberal Party. Of course the Liberal Party, like almost all parties, was in a sense a coalition; Paton explained to Duncan before he ever joined the party, 'a Wing Party throws up a great range of views in a small number of individuals, and thus throws up a disproportionate number of individualists'.[31] But Duncan was, even in a party of individualists, exceptional; he would have found it hard to fit into any political party; 'I was always a bad combiner,' he told Lewin, 'but I have decided that nothing is ever done in politics without combination, and I'd damn well better start now.'[32]

That alone was one reason for his wanting less of a political party and more of a movement, something for 'All People', combined in the one aim of getting rid of the colour-bar, but not doctrinaire, not too closely committed to a single programme. Of course one sense of 'liberal' includes this individualism; but Duncan's extremism was illiberal in many other senses. For instance, a few years later, on party business in Kimberley, and finding a few hours to spare, he and his companion went to see Brigitte Bardot in *And God Created Woman*; Duncan was disgusted and appalled by it, and said, 'When we have freedom here we'll put a quick stop to Bardot'.[33] He was in many ways authoritarian; though he thought it important that children should run wild, he is remembered by his children as a strict father, who laid down rules of conduct which had to be obeyed. Albie Sachs remembers that in Cape Town he thought of Duncan as a 'patriarch' in relation to his family, and that the Duncans lived very differently from most of his friends, liberal or socialist.[34] In political things, too, he could be very much the authoritarian. The undergraduate who had admired Frederick the Great above all men had not entirely disappeared: for instance, in 1957 he wrote for Anthony Sampson a few notes on Arden Clarke (by then Sir Charles), the Resident Commissioner whom he had so admired in his early days in Basutoland and who was now Governor of what was soon to be Ghana, which made it plain that his admiration was for a non-racialist who was also capable of ruthlessness, a 'tough man' of physical and moral courage, without 'a shred of condescension' to blacks but also with 'masterful control'.[35]

That he was capable of advocating authoritarianism even in the Liberal Party is clear from a letter he wrote Paton as President of the party in November 1957, when he argued that a particular issue was so important 'it needs the exercise of your leadership, and [can] not ... be left to majority votes'.[36] He goes on to quote approvingly a description of Gandhi 'in his best dictatorial vein' from Nehru's *Autobiography*. Gandhi said: 'So long as you choose to keep me as your leader you must accept my conditions, you must accept dictatorship and the discipline of martial law. But that dictatorship will always be subject to your goodwill and to your acceptance and co-operation.'[37] (Whether Duncan would have given his goodwill, acceptance and co-operation if Paton had used his authority in a cause Duncan disliked is by no means clear.)

Nor was he a liberal in a literary sense. He read voluminously all his life, but as an adult he read biography, politics, history, science and en-cyclopedias, not fiction (he did not quite count the great novels of the nineteenth century as fiction; they were literature), nor poetry, nor drama. In *Contact* he said of Khaketla, the Basotho intellectual, that he wrote 'books both serious and fictional',[38] which describes exactly his attitude. In his aesthetics, 'Picasso' was synonymous with 'infantile',[39] modern art nonsense, modern music cacophony. The supreme art was Bach's, controlled, orderly, formal. He was an intellectual in a sense, but not really a liberal intellectual at all.

If he was not entirely a liberal, what was he? The problem (and the pleasure) is that one cannot tie any one label to him. His individualism was an aspect of liberalism, his extremism not. In many ways a conservative, he was prepared to tear down past and present to achieve a future he approved of; according to Paton, he would have been quite prepared to destroy the South African economy to get rid of the colour-bar. His politics were too impatient for him to be called a gradualist; the big change had to happen fast. He was not a communist, nor any kind of socialist, yet he was not simply a capitalist: though he had given up the struggle to understand economics in his first term at Balliol, he disliked state control and nationalization, and approved of free enterprise; however, although he had some capital himself, he was an advocate of the Liberal Party policy of redistribution of land and wealth in a post-Nationalist South Africa and, unlike most South African capitalists, he was a strong advocate of economic boycott. He approved of America and Britain, and so was – in one terminology – an 'imperialist'; but he applauded the end of colonialism: in his Cape Town days, he kept a large map of Africa on the wall of his office, and one of his greatest pleasures was to 'black' in another country which had achieved independence, to show the 'tide of freedom' sweeping down towards the south. In short, if one tied labels to him, one would hardly be able to see him at all.

In the autobiography, Duncan calls his years at Riverside a 'waiting move',[40] of the kind one has in chess. His 'waiting' was an odd kind. He was a busy and successful bookseller and a farmer, running a small milk-business, growing potatoes, planting trees: in his diary he records that 'this season we have planted 1000 deltoidea poplars, about 250 honey-locusts and about 50 pines halepensis. I am collecting fruit-stones to sow all over the farm.'[41] He was a part-time journalist, writing on Basutoland for the *Friend*, on the Union for *Mohlabani*, for the Liberal Party newsletter, for *Indian Opinion*, and elsewhere. He was an active member of the Liberal Party, urging changes of policy and courses of action on the party, being co-opted on to the National Committee in January 1956, speech-making in Natal in March, and setting up a branch of the Liberal Party in the Orange Free State in March, too. (One of the replies to the invitations sent out said, 'If Christ himself came to Harmony in an election as a candidate [for the LP] he would lose his deposit'.) He was a family man, finding time for wife and children, entertaining his parents-in-law when they visited Riverside in March and April, and being delighted to hear that his brother John and family were returning to South Africa from Canada, to which they had emigrated in 1953; Patrick predicted a fine political career for John and looked out for a farm near Riverside, though John in the event went into business in Cape Town. He continued to be deeply involved in Basotho politics. He had hordes of friends to entertain – Basotho, South Africans, visitors from abroad – and he was too courteous to turn visitors away or ignore them. As he wrote on 3 March 1956 in his diary, abandoned since his mother's death in 1948: 'My life is again becoming leisured enough and with enough routine for me to begin a diary again.'

The so-called leisure was not to last very long. Seeing in its newsletter that the Liberal Party was looking for an organizer, he wrote, tentatively, to Paton to put himself forward:

> I would love to do this work – providing that I can iron out certain private matters – and providing you want me. I should have to sell this book business which would be a very hard thing to do, as it has taken such an immense amount of hard work.... But if the way opened for direct political work I should do it.[42]

The 'private matters' were mainly to do with Cynthia, who was on the point of leaving for England for a holiday with the children and her parents, and who neither wished to leave Riverside nor have her husband away most of the time, but the attractions of the job were many: influential in the party, in touch with political developments around the country, able to talk and travel, to see a variety of South Africans ... it might even be more suitable as a role than the chance of a senatorship he had had to forgo.

On the side of the Liberal Party, there were obvious difficulties: as Peter Brown told him, 'there will almost certainly be opposition to your application from some quarters. No doubt you can guess which!'[43] Although everyone knew Duncan would commit himself wholeheartedly to the job, could Liberals be sure *how* he would commit *them*? He was, in some things, to the left of the party; he had virtually been a Congress-man; he was a defier; he was known to be an individualist of an extreme kind. Following his own lead, he tended to put people's backs up, for all his charm and ability. Yet, if they appointed him, might he in fact not get so much more done than anyone else? And he was Sir Patrick Duncan's son ... and many blacks trusted him personally as much as they distrusted most Liberals ... and he did speak Sesotho fluently ... and he wasn't poor ... and, though his anti-communism could be embarrassing, the Liberal Party was hardly full of fellow-travellers, was it?

In the end, the decision was to appoint him, and to be grateful for someone of his stature. He was to work for the party two weeks in every four, travelling around the country, acting as messenger and information-gatherer for the

National Executive, starting new branches and encouraging old, finding new members, raising money for the party, and indeed for his own salary, which was to be £1000 per annum and travelling expenses up to £500 per annum. He would keep on the farm and the book-business, and devote himself to them in the fortnights when he was not organizing; Doris Paterson would continue to do much of the book-business, and Cynthia would do what she could in running the farm.

He was frank with both Brown and Paton about how certain he was that it was the right job for him. He wrote to Paton: 'Although I feel that it is now or never if I am to do anything in politics, and that this is the way I ought to do it, I also have a conviction that if it is *not* right the way will not open, but if it is, it will....'[44] In other words, if the job works out well, it will be the right job; if it doesn't, it won't be for lack of trying, but because it's the wrong job. The winner would take all, the loser nothing but his self-respect.

Shortly before his application to be organizer, Duncan had got involved in an imbroglio of exactly the kind which was to make him a difficult member for the party. First, he wrote privately to Dr Xuma, the old right-wing ex-leader of the ANC, congratulating him on his open letter to the ANC Conference of December 1955: 'It is the beginning of the comeback against Communist control,'[45] he said. That was private, so permissible; but then, replying to an attack on the Liberal Party in *Fighting Talk*, and after acknowledging the newness of his membership and his own dissatisfactions with some Liberal policies, he himself made an outspoken attack on the communist influence on the ANC, saying that the communists were deliberately using the Congresses for their own ends.[46] Both attacks brought bitter scorn and anger down on Duncan. Some of the attacks did not worry him, since their authors were obviously communists; but Christopher Gell's scornful dismissal of the LP and angry accusations that Duncan was aiding the government in persecuting the left did hurt, not just because Gell was attacking the LP for faults he knew very well himself, but because Gell was attacking him personally.[47] Gell at the time was privately scathing about Duncan, regarding him as a fool and politically irresponsible,[48] and Gell's and Duncan's friendship did not survive much longer. In April, the Minister of Justice made use of Duncan's attack to justify a series of raids on ANC members and others by the security police, raids which led eventually to the 'Treason Trials' (in which Duncan was not included, for all that the Minister had described him as 'a dangerous little fellow ... a very good friend of the African National Congress'[49]). In the view of Gell and many others, both inside and outside the Congress movement, Duncan's attacks on those already under attack by the government were unforgivable, and none of the explanations offered earlier will justify to them what he did, then or later. Within the Liberal Party, even some strong anti-communists thought his timing at fault; attacking the communists in the Congresses when they were under attack by the government would inevitably make the Liberal Party seem reactionary. Even those who approved his attitudes were sometimes embarrassed by his outspokenness.

Yet a letter to Ngubane makes it clear that he was actually considering at the time a closer link with communists, not a break, because of what he calls the 'new Russian policy':

Nehru ... believes ... that the Russians are giving up the aim to impose Communism on the world by force ... if this is an honest policy, and I believe it may be, it involves also pulling out of the idea of imposing Communism by international subversion too. If they actualize this policy, the results for Africa are immense. It means that the US will not be able for much longer to hold African liberation at arm's length, and that the two questions (1) will the world go communist, and (2) will Africa be free, become quite discrete and separated ... petty bosses like Strijdom will no longer be able to play the anti-communist line. And, if the Russian policy is honestly accepted by our local Communists, it means that they can form part of a really broad liberation front.[50]

This is an important qualification of his attacks on communism in 1956 at least, and it is worth noting that many South Africans 'of the left' and some communists themselves felt the 'party line' in South Africa to be uncritically pro-Stalin and pro-Russian. A statement Kotane made to *Advance* in 1953 about the death of Stalin typifies this line:

The working people of the world and the cause of freedom and peace have suffered a grievous loss. We who belong to the oppressed, exploited and despised Non-European races feel the loss more than any other people because it was in his policy of racial equality that we found inspiration. Those who traffic in human lives – the warmongers, profiteers and apostles of racialism – dreaded his name. They feared him because he was an indefatigable worker for world peace, and the architect of the freedom of the common man and the exploitation of man by man.[51]

Stalin? Even if one accepts that the full extent of Stalin's 'traffic in human lives' was not widely known in 1953 (though it was certainly not unknown), and even if one accepts that judgements of Russia were not made solely on ideological grounds but on the practical evidence of its policies towards and in Africa, Kotane's statement is slavish stuff, and helps one to understand some of Duncan's reluctance to work too closely with communists, and some of his reasons for attacking them, even though it lost him friends as admired as Gell.

A greater sadness than the breaking of living friendships was the death of Manilal Gandhi on 5 April: Duncan wrote an obituary in *Contact* of 'one of the finest human beings I have ever known ... [whose] death leaves me with an acute sense of bereavement'.[52]

Soon afterwards, Duncan left South Africa by air to join Cynthia and the children, who had gone two months earlier to stay at Hexton Manor with her parents. He took the opportunity of doing an African tour, and both what he saw and the people he met made a profound and permanent impression on him. In his autobiography, the account of the tour is the longest single section of the manuscript, though he was only a little more than three weeks in Africa north of the Zambesi. It was of course a time of great excitement and optimism in Africa, despite (or because of – it depends where you stand) the Mau Mau rebellion, the Algerians' long struggle against France, the débâcle of the Central African Federation: independence was coming, and with independence a brave new world of economic progress and social emancipation. With hindsight, it is easy enough to see the naïveté of much of Duncan's response, and the more recent history of much of Africa makes some of his optimistic predictions seem very ironic.

He started in Bulawayo, seeing Hugh Ashton, author of the *The Basuto*[53] and a former colleague in the Colonial Service who was now head of the Department of African Affairs in Bulawayo. Although Duncan was fully aware that Southern Rhodesia was still an '*apartheid*-state', he was nevertheless impressed, particularly by the new African townships of Bulawayo, which he felt were so much better than the shoddiness of Soweto. In Salisbury, however, he stayed with an old friend from Bishop's and Balliol, Ranbir Singh, whose father had been Indian Agent-General in South Africa in the early 1930s; Ranbir was then Assistant Commissioner for the Indian government in the Federation, and he and his wife were continually subjected to the underhand *apartheid* of Salisbury – Mrs Ranbir Singh was particularly enraged by it. Ranbir had recently moved from Egypt, and was able to tell Duncan much about Nasser, whom he admired greatly, and about the impending collapse of the Central African Federation.

From Salisbury Duncan travelled on to Nairobi with Philip Mason, later Director of the Institute of Race Relations in London; they stayed together with Sir Evelyn and Lady Mary Baring in great comfort and splendour at Government House. He renewed acquaintance with Kenneth Mackenzie, later Minister of Finance, met Sir Ernest Vasey, then Minister of Finance in Kenya and later Minister of Finance in Tanganyika, and Ibrahim Nathoo, Minister of Works; he met, too, Tom Mboya, of whom he wrote in 1960, 'he must be Prime Minister of Kenya, within two years'.[54] He visited his old Balliol friend Eliud Mathu, who was on the Kenyan Legislative Council but whose opposition to the Mau Mau was such that he had ruined his chances of a continued public career. Although many of those he met in Nairobi were deeply depressed by the Mau Mau crisis, Duncan was apparently not. He was impressed both by Baring's toughness in dealing with the crisis and by what was being done to eradicate the sources of discontent.

From Nairobi he went to Uganda, to stay with Brian Gray, also a former colleague in Basutoland; the Grays introduced him to Noni Jabavu (Mrs Nontando Crosfield), the writer, whose autobiographical book *Drawn in Colour* he found 'enchanting', and whom he liked personally, too. Uganda he describes thus: 'their jewel-like country, fabulously rich in soil and water, must have a future, if anywhere has a future'.[55]

From Uganda he went to Khartoum, where he saw Peter Kilner, then working for the *Morning News* of Khartoum, and was reported as saying how much he enjoyed the non-racialism so evident in the city, and how he welcomed Sudanese independence.[56] Then to Cairo. What he saw of modern Egypt confirmed what Ranbir Singh had told him of Nasser; but even more impressive was the recumbent statue of Rameses II:

I spent about an hour looking at it, marvelling. Ages seem to have worn it not at all, and parts of it shine as if the sculptors finished their final polishing processes yesterday. His face blends serenity with power and authority. What has happened to the art of the world when one compares magnificence of this order with the fraudulent and contemptible 'sculpture' and 'painting' that is being produced today?[57]

And so to London. A few days later came Nasser's nationalization of the Suez Canal – 26 July 1956: 'I was appalled at the stream of jingoism which I witnessed. I looked up a few books, and it seemed to me that Nasser had as much right to nationalize the canal as Britain had had to nationalize the coal mines.'[58] He wrote to *The Times* on 6 August: 'As one who has always been a proud partisan of the British idea ... I pray that this country will do nothing to begin a war with Egypt': 'Nasser has broken no law and abrogated no treaty. He already enjoys outspoken support in many countries. If at Suez "Imperialism" grapples with "Anti-colonialism" I have little doubt that "Imperialism" will be defeated.' It was one of his more accurate prophecies; at a talk at Chatham House on 'The breakdown of white domination in South Africa', he prophesied an end to racial tyranny 'within our lifetime'.[59] He went to talk to the Africa Bureau and to Fox-Pitt of the Anti-Slavery Society. He recorded a talk for the BBC on Strijdom, then Prime Minister of South Africa. He visited family and friends, and went so briefly to Oxford that he did no more than enter the Porter's Lodge at Balliol.

One thing he did not do was to speak out in favour of expulsion of South Africa from the Commonwealth, as had been advocated recently by Huddleston and taken up by some Commonwealth leaders. Duncan himself believed expulsion would have 'profound effects': first, it would complete the isolation of white South Africa, and 'make the white minority think very hard'; secondly, it 'would probably remove a considerable brake on Nazi acts'; thirdly, it would probably endanger the High Commission Territories; fourthly, it would shake up the whites of Natal, with their strong feelings about the British connection. Although not all the effects would be good – removal of a brake on Nazism, endangering the Territories – initially he was very much in favour of expulsion: at least *something* would happen, even if all the consequences could not be foreseen. But almost no one he consulted approved, even those who approved the sports boycott, like Gell. Paton and Brown both felt that as a member of the Liberal Party he could not support expulsion. Duncan wrote to Ngubane, 'Well, there it is. I shall have to abide by their views. And perhaps it is premature' – but, all the same, he goes on to tell Ngubane why he thinks expulsion might help, and asks: 'What do you think, Jordan?'[60] Party discipline was already beginning to rub.

The most important part of his experience of Africa was not yet complete, for on the way home he and Cynthia went to Accra to stay with the Arden Clarkes. They stayed in the castle of Christiansborg (now Osu), enjoying the vice-regal life, Accra and the hospitality of the Arden Clarkes. Duncan's admiration for Sir Charles, the 'tough guy by nature', was confirmed but, more important even, was his meeting with Nkrumah, then Prime Minister of the pre-independence government. Arden Clarke's own admiration for Nkrumah (whom he had released from jail to become Prime Minister) was well known, and Duncan felt exactly the same regard:

> ... he [Nkrumah] was planning the celebration of independence early in 1957. I said to him: 'You won't forget South Africa, will you?' He said 'Of course not. Without South Africa we could not celebrate our independence properly. But I don't trust those posts of yours. I shall send an invitation to Mr Strijdom, and I shall send it with my own personal messenger, with instructions to take it right into his own office, and to give it to him

personally.... And for that messenger ... I pick the Blackest man in Accra.'[61]

Duncan was amazed to hear from Nkrumah that in Cabinet he had taken Eden's side over Suez, but noted (approvingly) in the autobiography that since 1956 Nkrumah had moved 'appreciably away from his strongly pro-Western point of view'. Part of the reason, thought Duncan, was the influence of Sekou Toure, but part his 'genuine passion for a truly African policy ... subservient neither to the east nor the west'.[62] He was never to lose his admiration for Nkrumah, even when he ceased to be the darling of the liberal West.

Duncan took three things from his trip through Africa and his meetings with colonial administrators and African leaders: first, he began to think of himself as an African, and to think in continental terms. After the repression going on in South Africa, the mood of Africa was so much more exciting; 'forward-looking' was the kind of word he used. Secondly, he learned to admire African leaders like Nasser and Nkrumah; in part this was his natural respect for authoritarian figures, for people like Arden Clarke and Baring, but it was more than that, because he would not have admired just any authoritarian figure – it was the combination of the popular leader with the authoritarian he so admired. Thirdly, he began to think of Africa as a 'third force' in the world, neither pro-West nor pro-East, but specially African; again, this attitude was to dominate his political thinking until near the end of his life – it was one of his first steps to Pan-Africanism.

From Accra Duncan and Cynthia flew to Kano, where they picked up the children, and so back to Johannesburg, Riverside, and Duncan's new role in the Liberal Party.

Duncan was national organizer of the Liberal Party for sixteen months, from September 1956 to January 1958. He worked very hard, often doing more than his statutory two weeks in each month; he travelled forty-two thousand miles in the Volkswagen 'Kombi' which the LP provided, sometimes staying with friends, but often sleeping in the 'Kombi'; he raised money, he made speeches, he talked to the press, he recruited new members, he encouraged old ones (and offended others, too), he wrote letters, he wrote report after report on fund-raising, local activities, visits to sympathizers, attendances at conferences, matters of policy, and more. Yet, as Duncan himself wrote, 'it was an expensive operation, and after a year it was clear that it was not justifying itself'.[63]

First, it was an ill-conceived job. When Duncan took it on, there were about a thousand Liberal party members and many times more miles dividing the provincial groups than there were members. Duncan's fund-raising (which he loathed anyway) ended in being more for his own salary than for anything else; for instance, from September to November 1956 inclusive he raised £472.17 in donations and what Brown called 'the thorny old matter of our financial difficulties'[64] continued throughout his period of office. Moreover – and it affected more than fund-raising – while the visits of a national organizer were often encouraging to local branches, the fact that he served such a huge area meant that visits were not followed up sufficiently;

what he did on one visit would often have to be repeated on the next.

Secondly, and more importantly, Duncan was the wrong man for the job; he was more interested in ideas than organization, he was impetuous and impatient (in one case he walked out of an appointment after being kept waiting five minutes, in another did not wait because someone had not arrived ten minutes after a prearranged time), he was a loner not an organization-man – rather than hand over a piece of work to someone who might not do it quite as well, he would do it himself, which meant that he had to spend time on what other people thought trivia. He took everything at crisis-pace, and could not realize that most people had neither his energy, nor shared his certainties, nor were aware how close each next crisis stood. Bewailing the lack of members in the Transvaal, even of white members, he wrote to Peter Brown: 'There seems to be insufficient realization that the very existence of a settled white minority in Southern Africa is at stake and will be settled in our time.'⁶⁵ Everything was crucial; it was the 'here-and-now' mind in operation. He wanted red in the Liberal Party flag. After all, '¾ of all buses in Basutoland are red. I have looked at the first 17 national colours shown in Whitakers. *All but three* have red. . . . It is really essential, and if there is any doubt about it I shall have to fight as hard as I can. . . .'⁶⁶ In short, the party needed a workhorse, and had employed a firecracker.

Thirdly, and most importantly of all, he was in considerable disagreement with crucial policies of the party. Other people were, too, of course, including in some things Peter Brown and Alan Paton themselves; but they did not live at quite the pace Duncan did, and did not see that each issue he raised with them had to be settled now, not tomorrow. From their letters one senses again and again how gently they handled him, for he was a valuable member of the party; yet one also sympathizes with their occasional impatience with his perpetual impatience.

The first area of disagreement was over policy on the franchise. By 1955 Liberal Party policy aimed 'to achieve the responsible participation of all South Africans in government and democratic processes of the country and, to this end, to extend the right of franchise on the common roll to all adult persons'. That was clear enough; but the policy was hedged about: 'As it may be impracticable to introduce universal adult suffrage immediately, it may have to be achieved by stages during a transitional period.'⁶⁷ The statement of policy went on to discuss 'interim qualifications' which 'would be educational, economic or age', and so on. That was in Duncan's view wrong, first because it *was* simply wrong: if franchise was a right, then it could not be qualified. His Basutoland experience had taught him that even ordinary peasants without any formal education were capable of intelligent decisions about their own futures and needs; if universal adult suffrage worked in India, it could work in South Africa. Secondly, the policy was inexpedient, because it repelled potential African supporters.

The second area of disagreement was over a clause which limited the party to constitutional action only: 'The Party will employ only democratic and constitutional means to achieve the aforegoing objects, and is opposed to all forms of totalitarianism such as communism and fascism.'⁶⁸ As a defier himself, Duncan loathed the first part of the clause: it was vague (were strikes 'unconstitutional'?); and it missed the point – 'To suggest that in our critical situation we can achieve our aims more gently than the working class achieved its aims in the UK is not in my view realistic'; 'if "unconstitutional" means "illegal", think what a weapon we place in the hands of the Government. . . . With their synthetic majorities they can and do pass any law they feel like passing'; lastly, 'the Party by adhering to this will forfeit immense support among the Africans if there is another defiance campaign . . .'.[69] Again, it was both wrong and inexpedient; under it, *satyagraha* became impossible.

Thirdly, the LP still saw itself as primarily parliamentary; Duncan was convinced this was nonsense. Again and again in his letters of the time he returns to the theme:

> In the long run the White minority can only live on in South Africa on the terms of the majority, which by definition is largely Black. If we succeed in building a large Party we will be able to build the Party into the nation, on the terms of fairness enshrined in our principles. These terms are the best that the White minority can expect reasonably. If White joins now with Black in fighting for them (*a*) the party's power will grow and make those terms stronger and more likely of acceptance, (*b*) by blurring race lines the issue on the day of victory won't be a racial one, and (*c*) by fighting together such comradeship will have been created as will largely negative disruptive influences.[79]

In 1958, when he had left the job as national organizer, he told Paton:

> Our difference is this; that I see that power is the necessary ingredient of our struggle and that you don't. You are decent and believe that when others' cruelty has been brought to their notice they will change. You leave it there. I see the appeal as being necessary, but as not even worth making if one has not put all one has got into the *organizing of power*. I think our whole futility as a party is due to a neglect of the factor of power. I am *not* obsessed with power. In the *long term* it takes second place to decency and consent and goodness. But in politics it is . . . *the essential* ingredient. . . . Until the LP realizes this it will remain a weak, well-meaning group, making the right gestures and remarks, but listened to by no one.[71]

The only real source of power was in the hands of the Africans; only they could make non-violent resistance to the Nationalist government work. Yet many Africans scorned the LP, and the LP would not see why; few of those with this potential power were coming into the party, just because it was held back from true radicalism by its clinging to a 'European' idea. In May 1957 he told Ngubane:

> I have decided that the next thing that must happen is a pruning of certain elements from our party whose presence merely means that we are all reduced to imbecility. If it is done properly the loss can be limited to a few individuals; but even if it means a loss of whole elements I am sure that it will be worth it.[72]

His disagreement went much wider than just these issues; among his papers is a copy of 'The policies of THE LIBERAL PARTY of South Africa',[73] which is annotated in his handwriting. Comments include: 'rambling', 'irrelevant', 'Removal of all colour bars not even mentioned!!' 'Diffuse and irrelevant cf. the trumpet call of the Communist Manifesto',

'Why?' (against a suggestion for replacing the pass laws with a 'voluntary system of identity cards'), 'gabble', 'feeble', 'What is primitive?' (against a point about 'simple and even primitive peoples'), 'so there is a realistic colour policy' (against a point about 'the unrealistic wage and colour policy pursued by all past governments'), 'wash out this ambiguous chapter', 'but this is what it is all about', 'detail', 'Utopia', 'never heard of this word', and so on. To 'Economic policy', he adds 'sharing of wealth through taxation', to 'Agriculture', he adds 'Redistribution of land??', to 'Health', 'redistribution of wealth ...'. Against some points he has put ticks, against the word 'liberation', 'GOOD' – and the two crucial comments are 'abolition of discrimination – nothing less' and 'The new handbook must not PATRONIZE'. Even if he were rewriting the handbook (he did, though not surprisingly his version was not acceptable), one wonders that someone so critical of so many policies could have joined the party in the first place, much less become its national organizer.

One needs to add a corrective to Duncan's views. The LP did get a working-class African following; there was even a time in the 1960s when it had a majority of black members, and this was not done by having good strong policy, charismatic leaders, and radical action, but by slow, patient, hard political work, legal advice and aid, welfare work, joint committees to solve local problems or to fight local injustices. For example, in the northern Transvaal there was to be a branch of nearly two hundred black peasants, because a Liberal lawyer had fought a land-tenure case for them. Such people joined the party because it could help them with everyday problems (no less real for being everyday). The first provincial branch of the party to get substantial black membership was Natal; although from the start the Natal branch was unequivocally in favour of universal adult suffrage and much closer to the ANC than in other areas (except East London for a time), it was less a radical policy and more Peter Brown's quiet and patient political work (conducted mainly in Zulu) which brought in a working-class black membership. Ronald Segal, in *African Profiles*,[74] singles Brown out as the most politically minded Liberal, not only because of his views, but also because of his effectiveness; in keeping him banned as long as it did, the government seems to have agreed.

Still, there were compensations for Duncan in his job. In a sense he was having the best of several worlds: there was the farm, the books, the family, and he was doing something for his political aims, too, if not nearly as much as he wished to or felt himself capable of. He enjoyed seeing more of South Africa than he had yet been able to do and, having until then 'dismissed all the talk one hears of "beautiful South Africa" as the usual tourist propaganda', he now 'suddenly awoke to the fact that ours is one of the loveliest countries in the world' – high veld, Karoo, the mountains of the Western Cape, the Drakensberg, the Transkei, Natal, the coastline everywhere: 'One day, when we have got our racial obsession out of our system, scenes like this will awaken a vivid patriotism, a patriotism of the whole people for the whole land.'[75] He learned a great deal about public speaking, and talked in a variety of places to a variety of audiences, learning to cope with attacks from right or left: a polite audience of five hundred in the Grahamstown City Hall; a house meeting in Pretoria broken up by a crowd of toughs from Pretoria University, some of whom stayed to talk and listen; a meeting of seventy in Alexandra in Johannesburg, where he and Jordan Ngubane were attacked by an ANC Africanist who told Duncan to 'get out as fast as you can'.[76] He made a point of living in the areas of those people he was trying to recruit to the party, spending three days in Sophiatown in April 1957 and taking a room in Athlone, a 'Coloured area' in the Cape, in September 1957, since he was recruiting mainly coloured members. He was applying the lesson learned from Francis King at Winchester, years before: one needed to live with people before one could understand their problems, whether they were Welsh miners or African labourers.

Despite his earlier attacks on communist influence in the Congress movement, he, Ngubane, Paton and Brown and others were all convinced of the need for as close co-operation as possible between the Liberals and the Congresses; in November 1956 Paton and he were interviewed by *New Age* and urged publicly the need, not simply for the kind of concerted campaign which was already taking place on specific issues (opposition to the Group Areas Act in Natal and the Transvaal, membership of the Civil Vigilance Committee in Johannesburg), but for unity as 'an effective fighting front against oppressive measures'. Duncan added: 'The best corrective to doctrinal differences is hard work.'[77]

In December Duncan asked for, and got, persmission to attend the ANC Congress in Queenstown, though Brown warned him: 'we feel you should go with the object of making personal contacts but not to make any statement or speech on behalf of the party ... observe rather than participate'.[78] On 15 December he drove to Queenstown, where the ANC was meeting in the absence of the many delegates who had earlier in December been arrested and charged with treason – 156 Congress leaders altogether: Luthuli, Z. K. Matthews, Mandela, moderates, communists, intellectuals, labourers, housewives, lawyers; 'the other Parliament', it was called at the time.

The ANC Conference in Queenstown was badly disrupted by the arrests and started late on the Saturday. Duncan, the only white observer, helped search the meeting-place, a small hall in the Queenstown location, for microphones. The meeting was opened by its chairman, and went on until lunch-time. Duncan went back to his hotel for lunch, and immediately afterwards was arrested by the security police and charged with having entered the location without a permit. He was taken before the commanding officer, Colonel Huxham, who, after sending the other policemen out of the room, showed Duncan a dried flower which he had taken from a wreath on the coffin of Sir Patrick – he had been one of the guards over the body in the cathedral in Pretoria. They talked of the state of the country, and finally Huxham said, 'Duncan, *what* is going to happen in our country?'[79]

Huxham offered to release Duncan if he paid an 'admission of guilt' fine, but he refused; so he was held over the weekend, to appear before a magistrate on the Tuesday (the Monday was a public holiday). However, on the Monday Duncan was released because, as the jailer told him, 'Some Kaffirs have paid your fine'. He left the jail to be greeted by a small deputation from the ANC Conference; members had collected £5 in pennies and tickeys to pay the fine. Although Duncan had been determined 'not ... to shirk anything', since he felt the arrest and charge were 'an act of aggression against me and the Conference',[80] he felt he could not refuse such generosity.

The Conference had moved to a mission outside the location and Duncan went back to be greeted by a double line of the delegates, who all shook hands with him, then formed up into a round dance, and sang a victory song, with their wrists together in front of their faces, as if handcuffed. In high spirits, the Conference then resumed in the mission-hall, where Duncan said his thank-you in Sotho, and the security police looked on. In his report to Brown and Paton, Duncan added touchingly: 'I remembered your instructions not to make a statement of any kind and limited myself to the remarks reported above.'[81]

All the same, the action distressed many white Liberals, who raised questions of party discipline and illegal action. Alan Paton, with the unenviable task of holding his heterogeneous party together, wrote to Duncan, 'I do not hide from you that many members of the party, who are not antipathetic to you, were very disturbed by news of your arrest,'[82] and sent him a copy of a statement he had issued to allay some of the objectors' fears. Duncan, he wrote, 'did not go there with any deliberate intention of breaking the regulations but that he did in fact break them, because of his own nature and temperament . . . any official of the party or any person acting on behalf of the party cannot expect to enjoy complete freedom of choice in these matters . . .'.[83]

How Duncan answered is not known; perhaps he did not bother, because by the beginning of February he was deeply embroiled in helping the bus boycotters in Johannesburg. The bus boycott was a spontaneous reaction by the black people of Lady Selborne and Alexandra townships to an increase in bus fares into the city; there was no alternative transport, so they walked, or cycled, or begged lifts, until eventually the boycott succeeded and the fare increases were abandoned. The Congress of Democrats and the Liberal Party, and many white Johannesburgers who belonged to neither, helped with transport, despite considerable police intimidation, and brought what pressure they could to bear on the City Council, on Chambers of Commerce and of Industry, and on firms who got tough with boycotters. Paton and Duncan went to a meeting of the Johannesburg Bus Boycott Committee and together they went to see Luthuli and Z. K. Matthews about ANC–Liberal Party co-operation. It was, Duncan said, the 'best thing that has happened to the party for years . . . the idea that passive resistance is the way forward is accepted here . . .'.[84]

But the problems with party discipline continued; in May Alan Paton wrote to Duncan in his most schoolmasterly tones: 'Now Pat I have a bone to pick with you. I thought that at Cape Town we agreed that we would not say in public that it was impossible for the LP to be voted into power. . . .'[85] Paton knew as well as Duncan that the Liberal Party would not be voted into power; but to say so publicly meant an acceptance of the kind of role which many members would not accept. Duncan was prepared to lose them; Paton preferred not to. Similarly, after an article in *Liberation*[86] in which Duncan said that the Liberal Party stood unequivocally for universal adult suffrage, Paton wrote to tick him off roundly.

I am quite sure – I mean, I accept your assurance – that you forgot about our arrangement. Whatever else I may think about you, I have never thought you would depart from a contract unless through impetuosity, generosity, or bellicosity. At such times a wind sweeps through your soul and lots of things go flying out of the window, but this is what you are, and by now I accept it. After this fine tribute to you I must point out to you that in your article in *Liberation* you specifically stated that there would be no barrier to the introduction of universal franchise tomorrow, and if you think that is what the handbook says, I give you up. Do please be careful, Pat.[87]

In the matter of the National Workers' Conference which eventually took place under the aegis of the Congress movement on 16 March 1958, Duncan did submit to party discipline. The purpose of the Conference was to support demands made by blacks for a minimum wage of £1 a day, and there had been considerable activity for increases of wages in various parts of South Africa; in East London, for instance, a Liberal Party member, and a Member of the Provincial Council, B. P. H. Curran, had worked with the local ANC on a successful wage-raising campaign. There was some hope that the Conference would call a stay-at-home which might influence the impending general election.

On 5 January Duncan wrote to Yusuf Cachalia to say that, though the Liberal Party 'was not in at the birth of the idea of the Workers' Conference', he thought an invitation to Alan Paton and Peter Brown might bring the party in; Duncan offered his own services, for instance with transport or in helping call a local meeting in Ladybrand to elect delegates to the Conference. On the same day he wrote to Brown, saying that it was 'incalculably the most important plan since the Defiance Campaign'. Brown was less happy about the Conference, not its demands for a minimum wage of £1 a day, but its timing, since he felt the effect of a strike would be to strengthen not weaken the Nationalists. Duncan seemed to accept this point, for he told Curran, 'I am against this strike timed for then. . . . But I am for one at a later stage when it can be organized up and down the country . . .'[88] and on 29 January told Cachalia that, as he was a paid organizer of the LP, 'I have not enough freedom to go against the wishes of my party', which were caused, he explained, by the contradiction involved in the LP putting up candidates against the UP in a general election while at the same time helping the Conference which was designed to weaken the government and strengthen the UP, or so Cachalia had told him when they met briefly in Cape Town. A few days later he wrote to try to persuade Cachalia to put back the date of the stay-at-home until after the general election. While it is true that he was still talking in concessionary terms ('I want White South Africa to give concessions to very greatly stepped up pressure from the oppressed'), and did not want the Nationalists to do better in the election than they had to (he knew they would win), he had other reasons:

(a) The ANC at the Cape don't even *know* about the plans for the National Workers' Conference – see the ARGUS of 27 January, reporting a speech by Thos Ngwenya. Thomas was not trying to sabotage the plan, he genuinely did not know of it. I saw a good deal of him and asked him.
(b) All Africans I have discussed this with confirm my view that a call to

them to help the UP will fall on deaf ears. Whereas a call to them to fight for higher wages will succeed. I don't think you can aim at two objectives in such a great undertaking. That is, you must *either* try to help the UP, or you must aim at higher wages. Don't try to hunt two hares, as the Basuto say.

(*c*) I have found out that the East London Higher Wages campaign is unlikely to fall in with SACTU's plans, though I wrote there some weeks ago suggesting that it should do so.[89]

Instead of the projected date, he urged 26 June, 'Freedom Day', anniversary of the miners' strike of 1946 and the official start of the Defiance Campaign.

In the event, the stay-at-home went ahead for 14 April and virtually flopped; bannings on meetings and individual leaders, police and military intimidation, threats from employees, inefficient organization and lack of communication, disruption by Africanists in and out of the Congress, all contributed.

It is presumably because of this letter to Cachalia that in Bunting's account of the Conference Duncan appears, though very briefly:

> ... there were many groups attempting to divert the ANC from its course.... The Africanists were undoubtedly trying to harness black militancy to take over Congress for their own purposes, and in this aim they were encouraged and supported by agents of the South African Government and the US Central Intelligence Agency, as well as virulent anti-Communists like Patrick Duncan and the *Contact* group in the Liberal Party.[90]

Duncan was in fact one of those in the Liberal Party most strongly in favour of co-operation with the ANC; equally, he was at this stage deeply suspicious and afraid of the Africanists. Furthermore, his attitude to the Liberal Party's contesting the general election at all was such that he virtually withdrew from the party during that time. In November 1957 he wrote a long letter to Paton about political strategy, arguing that in fighting the election the Liberals were ignoring the mood of the country; even the ANC wished not to impede the United Party, for all its inadequacies. 'Quite frankly I am appalled at the political unreality and naivety of us Liberals,' he wrote. 'Our task is to become accepted in all South Africa, and among all races, and to earn the trust of the people. We will not do this if we fly in the face of a tidal wave such as is now sweeping the country.' He goes on to argue that 'the correct strategy for our party at the present moment of history is *reculer pour mieux sauter*, or, as the Basuto say, *ho checha ha ramo* (the step the ram takes backward when he is going to attack)'. Then he argues the second part of his case, which is for 'closer relations with the ANC.... I believe that it is our duty to enter into the same sort of relations, as a party, with the ANC, that the COD has. I know this is a terribly difficult question, but if I am right then we must explore now ... with the ANC, what the chances are....'[91] He told Peter Brown, too, that he could not bring himself to collect money 'from harassed Indians for an election campaign that I feel to be more harmful than useful.... If HQ feels I am wrong there are two things to do, (*a*) give me two months' unpaid leave, or (*b*) let me resign.'[92] In the event, he was given two months' unpaid leave of absence during January and February 1958, and used them to finish, at last, his work on Basotho law. (*Sotho Laws and Customs* was eventually published in 1960. While as an academic law-book it has considerable failings, since Duncan was apparently unaware of much of the recent discussions of customary law, and of course was not a lawyer by training, it was a useful handbook of case-law and as such was much used by District Officers and others in Basutoland in the 1960s and is still used by students in the University in Lesotho.)

Duncan took no part in the general election of 1958. Similarly, when in February 1958 the South African Coloured People's Organization (SACPO) suggested he stand for one of the parliamentary seats representing the Coloured people of the Cape, he turned it down, telling Paton his decision was 'largely instinctive', but he thought it also 'distaste for the fraud that set up the seats, plus even more for the disgusting race going on to climb to Parliament and £1500 a year on the backs of defenceless and harmless people'.[93] But the major truth was that he had given his heart completely to a new venture, which was at last going to fulfil his role in the 'great aim' of ridding South Africa of racial oppression. Though he remained loyal to the Liberal Party, it was in part because he had nowhere else to go.

CHAPTER 8

1958–9
'There can't be a Contact without me ...'

Duncan started thinking about a Liberal newspaper early in 1957, and soon was deep in discussion with Cynthia about it; in June he wrote to Paton to say that Cynthia had decided to give enough money to found a newspaper to support 'the Liberal cause'.[1] Cynthia, he said, made the gift on certain conditions: first, that he himself should be Editor and, secondly, that there was to be an editorial board mainly of Liberal Party members, though the paper was not to be controlled by the party *per se*. Initially it would be published fortnightly, but as soon as possible weekly; initially it would have eight pages, and be 'written in a popular manner and generously illustrated'.[2] Since he hoped it would start in three months' time, he wished to resign as National Organizer from 16 July.

On 27 June he sent a telegram to Paton withdrawing the original letter, and the same day sent an amended version of the letter: the newspaper would support 'in every possible way' the Liberal Party, though not be an official organ of the party, and a company should be formed, the directors of which would be the editorial board. The Editor would be paid £1500 per annum, the business manager £750. In a covering letter he said that he had decided

> (*a*) that you were right and that the editing just can't be done from Ladybrand [a small town near Riverside]
> (*b*) that my original intuition was right, and that I'd make a frightful editor.

He withdrew, too, his resignation as Organizer; no doubt Paton helped Duncan recognize his 'original intuition'. Duncan now approached Anthony Sampson, former Editor of *Drum* and then with the *Observer*. Sampson turned the job down, and so Duncan approached George Clay, *Observer* stringer in South Africa and Political Correspondent of the *Cape Times*; he was interested but not entirely sure – there was a possibility of a job as African correspondent of the *Observer* coming up, and he would take it if offered. By July, however, Clay was fairly sure he would edit the Liberal newspaper, provided he was allowed a certain independence, and in late July he, Paton and Duncan began talking firm dates, format, plan of publication and so on.

Part of the reason for the Duncans' wanting a newspaper is clear from a

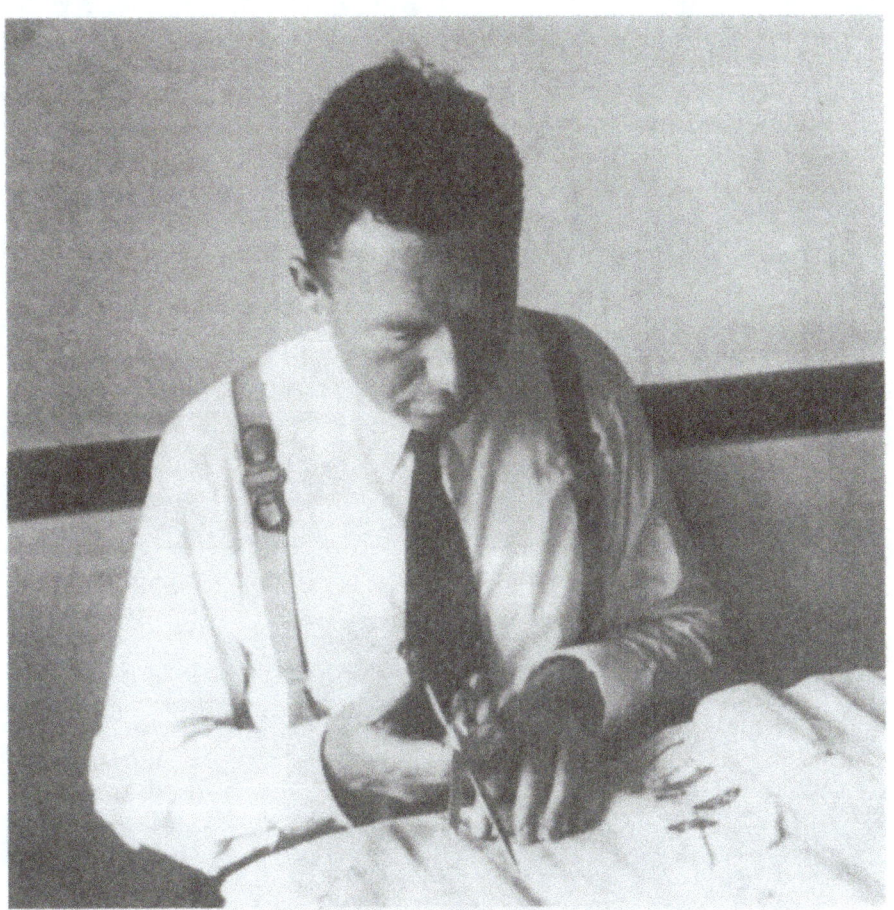

15 *Pat Duncan at work in the* Contact *office*

16   *Pat Duncan speaking at a Liberal party meeting, Nyanga, Cape Town, 1959*

17   Pat Duncan ana Harold Macmillan at the UK High Commission garden party, Cape Town, February 1960

conversation between Clay, Paton and Duncan in July, which Duncan
recorded afterwards:

> GC: I do not believe it is possible to fight the *New Age* [the successor to
> *Advance*].
> PD: There would be no fight. But the public appealed to would be largely
> the same.
> GC: This fact alone would provoke *New Age* into fighting. It would also
> create hostility with the Congress movement which has established its
> claim to be *the sole* representative of non-White bodies.
> PD: I dispute the right of any politcal body to claim a monopoly of any
> field.
> GC: They may not have a right, but they believe they do.
> PD: I can see this needs a basic appraisal of the role of the LP.
> A long discussion followed, PD maintaining the LP's destiny was to
> become a mass movement with non-racial leadership, GC saying it was
> quite impossible at present.
> AP: supported PD generally....[3]

Abandoning that subject, the three men talked practicalities; Clay outlined
his plans for the paper, 'to appeal to a middle class, mixed white and non-
white readership. This would grow in time into a popular paper of mass
appeal.' They should expect a loss of £200 an issue, and would have to pay an
editor £1500, a business manager £750, and a reporter £900, that is, a loss of
£7950 per annum.

In August, Duncan outlined his 'General lines of policy', which make it
clear that the paper – still not named – was to be an expression of Duncan's
own views: against totalitarianism; for universal suffrage immediately; for a
mass-membership of the Liberal Party; 'No doctrinaire adherence to
"capitalism" or "socialism" ... *fair shares*, thro' taxation of rich and land
redistribution'. Under the heading 'US' he writes: 'Generally friendly
especially to NAACP [the National Association for the Advancement of the
Coloured People] *Exceptions*: Dulles and H Bomb. Colour Bar in South.'
The coincidence between his own views and the policy of the paper is very
plain. Even if it was not designed to oppose *New Age*, it would be in
competition; and Duncan's views were not the same as those of *New Age*.
Even if it was to be a Liberal newspaper, it would take a harder line than the
Liberal Party.

The other major influence was Jim Bailey's news-magazine for Africans,
Drum. Duncan admired *Drum* for its popularity and populism, its campaigns against injustice (the famous exposés of condition in the Fort,
Johannesburg's prison, and of slave-labour in the Transvaal), its commitment to Africans as people and to Africa. What he wanted was a political
Drum, popular and radical; as the first 'Memo to correspondents' from Clay
said, the paper would 'try to avoid the "highbrow" approach which has
characterized so many liberal periodicals. It will try to put the liberal
viewpoint across in "down to earth" terms.'[4]

In October 1957, at the first formal meeting of Selemela Publications (Pty)
Ltd (Selemela was the Sesotho name for the Pleiades, the dawn star; when it
appeared, it was time to go into the fields to begin ploughing), Duncan
opened the meeting by saying that Cynthia had 'made available' an amount of

£7500 per annum for the newspaper. In fact, what happened after the initial grant was that Cynthia gave him money for the paper as and when he needed it, though she never gave him much more than he had given her (he had, after all, put the book-business in her name, and transferred all his money to her when he went into South African politics). In short, it was really their money, not just Cynthia's; however, others, too, gave money, either as gifts or advertisements, and when Duncan went abroad he often raised money for *Contact*. David Astor, for instance, gave £100 a month in 1960–2, and other larger sums, to enable Duncan to increase the print order. (Although Astor did not realize the connection between Helmuth von Moltke and Patrick Duncan, he had in fact helped finance some of Moltke's work against Hitler before 1939.) There was also an American source, though exactly who or which organization is unknown; it is commonly thought (even by some Liberals) to have been the CIA, through one of its front organizations; certainly *Ramparts*, in its exposé of the CIA, showed that other South African organizations and periodicals were being financed in part by organizations given money by the CIA (for instance, the Congress for Cultural Freedom), but those were generally later developments – Duncan visited America for the first time only in January 1961, though of course he could have got CIA money beforehand.

Clay's first 'Memo to correspondents' said that the establishment of the newspaper had been made possible

> by the generosity of a member of the South African Liberal Party who is prepared to underwrite the loss which, in the present political climate ... any such journal must be prepared to sustain.
> The sponsor wishes to remain anonymous, but there is no sinister secret about the source of this money, and I have authority to reveal the sponsor's identity to anyone who has good reason to require this information.[5]

So, it is certain that initially the money came from the Duncans, and that later they had other help. It is also certain that, when Duncan left South Africa in 1962, the money for the paper dried up. Duncan told Paton in 1963 that the 'principal backer' felt no longer able to support *Contact*; although he said this was nothing to do with his leaving the Liberal Party, it would be very strange if it did not have something to do with his leaving South Africa. David Astor had withdrawn his help in 1962 (it was only intended as short-term), so perhaps Duncan meant Astor, or perhaps he meant Cynthia. Writing from his exile in Basutoland to Paton in South Africa, and with Cynthia still in Cape Town, it would have been sensible not to name her; the letter to Paton makes it clear that the money was given to Duncan personally, rather than to the newspaper or to the Liberal Party.

In short, if there is a mystery about where some of the money came from after the initial founding of the paper by the Duncans, it is only a small mystery; and, wherever it came from, it did not have much effect on Duncan's political beliefs.

Initially, Duncan planned a board not only of Liberal Party members; he was very keen to have, too, Luthuli and Z. K. Matthews, but neither seemed to want to join and, though Duncan continued to want non-party members of the Board, he accepted others' opinion that only Liberals should run the company. Some of those involved in the early discussions dropped out; the Board then became: John Wilson (a Liberal and a Johannesburg lawyer) as Chairman, George Clay, Jordan Ngubane, Alan Paton, Walter Stanford, MP (one of the Coloured representatives in Parliament and a Liberal), Cynthia and Duncan himself. (Cynthia's presence on the Board is another indication of her role as financier.) There was discussion of their taking over the ailing *Forum*, a liberal magazine, or Gell's *Africa X-Ray Digest*, but eventually it was agreed that they would take over *Contact*, the Liberal Party newsletter; George Clay liked its title and its actual connection with the party, which he thought might make it easier to get subscriptions.

After various delays, the first number of the new *Contact* appeared on 8 February 1958, a twenty-page tabloid, with a full-page photograph on the front page of Archbishop Joost de Blank surrounded by black children in a location, details of writers (Gell, Paton, Harry Bloom the novelist and lawyer, and others), stories about the Liberal Party candidates for the elections, the Anglican Church, job reservation, a discussion of the Prime Minister's state of health, Alan Paton's column 'The long view', international and African news. Duncan told Clay he was delighted with the first issue;[5] but trouble between Clay and Duncan was already in the air. In Duncan's original memo of policy he had written, 'support for democratic front, but never of COD': 'After discussion I agreed – and I am sure that it was wise – that we should also not attack the COD – i.e. begin hostilities. But that did not cancel the original article, to which I attach great importance.'[6] However, on 8 March Clay published a very sympathetic profile of Piet Beyleveld, a Treason Trialist and a COD member who was, despite being banned, standing as one of the coloured representatives for Parliament. There followed what Duncan described in his diary as the most hectic week of his life: due to leave on 18th for London to raise money for *Contact* and the Liberal Party, he felt he had to settle the matter of the policy of *Contact*. There was a huge row, involving everyone else on the Board, in which Duncan made it quite clear that, if it was *his* money, it was *his* paper, and it would follow *his* policy, and Clay and the Board made it clear that no Editor or Board could possibly work under those conditions.

It is commonly thought that Duncan sacked George Clay. This is not so, since Clay had told Duncan early in February that he had after all been offered the post as African correspondent of the *Observer* and, as he had originally warned the Board, he would want to take it up in due course. It was, however, an unpleasant business, as Duncan told Cynthia: 'I've been through an experience that I never want to repeat. All is happy down here, and George is staying on, at least for two months, possibly until he goes to the Observer, which looks like being June or July or August....'[7] Duncan had in fact decided that he was going to be Editor after all, and at the Board meeting on the 16th it was agreed that he would take over on 1 May, and that Clay would help him bring out a couple of issues before he left.

It was not a decision which pleased everyone on the Board: Walter Stanford recorded his vote against, and later Alan Paton had second thoughts. He and Duncan exchanged letters which showed both Paton's worries about Duncan's suitability and also Duncan's own stubborn determination to do what he thought best. Paton wrote that after visiting *Contact* and seeing the Editor's job in practice, and since he feared a repetition of the crisis of March, he doubted Duncan's capacity for the job:

> ... though I fear your unpredictability, I am attracted to you by your courage and honesty, and would not lightly hurt or abandon you. I am beginning to understand the compulsions that sometimes drive you into impetuous action and speech, and I believe that you seek endlessly for a noble and useful way to use your life. The National Organizership has not satisfied this hunger, but now you hope that the editorship might. I would ask nothing better than to be able to help you find what you desire, but I do not think that the editorship of CONTACT is the answer. I do not think you have the right temperament or experience for it.[8]

Duncan replied that he was still absolutely resolved to take over *Contact*:

> I am not looking for a noble way of life. I have a message which I want to put over. I have a vision – a non-racial, free South Africa – which I want to realize. *I see how to get there with clarity.* 'Contact' is the answer. Also, you will realize that there can't be a 'Contact' without me. . . . I want 'Contact' to help the party to grow in power and strength. I hope the party will maintain its support of 'Contact' through the existing board. But even if it does not 'Contact' is going ahead, with or without the LP.[9]

One understands both Paton's fears and Duncan's determination; it is also interesting to see Duncan showing muscle: 'you will realize that there can't be a "Contact" without me. . . . "Contact" is going ahead, with or without the LP'. There could be no answer to that; and in a sense he was very consistent: he might have been making yet another change, but this one was the 'great aim' at last; he was sure of that, as sure as he was that a newspaper financed by the Duncans was not going to 'support Communism' in any way.

In 1957 he had applied for a renewal of his passport, and it had been refused; there was much public criticism of the government for the refusal, so much so that the Department of the Interior did what it normally never did, which was to issue a statement explaining that the passport had been refused only because Duncan had not been planning a trip abroad in the immediate future. However, since he had, as some South Africans were then entitled to, a British passport, too, he could travel on that if he wished.

Leaving Patrick junior behind – he was at boarding school – Patrick, Cynthia, Alex and Ann flew first to Lourenço Marques, then Beira, and then Dar es Salaam. In Dar es Salaam Duncan had two meetings with Julius Nyerere ('a real statesman and something of a Gandhi. . . . He is bound to be PM in five years'[10]) and talked to other Tanganyikans. In Zanzibar he met the editor of the local newspaper, and arranged exchanges of articles with *Contact*; in Nairobi Tom Mboya, Vasey, Baring, and others, Africans, Colonial officials and settlers. The family then flew to Germany, where Duncan stayed to raise money for *Contact*, while Cynthia and the children flew on to England. After finding sympathy but no actual support he, too, flew to England.

Originally, he had planned to visit Algeria, 'to see the Algerian war, preferably from the National Liberation Army viewpoint'.[11] The decision that he would take over the editorship of *Contact* had not entirely changed his desire to see Algeria, though quite how he planned to join the Liberation Army and be back in South Africa by 1 May is not clear. However, with Alan Paton's injunctions to consider, he abandoned his plans for Algeria. But he then fell very ill, with osteitis again in his bad leg and infective hepatitis. Many of the plans he had made for England had to be cancelled, though he contrived to see some of his friends and sympathizers – Astor, Anthony Sampson, Colin Legum of the *Observer*, the Africa Bureau and the Anti-Slavery Society. He did a telephoned interview with Bertrand Russell, trying to recruit Russell's support for the boycott of racially selected teams. He did not get an answer on this, though Russell did say that the difficulty in South Africa was caused by the whites being 'total beasts' and that he would like to see South Africa out of the Commonwealth; Russell predicted, too, that whites would hold their supremacy over non-whites 'until there is a war between Russia and the West. Whenever that happens all white men, throughout Africa, will be murdered.'[12] Duncan did not publish the interview in South Africa.

Illness and his desire not to cut short his trip meant that he had to tell Clay that he would not be back as planned, and Clay – now committed to leaving by the end of May – warned Duncan that he was taking on a harder job than he seemed to realize, and that the longer he had before actually taking over the better it would be. So, though there was much else he would have liked to do, particularly about fund-raising, early in May he flew back to South Africa; the family followed shortly afterwards. From Riverside he went to Cape Town and *Contact*, taking over the actual editorship at the end of May, and producing his first issue on 14 June.

Cynthia, Ann and Alex stayed behind in Riverside to get ready for the move. While for the children the change was something of an adventure, for Cynthia leaving Riverside was a great unhappiness. Fortunately, they were able to rent in Cape Town a house interesting enough to compensate a little for the loss of Riverside, a four-bedroomed, slightly eccentric place, between the coastal railway-line from Cape Town to Simonstown and the sea at Kalk Bay on the False Bay coast, looking out over the Indian Ocean; it was the only house which stood on the sea-side of the railway-line, which they had to cross to get to the road or station, watching out for trains as they did so. Its name was 'By the Sea', though Duncan renamed it 'On the Rocks'. For Duncan himself it was an echo of the years of childhood when his family had lived part of the year at Sandhills, a little way along the coast at Muizenberg. An added compensation was the arrival, later in the year, of Nanny Maxim, Miss Agnes Maxim. She had come to help Cynthia when the family stayed in England; when the death of her mother had left her free to travel, she went out to South Africa and soon became an indispensable member of the Duncan household, more a family-friend, companion and housekeeper than a nanny, and quite capable of running home and family when Cynthia was called away to help her husband, as she often was.

For Duncan himself, being in Cape Town meant he could see more of his brother John and sister Deborah Cowen; he would meet John on the station each morning and together they would travel into Cape Town. Although he and Cynthia had seen something of the John Duncans when they farmed at

Fortrie, Deborah was still virtually a stranger – Patrick had left home when she was a little girl and, though they had seen something of each other in his days in Pretoria, neither felt he or she knew the other well. Furthermore, Duncan had interests in common with Deborah's husband Denis Cowen, who was by now deeply involved in working with the Basutoland National Council in drawing up plans for the independence of Basutoland. So the three remaining Duncan children and their new families were closer than they had been since early childhood.

In April 1959 Emma, their second daughter, was born, and at the end of 1959 the Duncans bought a large and elegant house in Retreat, also on the Cape Town–Simonstown line, but closer to town and looking up to the Constantia mountains and the Tokai forests. Keyser House stood in a pleasant garden of indigenous trees which ran down to the edge of Keyser vlei, a lake which in winter served as sanctuary for thousands of water-fowl, and which was bordered by water-flowers. There was a paddock and stables, and Cynthia kept a pony for the children. In the garden the Duncans built a swimming-pool in the shape of Africa, though they were only five minutes by car and two stops on the coastal railway-line from the beaches of Muizenberg. 'It is a house that fits us like a glove,' Duncan wrote in his diary.[13]

The months of June–November 1958 were among the most unremittingly busy of Duncan's life. Although he was a trained administrator and had learned something of business methods while running Africa Books, although he had done much freelance journalism and had a scholar's interest in typography and printing, he was neither a trained journalist nor an editor, and there was much to be learned very quickly. Clay helped him with one issue, and then Duncan was on his own, dealing with the editorial work and the staff, with the Board of Selemela (scattered widely over the country), with the Liberal Party itself, his writers, his fellow-journalists, his printers, and his readers – who hardly existed yet. Most of all, his problem was to transform the paper from one directed at middle-class readership (white and black) to one directed at a mass-following for the Liberal Party. To be popular, radical, political and still intelligent is a problem for any newspaper. The example of *Drum* did help, but *Drum* was not specifically political in the way Duncan wished *Contact* to be, and was aimed at a more homogeneous audience than Duncan hoped *Contact* would have. Nor did the conditions in South Africa in 1958 make it easy to run a newspaper, particularly a very political one; although the press was relatively free, (within the context of its ownership at any rate) and although there was a tradition of outspoken criticism of politicians in and out of government, established in earlier struggles by the press in the Cape, it remained both a hide-bound society and one in which there were an increasing number of regulations and statutes – for instance, under the Prisons Act and Suppression of Communism Act – which made it necessary for editors to beware.

Initially, as Clay had planned, *Contact* had been a tabloid of twenty pages, a mixture of news, commentary and reviews; the sub-title was 'The news behind the news'. Soon a lack of money forced Duncan to reduce the number of pages, though he kept the price at ninepence. The first few issues sold about 2500 copies, though by April this was up to 4000, where it stayed steadily until 1959, when it began to rise, to 9000 at the end of October 1959; in 1960 the print order was up to 11 000 and the sales comparable. Clay's first issue had advertised four regular writers – Gell, Harry Bloom, Alan Paton and Ralph Horwitz (the economist) – and he had arranged a network of other journalists, some on small retainers. Duncan's first big success was to get Lewis Nkosi, the young Johannesburger who wrote mainly for the *Golden City Post* and *Drum*, to contribute a weekly column, 'My world', a witty and exciting view of township life in the Transvaal and a satiric examination of South African *mores* and manners; he had, too, Anthony Sampson, Jordan Ngubane, Benjie Pogrund, a young journalist knowledgeable about the ramifications of local African politics, David Marais the cartoonist, Liberal Party people, and various academics (especially Julius Lewin). Soon he began to draw into his orbit various of the more energetic and radical of the Cape Town Liberals: Randolph Vigne, a publisher and writer who became his literary editor, Peter Hjul, a trade journalist and deeply involved in the politics of the coloured community (he was actually a member of SACPO despite being white), and others. Soon, it became common to talk of a *Contact* group of Liberals, radical, anti-communist, energetic, committed, very different from the traditional Cape Liberals with their beliefs in gradualism, a qualified franchise and constitutional change. The *Contact* offices, which were in an old building in Parliament Street, overlooking the House of Assembly itself, became a centre of discussion and argument, as well as newspaper offices.

By mid-1959, soon after the number of pages had been dropped to twelve and the price to sixpence, a typical issue of *Contact*[14] was made up thus: on the front page a three-quarter-size photograph (one of Chief Luthuli of the ANC on his way to the ANC Conference) and a headline, 'What our students are really thinking'. Inside were three pages on South Africa: a full-page story on the ANC Conference in Johannesburg; an article on the racial views of a sample of university students in South Africa; stories on the use of Afrikaans in African schools, on Kozonguizi's fleeing from South-West Africa, on moves to exclude South Africa from the Olympics, and on the South African Foreign Minister's response to a speech made in America by Denis Cowen. Then came three pages of news of Africa: two stories on Ghana, one on Nyasaland, one on Kenya, two on Tanganyika, and one on French Africa. The leader pages had: two leaders, one comparing South Africa and Brazil, one condemning the banning of Luthuli; a cartoon by David Marais; three columns – one by Herbert Mofulatsi (this was Lewis Nkosi's usual spot), Peter Brown's 'Long view', and Patrick Duncan's 'Fair comment', a round-up of views and news; and then *Contact*'s version of the *New Statesman*'s 'This England', called 'South African looking-glass'. There were two pages on African writing: 'Sam Sly's' column, written by Randolph Vigne; various reviews – Mphahlele's review of a new translation of Venter's *Dark Pilgrim*, Olga Meidner on Lawrence Lerner's new novel, *The Englishmen*, Peter Hjul on Cyril Dunn's *Central African Witness*, and a poem by Sydney Clouts, 'Roy Kloof went riding'. On the back page were letters to the Editor and small ads (by June 1959 there were hardly any advertisements other than from publishers and small organizations; the advertisements of the bigger companies like Rothmans and Shell were not renewed after the first year).

There were two criticisms commonly made of *Contact* (other than ideological criticism from right or left). First, that it was dull. This was often the attitude of those who took *Drum* or the *Golden City Post* as model, and certainly *Contact*, except in Nkosi's column, rarely had the kind of linguistic vitality which made *Drum* such a remarkable achievement. (A similar criticism could well be made of *New Age*.) The cause of this was partly in the talents of the regular writers, whose language tended to be modelled on the *New Statesman* rather than on *Drum* or the *Golden City Post*, but mainly in the heterogeneity of the audience; Duncan wrote to Julius Lewin praising an article he had written for its 'crystal style' which fulfilled 'our ambition of pleasing the Professor and the standard 2 man'[15] (the South African education system runs from Standard 1 upwards), and that exactly explains the problem. He was aiming at a mass black audience; yet many of his readers and writers were in fact highly educated. He could of course have aimed at a different audience, at a lower level of literacy, or at the audience reached so well by *Drum* – the new townspeople, lively, sophisticated, politically conscious because they had to be. But *Contact* could not compete with *Drum* nor did it wish to; it was trying to create a non-racial readership as well as preach non-racialism.

The second criticism was of its amateurishness. Though there were occasional articles or news stories which were effective, too often if was badly produced (poor layout, murky photographs – though the front-page photograph was nearly always excellent) and poorly written.

This amateurishness was the cause of Duncan's first major crisis as Editor. When he took over from Clay in May 1958, he had of course inherited Clay's staff, the Business Manager Anthony Clarke, who had before been with *Drum*, and Ronald Legge, a professional journalist who acted as main sub-editor. Duncan's inexperience as an editor led to Clarke's sending Duncan a memo in August 1958, complaining of 'the appallingly low standard of copy we are using', 'living from hand to mouth', that *Contact* was unplanned and was missing good stories, and that Duncan was not treating his staff as he should. According to a note Duncan wrote himself at the time, Clarke in conversation after his memo made even harsher criticism: 'I have never done anything for *Contact* – except (this said in an attempt to be biting) given the money.... I am impervious to all advice and suggestions.... I sit all day in my office and interview people who butter me up.'[16]

Soon afterwards, Legge decided to leave; he was replaced, first, by Oswald Blake (until December 1959), then by Collingwood August (until April 1960 when he left the country), and then by Tim Holmes, who stayed on as Assistant Editor until Duncan went into exile in Basutoland, when he took over as Editor. Clarke had already decided by the time of his memo to leave, and did so at the end of the year. After various temporary arrangements, he was eventually replaced by Joe Daniels, who remained as Business and Circulation Manager until Duncan left the country in 1962.

Another unsigned critique, written in August 1958, goes through the problems: the shortage of money, and poor book-keeping; the lack of real news and the missing of news stories; the small number of subscribers; the staffing problems: 'I am very worried about what may happen when there is nobody left on Contact who is a real Newspaper man and who has any real business experience. Of all the competitive businesses, manning a newspaper is one of the hardest and needs the most competence.' Yet the last paragraph of the report shows clearly that what was being argued was not just journalistic competence, but political line:

> Patrick believes – and I think there is evidence to show that he may be right – that the circulation in the African areas can be increased. But I believe that if we are ever to build a common society it is necessary to get the acceptance by the Whites of this point of view. I think that without a demonstration of the power of the non-whites this is likely to be a lengthy process. But I believe that the real bogey in this country is Apartheid, Baasskap, the apathy of those with a British heritage and not communism. And so I believe we should be chiefly concerned with 'converting' whites....[17]

And that was the real rub.

In a sense, what Duncan did with *Contact* from 1959 onwards was to make the most of exactly its amateurishness. Although for a time he held on to the slogan which Clay had used, 'The news behind the news', his interpretation of the idea was very different, for he was interested less in commenting on and analysing the news than in trying to discover a new kind of news, that is, the news of a South Africa usually invisible to white people's eyes, and the news of an Africa usually invisible to all South Africans' eyes. Of course there were other papers doing the same thing – *Drum*, the *Golden City Post*, the *Bantu World*, the Indian newspapers in Natal – but *Contact* was not quite like any of these, because it was aimed at an inter-racial audience, increasingly a black audience, though never entirely so. What *New Age* (its great ideological rival, though it sold much better than *Contact*) did was roughly similar, in that it, too, tried to make a new version of South Africa visible to an inter-racial audience; but *New Age* did so mainly in terms of its own ideological commitment – it carried news, of course, and like all news it was interpreted, but it was interpreted from a much firmer position than *Contact*'s was. The kind of policy Duncan represented to Clay did of course represent an ideological position (muddled or flexible, depending on where one stands); but the visibility *Contact* tried to create, especially later in Duncan's editorship, was not so much interpreted from a centre but from the edges of visibility itself: to create a sense of the South Africa which otherwise voiceless people had. Duncan called this 'the location front':[18] the news was to come from the black townships, and that is where he wanted to sell *Contact* most of all. Largely this was done by using semi- or non-professionals as the source of the news – a young Indian from Stanger, a priest from the Transkei, a student from Fort Hare, an ANC man from Port Elizabeth. One of Duncan's first acts as Editor had been to dispense with the professional journalists to whom Clay had been paying retainers; he knew that what the new readership did not want was white liberals theorizing from their armchairs. He was less sure of what should replace their professionalism, but grew more and more to depend on local 'amateur' correspondents. It was this which the regular

Contact team, Duncan, Daniels, Holmes, with help from Randolph Vigne, Peter Hjul and others, were to build up.

The continental network, the other outstanding characteristic of *Contact*, derived partly from Duncan's own interests in Africa, and partly from the encouragement of the *Observer* journalists Colin Legum and Anthony Sampson, who suggested to Duncan that *Contact* should become a 'Pan-African journal'.[19] From 1958 to 1962 it was probably the most reliable source of information in South Africa on political developments in Africa; this is particularly significant because it pre-dates any admiration which Duncan had for the Africanists in the ANC and their formation into the Pan-Africanist Congress in 1959. It is significant, too, that a proportion of *Contact*'s readership was elsewhere in Africa, at least by 1960; in a file of sixty-five letters from readers, all of about mid-1960, half are from other African countries.

The way *Contact* was sold and the way it found its band of correspondents connect closely. The breakdown of sales before 1960 is not known, but one number in February 1960 sold 1822 copies by subscription, 1700 through the commercial distributor, the Central News Agency, and 7300 through local agents all over the country; that is, about three-quarters were sold by local agents, each of whom would tell the *Contact* office how many copies he or she would like to sell. Of the sale-price of 6d each agent kept 3d and returned money or the corner of the front page of each unsold copy. Often these agents doubled as sources of information; clearly they had a stake in this, since selling locally was likely to be easier if there was an item of local news.

In one of the *Contact* files there is a collection of two hundred and fifty letters from local agents to the Business Manager; there are letters from seventy-eight agents in South Africa, two in South-West Africa, three from Southern Rhodesia, ten from Nyasaland, seven from Northern Rhodesia, two from Tanganyika (one was from the Tanganyika African National Union, which often ordered a great many copies), three from Bechuanaland, three from Basutoland, and one from Kenya. Of the South African agents, a great many were Africans, both from urban and from rural areas; in other words, by 1960 Duncan (mainly through the patient work of Joe Daniels) had achieved part of his aim of reaching a new audience, even if it was not a mass one, because its sales rarely rose above 15 000. Readership, especially in the black townships, was substantially higher than this; the less money there is, the more people will read a single copy and, despite all the stories about how rich black South Africans are, at least relatively, 6d a fortnight in 1958 was more than it may seem. The letters reflect, too, the difficulties of selling *Contact* in South Africa: agents were harassed by police, had to encounter African apathy as well as illiteracy in the rural areas, and were sometimes arrested, though there was usually a relative or friend to take over; even white agents would take risks in selling *Contact* – one of the detentions in 1960 was made on the basis of a pile of *Contact* ready to be sold. Yet there were not many resignations from the agents, most of whom had a stubborn political commitment to selling *Contact* as well as a small financial interest.

In December 1958 Jordan Ngubane, Patrick Duncan and Cynthia flew to Accra to represent the Liberal Party on the South African delegation to the

All-Africa People's Conference. The senior member of the delegation was Zeke Mphahlele, then teaching in Nigeria, and others were Alfred Hutchinson (the author and a co-defier of Duncan's in the 1952 campaign), Mrs Mary-Louise Hooper, Luthuli's secretary until her deportation from South Africa (these three representing the ANC), and Michael Scott, representing the Hereros of South-West Africa. From Basutoland came Ntsu Mokhehle and two others of the BAC. In itself, the composition of that South African delegation is a comment on the leadership of the anti-*apartheid* forces in southern Africa at least in the 1950s and 1960s. In concentrating on ideological differences – and there were many; for instance, the organizers of the Conference had to persuade Mphahlele not to include a bitter attack on liberals in his draft of the ANC 'declaration' for the Conference – it would be very easy to ignore the kind of relationship which existed between, say, Mphahlele, Mokhehle and Duncan from the days of their friendship at Riverside and Maseru.

The All-African People's Conference was the brainchild mainly of George Padmore, the veteran Pan-Africanist from the West Indies then acting as adviser to Nkrumah, and was in effect the sixth meeting of the Pan-African movement and the first to take place in Africa itself. To the Conference came two hundred delegates representing sixty-two organizations from twenty-seven African countries, the organizations ranging from small trade unions to huge national political parties; there were a number of international observers, from the Soviet Union, the United States of America, and including the wives of Paul Robeson and W. E. B. Du Bois, the most celebrated of the early Pan-Africanists. Among those Duncan met at the Conference were Fanon, Holden Roberto, and Patrice Lumumba. He spent some time talking to Potekhin, the Russian Africanist (and on his return to South Africa conducted a correspondence with him on Russian attitudes to southern Africa).

On various issues, such as Pan-Africanism itself, racialism, colonialism and imperialism, the Conference was largely in accord: they were to work for an independent Africa which would eventually become a Commonwealth of African states within five regional groupings – North, West, East, Central and South; they were to use all means possible to break down southern African intransigence – boycott was an especial theme of Mboya's, who was Chairman. In world affairs, the new Pan-Africa was to be neutralist. On the issue of means there was much more controversy, and a discussion of the use of violence had most North African delegates threatening to walk out; after all, the Algerians were fighting a war of independence, and to be told – as the draft agenda stated – that the 'main purpose' of the Conference was 'to formulate concrete plans and work out the Gandhian tactics and strategy of the African Non-Violent Revolution . . .'[20] was intolerable to them and their supporters.

Eventually, the Conference left possibilities open in a resolution which read:

Recognizing that national independence can be gained by peaceful means in territories where democratic means are available, the conference guarantees its support for all forms of peaceful action. Their support is pledged equally to those who, in order to meet the violent means by which they are subjected and exploited, are obliged to retaliate.

The South African delegation voted for the resolution, though whether they all understood the resolution to mean the same is uncertain.

For Duncan himself, not only the Conference but also the renewed experience of non-racial Ghana was very satisfying. On his return to South Africa he told the press that Ghana was 'the nearest thing to Utopia I have seen'.[21] He was even more impressed when the South African delegation was called to see Nkrumah, who spent forty minutes talking to Mphahlele, Ngubane, Scott, Cynthia and him and then gave Duncan a message to deliver to the people of South Africa: 'I strongly advise you South Africans not to resort to violence [in your struggle against racialism]. Otherwise you will be the losers.'[22]

There was considerable publicity about the Conference in the South African press on the Duncans' return (Ngubane stayed behind in Ghana for some time before returning), and most South African newspapers carried versions of the Conference; *Contact* itself devoted three full pages to it, its background, its resolutions, its significance. Duncan was attacked from both right and left. The right said he had ignored the thousands of people Nkrumah had locked up – was he not a hypocrite to curse South Africa and praise Ghana in the same breath? (This was a favourite theme in South Africa in those days.) From the left came an attack on Duncan by the ANC Youth League, always more militant than its parent organization: the Youth League wrote to Padmore saying that Duncan was trying to 'present a picture of a conference riddled with divisions and hostility'.[23] Duncan was angered by the attack, and wrote to both Padmore and to *New Age* to protest: he had, he said, reported the Conference objectively, and in fact had stressed its unity on the essential issues. Of course, the point was not whether or not he had been objective, but that he had reported any argument at all. As Achebe's character Odili says of the expatriate critics of Nigerian corruption, 'Your accusation is correct; but you have not the right to make it'.[24] It was exactly this lack of right which Duncan could not accept. Had the Conference not described as an African anyone who owed his primary loyalty to Africa and nowhere else? Had he not demonstrated his right to be an African?

It is in part out of his visits to Ghana and his personal and political respect for Nkrumah that Duncan's increasing commitment to the Pan-African idea grew. Alongside this commitment began to emerge a new side of policy and practice in *Contact*: interest in the Africanists in the Congress movement. If that was the positive side, the negative side was his conviction that communists were controlling and directing the Congress Alliance to their own ends. He had felt this ever since his decision to take part in South African politics, as his statements before the Defiance Campaign show; in 1953 he had refused to write for Bunting and *Clarion* (the predecessor to *Advance* and *New Age*); in private and public he had spoken out against communist influence and, though he told Sampson in May 1958 that he would not attack the ANC, he made it clear to Gell in the same month just where he stood. Gell had written to advise him against an 'editorial anti-Commie ... line',[25] and

Duncan replied, arguing that Gell had 'allowed evil in South Africa to obscure and distort your wider view of evil'. Since all governments were 'essentially selfish', the best objective tests of them were to ask:

(1) how many people has Government killed for non-conformism?
(2) how many exiled? You apply that to Hitler, and you get a horrifying answer. You apply it to Stalin and you get a similar one. You apply it to Strijdom, and you get a different one. He and his government are evil; they are on the same path as Hitler; but no one who has kept a sense of proportion could equate the evil of the two systems. In brief, as I see things, the menace in the 20th century is the armed fanatic – the semi-educated fascist, hitlerite or communist who irrespective of human suffering is prepared to pull down the world to get his stupid way, to torture, to 'liquidate' (whose word is that?), as Serov (still the head of the USSR security police) 'liquidated' the entire middle class of the Baltic republics in 1940.[26]

He was making much the same attack in public. *Counter-Attack*, voice of the COD, reported that in a lecture on 'The Liberal Party and co-operation' he had delivered 'a 45 minute tirade against international communism'.[27] When asked if it were not possible for two organizations differing on 'foreign policy' to unite on local issues, Duncan 'admitted that he would not co-operate with any organization which he considered to be run by, or contained communists because he considered communists a greater danger than Verwoerd'. Duncan replied to the report:

I did *not* say that I considered communists a greater danger than Verwoerd. I said that I considered them a greater danger potentially, which is a very different thing.
  ... you have made my talk appear as if it was an attack on the ANC ... [it] was a straightforward attack on communism, and it laid the blame for the disunity of the freedom forces on the doctrinaire determination of certain newspapers to grind out regular pro-communist articles on foreign policy....
  I have also all along stressed my support for the ANC.... But if individuals within the ANC follow the line ... they cannot expect to be immune from criticism.[28]

Duncan's hard line was by no means approved by everyone in the Liberal Party, which was in most areas of the country working closely with the Congress Alliance on local issues; nor did it have the unqualified approval of even all members of the editorial board, though Jordan Ngubane felt much as Duncan did.

In late 1958 he began to refuse to accept advertisements which COD tried to place in his newspaper for their meetings. When Paton questioned the decision, Duncan wrote, 'Some weeks ago when I addressed a house meeting of COD, it was quite apparent that they proudly, unashamedly, backed the communist cause. In view of all this I refused this ad. I am pleased I did. The "mass meeting" they called was attended in fact by 51 people, most of them members. If the ad had appeared in CONTACT this figure might have been doubled.'[29] The only compromise he was prepared to make was in not imposing a blanket ban on all COD advertisements; he would, he said, accept 'only the most innocuous ads'.[30]

This was too much for Paton, who answered:

> If you feel it is important to have nothing to do with the COD, even to the length of not accepting an advertisement from them, then this is not a matter of purely editorial concern, because it affects the relationship of the Party to other organizations. The Party has already decided to co-operate with the Congresses on defined objectives.... I think there is a clear-cut choice before us. If you insist that CONTACT should take up this unco-operative attitude to COD, then either you should have no Board, or you should have a Board having no firm connection with the Party. I add a further comment of my own. If we have an open breach with COD, the doors of the other Congresses will be slammed in our faces....[31]

Eventually, in January 1959, after several more arguments, the Board of Selemela Publications was substantially changed, and became a purely Cape Town Board; though its membership changed occasionally, as various people resigned or were co-opted, by 1960 the firm nucleus was Peter Hjul, Randolph Vigne, James Currey (a Cape Town publisher), Joe Daniels and Duncan himself. Cynthia left the Board in late 1959, because Duncan felt that she should be protected as much as possible from the dangers involved in sharing his opinions publicly. With the *Contact* Liberals now in complete control, the newspaper could take its own line without internal criticism.

The culminating point of his policy of open opposition to the communists in the Congress Alliance was Duncan's 'Open letter to Chief Luthuli' in *Contact* of 2 May 1959. The 'open letter' took as its occasion an appeal by Luthuli, published in *New Age*, that the Liberal Party should 'drop its anti-communist plank' in the interests of co-operation between the Liberal Party and the Congress Alliance. Duncan replied: 'Chief Luthuli is not a communist. Nor, I think, would he wish communism to take over this country. He must therefore believe that the tensions between the West and the communists are not relevant to this country, being too far away. I would reply that in this sputnik age distances are no longer important....' Nor, he continued, did *New Age* think the 'cold war' irrelevant, since it 'pours out anti-West propaganda, and holds up the "peace camp" or "socialist camp" as utopia'. Therefore, Luthuli wanted the Liberal Party to abandon its 'loyalty to democracy' but did not seem to want communists to abandon their loyalty to the Soviet Union. 'Far, therefore, from accepting Chief Luthuli's appeal, I appeal to him to use his eyes, and to see where he is allowing his congress to be led.' Arguing that communists were using the Congress Alliance as a 'front', he went on:

> From the events of the thirties ... we know that if Stalin had told the South African communists to climb a Karoo koppie and pretend to be baboons they would have obeyed immediately. From the events of the forties we know that Stalin, if he had had the power, might easily have decreed the liquidation (a *Soviet* word as applied to people) of the Africans in our country.

The polemic grew even stronger: 'How many times has the ANC followed a line during the last five years which would displease the Kremlin? – surely not once.'

Communists, he continued, were the 'worst oppressors of the modern age', and he specified: the imposition of collectivism in the Ukraine; the destruction of subject peoples, the Kalmyks, the Chechens, the Ingushes, the Crimean Tartars, and the Balkars; the 'Communist rigidity' imposed on the Chinese 'with a barbarity that makes Dr Verwoerd look like a Sunday school teacher'; the slave-camp system in Russia; the 'stupid, inefficient and cruel system' imposed on Hungary, East Germany and so on. The result? Even those once sympathetic to communism, like Nehru, Nasser and Nkrumah, have learned 'that in 1959 the only real imperialists are the communists'.

At the end of the open letter, he softens his line somewhat:

> It is the duty of all responsible men outside the socialist camp so to behave that a third world war is avoided. What is needed is peaceful co-existence.... Nothing ought to be done to interfere across the line in the territory of the others. I deplore the few attempts of some unwise westerners to subvert Eastern Europe, just as much as I deplore the many attempts of the communists to continually expand their sphere.

Liberalism, in short, is the best opposition to the totalitarians, the fascists and the communists; therefore, 'so far from collaborating with totalitarians I hope that the [Liberal] Party will intesify its determination to allow no sort of totalitarians to get the smallest foothold in our movement'.[32]

The 'open letter' caused great offence and bitterness. Luthuli himself, who had had lunch with Duncan the day before it appeared, and to whom Duncan had said much of what he had written but not that he was publishing it, was deeply offended. Paton, too, criticized Duncan, as did many other Liberals, especially those who were struggling to build up local co-operation with the Congress Alliance, as in Natal and the Transvaal. Even Eddie Roux, veteran ex-communist whose *Time Longer than Rope* Duncan had referred to in the 'open letter', wrote to object: he disliked Catholicism, he said, thought it, too, had totalitarian tendencies, but was quite prepared to work with Catholics, and in the same way thought Liberalism was best served by 'active association with other groups in a common struggle'.[33] The Congress of Democrats and Communists, both Stalinists and non-Stalinists, were very angry; and the next number of *Contact* exacerbated the anger, since it claimed the Liberal Party as the only non-racial party in South Africa, and said that the multi-racialism of the Congress Alliance meant seeing 'each human being first and foremost as a member of a racial block, and only later considers his humanity ... in this (though of course not in other respects) the Congress Movement is no whit different from the racialists of the Nationalist Party'.[34]

Again Paton wrote accusing Duncan of 'verbal trifling' and of confusing 'political principles with organizational methods'.[35] But, in fact, it was for Duncan the old argument about the nature of the Liberal Party. Was it aimed at a mass black membership or was it not? For Paton it was a much more complex argument: *Contact* was thought of as the organ of the Liberal Party, and what *Contact* said was taken as Liberal Party policy; yet often Duncan abandoned Liberal policy. There was even talk of expelling Duncan from the Liberal Party at a National Conference in Cape Town later that year, along with much talk of resignation on all sides; only Peter Brown's sense of humour saved the meeting from complete disruption, when he said gruffly from the chair, 'I'm taking resignations at the end of the debate'.[36]

In one sense Duncan had a powerful argument on his side, for the *Contact* Liberals seemed at the time to be gathering a considerable following among black Capetonians. For instance, at an Africa Day celebration in Cape Town in April, at least five hundred people, many of them black, turned out to a meeting on the Grand Parade (*Contact* claimed an attendance of eight hundred), at which Senator Leslie Rubin, Joe Nkatlo and Patrick Duncan spoke for the Liberal Party, and Thomas Ngwenya for the ANC. A telegram from Nkrumah was read out and applauded. Similarly, at a Grand Parade meeting on 30 April, at least six hundred people, possibly more, heard Joe Daniels, Joe Nkatlo and Patrick Duncan attack job reservation (the Industrial Amendment Act of 1959, which extended provisions by which the government could limit certain occupations in certain areas to members of particular race-groups). But for many Liberal Party members what the *Contact* Liberals were doing positively was still not enough to compensate for their hard line on communists in the Congress movement.

One needs to add a proviso, not so much to Duncan's attitude to communism as to his attitude to communists. Always, when he was faced with a flesh-and-blood person, ideology mattered much less. In contrast to his abomination of Afrikaner Nationalism and communism are his friend-ships with Afrikaner Nationalists and communists. For instance, once a week he would lunch with Piet Cillié, Editor of the Afrikaans newspaper, *Die Burger*, the most 'liberal' of the Afrikaans papers admittedly, but still Nationalist. For instance, the night before Lionel Forman, Editor of *New Age*, devoted communist, brilliant young lawyer (he was only thirty-one), died in Groote Schuur Hospital during a heart operation, Duncan went to visit him. After Forman's death, Duncan wrote an obituary which quoted the letter Forman had written to his wife in case of his death: 'I want it trumpeted from the roof-tops that Lionel Forman believed in communism for South Africa with a burning passion till he died and in all his adult years that passion never once diminished.' Duncan commented:

> His political standpoint was mellowed and humanized by a remarkable sense of humour and he seemed to enjoy the company of those who, while opposing *apartheid*, were most unfriendly to his own ideas. I liked him for this, and admired his truly magnificent courage. One felt that his illness had purged him of fear, that he had no fear even of death, and that he looked down on people who were afraid.[37]

One needs to add, too, that in a perverse way Duncan earned the admiration of many South African communists; they disagreed violently with him, they thought his anti-communism both wrong and ill advised, they thought his individualism as fanatic as he thought their ideology, but they admired him for his courage and steadfastness. This was no one's fellow-traveller.

It has nothing to do with his anti-communism but something to do with his attitude to people that, when he read in a newspaper that a Japanese sailor who could speak no English had been taken off a Japanese ship and put into Groote Schuur hospital, where he was dying, he took it on himself to go to visit the man; he could speak no Japanese, and the Japanese no English, but Duncan took him fruit and flowers and sat by his bedside during visiting-hours trying to communicate in sign-language. As he told friends when they discovered what he was doing, it could not be much fun dying alone in a country you did not know, the language of which you did not speak, and with none of your own people around.

If Duncan's increasingly open attack on communism was a negative side of his development during this time, a positive side was his growing interest in the Pan-Africanists. For some, particularly those in the Congress of Democrats, but even some Liberals, his interest was simply opportunism: the Pan-Africanists were attacking communist influence in the ANC, so Duncan listened to them, although they were anti-white and reactionary. Paton, for instance, criticized what he called Duncan's 'flirtation with Africanism'.[38] Obviously, given the depth of his opposition to communism, Duncan was attracted to the Pan-Africanists because of their attacks on communists; but the attraction is much more complex and lies not only in his sympathy for Nkrumah's Pan-Africanism.

The history of the Africanists in the ANC is usually traced to the formation of the ANC Youth League in 1944. The Youth League had been formed largely as a 'ginger group' to persuade the leadership of the ANC to base itself more on African Nationalism than on an ideology of class; its opposition to communists was based on an idea that communists served a master other than the needs of the Africans themselves. In 1954 disunity within the ANC was becoming a serious problem, especially in the Transvaal. The Africanists, who were concentrated in the lower echelons of the movement, particularly in the Orlando branch of the Youth League, were becoming increasingly outspoken in their criticism of the collaboration between the ANC leadership and sympathetic Indian and white organizations. The National Executive tried to discourage this sentiment by expelling P. K. Leballo, leader of the Orlando branch of the Youth League, from the movement. The branch immediately insisted on his reinstatement. Matters were not improved the following year when the national leadership were accused of hesitation, lack of militancy and poor organization in their handling of attempts to oppose the Bantu Education Act and the 'Western Areas Removals'. In 1956, the year of the Freedom Charter, the split in the ANC widened, and it became customary to talk to two groups, the 'Charterists' and the 'Africanists', the latter concentrated in a few Johannesburg branches (notably Orlando) and in the Western Cape, and talking (and writing in their periodical, *The Africanist*) in racially exclusive terms: even the most sympathetic white could not help but dissipate the power of the purely African movement; what was needed was to harness the power of the black people as a coherent national group, without any white sympathy or guidance. Discontent was made even stronger by the failure of the 1958 stay-at-home campaign when branches of the ANC dominated by Africanists refused to participate (whether the Africanists caused the failure or merely recognized how inadequately the campaign was being planned is a matter of argument); in November 1958 Luthuli called on the Africanists to reject 'racial chauvinism' and, after a great deal of argument and indeed violence, the Africanists, including the entire Orlando branch, were expelled from the meeting, and set themselves up as an organization to be 'custodians of ANC policy as formulated in 1912' – that is, to act for Africans exclusively.[39]

In April 1959 the Africanists held a conference in Johannesburg at which the Pan-Africanist Congress was formed; the name alone reveals how the new ideas of continental Africa were beginning to influence South African political thinking. Nkrumah was the major hero in the PAC view of Africa – their flag, of Africa and a symbolic star, shows the star growing out of Ghana. The two major figures at the conference were Mangaliso Robert Sobukwe, a lecturer in African languages at the University of the Witwatersrand, an articulate and thoughtful man, and Josias Madzunya, much more demagogic and fiercely anti-white. Sobukwe was elected President, and in his statement of PAC policy argued against multi-racialism, against communism, for Nkrumahism and African socialism, and said, 'There is but one race – the human race – politics is not a matter of race or colour but of vital material and spiritual interest.'[40]

In the matter of his attitude to the PAC Duncan moved much more slowly than he usually did. He had known some of the Africanists a long time; for instance, as early as 1952 he had known Potlako Kitchener Leballo, a Mosotho, whom he had met through Cyprian Thorpe after Leballo had been 'named' as a communist by the government liquidator of the Communist Party; in 1953 he met Matthew Nkoana, a journalist and later to be on the PAC Executive; from 1954 he had known Zeph Mothopeng, who after being thrown out of his teaching job had come to Maseru with Mphahlele; from 1954 onwards he had become increasingly close to Jordan Ngubane who, as an old friend of Robert Sobukwe, was invited to attend the inaugural conference of the PAC, and did so, much to the upset of Johannesburg Liberals, one of whom asked at the 1959 Party Congress for his expulsion.[41]

As early as January 1958 Duncan wrote to Ngubane: 'My instincts tell me that the Charter has had it.... In so many ways – ideologically especially – the Liberals ought to be able to ally themselves with a non-chartist ANC.'[42] However, he went on to tell Ngubane that he had met Sobukwe the previous week, and 'felt that after talking to him there was little common ground between his views and ours. Co-operation with other race groups could come after reconquest....'[43] Still, he remained in touch with Sobukwe, who sent him some of the Africanists' publications. When the first two editions of *Contact* (before Duncan's editorship) appeared, Sobukwe wrote to him:

> I do wish to say that I found your first issue of *Contact* honest sincere and fearless. I cannot say the same for the second issue ... to be accused of fascist intentions and designs makes me sad rather than mad, for the simple reason that thousands of Africans hold precisely such views and when they learn that there is an organization accommodating such views they will not only support it but demand that the leadership of the Africanists should come out openly in favour of such sentiments. And once that stage is reached there will be no going back. And it will be White propagandists and their African stooges who will be responsible for such a state of affairs. The article on Congress could have been written by a COD propagandist. By stressing our *hatred* of the white man per se, you identify us with the masses who do not distinguish between oppressor and oppression and you, therefore do not discredit us but raise our stocks.[44]

Ngubane and Benjie Pogrund wrote fully about the development of the PAC in *Contact*, and Sobukwe and Nkoana wrote for it, too, the latter regularly. Moreover, when Duncan met Z. B. Molete, the PAC Publicity Secretary, and Jacob Nyaose of FOFATUSA (Federation of Free African Trade Unions of South Africa) he was impressed, this despite the fact that the month before Z. B. Molete had called Duncan a representative of a 'foreign national minority' and had accused him of trying to 'cash in' on his 'so-called participation' in the Defiance Campaign.[45]

There were two other strong personal influences on Duncan, one Joe Nkatlo, who had been expelled from the Communist Party in the 1940s and who had been on the Africanist side of the ANC until he joined the Liberal Party, the other Randolph Vigne. It was in Joe Nkatlo's house in Woodstock that Nana Mahomo lodged (Mahomo, a Transvaaler, then at the University of Cape Town and an executive member of the PAC, was at the time doing much to establish the PAC in the African locations) and it was through Nkatlo that Randolph Vigne, one of the most radical of the *Contact* Liberals, met Mahomo and later Philip Kgosana, who was by March 1960 to be the main leader of the PAC in the Cape.

From the start Nkatlo and Vigne were strongly for the PAC. Nkatlo was deeply disillusioned with the ANC; and Vigne, unlike Duncan, had no links with the ANC – he had come direct to Cape Town from Oxford, and the ANC was relatively weak in Cape Town, except in the person of Thomas Ngwenya, an old trade unionist more liberal than most Liberals but fiercely loyal to the ANC and especially to Luthuli himself. Vigne describes himself as having been 'number one white pal' to the PAC from 1959, when he had been very deeply impressed by two PAC organizers, Mlokoti and Matros, both labourers, who had come to visit him, uninvited. Vigne wrote a report for a Liberal Party National Executive meeting which he persuaded Duncan to present for him, particularly since Sobukwe had also written to the Liberal Party asking for their support in the Anti-Pass Campaign planned for March 1960: Vigne wished the PAC to be treated very seriously; it was not at all the joke that many thought it at the time, and he was convinced that it would have an enormous influence.

With all these pressures on him, one might have expected Duncan to commit himself much more wholeheartedly and instantaneously to the PAC. His commitment did tend to come very suddenly; yet it is clear that he went very cautiously with the PAC. For instance, when he delivered the report on behalf of Vigne, he did so critically; and, in dealing with the letter from Sobukwe, he was for the majority view that the reply should be friendly but non-committal. Matthew Nkoana recalls that when he saw him in 1959 Duncan was critical of Sobukwe:

> He was pointing out that Sobukwe was carrying on as a lecturer at Wits and this seemed to him to be in conflict with the other things that Sobukwe was doing. When I said to him, 'You give an example of colonial leaders who acted the way Sobukwe should have,' he said, 'Mahatma Gandhi.'[46]

It is evident, too, that despite the fact that *Contact* published a great deal of material on the PAC and some by PAC members it remained largely neutral, for instance stressing inconsistencies in its racial attitudes and denying its claims to a membership of twenty thousand. Like the ANC leaders, Duncan thought the PAC had only about two or three thousand members.[47] Some articles on the PAC were fiercely critical – for instance, one headlined 'Africanist flop' about one of Madzunya's Durban meetings.⁴⁸

The major proof is in *Contact*'s handling of the build-up to the Anti-Pass Campaign of March 1960. The issue of *Contact* immediately before the Campaign had as its cover photograph Huddleston, Makiwane of the ANC and Gaitskell at a meeting in London calling for a boycott of South African goods; the headlines are 'The Federation – end in sight', 'Boycott of Union Festival gains ground'. The story about the PAC Campaign is at the bottom of page 2, headlined 'Only a few weeks away? PAC Campaign will be test'. The *Contact* correspondent (obviously not a PAC man) wrote:

> It is impossible to estimate what hope of success the campaign has.... It is possible that with large numbers of PAC members offering themselves for arrest, other Africans will follow suit.... This could catapult the Pan-Africanist Congress into national prominence almost overnight. It could lead to a massive build-up of support.... If, on the other hand, the Africanists fail to rally a substantial number of people to their campaign call, the result could be their total eclipse....
>
> At the moment, there are no ready answers.... [They] will come when the campaign begins, until then, no one knows.⁴⁹

This is hardly the report of a paper which has given wholehearted support to a movement. The next issue of *Contact*, with its banner headline, 'Apartheid – the end approaches', a photograph of 'The man – Mr Mangaliso R. Sobukwe talks with supporters', headlines that 'United Nations must intervene', and 'The truth about Sharpeville – only eyewitness account of massacre, exclusive to *Contact*', ⁵⁰ is the first real commitment by Duncan and *Contact* to the PAC.

Duncan's first worry about the PAC was the use it made of anti-white feelings among Africans; as early as 1958 *Contact* had reported a 'leading Africanist' as saying:

> Even if we grant the sincerity of the whites, Indians and Coloureds, who want to collaborate with us, the fact remains that the only way in which white domination will ever be broken is by black force. When that day comes, if we have to stop and ask ourselves whether a particular white man was a friend of ours in the past, then we will never be able to act.⁵¹

On the other hand, Duncan knew many PAC men personally, and personally they were not racialists; moreover, he was enough of a political realist to understand the problems of African politicians. For all his attacks on 'multi-racialism' in the Congress Alliance, he had written in 1957: 'The Liberals ... must realize the very difficult position with Africans that African leaders get into when they become dependent on white support. There is trouble in the ANC at the moment over this.'⁵²

A second reason for his holding back is more probable. Although it suited the communists to equate Duncan's attacks on the influence of communists in the ANC with attacks on the ANC, Duncan was in fact deeply loyal to the ANC and some of its leaders; his attacks on communists were made in loyalty to his idea of the ANC. After all, he had gone to jail for the ANC in 1952; he had been jailed for attending the ANC Conference in Queenstown in 1956; he had tried hard to get the ANC to accept him as a member; he had been one of the strongest advocates of the ANC and LP co-operation; he admired Luthuli – even after his 'Open Letter' he again and again expressed public admiration of him, as in *Contact* of 13 June 1959, with Luthuli's photograph on the front cover, a lead story on a successful ANC rally, and a leader attacking the banning of Luthuli. Moreover, if he was influenced on the one hand by Vigne, Nkatlo, Ngubane, he was also very close to old Thomas Ngwenya of the ANC, whom he regarded as one of the finest men he had ever known, nor did he lightly disregard the advice of men like Jock Isacovitz, Eddie Roux, Peter Brown and Alan Paton, who shared so much of his political thinking and who had little regard for the PAC. For instance, writing to Paton in November 1959, Duncan stressed how important he felt it for *Contact* 'to be impartial on the subject' of the split between the ANC and the PAC.[53] This was not simply an editor speaking; this was a politician.

The third reason is the simplest. Although he liked and admired some of the PAC leaders for their energy, dislike of communism, attitudes to Africa, he was not at all sure any of them had the potential to be *satyagrahi*, and he was still a devoted Gandhist. As he told Nkoana, Gandhi would not have kept on his job in the way Sobukwe did; and, if their leader was not a Gandhi, would their movement succeed?

These three reasons were more than enough to hold him back from the commitment some of his friends urged on him. It was not until the PAC demonstrated in action that it had two qualities that he was most in search of – first, the ability to gain a mass-following, to tap the source of power that he knew was the one hope of change and, secondly, the ability to practise non-violence as the Mahatma would have advised – that he began to commit himself.

After his refusal even to consider standing as a coloured representative in 1957–8, and his insistence that during the general election of 1958 he should be allowed either to resign as National Organizer or to take unpaid leave, and in the light of his conviction that the only real power lay in the hands of black mass-movements, Duncan's decision to stand in the white elections for the Cape Provincial Council in late 1959 was surprising.

There were several reasons. First, there were murmurings of political change. There were rumours of an impending split in the United Party, which did in fact occur in 1959 when a group of more liberal United Party MPs and their supporters broke away to form a new Progressive Party. There was increasing international pressure on South Africa, both in the United Nations and in the boycott of South African goods. The PAC had broken away from the Congress Alliance. The Liberal Party seemed to be gaining black support. Even within the Nationalist Party there were rifts between hard-liners and those who wanted to push Verwoerd's version of *apartheid* ahead faster. Secondly, the Cape Liberal Party was now mainly in the control of the *Contact* Liberals: the constituency the party chose to fight was Sea Point, where Randolph Vigne was Chairman of an active branch which had already made some impression on the constituency (in the general election of 1958, the Liberal Party candidate, Gerald Gordon, had taken 1642 votes); the election agent was Peter Hjul; and, as well as some of the older Liberals like Oscar Wollheim and Gerald Gordon, the main team for the election included

Joe Daniels and Joe Nkatlo. Thirdly, Duncan made one condition in accepting nomination: he would be free to say what he really believed, to take a hard line, not give woolly answers in the hope of catching votes. The *Liberal Party Cape Divisional News* said:

> We are well aware that some members might occasionally find Mr Duncan's political forthrightness a little disconcerting, but this is not the time to soothe the electorate with empty phrases or with lofty sentiments so ambiguously phrased as to be meaningless.[54]

The election campaign was active: more than 140 canvassers went out (including some COD members) and visited some 5000 voters; there were a number of well-attended public meetings; there was much discussion and argument, both among Liberals, their supporters, and their opponents. The United Party was shaken by the defection of the Progressive Party, and its original candidate for Sea Point withdrew and was replaced by Dr Jan Dommisse, an actuary and formerly Smuts's private secretary. As the party news-sheet had predicted, Duncan did manage to disconcert even his supporters: when asked if he were in favour of the boycott, he replied that, although his party was uncommitted, he personally thought it 'a thoroughly good thing'. Asked if 'Natives and Coloureds' should be allowed to use the famous Sea Point swimming-pools, he replied, 'I do not like the idea of a colour bar in South Africa, including baths. Only in Southern Africa could such a question be asked.'[55] When he was asked the question subsequently, he took to replying simply 'Yes'. Even some *Contact* Liberals said this answer was impolitic; he could so easily have answered, 'I'd prefer it if only clean people use the swimming baths', and so turned the question back on the questioner. But he was trying to tell the truth, and so win votes, not lie to win them. Of course the election at once became the 'swimming-bath election', and the United Party canvassers and speakers worked hard to use Duncan's answer against him.

What nearly ruined Duncan's campaign was not his honest answers, but a serious illness. He had in fact been very ill in April 1959, just before the time of Emma's birth, and had had agonizing stomach cramps. Instead of seeing a doctor, he took off from Cape Town for Miss Murray's farm in Elgin, where he stayed five days walking, sleeping, and reading Trollope; he refused a special diet, just asked for time on his own. To Lewin he wrote, 'I cured myself'.[56] On 2 September, just before speaking at a public meeting in Hout Bay, he told Cynthia he was feeling so ill that he would stay outside in the car until it was time for him to speak; she sat with him, and he was grey with pain, and shaking. Then he went in to speak, and Cynthia remembers it as the very best speech she ever heard him make, funny, passionate and very moving. Later that night, he woke Cynthia and said he would have to go to hospital; by the early hours he was in a nursing home, and next morning the surgeon operated from 8.30 a.m. to 1.45 p.m. on a set of badly perforated duodenal ulcers. At one stage, the surgeon and anaesthetist thought he might even die under the anaesthetic and, soon afterwards, the surgeon told Cynthia that Patrick would be in hospital at least a month, and would need six months' recuperation. In fact, he was back on a public platform in eleven days, having made a miraculous recovery from what was after all a major abdominal operation; he had his usual row with his doctor, because he refused to take any of the pain-killing pills prescribed for him after the operation.

In the voting on 14 October, Duncan polled 1505 votes, something less than Gerald Gordon had polled in 1958, but the United Party majority was down from 5625 to 4476, so the Liberals could count it as a victory. Looking back on the election in 1966, he wrote to Peter Hjul:

> What did we try to do? We tried to enlist the consciences of white voters to vote against their stomachs, their tribes and their fears. Obviously, in retrospect the attempt could not have succeeded, but it was worth doing, just for itself, even if there are no long-term good effects. But, even here I believe that there will be good effects, to a tiny degree, in the future of South Africa.[57]

However, in the immediate future of the next four or five months of 1959 and 1960 it was all to seem very insignificant.

CHAPTER 9

December 1959–62
'We are not leading corpses
to a new Africa'

In December 1959, at a PAC conference in Johannesburg, Sobukwe announced that 'positive action' would begin with a campaign against the passes that all adult Africans were required to carry; passes would be left at home, and PAC volunteers would seek arrest. Their slogan was to be 'No Defence, No Bail, No Fine'; the leaders would set an example by being the first to submit themselves for arrest; and this was to be a campaign, not a demonstration, since the aim was to compel the government to repeal the pass laws by making the system impossible to enforce. After this would come a series of other campaigns, which would lead to 'independence' by 1963. No date was specified for the start of the Anti-Pass Campaign; only Sobukwe and a handful of those in the leadership knew the date.

Afterwards, Duncan was to write that the Anti-Pass Campaign 'wore the face of Gandhi not of Hitler'[1] but, as we have already seen, *Contact* treated the build-up to the Campaign very cautiously. Indeed, in January and February Duncan was more involved in two other activities, the first visiting Basutoland and renewing his political connections there, the second trying to influence the views of Harold Macmillan, the British Prime Minister, who was then visiting South Africa for talks with the government. It was not until the Campaign was under way that he even began to think of an alliance between the Liberal Party in the Cape and the PAC, or even to regard the PAC as at last providing the mass-movement he was in search of.

The main purpose of his visit to Basutoland in January 1960 was to study the elections, the first under the new constitution, largely the brainchild of Denis Cowen, in which the Basotho and other voters in 162 constituencies voted for the nine District Councils, which would then elect forty members to the new Legislative Council; also on the Legislative Council would be twenty-two senior chiefs, fourteen people nominated by the Paramount Chief, and four by the Administration. The Legislative Council would then in its turn elect three members of the Executive Council of eight; one other would be nominated by the Paramount Chief, and four by the Administration. It was, in other words, the first time in southern Africa that a large share of political power was being granted to an overwhelmingly black electorate. Duncan was very impressed by the election, and saw it as

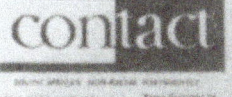

APARTHEID—THE END APPROACHES

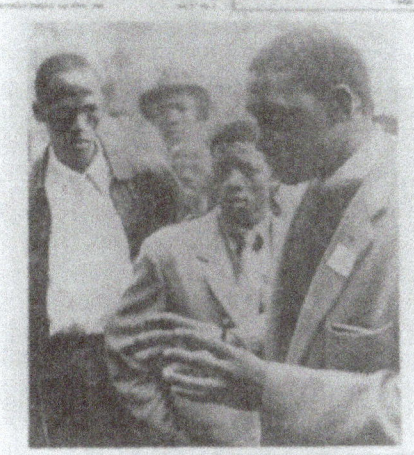

THE MAN—MR. MANGALISO R. SOBUKWE TALKS WITH SUPPORTERS

18   (above left) Cover page from Contact, *2 April 1960*

19   (above right) Cover page from Contact *16 April 1960. 'PAC campaign reveals the power of non-violence'*

20   (left) Philip Kgosana

21   (below) Philip Kgosana leads part of the crowd of 30 000 on his way to Caledon Square, Cape Town, on 30 March 1960

22   *Chief Leabua Jonathan, 1960*   23   *Jordan Ngubane*

24   *The Duncan children. From left to right: Emma, Ann, Alex, Patrick*

justifying his longstanding belief in universal suffrage; he renewed his friendships with Ntsu Mokhehle, Khatetla and Leabua Jonathan, and said that the results, which gave Mokhehle's Congress Party seventy-three seats and the National Party only twenty-two, were both a 'shattering set-back for Chief Leabua Jonathan'² and an enthusiastic endorsement of Mokhehle's potential as a leader and of the Congress Party's programme for independence soon. He argued that the BCP's success did not mean a spurning of the chieftainship, as other commentators had said, and pointed to the fact that the BCP had not exploited the issue of whether or not Constantine Bereng Seeiso be 'placed' as Paramount Chief and take over power from his father's senior wife, the Regent. What was happening in Basutoland would, Duncan was sure, influence events in South Africa in the direction of racial sanity.

The other event which preoccupied him in late January and early February was the visit to southern Africa of Harold Macmillan, at the end of his extended African tour. Duncan had an introduction to one of Macmillan's entourage, John Wyndham, and wrote a letter to him in Pretoria to await his arrival; but, because there had been controversy in the press over the extent to which Verwoerd was controlling whom Macmillan would see, he then telephoned Wyndham and urged that Macmillan see black leaders (other than government stooges) and the Liberal Party; he gave Wyndham the names and addresses of Luthuli, Paton and Mrs Ballinger (he was then still taking Luthuli as the crucial black leader). Wyndham promised to pass Duncan's comments on, but said no more. Duncan was not hopeful.

It transpired in fact that Macmillan and his entourage were annoyed at just how tight a rein was being kept on whom they saw; but, diplomatically, there was little they could do, until they reached Cape Town. There, the High Commissioner, Sir John Maud, had included among those invited to a garden-party for Macmillan the Anglican Archbishop of Cape Town, Joost de Blank, known for his outspoken opposition to *apartheid*, the Ballingers and the Duncans. Since the garden-party included Cabinet Ministers, diplomats, and so on, it seems that Maud's invitation to the Ballingers and Duncans was deliberately intended to enable Macmillan to meet at least white opponents of the government. Duncan managed to get hold of Wyndham at the garden-party, and argued that there was still time for Macmillan to see black leaders; with Anthony Sampson and Thomas Ngwenya he had already concocted a plan to bring Z. K. Matthews to Cape Town to see Macmillan, and he urged this on Wyndham, who argued not that it was undesirable but that it would be dishonest of Macmillan to pretend to be consulting black leaders when in fact he would hardly be able to see them. (Once again, it is worthwhile noting that Duncan fixed on an ANC leader as the potential spokesman – Luthuli's ban of course prevented his leaving home.)

A little later at the garden-party, Wyndham introduced him to Macmillan, who had already taken Margaret Ballinger aside for a twenty-minute discussion, and had talked to the Archbishop; now Macmillan did the same with Duncan, saying to him, 'Let's get away somewhere where we can talk . . . tell me, when did your father die?' When they had found somewhere more private to sit, but still in view, he talked to Duncan about politics; Duncan wrote up the conversation soon afterwards:

HM   Tell me. *What's* going to happen in this country?

PD   Total breakdown of the present set-up in ten, or at the outside fifteen, years.

HM   What can we do to help?

PD   I think the vote at the United Nations is the most urgent thing.

HM   I told 'him' this morning that we'd probably have to abstain in future. You see, while Cyprus was still in the way there was a good political reason for saying it was a purely internal matter. But that's no longer so, and it is now a purely legal question. Some have one idea and some have another. In any case I'm not sure what is an internal matter. As I said to Jooste (External Affairs Secretary) 'If Hitler starts massacring Jews, is *that* an internal matter?'

They went on to discuss whether or not Macmillan should see some black leaders, Duncan noting at one point that Macmillan 'had suddenly become totally deaf. But ... *with perfect courtesy*'. According to Duncan, Macmillan seemed 'very interested and sympathetic'.[3]

By the time Duncan reported this conversation to Brown, Macmillan had already made his celebrated 'wind of change' speech; so Duncan's version might have the advantage of hindsight. Certainly, immediately after the garden-party he told Dot Cleminshaw, a fellow-member of the Liberal Party, that he did not think Macmillan would take the outspoken line which Liberals and others had been hoping for. Macmillan's speech had been written with the help of Sir John Maud and others, partly before his arrival in South Africa, though Macmillan worked on the speech himself up to the last stages of the tour; the big discussion in the entourage was whether the attack on *apartheid* would be 'in or out'.

In the event, Macmillan's speech to the House of Assembly next day did includes an attack on *apartheid*, albeit in the most gentlemanly and moderated of British tones.

> The wind of change is blowing through this continent ... this growth of national consciousness is a political fact ... it has been our aim ... to create a society which respects the rights of individuals ... in which individual merit, and individual merit alone, is the criterion for man's advancement, whether political or economic.... I hope you won't mind my saying frankly that there are some aspects of your policies which make it impossible for us to ... [support and encourage you] without being false to our own deep convictions about the political destinies of free men to which in our own territories we are trying to give effect....[4]

The speech had considerable effect, and at least one expression, 'the wind of change', seems likely to remain a permanent part of the language of colonial history (Macmillan had in fact used the phrase earlier in his tour though it was not noticed); the Afrikaans press, which had been hoping for, if not approval, at least a non-committal politeness, was very disturbed, and *Die Burger* reported as general reaction among MPs, 'We have been thrown to the wolves'.[5] The only Afrikaans paper which did not share the concern was *Die Landstem*, which had gone to press before the speech with the hopeful headline, 'Thank you Mac! Your visit is worth gold to us.'[6] In fact the price of shares fell. Part of the paralysis of will and the panic which affected the government and its supporters during the initial stages of the PAC Campaign was probably due to Macmillan's speech (though he could hardly have calculated this effect). The ANC welcomed the speech, especially its references to the United Nations, and Duncan sent a telegram to Macmillan which read: 'I have just listened with deep emotion and gratitude to your historic speech. You spoke for the human race and for all the best in British and South African traditions. I am convinced that your speech will over many years exert a profound influence for good in this country torn as it is by natural and synthetic divisions.'⁷ Although the PAC would certainly not have shared exactly those sentiments, it could not have avoided sharing some of the mood which the speech created: the South African government was on its own now; it could not look for a non-committal response from Britain to its policies; it was going to lose British support in the United Nations; it might be forced out of the Commonwealth; it could be shaken very easily.

On 18 March Sobukwe and Kgosana announced simultaneously in the Transvaal and Cape that the Anti-Pass Campaign would begin on 21 March: there would be no violence; campaigners would obey reasonable instructions from the police; and the slogan, 'No Defence, No Bail, No Fine' was reiterated. Kgosana said: 'We are not leading corpses to a new Africa.'⁸ Men were to leave their passes at home and present themselves for arrest, women were to stay at home, no one was to go to work until the pass system was abolished and a minimum wage established.

No one – outside the PAC – was sure how seriously to take the Campaign. ANC leaders derided it, saying it was no more than an attempt to pre-empt their own campaign, due to start on 31 March. The white press largely ignored the call; after all, the last stay-at-home in 1958 had been a flop. The police took few special precautions. Even *Contact* would say no more than 'if' and 'could', and only a handful of *Contact* Liberals like Vigne were prepared for what happened. Although Z. B. Molete had claimed a membership of twenty-four thousand for the PAC, Duncan himself accepted the ANC's estimate of two or three thousand only; however, he knew that the PAC in the Western Cape was stronger than in most areas except the southern Transvaal, and that there were PAC men active in the Cape. One of them, Philip Kgosana, a first-year student at the University of Cape Town in 1959, had approached him in that year for financial help: he had only a grant for fees from the institute of Race Relations, and was in fact having to live in one of the Langa's 'bachelor-flats' or dormitories, where most single migrant workers were housed in conditions of great discomfort. Duncan gave him £2 and appointed him an agent for *Contact*. Duncan was, through Vigne and Nkatlo, also in touch with Nana Mahomo, though by March 1960 he had left Cape Town on his way overseas to represent the PAC. Vigne, Hjul, Nkatlo and other Liberals, too, were in touch with other PAC organizers, and some were working actively with them. Some PAC meetings had been reported in *Contact*; but how far the extent of PAC organization was known to Liberals is uncertain. Part of the reason for this is that many of the PAC leaders were in fact workers, and not intellectuals or students: twenty-nine of the thirty-one PAC leaders later tried in Cape Town for incitement were described as 'labourers' and Vigne's contacts in the PAC, Mlokoti and Matros, were both manual labourers, though the first was an educated man. After the event, it became known that there were PAC branches in a number of Cape locations, even outside the immediate area of Cape Town – for instance, in Paarl – though still the best estimate gave the PAC in the Cape in late 1959 only about a thousand members.

In the event, actual membership was to be of little importance, though lack of extended organization was to be more serious. By February, when Sobukwe and Leballo (then National Secretary) visited the Cape, the PAC was capable of drawing three hundred to a meeting in Nyanga. At the trial of the thirty-one leaders, a diary of one, Ralph Mbatsha, was produced as evidence and showed that he had done some organizing in Worcester and in Sea Point (Worcester was one of the few places where coloured workers joined Africans in striking, but this was probably more due to the established activities of the Food and Canning Workers' Union, which had both coloured and African members, than to PAC organization). PAC members had distributed pamphlets to Cape Town dockers on 19 March to persuade them to stay away from work. Most significantly, a 'Task Force' of young PAC volunteers had been set up in the Cape Town townships, and on the day before the Campaign officially started, Sunday 20 March, Kgosana addressed large PAC meetings at both Nyanga and Langa.

Early in the morning on Monday 21 March about six thousand men began to gather in the rain outside the bachelor-dormitories at Langa New Flats. When Kgosana arrived, he told the crowd that they would go to Langa police station to be arrested; then Makwetu, Secretary of the New Flats branch, reminded the volunteers that there was to be no violence. Soon afterwards the police arrived; they warned Kgosana that a march on the police station would be taken as an attack, and he dispersed the meeting, but also told the police that no one would be going to work that day.

At Nyanga, PAC supporters gathered on the rugby field; at 7.30 the first volunteers started for Philippi police station, a mile from the field, where a number were arrested. Collingwood August, a *Contact* Liberal who lived in Nyanga and who sympathized with the PAC, wrote in his diary:

> I am surprised at the large number of peasant-type demonstrators. Normally they take little interest in politics. They are the migrant labour and they are the section of Africans hardest hit by the pass laws. But it is still surprising and a revelation that at last a political call that appeals to them has been raised.[9]

In white Cape Town itself there was no need for anyone to bring news that the stay-at-home was working; very few African workers had arrived that morning. In the *Contact* office there was great excitement; perhaps the PAC claim had not been exaggerated after all. By one o'clock, when the first news of the massacre by police of campaigners at Sharpeville came through on the radio (forty dead, said first reports, not the actual sixty-eight), the excitement had changed to something else. Similarly the feelings in the townships also underwent a subtle change; whereas in the area around Sharpeville and Orlando the killings effectively ended the Anti-Pass Campaign almost before it had begun, in the Cape the PAC gained new determination.

Kgosana then left the townships and went to the *Contact* office, on his way to visit some of those PAC men who had been arrested at Philippi police station and taken to Caledon Square, the headquarters of the Cape Town Police. His account has Duncan in great excitement and saying to him, 'You have poked the bees but you must be very careful. Anything can happen tonight.'[10] According to Duncan's diary, Kgosana 'understood the dangers of the situation and the ever present possibility of violence erupting'.[11] According to Peter Hjul, also there at the time, Kgosana was very worried about the possibility of violence; he told *Contact* that afternoon:

> The senior officer in charge of the police [at Langa] refused to arrest me. He wanted to know who would control the demonstrators when I was in gaol. I told him that our demonstration was opposed to any form of violence. At this he shook my hand in congratulation.[12]

Immediately after this interview, Duncan took Kgosana off to the *Cape Times* where he told reporters what had happened that morning and repeated that the PAC abjured violence.

By 5.45 p.m. on the 21st, while Kgosana was on the train returning from his newspaper interviews, six thousand people had gathered in the open space in front of Langa police station. The police tried to disperse the crowd by driving into them with their vans and Saracen armoured cars; stones were thrown at the police, and some of the police picked up stones to throw them back, while the crowd chanted 'Cowards' and 'Kill the white men'. Firing started after the police command for the crowd to break up in three minutes had been ignored. Four people were killed instantly.

That night, as Duncan and Kgosana had feared, rioting broke out in Langa. Public buildings were burned and the mutilated body of a man who had driven two white journalists into Langa was found the next morning.

Paradoxically, the main reason that the Campaign kept going in Cape Town after the shootings was the efforts the government had made to drive Africans out of Cape Town and back to their reserves, mainly in the Transkei; from 1957 the 'influx control' laws had been very much toughened up and were enforced by the central government, not by the municipality (which was more inclined to feelings of humanity). Anything which might encourage a settled African community was discouraged; men who came to work in Cape Town were not allowed to bring their families, and people illegally there were ruthlessly 'endorsed out' to the reserves. The proportion of migrant labour in the African population in the Cape is the highest in the Republic. The men's communal hostels, the 'bachelor-flats', which in 1960 held 18 276 men in Langa, were such unspeakable places – cold, crowded, squalid, disease-ridden, without any privacy for anyone – that it is not surprising the men who lived there were more reckless than settled householders. Kgosana, who assumed the overall leadership of the Cape Campaign, lived in the 'bachelor-flats' himself – at such close quarters, organization was a relatively easy matter, once a mood was established. Certainly, the strike was to gather momentum throughout the week. On Tuesday morning the hostels in Langa were raided and white and black policemen burst into people's rooms and beat up whomever they found in them and, later that day, the PAC 'Task Force' put up road-blocks in Nyanga to prevent the police coming in.

Some time before, Duncan had planned a dinner-party for the Wednesday night at which he planned to introduce Thomas Ngwenya of the ANC to Anton Rupert, the Afrikaans tobacco magnate and financier who Duncan thought had liberal leanings; now he invited Kgosana, Randolph Vigne and another black student at the University, Fikile Bam, to join the dinner-party, which they did. In his diary, Duncan wrote, 'a useful and friendly meeting',[13] though Vigne remembers a much less comfortable occasion. Certainly, the conjunction of old Ngwenya of the ANC, young Kgosana of the PAC, Anton Rupert the rich man of Afrikanerdom, Vigne, Fikile Bam and the Duncans must have made it one of South Africa's more extraordinary dinner-parties, particularly as it took place while the townships were on strike. In some countries, it is possible to imagine such a combination plotting a coup; in South Africa in 1960 it was merely ludicrous, and Duncan's hope that Ngwenya and Kgosana would persuade Rupert to put pressure on the government to negotiate with the strikers was not fulfilled.

On Thursday 24th, Kgosana was again in Cape Town, both at the *Contact* and the *New Age* offices; Duncan was very displeased when he heard that Kgosana had been in touch with Bunting and *New Age*, and would have been even more displeased to find out that, the day before, Kgosana had arranged for COD to bring a truckload of food into the township. Duncan in his diary says:

I spoke to him about Bunting. I said that the PAC campaign was his campaign, and he must run it the way he wanted, but that if he were to work closely with Bunting he would have to count us out. I reminded him that Sobukwe had split with the ANC over the question of communist domination, and told him that the Liberal Party was firmly anti-communist. He was extraordinarily nice about it, and thanked me for the advice. 'I am still very young,' he said, 'and shall always be grateful to you for advice when you see any way in which you think we are going wrong.'[14]

Kgosana's version is rather different:

In his presence, and unaware of his irreconcilable relations with Brian Bunting, I telephoned the latter and informed him that I was calling on him shortly. I did not complete my telephone conversation with Brian when Duncan jumped onto his feet and literally pounced [sic] the telephone receiver from my hand and cut it off with a bang, in great flurry. He was furious that I had any deals with 'communists' at all.

I took him coolly and left the office. I rushed into the nearest telephone booth and called Bunting....[15]

While Kgosana was in Cape Town, a hundred and one PAC volunteers left Langa and presented themselves at Caledon Square for arrest. By the evening the government had banned all public meetings. By the end of the week half the African labour force in the Cape Peninsula was to be away from work, the most successful strike in South Africa at the time.

On Friday 25th, Kgosana, Makwetu and others led a demonstration of PAC supporters to Caledon Square; there were between two and five thousand of them, and most came by train. At 9.30 a.m. Kgosana telephoned Duncan from the Grand Parade in central Cape Town to warn him that the demonstrators were on their way to hand themselves over to the police: 'They have seen yesterday the police had room to arrest 101 men and they want to join them. Come quickly,' he said.[16] By the time of the telephone call only a small group had arrived, but soon the street was dotted with small groups of men, and when Kgosana approached the police station from the Grand Parade they gathered in a crowd in front of it. (It is important, in view of later recriminations, to note that Kgosana actually *asked* Duncan to join him outside the police station.) Duncan arrived to find a good humoured and relaxed crowd; he noticed many dockers and saw approvingly that 'Task Force' runners were preventing the demonstrators from blocking the pavements or disturbing the traffic. Kgosana, however, had already been arrested and taken inside the police station. Colonel Terblanche, who was facing the crowd, then asked Duncan for advice, and was told to speak to those PAC leaders who remained unarrested. This he agreed to do, and at 11.40 a.m. five PAC men, Terblanche and Duncan went into the building, where Makwetu told Terblanche that the people outside were ready to surrender themselves for being without passes. Terblanche replied that he had no intention of arresting anybody who was breaking pass laws at that moment and then went on to promise that until things returned to normal he would see to it that no one would have to show his pass in the Cape Town area. The PAC leaders then demanded the release of Kgosana and the other leaders, and with Duncan's help they managed to persuade Terblanche to let them go.

At 12.10 p.m. all the PAC leaders and Duncan went out in front of the crowd, who were told by Makwetu that they should return home. The crowd at first booed the speaker but then marched off chanting, singing, and carrying Kgosana shoulder high. Police armed with sten guns escorted the men to the location, where they were greeted by women and children doing what the white press called 'screaming' but in fact ululating.

Kgosana was to say later that Duncan's part in the events angered him, that he was furious Duncan had taken it on himself to negotiate for the PAC.[17] There is no evidence he felt so at the time and there was no break in their close co-operation at that point. Certainly, the PAC had scored a considerable victory; they had forced the police to negotiate and make concessions. Moreover, Terblanche's statement that pass laws would be suspended was soon afterwards backed by the Chief of Police, Rademeyer, and then extended to the whole country by the Minister of Justice, Erasmus. In a sense the Campaign had been won, albeit temporarily.

A curious relationship was beginning to develop between the PAC leaders and the police authorities, one that is confirmed by Terblanche's own version of the events of the 30th; Duncan's part in getting the two sides to talk to each other was crucial in this. Though it is untrue that he took decisions out of the hands of the PAC, nevertheless it is unlikely that any such negotiations would have taken place without his intervention. One version of events has it that Terblanche had some reason to be grateful to Duncan's father, who had apparently helped him in some way; but Duncan did not mention this in his diary, and Cynthia does not recall his saying anything like this at the time. It needs saying that Terblanche was a conscientious policeman who did his best to prevent violence, at any rate in the early stages of the Campaign, if only because he knew how shaky his control of the situation was; compared to some South African policemen, he was a model of sympathetic tolerance. It is also an aspect of the Gandhian version of passive resistance that co-operation between authorities and resisters is necessary.

In the short term the relationship of the police and the PAC leaders was to strengthen the PAC hold on the townships. Hjul claims that Duncan's object was to enhance the importance of the PAC – to make the police recognize that the PAC controlled the townships.[18] Judging by the increasing success of the strike in the days that followed, it seems that the police did harass the campaigners less, and the degree of PAC control is apparent from an entry in Collingwood August's diary: 'I put in a brief appearance at the [*Contact*] office, I must leave soon. The permission given to me by the task force, the youths of the PAC who have complete control of the township, is due to expire.'[19]

By Saturday 26th food in the locations was getting desperately short; traders were no longer willing to replenish stores and men were not bringing home pay-packets. Duncan began raising money from Cape Town businessmen to buy food, and Eulalie Stott, a Liberal Party member though not of the *Contact* group, successfully persuaded some wholesalers to replenish stores. Relief supplies raised by Duncan and Mrs Stott were taken in on lorries driven by volunteer white women escorted by PAC 'Task Force' men and Kgosana himself; two food-trucks were unloaded that afternoon in Langa, where food distribution was in the hands of the PAC Committees. Altogether Duncan raised £1800 for food and for the PAC, with the specific purpose of prolonging the strike and the control by the PAC of the locations.

Duncan's diary entry for Saturday 26th is this:

> The Nyanga East Committee came into the offices of Contact.... They asked us to introduce them to the police and I rang Colonel Terblanche.... He was obviously glad to know they wanted to see him, and made arrangement to meet them at Caledon Square. He assured me of their personal safety. Before the committee went off to see Terblanche I told them that I had sensed, on the Wednesday, that the police were very worried about the road blocks that had been built in Nyanga. I said it was difficult to see the point of them, that the police could only regard them as a provocation and as a challenge to their authority and that it might be wise to pull them down. They claimed that they had been put up by the 'Tsotsis' (gangs of youths) but that they would do what they could.

It is a passage which defines the limits of the Campaign, both on the PAC side and on Duncan's. Some will see in Duncan's trust of the police and his desire for the maintenance of law and order a manifestation of his class and of the way in which Liberals, perhaps unconsciously, always tried to moderate black radicalism, though, of course, if Duncan had merely acted in the interests of his class, he would not have helped to get food and money to the strike-bound locations. More importantly, however, Duncan's anxiety to co-operate with the authorities when they behaved in a way that he considered to be honourable and gentlemanly arose from his belief in *satyagraha*. Unjust laws could be disobeyed, but those who disobeyed them had to be willing to accept the penalty and by their example of suffering induce a change of heart in the authorities. Road-blocks implied defiance of the state's authority, not a willingness to accept it and suffer the consequences.

On Sunday 27th, the seventh day of the Campaign, Kgosana and the Langa and Nyanga PAC Committees visited Duncan at Keyser House. Later that day a Cape Liberal Party Executive meeting was called in Sea Point which discussed the possibility of the party being banned, and which agreed that a ban would be ignored; Duncan also got approval of his plan for the Liberal Party to spend the next few days raising money for the PAC.

By Monday 95 per cent of the African workers in the Cape Peninsula were on strike; Luthuli's call for a one-day stay-at-home on Monday 28th to mourn the dead of Sharpeville and Langa contributed to the high percentage, although PAC leaders derided his call as 'moderate'. On the other hand, coloured workers, except at Worcester, were black-legging.

The same day, yet another appeal was made to Duncan for help, this time by the Nyanga PAC Committee; their Chairman, Mlokoti, and his deputy, Matros, had been arrested at Philippi police station early in the Campaign. Duncan again telephoned Terblanche, though what Terblanche's answer was Duncan did not record; he did, however, tell Terblanche that the Liberals would co-operate with the police provided they kept the peace 'by reasonable and humane methods'.[20] Terblanche now fulfilled his side of the bargain by helping Duncan and Kgosana hire a public-address system for the Langa PAC Committee without the normal guarantees about its safe-keeping; the system was needed for the mass funeral of the Langa dead. Terblanche also agreed to keep the police away from the funeral, which he did.

The fifty thousand who attended the funeral in the open air on Monday at Langa included ANC supporters – once the Campaign in the Cape was under way, individual members of the ANC and PAC seem to have forgotten their differences, though the leadership remained in the hands of PAC Committees. The funeral was mainly peaceful; non-violence was still the order of the day, as PAC speakers at the funeral reminded their followers. On the same day, legislation to ban both the PAC and the ANC was introduced into Parliament; the government was beginning at last to react. Two days later, a State of Emergency was declared and hundreds of people all over the country were detained, mainly members of the Congress Alliance, though some Liberals, too. No Cape Town Liberals, however, were detained; apparently the Minister of Justice asked for Duncan's arrest, but Colonel Terblanche advised against it, since without Liberals to provide a link with the townships he could not guarantee law and order. Though this may have been true, it was not enough to prevent Terblanche's men from repeating their attempts to break the strike. Police had broken into houses in Nyanga on the 28th and had shot at those who attempted to escape; then, early in the morning of Wednesday 30 March, the police raided Langa with immense brutality, breaking down doors, pulling people out of bed, beating them up, throwing them into the streets.

It was this last action which was the immediate provocation of the march of the thirty thousand into central Cape Town. It came after ten days of political crises, after a strike which had brought Cape industry to a standstill, after mass demonstrations had wrung concessions from the government, after Africans in Cape Town had had a chance to feel their power in a way that had never happened before. To call it 'spontaneous' as some commentators do is to ignore the events of the previous ten days; yet the march was (at least in part) the result of the growing groundswell of political elation among Africans, not simply a reaction to the cruelty of the police that morning. The Langa Committee claimed at the time that a massive march had in fact been planned – though for Thursday rather than Wednesday. The marchers moreover were not only from Langa; a contingent from Nyanga also began the long journey into Cape Town, though later in the day.

Whatever plans had been made beforehand, the PAC leaders were taken aback when the march began. Kgosana admits that when he first heard about it he was in bed and had to be given a lift by an American reporter to get to the head of the procession. He caught up with the marchers as they came to the Athlone–Pinelands railway-line, asked why they were marching, and was told it was to protest to the police in Caledon Square about the attacks of the morning. Kgosana then suggested that the objective should not be Caledon Square but the Houses of Parliament where they could find the Minister of Justice.

Some commentators argue that if the marchers had gone to Parliament there would have been a bloodbath; their version has it that, though the men were quiet, they were tense, and the slightest provocation would have broken their self-restraint.[21] There were enough armed policemen to have ensured a massacre. Duncan's diary says: 'Cape Town became like a city of war ... Parliament surrounded by armoured cars, and tense troops.'[22] Others argue that the police were weak and afraid and that the marchers could have taken over the whole of central Cape Town quite easily; certainly Terblanche's account of the march admits that at one stage he went on his knees to pray for guidance, and that he kept his policemen together rather than dispersing them to control the crowd. Still others argue that the mood of the crowd was not volatile, but peaceful, almost joyful, and genuinely non-violent. The phrase that Kgosana used again and again was (in English, since he did not speak much Xhosa, which was the language of most Cape Town blacks): 'ab-so-lute non-vi-o-lence', each syllable equally stressed, and even now he insists that the whole Campaign and the march of the 30th were essentially non-violent: 'I think we did our best to demonstrate our opposition to white domination and oppression. We were shot at, we never fired back; we were killed, we never killed a soul. . . .'[23]

As things turned out there was no attempt to march on Parliament; the march was to end peacefully at Caledon Square. Thousands of people joined the march at Mowbray railway station and then the procession took the De Waal Drive route into Cape Town, because there was less traffic that way. When cars came, the line of marchers good-humouredly made way for them, even if they contained whites. At an early stage of the march Eulalie Stott had tried to persuade Kgosana not to take his men to Parliament – the police reaction, she insisted, would be too awful.[24] Kgosana refused to reassure her, saying the matter was out of his hands. But when he was confronted by Detective Head Constable Sauerman at the intersection of Roeland and Buitenkant Streets, he agreed, after some argument, not to go on to Parliament.

At Caledon Square, Kgosana had another meeting with Terblanche and again he agreed to send the marchers home, this time in return for a promise of an appointment to see Erasmus, Minister of Justice, at Caledon Square at 5.00 p.m. Again, some have said that Liberals were directly responsible for persuading Kgosana to disperse his men and have praised them for doing so. More hostile versions view this as a betrayal: the Liberals got Kgosana to negotiate and turn back the men, thus surrendering power.[25] But no Liberals were directly involved on this occasion; Duncan was in fact in his office at the time.

After the marchers had gone home, Kgosana stayed in town; at that stage, some Liberals advised PAC men that Kgosana should not keep his appointment. However, at 5.00 p.m. he went to Caledon Square and was arrested. Cordons of troops and armoured cars were then thrown round Langa, though Nyanga was to be sealed off only three days later. Despite these events, both Hjul and Duncan believed that their faith in Terblanche had been justified, that Terblanche was overruled by his superiors.[26]

Despite the cordons – so strict that when two parents tried to carry their sick baby through the cordon at Nyanga to the Red Cross Hospital they were shot at and the baby killed[27] – resistance went on for a week. By 2 April both Nyanga and Langa were completely cut off; water and electricity to the townships had been turned off, and no one was allowed to enter or leave. The government called up the military reserves to reinforce the cordons and to guard the towns, and on the 4th the police moved into the townships. Men and women were beaten on the streets of Langa, were dragged from their homes and beds at all hours of the day and night, chased, arrested, shot. It took most of five days of continuous brutality to break the strike. *Contact* recorded twenty-eight cases of 'severe assault and injury' and claimed that this was only a fraction of those who had been beaten up. Now and then the people fought back using what weapons they had – on the 5th men began stoning a Saracen, which immediately opened fire on them. But by the 7th, when the suspension of the pass laws was revoked, the situation was 'normal' enough for the cordon to be lifted, though more police and military reinforcements were sent to Langa at the same time.

By the following Monday the strike was virtually over. For nearly three weeks the people of the Cape Town locations had presented the biggest challenge to face the government since the Defiance Campaign in 1952. Their non-violence had met with violence, and their resistance had been countered with all the machinery of the state; from that moment on, though passive resistance and non-violence remained techniques (necessary since the people had no weapons to fight with), they were only techniques and ceased to be principles. *Poqo* (the Xhosa word meaning 'alone', and used to describe the new underground PAC) was born.

Duncan was at the time still committed to the principles of Gandhism: he believed in *soul-force*; he believed in the essential decency of at least some Afrikaners (witness his attempts to influence Rupert, his trust in Terblanche's sense of honour, and a meeting he had on the afternoon of 25 March with Piet Cillié of *Die Burger*, in which Cillié apparently talked of 'concessions on wages, passes, housing to satisfy the town African'[28]); he believed that the power of the Campaign would make the government see reason and behave decently. When the State of Emergency was declared, he wrote in his diary: 'In my view the Government was compelled to do this, and I defended their moderation (up to date) in dealing with the Cape Town situation.'²⁹ In short, he was not in 1960 a revolutionary; when he supported the PAC, when he raised money for it, when he helped organize supplies of food to the townships, when he helped establish links between PAC Committees, when he talked to the police on their behalf, when he negotiated on the 25th for the release of their leaders, he was helping passive resistance, not encouraging a revolution.

He was in no way exceptional in this; the PAC Anti-Pass Campaign had been based from the start on passive resistance, on making the system unworkable by withdrawing labour and by overloading the machinery of oppression. The PAC leadership as much as Duncan himself failed to realize how far the government would be prepared to go in not making concessions: Kgosana and the PAC Committees in Langa and Nyanga themselves turned to Duncan for help, and Kgosana's later attacks on Duncan, in 1963 and afterwards, seem merely self-justificatory. When Kgosana asked for assistance, he asked for it in the terms that Duncan himself used at the time: passivity, negotiation and concession. To talk of Duncan and the Liberals betraying a revolution, which some of their critics do, is to add a revolutionary theory to a situation in which there was no revolutionary theory: it may possibly have been a revolutionary moment (though even that is a matter of dispute), but the leadership – whether PAC or Liberal – did not see it as such.

Much of Duncan's time and energy during the Campaign and the Emergency which followed went on keeping *Contact* in production. On 28 March he produced the 'Sharpeville' issue of *Contact*, with a picture of Sobukwe on the front cover, eye-witness accounts of the Sharpeville massacre, and a story of the Anti-Pass Campaign in the Cape, with a subheading, 'Peaceful meeting – until police arrived', and a long leader blaming the government and the police for the violence:

> Responsibility for the bloodbath of Sharpeville lies squarely on the authorities.... It does not lie with Robert Sobukwe and his Pan-Africanist Congress. They have done nothing more than to call on the people to challenge the pass-laws with non-violent resistance. It is true that they might have done it more wisely – there is much in the detailed planning of the campaign which is plain crazy. But they have chosen a noble and mighty weapon, the weapon of non-violent non-co-operation.

The leader goes on to defend Sobukwe and the PAC from some of the criticisms made of them, to praise them 'for their single-mindedness, their discipline, and their anti-communism', to warn them against racialism and to urge them to open 'the doors of their movement to all races ...'. On the back page is another editorial, 'UNITED NATIONS MUST INTERVENE'. Macmillan's speech had been 'the first blow at Dr Verwoerd's authority ...', the PAC Campaign the second, Sharpeville the third, and now the United Nations was calling South African *apartheid* a threat to the peace of the world. The choice was a bloodbath in South Africa or the intervention of a 'United Nations Emergency Force'.

On 29 March, with the declaration of the State of Emergency, Duncan and the rest of the *Contact* Board and staff decided that the production of the paper should be moved to another address, and most of the next day, the day of the great march, was spent, first, with the help of some of the PAC 'Task Force', in getting the number of 2 April, with publication date advanced by three days, wrapped and distributed and, secondly, in moving the production side of the paper to a secret address, where it stayed for a fortnight. Duncan himself went into hiding, as did other *Contact* Liberals, and worked on the next number, which came out as planned, though shorter than usual, on 16 April, with a front-page photograph of part of the crowd in Caledon Square on 30 March, a headline 'PAC CAMPAIGN REVEALS THE POWER OF NON-VIOLENCE', the text of Kgosana's speech which opened the Campaign, and detailed stories of the police brutality in Cape Town, including one which Duncan witnessed himself, in which a policeman

> began chasing [an] ... African whom he had seen. He had a heavy 3-ft sjambok made from a motor car tyre. He chased the African past the front of our taxi. I put my head out and roared: 'Stop it, you swine', in a voice that reached several hundred yards. The policeman did stop it, and came to me in a menacing and extremely angry spirit. He shouted at me and asked me if I knew there was a state of emergency, said I was obstructing the police, and threatened me with imprisonment. He was joined by a Sergeant, who said much the same. I said to him, in a peremptory tone: 'Your men are behaving like swine. Call them off.'

The story also quoted Colonel Terblanche: 'Under the new regulations Natives who cannot account for themselves where they might cause trouble can be dealt with on the spot.'[30]

Alan Paton took over Peter Brown's usual column, 'The long view', and made it clear that Brown was in detention, though it was an offence under the Emergency Regulations to mention even the names of those in detention. The leader page carried three comments. Under the title 'The power of non-violence' Duncan returned to the basic theme of *satyagraha*: 'the Afrikaners are no worse ... than ... other people. Like other members of the human race they have a conscience, and want to do the right thing.' The proper use of non-violence would 'melt their hardest hearts, and ... show them what is right for the oppressed people is also right for them and their children'. Under the tile 'Betrayal (1)', Duncan asserted that the reimposition of the pass laws on 7 April was 'another solemn pledge ... dishonoured': 'It is because human society is built on good faith and an instinctive revulsion from treachery, that *Contact* has recorded these plain facts.' Under the title 'Betrayal (2)', he compared the arrest of Kgosana on 30 March when he went to Caledon Square to keep his appointment with the Minister of Justice with Dingane's betrayal of Piet Retief in 1838: '*Contact* therefore appeals to Mr Erasmus [the Minister of Justice] to erase this foul blot on his Government's and his own reputation and to see Mr Kgosana.'

Honour, treachery, or whatever, almost every word *Contact* published was breaking the Emergency Regulations, which laid down what the press could and could not publish. Journalists on other newspapers fed Duncan news that their own editors and publishers did not dare to print (though other editors, too, like John Sutherland of the *Evening Post* in Port Elizabeth, were later charged with breaking the Regulations); *New Age* was not being produced (most of its staff were in detention and it was banned on 8 April) and *Contact* was virtually the only source of published information of what was actually happening in the Emergency. Knowing this, Duncan increased his print order to 16 000 and then to 25 000. A few days after the publication of the number of 16 April, the police raided the *Contact* offices and removed what copies were left of the number of 2 April; they also advised the Central News Agency not to distribute the number of 16 April, and seized 800 copies of the same number from the Post Office. Duncan arranged to have more printed, and went ahead with writing and printing the next number. The police again raided, publication had to be suspended for a week, *Contact* was dissociated from the Board of Selemela to give the Board some protection, and *Contact* was now published by the proprietor, Patrick Duncan himself, at the usual address. Police and Post Office seized more copies; Duncan printed them again, and found new ways of distributing them.

In short, he simply ignored all but one of the Emergency Regulations; as he wrote in his diary,

> I continued to report what I felt important, and to comment, regardless of the law. On only one occasion I bent before the hurricane of government dictatorship: it was forbidden to mention the names of any detainees. Despite this veto we published many such names. Then George [Clay] gave me a list of hundreds [of detainees]. Rightly or wrongly I funked publishing it. I felt that to have published would have compelled the Police to close the paper ... with this exception we never bent once....[31]

On 7 May, in a front-page leader in large type, *Contact* carried 'Our message to the Commonwealth Prime Ministers' Conference', calling for the suspension of South Africa from the Commonwealth 'until a non-racial government comes to power'. The same number began a detailed account of statements and affidavits of Africans shot and beaten during the police attacks on Langa and Nyanga, which was continued into the next issue; once again this was a deliberate breach of the Emergency Regulations. On the 4 June *Contact* carried more details of some Liberal Party members in detention; some detainees had been released, provided they accepted certain conditions, where they were to stay, not travelling, not revealing anything about conditions in jail. For breaking these conditions one could be charged under the Emergency Regulations, and sentenced to a fine of up to £500, or up to five years in jail. Peter Brown, offered his release on these conditions after sixty-two days' detention, refused; *Contact* carried his photograph and the story on the front cover of the issue of 4 June. The next issue, of 18 June, carried a photograph of Kgosana on the front cover, details of the trials of PAC leaders and a statement of PAC policy by Peter Molotsi, who had been sent by the PAC Executive to Ghana, and an account of more secret arrests and detentions.

Once again the police raided the *Contact* offices and seized all the copies of the number. Duncan reprinted and distributed it by what he called in his diary 'non-usual channels'.[32]

They were great days for *Contact*. Its sales had increased to a regular 14 000, occasionally more, despite the police harassment of the editorial office and intimidation and arrests of sales-agents. It was sold widely outside South Africa (vol. 3, no. 11, the issue of 4 June 1960, sold 1700 in Nyasaland, 375 in Basutoland, 275 in Bechuanaland, 75 in Swaziland, 200 in South-West Africa, 250 in West Africa, 1000 in the Rhodesias, and 150 in East Africa) and all over South Africa, even in more remote areas.

All this cost money, and the Duncans' supply was not limitless. In June 1960 Duncan wrote to David Astor to say that the increase in print order (for, given the nature of the sales-structure, the more *Contact* sold, the more it lost) and the various reprintings had cost about £1800. Could Astor raise £2000 to help them? A sympathetic answer made Duncan write more fully: with some financial help, he said, he could push circulation up to twenty thousand quite easily. In the event, Astor covered the loss incurred during the first months of the Emergency, and for the next two years gave *Contact* £100 a month and various lump sums; it was an enormous fillip to Duncan, not only for the sake of the increased circulation (in late July he was able to print 23 000), but also because he admired Astor personally and the *Observer* as a newspaper.

Contact was by no means Duncan's only activity. Having raised in Cape Town £1800 for food-supplies and for the PAC itself during the sixteen days of the Campaign, he turned his attention to the United States of America, wrote to George Houser of the American Committee on Africa for support, and asked Allard Lowenstein, a young American and former President of the US National Students Association, who had visited South Africa in 1959 and had become deeply involved in South-West African affairs, to raise $200 000 for medical relief for Africans, particularly those shot and injured in the Emergency. The American Committee on Africa in fact sent a great deal of money at the time. Duncan continued to do what he could for the PAC leaders in jail in Cape Town; on the 6 May Kgosana wrote to him from jail, asking for books, towels, washing-cloths, pyjamas, letters and cough mixture, and for Duncan to visit him. Duncan applied for a permit to visit him, but was refused; so he sent an assistant to Caledon Square with all that Kgosana had asked for, and some fruit; the assistant was allowed to take the parcel on to Roeland Street jail, where Kgosana and the thirty other PAC leaders were being held. Colin Legum of the *Observer*, who was in Cape Town in April, told Astor that 'the relationship between himself [Duncan] and the Liberal leaders and the Pan Africanists ... was one of the best things I saw in South Africa', though he thought, too, that Duncan 'was idealizing the leaders – some of them, like Kgosana, are unquestionably outstanding. But many are really rather shocking – but there is no point saying this to Pat.'[33]

On the 31 May, 'Union Day', Liberal Party members and others organized a march through the streets of Cape Town to the Old Drill Hall for a meeting to 'dedicate themselves on the 50th anniversary of the Union to "ridding the country of the scourge of poverty and achieving inter-racial justice on the basis of government by consent" '.[34] Duncan was one of the leaders of the march, along with Albert Van de Sandt Centlivres, a former Chief Justice, and Anglican Archbishop Joost de Blank, Alan Paton and others, and between eight and ten thousand Capetonians of all races joined them, far too many tor the Drill Hall, so an overflow meeting had to be held on the Grand Parade.

Duncan went to talk to students of the University of Cape Town who were holding a fast in sympathy with those detained under the Emergency Regulations; he was the kind of man who was very attractive to students, and he had a considerable following on the campus. He wrote letters to newspapers, issued statements about the harassment of *Contact*, was the main speaker at a Liberal Party meeting when he predicted 'that in five years there will be no colour bar in South Africa',[35] met Julian Huxley who was then visiting the University of Cape Town, gave a farewell party for the Ballingers who were going overseas, predicted again that the United Nations would have to intervene in South Africa,[36] and more; when he went to see his brother John who was manager of a large department store in Cape Town, he said loudly to the African man who worked the lift, 'Your freedom is coming', despite the other whites in the lift. 'When?' asked the lift-man. 'Soon', said Duncan, 'In a year.'[37]

An unpleasant disappointment came at a National Congress of the LP, held in Cape Town at the same time as the 'march of dedication' and despite the Emergency Regulations still in force; Vigne, supported by other Cape Town Liberals, proposed the election of Duncan as one of the three Vice-Presidents – the only honour the party could bestow – but was opposed by the Transvaal Liberals, who had their own nominee. Duncan was not elected. He managed to conceal his disappointment in public, but in private was deeply shaken; for both Vigne and him, it was a sign not simply of narrow provincialism in the LP, but of a rejection of the kind of leadership Duncan offered. Not only was this a refusal to honour Duncan for what he had done during the 'March days' and in defying the Emergency, but it seemed an espousal of a passive and naïve liberalism which feared defiance as much as it feared racialism.

In late July 1960 he and a companion, a young Liberal called Neil Ross, set off on a tour of South Africa, Swaziland and Basutoland. They had a number of purposes: political reconnaissance; visits to *Contact* agents; visits to Liberal Party members and branches; and some public speaking. One of their visits was to Potchefstroom, where Duncan called on Professor L. J. du Plessis, who was out, but talked instead to his wife and to the widow of Professor J. C. van Rooy, whom Duncan called the 'former head' of the Broederbond, the secret society of Afrikanerdom: 'They were very jolly, and we discussed the Congo and SA. I told them I thought that the same sort of adjustments would be made here, and made right soon. They all agreed that vast changes were coming, and my "extreme" views did not seem to shock them at all.'[38]

In Johannesburg, Duncan addressed a lunch-time meeting from the steps of the Johannesburg City Hall, telling the 1500 people who gathered that the Emergency must be lifted, and that freedom in South Africa would be won, by non-violence, within five years. He ended his speech in Sotho, praising Sobukwe and Kgosana, called out 'Izwe Lethu', and gave the PAC salute. He was trying to organize three separate meetings in the Transvaal: with Verwoerd, whom he wanted to interview for *Contact*, with leaders of the

PAC, and with Harry Oppenheimer of the Anglo-American Corporation. Only the last meeting came off, and he and the Pogrunds dined with Oppenheimer, though Duncan and Oppenheimer disagreed on almost everything discussed; Duncan had known Oppenheimer some time, had approached him for donations to *Contact* (apparently with no great success), and was fond of him though increasingly critical.

From Johannesburg he and Ross went on to Swaziland, going via the prison in Benoni known as 'Modder B', the great brutality of which had recently been exposed in the press, and photographing it and prison-vans. In Swaziland they saw Patrick van Rensburg, a Liberal Party member who had worked for the boycott movement in Europe and who, at the time of the Emergency, had fled to Swaziland, and other refugees, and interviewed Brian Marwick, then Resident Commissioner, for a report on Swaziland for the *Cape Argus*.

Then Ross and he went on to Basutoland; he saw various government officers, both British and Basotho, had an interview with the Paramount Chief, who was now known as His Highness Motlotlehi Moshoeshoe II, talked to Khaketla of *Mohlabani* about politics, and went to Morija printing works to discuss the possibility of having *Contact* printed in Basutoland if it were banned in South Africa. He also spent an evening talking to Joe Matthews, like his father Z. K. Matthews a committed ANC man; Matthews had taken refuge in Basutoland during the Emergency and, although Duncan's and his political views were very different, Duncan was impressed by him, describing him as 'calm, strong, humorous, sensitive',[39] so impressed indeed that when he wrote about Basutoland for the *Cape Argus* he stressed that the 'leftist' threat in Basutoland was very strong. His article did not mention Leabua Jonathan, but repeated a scurrilous story about Mokhehle – scurrilous and, as Duncan himself later admitted, untrue;[40] the article offended Mokhehle deeply and it was a year before their relationship was restored. Duncan was happy to be back and was once again convinced that 'in any future crisis the importance of these territories will be even greater than it now is. It is likely that anti-apartheid forces will go on to the offensive from these territories, since internationally the Union is on weak ground, and will find it difficult to hit back without provoking strong counter-reaction'.[41]

From Basutoland they drove down to Durban, where Duncan spent a day talking to Ngubane, next day addressed a lunch-hour meeting and attended a meeting of the National Executive of the Liberal Party in 'Maritzburg. From there Ross and he drove to Underberg, and thence into Pondoland and Tembuland.

There were four main reasons for Liberal party interest in the Transkei, three positive and one negative. The negative reason was that, although the ANC had strong traditional links in the Eastern Cape – for instance, with places like Fort Hare University College in the Ciskei, and Lovedale College – and, although some ANC men were deeply involved in the Pondoland rebellion of 1960 and 1961, most ANC theorists thought that the main hope of change in South Africa lay with the industrial workers in towns; they tended therefore to concentrate their efforts not in rural areas nor with peasants, and in 1960 there was something of a political vacuum in large areas of the Transkei. Secondly, the close alliance between the *Contact* Liberals and the PAC in the Cape, and the fact that most Africans in the Cape were migrant workers from the Transkei, meant that there were strong reasons for extending the links to the Transkei; when the *Poqo* phase of the PAC began, it was concentrated in the Western Cape and the Transkei. Thirdly, in the government's plans for establishing Bantustans as the realization of territorial *apartheid*, the Transkei was to lead the way. Fourthly, in many areas of the Transkei, Africans were deeply opposed to the first stage of the Bantustan scheme, the establishment of 'Bantu Authorities'. *Contact* and other newspapers had reported the month before a meeting at Ngquza Hill, in Pondoland, which had been violently dispersed by the police – according to official reports, six people had been killed; *Contact* claimed the figure was thirty, and at least thirteen seriously injured.[42] To these four reasons, Duncan added a fifth more personal one: the Transkei abutted Basutoland and, if he was right about the relation of the High Commission Territories to South Africa, the Transkei might be a weak point in the South African strategy.

The report Duncan wrote after his visit to the Transkei started from the premise that 'Dr Verwoerd's policy [there] stands in greater danger than anywhere else':

> The solidity of opposition to 'mazipathe' (Bantu Authorities) is something quite unique. In East Pondoland the *whole area* is out of control. To show defiance Pondos are hunting in the forests, normally highly taboo without a permit.... The chiefs can do nothing with the people. The 'Anti-Bantu Authorities Committee' ... has collected large sums of money, and is able to hold meetings of 1000 to 2000 in secluded spots. It has further succeeded in driving out two traders ... suspected of informing the Police of their meetings, and of helping scour the bush with dogs for fugitive Pondo. There was a great deal of hut-burning.[43]

After meeting a few African members of the Liberal Party in Pondoland, Duncan was invited to speak to a large meeting shortly afterwards. It was the beginning of what was to be one of Duncan's greatest concerns for the next two years, and Peter Brown gives Duncan a large share of the credit for the way in which the Liberal Party managed to establish itself as an influence in the Transkei, though in fact others of the *Contact* Liberal group were to take over a large part of what Duncan had initiated.

Duncan and Ross visited Tembuland, too, addressing a house-meeting of Liberals and, next day, a meeting of about 200 local people:

> I called on them to resist Bantu Authorities, and to form an anti-Bantu Authorities Committee.... This they did, giving us the name of a man to correspond with. They will try to spread, and to call on us for a worker, for transport, money, and printed leaflets later if the response is good.[44]

From the Transkei, Ross and Duncan went to East London, Grahamstown and Port Elizabeth, seeing sales-agents and party members in all three, before driving back to Cape Town.

Duncan's final comment on his tour is that the Liberal Party 'has become tougher and more practical since the Emergency. It is now thinking purely in extra-parliamentary terms. With the Emergency, and with the recent clarification of its adult suffrage voting policy, the party has become, as to a majority, a non-white Party'.[45] (This last point is worth confirming: from late 1960 on there was to be a bigger and bigger black majority in the party; though it was never a mass movement, in the 1960s it ceased to be the 'white' party with a few black 'stooges' which its critics had called it in the 1950s.) Duncan said, at the end of his tour: 'the picture which I got was of a country which has already entered the final phase of the final showdown. Much is happening, and the pace increases. The end of *apartheid* is not more than five years away, perhaps less.'

Soon after Duncan and Ross left Cape Town for their tour of South Africa, *Contact* carried a story that 'a new communist movement has been established inside South Africa. It is called the "South African Communist Party" (the old, banned organization was called the "CP of SA")'.[46] The source of the story was a roneoed leaflet posted to some Capetonians in early July. On his return from the tour, Duncan wrote a short editorial, arguing that the reformation of the Communist Party was important, first, because it was an acknowledgement of the failure of the 'united front within the Congress' and, secondly, because it showed that the communists believed that South Africa was entering its 'final revolutionary period'. The editorial ended: 'When the list of committee members is examined, one interesting fact emerges; there is listed not one single fresh name, not one new recruit. Like the British Communist Party, now dying on its feet, the South African body is also an ageing party.'[47]

Duncan had been told by John Lang, a Liberal Party member detained during the Emergency, who the Committee of the 'new' Communist Party were; Lang had apparently picked up the information while in detention with members of COD. Almost immediately, the security police served a subpoena on Duncan which required him to give before 3 October the source of information of his editorial and the names on the 'list of committee members' he had 'examined'. At first, Duncan said he would consult his source before deciding, but then decided not to, since he felt he must take the onus of the decision on himself. When he appeared before a magistrate on 3 October, having refused to answer the questions put to him by the security police, he again refused to answer, and was jailed for eight days.

On the same day as his appearance, the publishers (Selemela Publications), Duncan, as Editor of *Contact*, and Joe Daniels, as Business Manager of *Contact* and Secretary of Selemela, were charged under the Emergency Regulations with having published 'subversive literature'; the charges related to the numbers of 2 and 16 April, the 'Sharpeville' issue and the 'Kgosana–March Days' issue, and mentioned specifically the two editorials, 'Betrayal (1)' and 'Betrayal (2)', the eyewitness account of the Sharpeville massacre, 'United Nations must intervene', the Kgosana speech, and Randolph Vigne's column, 'Sam Sly', of 16 April, which told the story of how he, Duncan and some visiting British MPs and a 'Panorama' team had taken two PAC men to the segregated Mount Nelson Hotel – the smartest hotel in Cape Town – for a drink and a talk. The charge did not include the articles on police brutality.

After eight days in Roeland Street jail, Duncan was again brought before the magistrate, again refused to answer the questions, and again jailed for eight days: 'I have already told your worship', he said to the magistrate, 'that it is politically impossible for me to appear as a police informer. I told your worship that I was prepared to stay in prison for 20 years, if necessary. After a week, I still think that.'[48]

At his third appearance, on the 18th, some of the wide publicity which the repeated detentions were getting began to make its effect felt, for the Crown prosecutor now said that Duncan was being held, not as the Editor of *Contact* but in his capacity as a citizen 'who possessed information which may lead to the detection of a crime'.[49] He was sent back to jail for another day, but when he appeared on the 19th he again gave no answer and was sent back for four more days. On the 24th he again refused to answer, and was sent back for another day. On the 25th he was released, the Crown prosecutor saying 'we have got the required information from sources other than Mr Duncan'.[50]

Duncan had never completely recovered from the shame of not serving his full sentence after the Defiance Campaign and, although he had too much of a sense of humour not to appreciate the oddity of his serving a term in jail for protecting communists when he was himself anti-communist (and he made it plain to the magistrate that he was), it was not altogether an unhappy experience. The worst of it was the lack of privacy when Cynthia visited him twice weekly: 'I was caged,' he wrote; 'she was put behind a barrier, while between us was a warder. There was no possibility of privacy'.[51] 'The best that I experienced was a repetition of the mental clarity and logical flow of thought I had experienced in Boksburg prison years before. This time I found, like a caged lion, that pacing up and down the 13′ × 9′ cell, hour after hour, helped the flow of thought.'[52]

Though he wrote to Cynthia, 'I am longing with all my soul for release', he was 'still prepared if necessary to stay here for years'.[53] (At the end of one of her visits, Cynthia was told by one of the warders, 'He's a nice enough man, your husband; he's just got into the wrong company'.)

There is some evidence that for years he had been putting himself in training for such an imprisonment; he had had to expect something of the kind, given the kind of political work he was involved in, and several of his friends believe that he deliberately taught himself to care less about personal comfort than he might otherwise have done. Of course the ascetic streak had been in him since he was quite young; as he had said disapprovingly years before, Oxford taught one to need luxury. When he was travelling, or even at home, he would often deliberately go without food and drink as a way of strengthening himself morally; while there was much of the Gandhian discipline which he was too European to accept, there was part of it which did seem worthwhile. In his diary he wrote of Roeland Street: 'I had no extra food (I did not want it), and I slept on a mat on the hard floor with no mattress. Yet it was a healthy life. I bubbled over with energy....'[54]

He was allowed books and a typewriter, and he got through a great deal of reading and writing; not only did he write articles for *Contact* but he also began his autobiography, covering the years up to 1958, and he worked, too, on the statement he intended to make when Joe Daniels and he were brought before the courts for publishing subversive literature. His brother-in-law

Denis Cowen, himself a believer in the concept of natural law, helped him
with precedent and legal argument, and Duncan added his own certainty that
political cases must be fought politically. The defence case and the autobiography were, in fact, intimately connected; 'before I can plead anything,' he
wrote, 'I must examine my own life to see if such a plea is in harmony with my
own destiny, and whether I am worthy to make such a public allegation
against our government, and its laws'.[55]

The trial of Duncan and Daniels for subversion opened on 4 November.
By agreement, Daniels pleaded not guilty; Duncan refused to plead, and a
plea of not guilty was entered on his behalf. The Crown's case was very short:
'the situation among the Natives was highly inflammable', said the police
witness (Detective Head Constable Sauerman). *Contact* was published, said
other witnesses; and it was subversive under the Emergency Regulations,
said the prosecutor. The lawyer defending Daniels asked for an adjournment,
which was granted for a fortnight. On the 17th, Duncan (on his own behalf)
and the lawyer (on behalf of Daniels and Selemela Publications) said they did
not intend leading evidence. At the close of the Crown case, Duncan made his
statement (later published as a supplement to *Contact* and, in 1961, as a
chapter in Blom-Cooper's anthology, *The Law as Literature.*[56]) Although the
magistrate interrupted once to say that Duncan's statement was not the
concern of the court, he was allowed to make it.

It was an important statement of his beliefs at the time. He started by
admitting surprise that the government would risk opening up again to
discussion 'large-scale murder by the police, and two treacherous breaches of
faith'. 'I would have thought that a government of guilty men ... would have
left these horrors alone, to be forgotten.' He accepted sole responsibility for
the articles in question, and had published them in the full knowledge that
they would conflict with 'government policy and regulations':

> I deny that the emergency regulations ever were or are law in the true sense
> of the word, or that they were or are in any way binding on the conscience
> ... [they] are lacking in two essential ingredients of true law ... firstly, the
> legitimacy of parliament, and, secondly, the morality of the law.[57]

Duncan's case rested on the principle that 'an unjust law is not law', and he
cited Sophocles, Aristotle, Cicero, Aquinas, Lucas de Penna, Theodore
Peza, Grotius and Locke for precedent (this was Cowen's contribution,
though elsewhere one detects Cowen's orotund prose-style influencing
Duncan's normally much plainer one). For evidence that the Emergency
Regulations led to violent injustice, he cited the assaults at Langa, and then
he turned his attention to the whole of *apartheid* legislation, some parts of
which were 'anti-life', and he gave instances of 'some laws [which] actually
seek to deny life to non-Whites' and of 'others [which], while not exhibiting
hostility of this extent, yet shamelessly deny justice'. Again turning to the
precedents, this time of Nuremberg, he argued that it was his patriotic duty
to protect his people and country against the 'group [that] has been able
temporarily to abrogate to itself the name of government ... by a series of
historic swindles'. 'In this trial,' he said, 'I am not the accused, though I
appear in the dock. On the contrary I am the accuser.' He then turned to the
articles which were specifically described as subversive, and looked at his

justification for publishing them. He claimed that 'the alternatives before South Africa are liberation with violence and liberation without violence. As a South African patriot and as a democrat I chose and I choose the way of non-violence wherever it is possible.' He praised Sobukwe, Kgosana and the PAC for non-violence, saying that 'white South Africa does not yet know how lucky it is' to have them; he argued that United Nations intervention was an alternative to chaos, and that intervention would end *apartheid* and bring 'democratic freedom'. Finally he said: 'I decided to publish all the articles in the heat of the crisis of April. Looking back from this somewhat calmer period, I would omit nothing, add nothing, and change nothing. I leave it to a future South Africa to justify or to condemn what I did.'

The magistrate, in his turn, said that the articles were 'treasonable', 'grossly insulting', 'distorted', and that they 'subverted the authority of the Government', 'ridiculed *apartheid*', and 'suggested anarchy'. The court had to assume that the laws and proclamations of the government were valid, that the will of Parliament was 'the over-riding factor', and could not question the regulations.[58] He found both Duncan and Daniels guilty, and sentenced them to fines or imprisonment: £350 (or 350 days) for Duncan as Editor, £100 for Duncan as a Director of Selemela, and £50 for Daniels as Secretary of Selemela.

Christian Action offered to pay the fines, and Duncan and Daniels accepted the offer; other donations covered their costs. *Indian Opinion*[59] criticized Duncan for not serving his sentence, but Duncan replied arguing that Gandhi never 'laid down a hard and fast rule that in every single case where a choice could be made between fine and imprisonment, it is absolutely obligatory to choose prison'.[60] He had told Astor beforehand: 'I shall fight the case politically, and shall win in my way.'[61] He had, in his way.

Was he at that point beginning to desert the doctrines of *satyagraha*, and to think that he should commit himself to joining those who were proposing to use violent means in an attempt to overthrow the *apartheid*-state? In the nature of things in South Africa in the 1960s, one did not make public announcements of this particular change of mind; nor, if one had any sense, did one record one's attitudes in letters or diaries. In Duncan's case, it is easy to put an end-date on his change of mind; in July 1963 he wrote to David Astor: '[I] have now lost hope in a peaceful transition, and [we] can expect an Algerian clash in our country. The best that can be hoped for is that a referee may be called in to stop the fighting when it gets too bad. . . .'[62]

It is much easier to say what had brought about this change of mind than when exactly it happened, because many more people than Duncan himself went through the same change. For some, the brutality with which the police and army put down the passive resistance at Sharpeville, Langa, Nyanga, Durban and elsewhere was the turning-point; after the Emergency of 1960 one could no longer ask black people to expose themselves unarmed to the Nationalist forces who had shown clearly that they would use any technique to defend their power and privilege. It was clearly this which provoked the PAC to begin to work under the slogan *Poqo*, and to kill, not to resist passively; although *Poqo* was not really active until late 1961 and 1962, PAC men were talking and plotting violence soon after the start of the Emergency.

With Duncan, too, this weighed heavily; *satyagraha* depended on the idea that the nobility of the suffering would induce the rulers to behave according to the consciences which, as basically decent and honourable men, they were assumed to have, so that when they behaved dishonourably – as Duncan felt Rademeyer and Erasmus had – *satyagraha* was made into nonsense.

Yet it was not this which changed his mind. Though he was aware of the brutality and treachery, he continued to believe in non-violence as a principle of action. After all, it had worked, albeit very temporarily: Terblanche had negotiated, the PAC had controlled the townships, some Nationalists had called for concessions, the pass laws had been revoked for a time. Perhaps more of the same tactics might work for a longer time, next time. So, when Robert Resha, one of the Treason Trialists, was quoted in evidence as having told volunteers at the time of the 'Western Areas Removal' that they must, if they were ordered to, 'Murder, murder', Duncan wrote in *Contact* that he was 'disgusted': 'This sort of speech is not only morally despicable, but is calculated to do the greatest harm to the cause of freedom itself, and to hurt, before any others, the Africans themselves.'[63] In his editorial in the same number, Duncan wrote: 'Violent revolution would smash our painfully built-up economic system, and would destroy our country. It would lead to a partition after indescribable massacres and the deportation of millions. It might harm the cause of the non-Whites more than that of the Whites.'

He continued to see intervention by the United Nations in its peace-keeping role as the great hope, though that in itself was a recognition that passive resistance alone would not bring about change; however, it might bring the country to a standstill and, in the vacuum which resulted, United Nations intervention would produce, if not immediate democracy, at least a non-racialist state. It was for this kind of reason that, much to the displeasure of many in the Liberal Party, *Contact* came out in favour of South Africa's becoming a republic. Of course the all-white referendum of October 1960, in which a majority of the whites voted for a republic, was a farce in itself; but it might be turned to the advantage of non-racialism, in that the greater the isolation of white South Africa the more open it would be to the pressure of passive resistance. Similarly with boycotts. Similarly in the matter of whether or not South Africa stayed in the Commonwealth; Duncan wanted South Africa expelled, not because he disliked the Commonwealth – he was too much a son of the 'kindergarten' ever to do that, even in his most Pan-African days – but because he wanted the isolation of South Africa. In his diary he wrote:

> I wrote to everyone I could – Nkrumah, Nyerere, etc. I telephoned Mrs Pandit and she promised to speak to Nehru. . . . The authorities desperately wanted the decision to be 'Yes' and this desire was betrayed in the slanted news we got. . . . Then, at 8 p.m. on the 15th, we tuned in to the BBC by pure chance and learned that Dr Verwoerd had withdrawn [from the Commonwealth]. This house has never heard such loud cheers.[64]

There were not many white English-speaking houses joining in the cheering that night.

The intervention of the United Nations in the Congo, four months after *Contact* had first called for intervention in South Africa, seemed to strengthen Duncan's case immeasurably. In his diary he wrote: 'When I look back on this [call for intervention] and remember it was written four months before the UN moved into the Congo, in all modesty I feel it was prophetic.' For many South Africans, however, it was the events of December 1960 to May 1961 which were the most significant in the change of mind about the use of violence. Late in 1960, Luthuli, Z. K. Matthews and other African leaders called a Consultative Conference of African leaders, which met in Orlando on 16 December. From Cape Town went Joe Nkatlo of the Liberal party, and Francis Mbelu 'representing Kgosana',[65] said *Contact*, which was a euphemism for 'of the PAC', since it was of course then illegal to represent either the banned PAC or the banned ANC. Other Africans in the Liberal Party, including Ngubane, also attended, though the Conference was largely dominated by ANC men. The main decision of the Consultative Conference was to call an All-African People's Conference for March 1961, to meet in Pietermaritzburg, and a Steering Committee, mainly of ANC men, but including PAC men and African Liberals, was set up to organize it.

The attitude of the Liberal Party to the Steering Committee and the 'Maritzburg Conference was generally to support it, though many members felt that the limitation to Africans alone was mistaken. While the PAC had initially seemed in favour, its leadership – then almost entirely in jail or in exile – was very much opposed. Matthew Nkoana, who had been sentenced to eighteen months' imprisonment or a fine for his part in the Anti-Pass Campaign, and who served his sentence with Sobukwe, was instructed to allow part of his fine to be paid so that he would be released a little early, with the specific purpose of withdrawing PAC co-operation from the Conference. He was told, he says, that 'this meeting must be crushed', because the Steering Committee was thinking in terms of the 'pre-1960 tactics of demonstrations', whereas the idea of the Anti-Pass Campaign had been to 'force' the government to revoke unworkable laws, to 'force independence'.[66]

Withdrawal of PAC support, the walkout by the two Liberals on the Steering Committee, the arrest of many of its organizers, police intimidation (the hall the Conference was to meet in was found to be heavily 'bugged') meant that the plans drawn up by the Conference in March 1961 were more or less doomed from the start, despite the presence of more than a thousand delegates representing 145 organizations, and despite Mandela's presence at the Conference (he was temporarily without a banning order) and his combination of inspirational leadership and dour organizing ability. The Conference's tactic was to call on the government to set up a National Convention to bring democracy to South Africa; if the government ignored the call (which it was bound to), demonstrations and a stay-at-home were to begin on 31 May, the day South Africa was to become a republic.

Sometime between March and May, Mandela, travelling widely and secretly around South Africa to organize the stay-at-home, had at least two meetings with Duncan. On one occasion Randolph Vigne was asked to collect Mandela from an address in Cape Town and to drive him out to Keyser House in Retreat; the main purpose of the visit was to enlist Duncan's support, both personally and as Editor of *Contact*, for the call for a National Convention or, failing that, for a stay-at-home to coincide with the republican celebrations. Duncan agreed readily to do this; while he shared the view of some Liberals that the closed nature of the 'Maritzburg Conference had been a mistake, he understood perfectly well why Mandela and others felt that the vanguard of the struggle had to be African. Peter Hjul remembers another meeting between Duncan and Mandela, on the same subject, which he attended, although he says, too, that the discussion soon got on to Duncan's favourite theme, communist attempts to direct the ANC – he remembers Mandela saying to Duncan, 'Do you think I'm so stupid that I can't run an organization without being influenced by people we've associated with?'[67] Duncan admired Mandela a great deal; they had met at the time of the 1952 Defiance Campaign, and several times since, and Mandela's no-nonsense, non-communist politics impressed Duncan considerably.

Certainly, *Contact* did support the decision to call a national stay-at-home on 29–31 May, announced by Mandela on 13 May, and its coverage of the stay-at-home, though not laudatory, did give it (and Mandela particularly) credit for what was done. Matthew Nkoana of the PAC, however, offers a very different picture of Duncan's attitude at the time; he remembers meeting Duncan in the 'shebeen' called the Classic, much frequented by African journalists and writers, soon after his arrival in Johannesburg after leaving prison. They talked there, and later continued their discussions in one of the offices of *Drum*; during their talks Duncan apparently said that he was prepared to help the PAC produce fifty thousand leaflets explaining the attitude of the PAC to the 'Maritzburg Conference. He did not actually do so, though leaflets were produced by someone, and widely distributed.[68]

One finds the answer to the inconsistency, as one so often does, in his fear that communists were manipulating the Congress movement. His editorial on the 'Maritzburg Conference makes this plain: after calling it 'another well-meant and well-planned attempt to defeat apartheid', he discusses the PAC walkout, and then goes on to fix the blame for the 'possible failure' of the Conference on the fact that 'the people organizing the conference were not truly neutral', rather than on the deliberate policy of the PAC. Yet, when he was approached by Mandela to give his and his newspaper's support to the actual stay-at-home, he was quite prepared to, simply because it was Mandela who did the asking; he knew that Mandela was not a communist and that he shared some of his own ideals. If Duncan's attitudes to the Conference and the stay-at-home seem inconsistent, they were not so in the context of his own mind.

The stay-at-home of May 1961 was, at the most, a limited success. Whether it would have been more successful even if the PAC and all Liberals had given it wholehearted support is doubtful, because the government had learned the lessons of 1960 well; this time it acted before threats became action, by introducing new laws, including one which empowered the holding of suspects for twelve days without a charge, by banning meetings, by calling up police and military reserves, and by using the police to intimidate. *Contact* reported: 'Saracens, police trucks, night-flying helicopters beaming into African houses and yards, 4 a.m. raids, arrests under the special 12-day laws, threats of deportation, "repatriation" and sackings.' After the event, the headline in *Contact* was 'Not a flop but ... WHY DID SO FEW STAY AT HOME?'[69] The answer was that, though the PAC was partly to blame, and though the stay-at-home was organized too hurriedly, it was really the effective repression by the government which ruined the chances of success.

This was, for many in the Congress Alliance, the turning-point. Mandela said at the time: 'Is it politically correct to continue preaching peace and non-violence when dealing with a Government whose barbaric practices have brought so much suffering and misery to Africans? ... Have we not closed a chapter on this question?'[70] For years the Congress Alliance had tried petitions, requests, pleas, then for years defiance and strikes and stay-at-homes; now, they had nothing left but force. In November 1961 some ANC leaders set up Umkonto WeSizwe, the Spear of the Nation, to be the military wing of the ANC, and Umkonto began its campaign of sabotage (aimed at things, not people) on 16 December. The African Resistance Movement, a small group of Liberals (mainly whites) and allies, began its sabotage in late 1961, blowing up telephone-kiosks, railway-lines, pylons, electricity sub-stations; when eventually they were discovered and convicted, those who were in the Liberal Party were expelled from membership, for the Liberal Party as an organization never wavered from its commitment to non-violence. Duncan was never an active member of the African Resistance Movement, though he was peripherally involved for a very short time during his exile in Basutoland. Randolph Vigne, one of the main organizers of the ARM, thinks that Duncan knew very little about it; and the ARM did not try to recruit Duncan, partly because of his long-standing opposition to the use of violence, partly because he was so well known that he might have been a liability in an underground organization, and partly because they did not wish to destroy the Liberal Party by compromising its leading members.

Duncan's reaction to the sabotage campaign of December 1961 was an editorial in *Contact*: 'STOP THE BOMBS!' After calling the government itself 'largely responsible', and noting that it was amazing 'that the oppressed people were not, long ago, driven to far worse excesses of violence', he went on to 'condemn the bombings with all the strength at our command, and to ask the unknown saboteurs to give up any plans that they may have for future violence ... violence will probably *delay*, not *hasten*, the day of liberation ... true *satyagraha* has not been tried ... victory against white supremacy is almost assured within a few years, providing the struggle remains non-violent'. Though the old idea of 'decent Afrikaners' being persuaded by *satyagraha* had disappeared, there was a new tack: 'White apathy' would assure eventual victory.

In continental African terms White South Africa is a military giant. This giant is asleep and will remain asleep (if the struggle remains non-violent) until after the whole country is closed-down by a total political strike, until the oil has ceased to flow, until South West Africa is detached, and until the world takes us over as its responsibility.[71]

A story told by Randolph Vigne shows Duncan taking much the same attitude in late 1960 or early 1961. One of the leaders of the banned PAC in Cape Town, at the time the PAC was beginning to think of itself under the slogan *Poqo*, came to tell Vigne that he was being asked by a number of young PAC men to 'get them guns'; he asked Vigne to go with him to Duncan to see if he would assist, Vigne assumes because Duncan was known to have money. 'L—— and I drove to Retreat', Vigne recalls,

> and L—— put his case, and Pat said to me, 'What do you think?' and I said, 'I think great care should be taken to find out what their plans are – I don't think dishing out weapons without real planning should be considered', and then L—— said, 'Well, what's your answer?' and Pat stood against the fireplace for something like five minutes in total silence and then he said, 'I am not able to take part in anything that would turn South Africa into a battlefield.' And L—— said, 'I'm sorry you aren't able to help', and he said, 'I'm not able to help.'[72]

Obviously, there were people who refused to answer questions of this kind because they did not trust the person asking, or because they thought someone else might be listening. But they did not usually think about their answers for five minutes in total silence – nor, indeed, did people who were not thinking about the possibility, however firmly they replied to the question in the end.

During 1961 Duncan made three secret trips abroad, two to America and elsewhere, and one other trip in Africa. In February 1960 he had been told that his application for a passport had once again been refused. However, since he had a British passport, it was relatively easy still for him to travel abroad, though his not wanting to fly from Johannesburg meant going to Bechuanaland or Basutoland first. There is some evidence that his trips abroad were known to the police: on the second of them he stayed with old Basutoland friends, the Temple Grievsons, then in Lobatsi, Bechuanaland; and, soon after he left, a policeman came round to ask where exactly he had been going to; the Temple Grievsons did not know, so were able to tell the truth. Given the close co-operation of police in the High Commission Territories and in South Africa, what one police force knew was likely to be shared with the other, and apparently officials in the High Commission were aware of both the visits to Washington. On the first trip, in January 1961, Duncan went first to Basutoland, where he tried to use his personal influence to heal some of the rifts which had appeared since the 1960 elections. He saw, too, a number of Liberals who were there either in exile or temporarily and, through the diplomatic offices of a young Liberal Party member, Peter Rodda, was able to have a meeting with two members of what he called the 'Mozambique Liberation Party'.[73] While there he wrote to Cynthia: 'I have decided to go.... I don't know when you'll see me back.'[74] From Maseru he flew by light plane to Rhodesia, staying with the Clutton-Brocks, an outspokenly anti-racialist family in Rhodesia, and then on. The next sure knowledge of his whereabouts is in Washington, where he stayed with Cyril Dunn, then the *Observer* correspondent in Washington. It is not even sure when he returned, though he sent Cynthia from Washington a Valentine Day's card with an unsigned typed slip inside to say 'See you well before this date'. On one of the trips he went to Maun, in Bechuanaland and near the borders of South-West Africa, before going north; and on another he gave a lift on his plane from Bechuanaland to Mrs Hadebe and her children, the family of Jimmy Hadebe, later the ANC representative in Dar es Salaam.

Even his hosts in America, the Dunns, were not sure of the purposes of either visit, though Dunn was able to arrange for him to see Senator G.

Mennen Williams (called 'Soapy' because his money was made from Mennen shaving cream), Kennedy's spokesman on Africa. The most vivid memories which the Dunns' daughter has of Duncan's first visit are that he bought her one ski in the hope of persuading her to buy the other, and that he could not sleep, and spent most of the nights pacing up and down his room, and would then come downstairs at dawn. The Dunns' impression is that he had two purposes: first, to raise money (though for what they were uncertain) and, secondly, to influence American foreign policy to Africa. 'Soapy' Williams had in fact already made some outspoken statements on Africa, and the reign of the Kennedys had made many people hope for a stronger American line on African affairs, which indeed they were to get; Williams said in Nairobi in February 1961 that the United States believed in 'Africa for the Africans' and defined 'African' exactly as Duncan wished: 'all those peoples who had made their homes in Africa, irrespective of race'.[75]

In May and June 1961 Duncan made a more extended trip abroad. About this visit more is known, partly because the trip was largely organized from London, partly because he arranged to have a number of letters posted in Swaziland to Cynthia, while he himself wrote to her from wherever he was, using the name 'Colin' and pretending to be a young man who had stayed at Keyser House shortly beforehand; whether the subterfuge fooled anyone is unlikely. During his January trip, Duncan had talked briefly to Astor, Legum and others in London about the whole problem of American attitudes, and they had agreed that in order to influence American politicians it would be necessary to set up in Washington the equivalent of the Africa Bureau in London, to keep those interested informed of what was happening, and to create interest generally. (Although there was already an American Committee on Africa, run by George Houser, with whom Duncan had been friends since 1952, it was felt that another pressure-group was needed, run by people from Africa themselves.) The plan was for Astor and Duncan to be together in Washington in May 1961, though in late March, because Legum was having some doubts about Duncan's own political reliability, Astor changed his mind. For Duncan, convinced that 'this is Act Five, and that the end is in sight',[76] nothing could stand in his way. At any rate, he went to Washington again, and this time apparently had more success. There was much coming and going from the Dunns' flat, with Duncan meeting English people from planes in the early morning and bringing them back to breakfast (the Dunns were away, and only their daughter at home, and Duncan never introduced his visitors to her); he went several times to Capitol Hill, trying to see Senators, sometimes successfully; he went once to the United Nations in New York. He saw something of Elliott Richardson, who has South African connections and who was later to be American Ambassador in Britain, George Houser of the American Committee on Africa, and others.

Another aspect of this second trip is even more significant, both in political terms and in terms of analysing Duncan's attitude to violence. From 1960 onwards Duncan, Hjul, Vigne and others had been in increasingly close touch with members of the South-West African People's Organization, mainly in Cape Town; the SWAPO people were closely associated with the Liberal Party and, since they had as their main aim of the time to persuade the United Nations to revoke South Africa's mandate to govern South-West

Africa, they obviously had close links with Duncan politically. Part of the purpose of Duncan's secret trips in 1961 was to raise money to set up a base for SWAPO in north-west Bechuanaland, near the borders of South-West Africa and relatively near the borders of southern Angola. 'This area', Duncan wrote to Astor,

> is the critical Southern Africa area, in that it is in this area that the future SA democracy can most probably be sown and grow, out of reach of the semi-Nazis who are taking our country over. From this critical area, our democratic movement can, when SWA is liberated, move in at speed, into SWA, and grow still larger, so that it, and not a communist movement, will be poised in SWA to nourish the freedom movements with SA and to thrust in when the moment is ripe.[77]

Duncan was convinced that increasing oppression in South Africa made it essential to have bases just outside the borders to which refugees could retreat and there regroup, and from which they could enter South Africa secretly. With arms? There is no evidence, and to infer that he meant armed infiltration needs caution, for in *Contact* he was still pleading for non-violence.

Initially, Astor was prepared to help, but eventually withdrew his support, mainly because of advice from Legum and Michael Scott. Scott was worried that taking sides too openly in the split between SWAPO and its rival organization, the South-West African National Union (SWANU), would damage the chances of influencing policy in the future if one organization or the other became dominant. Legum felt that putting a great deal of money into one project would be a mistake, since the police might already be aware of it, since control on the borders of South-West Africa was increasingly severe, since men sent out to the Bechuanaland camp might not be able to return and, if they were caught returning or going, would be savagely dealt with.

With hindsight, one knows that the scheme worked out by Duncan and the SWAPO people in Cape Town was exactly right, though premature; it is in the area of Ovamboland, which runs across the borders of Namibia and Angola, that SWAPO has been able to make most of its (now armed) attacks on the South African forces, and to send leaders in and out. The proximity of Bechuanaland (now Botswana) is, equally, of vital importance. Duncan was deeply disappointed by Astor's decision not to help with the Bechuanaland project, and he and Z. A. Shipanga, then Secretary of the Cape Town branch of SWAPO, wrote anxiously to persuade Astor to reconsider; but Astor felt he could not ignore the advice he was getting from Scott, Legum and others, though he continued to support *Contact* and to give Duncan his personal blessing in most of his activities.

Duncan did not abandon the scheme; sometime during 1961 (probably May) he went himself to the borders of Bechuanaland to look at possible sites for a refugee-camp-cum-staging-post, and in November 1961 made yet another secret visit, to see Nyerere of Tanganyika, whom he had seen briefly on his second trip in May. This time he did not write to Cynthia; but he took Nanny Maxim with him, for the adventure. From Kenya he wrote a long letter to David Astor which outlined why he wanted to see Nyerere. First, he wanted to raise about £10 000 to finance 'general organizational work' in rural areas of South Africa, because the Liberal Party had shown 'a buoyant ability to draw real mass support' in these areas, including South-West Africa and Tembuland. Secondly, he wanted an 'HQ' in Bechuanaland, a 'SWA action station' on the borders, and a 'refugee reception point inside Bechuanaland'. He said, too, that he had been 'mapping out inconspicuous escape routes' from the Transvaal into Bechuanaland 'for use when Verwoerd closes all vehicular roads into the territory which I learn will be done within three months' (where he had learned this from is unknown; but he did have close links with officials in the High Commission office, and there were rumours of this kind current in South Africa in late 1961). Thirdly, he told Astor ('for you alone'):

> ... we would need a station inside Basutoland, for political action into the Transvaal, Durban and Transkei when things hot up, as they almost certainly will next year. I have found the perfect place ... 20 miles from Maseru, where 20 active refugees could make a go of maintaining themselves for long periods with light industry and trading, and from which activists would sally forth to almost all the strategic areas of the Union.[78]

Though this letter still does not offer conclusive evidence of Duncan's preparedness to use violence (for the 'activists' could be organizing passive resistance), it offers conclusive evidence that his decision to go to Basutoland in 1962 was a more carefully considered operation than most of his friends and colleagues realized. Just how secretly he was working at this time is clear from the fact that Randolph Vigne and Peter Hjul, his closest political associates, had only a hazy idea of his movements and plans, and even his wife was unaware of exactly what his plans were.

His visit to the Congo on his way back from America in June 1961 was probably the most significant influence on his change of mind. The 'Angola War' issue of *Contact* appeared in the same month, with its headlines 'War in Angola involves South West and Union':

ANGOLA WAR!
Dead: 34 000 Angolans, 1000 Portuguese
The Fight: Angolan Freedom vs. Portuguese Imperialism
At stake: The whole of Southern Africa.

On the centre page was a story, 'By an observer lately in the Congo' – Duncan himself – which makes it clear why Duncan thought in 1961 that Angola was the key to the liberation of southern Africa: with the United Nations already in the Congo, with the situation in Angola increasingly vicious, with the United Nations already interested in South-West Africa, Duncan thought that there was a good chance of the United Nations moving, first, into Angola and, then, into South-West Africa. He was impressed to see United Nations troops in action in the Congo, was convinced that most of the atrocity stories from the Congo were being deliberately exaggerated in the South African press, and that the Congo was on its way back to prosperity. Duncan was even more impressed by Holden Roberto, commander-in-chief of the Union of the Populations of Angola (UPA), whom he interviewed at some length about the situation in Angola. Though his article discusses the role of the

MPLA (Popular Movement for the Liberation of Angola), which was 'not on good terms' with the UPA, he clearly favours the UPA: 'Both these movements are neutralist, but the MPLA has shown itself prepared to accept help from the communists, while the UPA has refused it.' From his discussions with Holden Roberto, Duncan concluded that the Nationalist forces held most of northern Angola, and called it a 'great breach ... torn in the defences of White supremacy and imperialism in Southern Africa'. The fact that the war of liberation had also spread to the south, and that South Africa had set up three army camps 'to try to insulate the southern Ovambo from the northern' was also very significant. The article ended: 'The Congo ... Angola ... South West Africa.... The next few years are swimming into clearer focus, and show us that the heroic nationalists now fighting for life and liberty ... are fighting the battle of all free men in South Africa.' That is hardly the language of a *satyagrahi*. Moreover, Peter Hjul was told by Duncan, on his return to South Africa, that having discovered that Holden Roberto was working without proper maps of Angola he had arranged for the *Times* maps of the Congo and Angola to be sent from London to the UPA. When Hjul asked him if this was not an odd thing for a believer in non-violence to do, Duncan replied, 'I've changed my mind'. What is even more significant about this conversation is that Hjul recalls Duncan saying it was a 'flash decision' he had reached in the Congo after talking to Roberto. Since that describes so exactly the way in which Duncan's mind usually worked, not by rational stages, but by imaginative leaps, what he himself called 'visions', one must accept this as the crucial point of change.

One needs to understand, not just the context in which the decision was made, or when and where it was made, but that it was intimately connected with his belief in United Nations intervention. This explains his reaction to the sabotage campaign by Umkonto WeSizwe later in 1961: his arguments were more tactical than principled – it was necessary to condemn the sabotage campaign because it would provoke the 'sleeping giant' of South African militarism, so make the incursion of armed raiding parties from the borders more difficult, and thus hold back United Nations intervention. The technique would be passive resistance inside, armed intervention from the borders; eventually the United Nations would intervene. In other words, though the decision about violence represented a leap, it started from earlier decisions. Of course it represented a considerable change from the principles of *satyagraha*, but for Duncan himself this was necessary: in 1962 he wrote in the *New African*, a magazine founded by Vigne, Neville Rubin, James Currey and others, that he was not a pacifist and that he believed in passive resistance only as a political technique which unarmed and powerless people could use against those stronger than themselves. He was, in a sense, rewriting his own personal history to fit in with his new vision; while it was true that he had never been a pacifist (as his attitude to Nazi Germany showed), his belief in *satyagraha* was based on principle, not just on expediency. In just the same way, his attitudes to Jews and Nazis had been more muddled before he met Helmuth von Moltke than he afterwards accepted, though once he had decided to loathe anti-semitism and National Socialism he rewrote his earlier beliefs, in the sense of picking out a different pattern from the process to make it more coherent. Self-justification is not unique to Duncan. Looking from the inside at what happened, one sees it as much more coherent and consistent than most people at the time did; it is too simple to call Duncan merely erratic. Cyril Dunn describes both the problem and the answer brilliantly:

> His changes of opinion seemed bizarre to many people. Yet they were logical – a steady progress towards extremism, dictated by compulsions which he accepted bravely. They probably seemed odd because his personality never changed. His enormous enthusiasm crackled away the same as ever, day after day, no matter how much the nature of the fuel might have changed overnight. The fact is he was always climbing on his gammy leg towards the same peak and was always the same person, no matter what giddy traverse he had made to join another and what he supposed to be a more promising group of climbers.[79]

In early March 1961, Duncan was summoned to appear in the Magistrates' Court in Cape Town to answer a charge under the Prisons Act that he had published in *Contact* the year before 'information concerning the behaviour or experience in the Modder-B Prison at Benoni, Transvaal, of any prisoner or ex-prisoner'. On 22 March 1961, the security police handed him a notice issued under the Suppression of Communism Act banning him from attending all gatherings for five years. He was of course not the first anti-communist to be thus treated, and had been expecting action of some kind for some time, but even he was surprised that it should be under the Suppression of Communism Act. When he wrote to the Secretary of Justice to ask for an explanation, he was told: 'You attended and addressed meetings, made utterances and participated in agitation as a result whereof, in the opinion of the Minister [of Justice], there is reason to believe that the achievement of the objects or some of the objects of communism would be furthered if you were to attend any gathering in any place.'[80] The reply makes the idiocy of the case clear: to call Duncan a communist in any shape or form was patently absurd. (Patently absurd it may be, but it is worth recording that even people who served in the British High Commission in South Africa are to this day apparently convinced that he was a crypto-communist whose outspoken anti-communism was a carefully nurtured front, and that his secret trips abroad included visits to Moscow to receive instructions.[81])

In fact, he had throughout the period been ferociously attacked again and again by Congressmen and communists for his anti-communism. A spokesman for SACTU attacked him in September 1960 for criticizing the ANC after its banning.[82] In December *New Age* launched what was to be a series of attacks on Duncan's attitude to Lumumba. Duncan had called Lumumba 'the man who tried to sell his country to the Russians',[83] and *New Age* said: 'Mr Duncan is spitting in the face of all genuine African patriots. He spits with the venemous [sic] spittle of Joe McCarthy, John Foster Dulles and the American State Department. . . . We hope that his views are not shared by the Party to which he belongs. Being anti-Communist is one thing. Siding with imperialist robbers in Africa is something altogether different.'[84] In February, an ANC spokesman said that 'In the catalogue of names of those whom we . . . associate with the murder of Lumumba, one is reluctantly compelled to include the name of Patrick Duncan . . .'.[85]

However, despite the original comment on Lumumba, *Contact* did in the event condemn the murder,[86] as even *New Age* admitted, and *Contact* also carried news items which showed links between Tshombe of Katanga and the South African government, making its attitude to such links plain; but, for *New Age*, Duncan's original attack on Lumumba was not to be forgiven, nor his equivocal attitude to the 'Maritzburg Conference, nor what the Congress people thought his opportunist alliance with the PAC. *New Age* asked:

> Why does *Contact* continually promote these views in its columns? The answer is that *Contact* is prepared to do anything to embarrass the ex-members of the banned ANC and frustrate their policies because it has for years dubbed the ANC 'Communist' and condemned the multi-racial Congress alliance as an instrument of Moscow.[87]

Duncan had never once called the ANC 'communist'; he had attacked what he thought the undue influence of communists on the ANC. To *New Age*, he replied: '... we are for *Congolese* nationalism and *for* the United Nations as the hope of the world.... We are against the way in which the USSR is trying to get a foothold in Africa, and in which it has tried to use the murder of Mr Lumumba to cynically whip up feeling against the opponents of the USSR.... You criticize us for anti-communism, as if that were something to be ashamed of. "Contact" is proud to be anti-communist ...'.[88]

Even after he was banned, the attacks continued: in October 1961 at a mass meeting in Durban called by SACTU a message from a banned trade unionist was read out which singled out Duncan, *Contact* and the PAC for attack as 'instruments of American imperialism'.[89] The Nationalists, too, continued their attacks, particularly over his work in and reporting of the continuing crisis in the Transkei, which had led to the reapplication of the Emergency Regulations in the Transkei in December 1960. For instance, in February 1961, De Wet Nel, then Minister of Bantu Administration and Development, said in the House of Assembly:

> 'The Native can adopt the Western way of life if he wishes, but it has been found that he prefers the system he understands and has therefore accepted Bantu Authorities. It is in no way a plan to hold them back, but rather to allow them to build on their own traditional system....'
> The Minister said he deplored the activities of people like Mr Patrick Duncan who did not hesitate to incite the Natives. Such people lived with the Natives in Pondoland and held secret meetings.
> Senator J. M. Conradie (UP): Why do you not arrest him?
> The Minister: It is not so easy to arrest a man in Pondoland.... Trouble is created by a small organized band of white communists and members of the Liberal Party who receive financial assistance from Russia.[90]

Duncan certainly did visit the Transkei regularly at this time, and established a complex network of political connections there, not only with the Liberal Party, but with the PAC and local ANC members, too, though most of his visits were so secret that not many details are known even now. Indeed, in the Transkei, 'Duncan' became a kind of generic term for all white politicians whom the government or Matanzima, prospective Prime Minister, did not approve of, and when members of the Progressive Party tried to force an answer from the Minister of Justice in the House of Assembly he could only reply in the same vague terms. Yet, from the point of view of the government, banning Duncan from meetings was an effective way of limiting his influence, and in his diary Duncan himself recorded: 'The press gave it some notice, then closed down on me and. . . . I have since then drifted out of the consciousness of South Africans, slowly.'[91] Part of this he felt was deliberate; in his press-cuttings book of the time he pasted an article from *Fighting Talk* called 'Landmarks in the Defiance Campaign' and under it he wrote: 'I have included this account . . . because it is the first history of the Campaign in which neither Manilal Gandhi nor myself is mentioned.'[92] But the Suppression of Communism Act did its work well; those banned became forgotten in the public mind, no matter how much they wrote – and Duncan, despite his preparedness to risk unpopularity for what he believed in, needed the warmth and encouragement of a public.

Not that the first banning made much difference, since it happened before some of the other activities discussed earlier, such as the second and third secret visits abroad. The banning had come just after an abortive visit to Swaziland, at the request of the Swaziland Progressive Party (SPP), whose cause he had taken up in *Contact*, and with the encouragement of Ernie Wentzel, a young lawyer and Liberal Party member in the Transvaal who acted as lawyer to the SPP, to put to the Paramount Chief of the Swazis, Sobhuza II, the case for constitutional advance. The Paramount Chief's advisers told Duncan what he called a 'cock and bull story' about Sobhuza's being in mourning for some relative; it was apparently a way of avoiding visitors. In April, after the banning, he went again: this time Sobhuza was 'praying for rain'. In May and June he was abroad. In later June he was visited by Bernard Sheridan, of 'Justice', the English committee of the International Commission of Jurists, to whom he put the idea of collecting affidavits of 'apartheid excesses, and keeping them until the excesses can be punished';[93] it was a reflection of the anger he felt at police brutality and the conditions in locations and prisons, and he was clearly thinking of Nuremberg, too. In August a Tembu chief, Zwelihle, came to Cape Town with his suite; the Liberal Party did much to entertain him and arranged for the *Cape Times* to interview him, during which Zwelihle made an impassioned attack on the shortcomings of Bantu Education, much to Liberal delight. During this time, too, he met Adam Hochschild, a young American, son of Harold Hochschild, one of the millionaires of the American metal industry; Hochschild worked for a time on *Contact*, and became an admirer of Duncan.

In October he and Cynthia went to Basutoland, she to visit friends, he to investigate on the spot the supposed kidnapping of Anderson Khumani Ganyile, one of the young Pondo leaders, and two of his companions, from inside Basutoland by six South African security policemen. After visiting the hut in which Ganyile and his companions had been staying, taking affidavits, sending blood-marked articles for analysis and asking awkward questions, Duncan became convinced that Ganyile and his friends had been kidnapped. Using all his influence in Basutoland, the pages of *Contact*, his friendships in London, his connection with the International Commission of Jurists, Duncan managed to exert enough pressure on the South African government and the British High Commission to get Ganyile and his companions released from detention in the Transkei and returned to Basutoland. It was one of *Contact*'s most important acts of crusading, and increased the strength of the Liberal Party in the Transkei a great deal, since Ganyile was a popular and important political figure there.

In Basutoland in October, too, he renewed his friendship with Ntsu Mokhehle of the BCP, who now forgave Duncan for the scurrilous story of the year before. The South African United Front, set up abroad by the exiled leaders of the various banned organizations, was in the process of breaking up, and as a result of what Mokhehle and others thought a well-planned attempt by communists (both South African and Basotho) to take over the BCP and establish themselves in Basutoland Duncan threw his weight behind Mokhehle; in the diary he wrote: 'I spoke for Mokhehle to Government, P[aramount] C[hief] Bereng Seeiso, B. M. Masilo (editor of the Protestant [newspaper] *Leselinyana*), Andrew Murray of the Catholics, in fact everyone I could think of.'[94] It was exactly the kind of role he most enjoyed, and once again reveals the position he held in Basutoland at the time. Certainly, Duncan's support both personally and in *Contact* was a factor in Mokhehle's managing to retain his leadership of the BCP, though once again Duncan's outspoken reporting in *Contact* of the struggle between Mokhehle and the communists, and of the way in which Mokhehle had broken with Mandela and the ANC over the issue of 'interference' and had transferred his allegiance to the PAC, made him exceedingly unpopular with both the ANC and the communists.

His crucial work remained the editing of *Contact*, and its importance and influence in those years were considerable; one of the reasons it came under such heavy attack from communists was simply that it had found an effective voice. For many it was the most reliable source of political information in South Africa, saying honestly and clearly what the problems in the exiled organizations were, what was happening behind the bland official announcements about the Transkei and other rural areas of South Africa, what was happening in the independence movements in the rest of Africa, how United Nations policies were changing. If the optimism of 1960, in which freedom and the end of *apartheid* were always imminent, in one year or five years, was gradually replaced by a greater realization of both how intransigent the Nationalists were and how powerful white South Africa was, it reflected what was a common mood in the South African opposition at the time. If its anti-communism seemed a little too strident to some – even those who held no brief for communism and who distrusted the machinations of communists in other organizations – if occasionally it placed more hope in the United Nations than that faltering organization seemed capable of fulfilling, if occasionally it went overboard for some organization or movement which seemed to have no power nor mandate but considerable antipathy to communism, at least it did not fawn on the West, as *New Age* so often did on the Soviet Union. If occasionally its advocacy of African neutralism sounded a little too like an apologia for capitalism, at least it was prepared to attack the British for their half-hearted dealing with the Ganyile case,[95] or their caution in the High Commission Territories,[96] or their lack of real commitment to the policies which Macmillan had spoken of in 1960.[97] Most important of all, it went on doing what it had done during the Emergency of 1960, publishing news that many other South African newspapers were afraid of, looking for news of a South Africa in which black people were visible human beings, not invisible units of labour or statistical entries (its policy of publishing the photographs of those who wrote letters to *Contact* was apparently a minor oddity and yet in fact a significant human action which went far beyond politics in any narrow sense).

In his diary for December 1961, looking back to February 1960, Duncan wrote 'Privately speaking these months have been months of the greatest family happiness I have ever known,' and he specifies Keyser House, the *vlei* at the end of the garden, the Constantia mountains and the Tokai forests, 'two glorious calm sunny winters', the children growing, flourishing, doing well at school.[98] Although he was sometimes ill – once badly with flu, which started on a camping holiday with the family soon after his first banning, then for some months with a cough which turned into a form of asthma, and then in December 1961 with a bad attack of malaria, probably picked up on his Congolese or Bechuanaland visits – his leg and the ulcers were no longer causing him undue pain. There was of course personal sadness, such as the death of his father-in-law, Sir Patrick Ashley Cooper, on his way home to England from South Africa in March 1961, and the banning and imprisonment of political friends and colleagues. But he was doing work he believed in, was fulfilling what he saw as his 'great aim', was defying an immoral government, was speaking out for freedom and democracy.

> And yet, on the most golden days at the back of our minds has been the knowledge that it cannot last. My course and that of the government are bound to collide, and at the first clash I shall come off the worse. And so the golden days have been more precious than they could ever otherwise have been.[99]

He had been banned once; the next stage was bound to come soon, and at the very least it would mean a ban on his travelling outside Cape Town. Since *Contact* had consistently ignored the Emergency Regulations in the Transkei, the government was sooner or later bound to take action against it. (In fact, the charge under the Transkeian Proclamation R.400 of 1960 was laid in July 1962, against Duncan, Hjul and Vigne, for subversive articles on the Transkei published in December 1961 and January 1962.) Since he often broke his ban on attendance at meetings to talk to groups of friends in the Liberal Party and occasionally to other banned people (for instance, in late 1961 he visited Luthuli in Natal), he was sooner or later going to be caught doing so, charged, and inevitably convicted. The General Law Amendment Act of 1962, the 'Sabotage Act', which provided for the death penalty for sabotage, house-arrest for opponents of the government, and the prohibition of any statement by anyone banned was a clear sign that the government was not going to respond to sabotage by making concessions. Duncan knew that he would sooner or later be prevented from writing and travelling as well as from going to meetings. But, most of all, he had made his decision about violence.

On 1 February he was arrested at Cape Town railway-station and charged with distributing Liberal Party pamphlets on the station without the proper authority; it was no more than a technical offence, and he was fined R10 (£5 approximately). Then, on 18 April, the security police served a second banning order on him, which confined him to the magisterial district of Cape Town for five years. Immediately, and almost without thought, he announced his intention of defying the banning order; he had no intention of being an unconvicted prisoner in his own country.

When the banning order was served, he had in fact been planning to go to the Transkei, and at first thought he should have to cancel his plans. But, discovering that the banning order allowed him a week's grace, he and Cynthia set off the very next morning with a load of posters calling on the people of the Transkei to continue their opposition to the phoney independence being offered them (the posters had been drafted by Transkeians themselves, and printed by Duncan, though carefully he cut off the imprints). Leaving Cynthia behind in Grahamstown, he drove on to his first stop in the Transkei – a mission-station, where he left posters – then drove on, picked up various companions and guides, and toured the Transkei, often taking the car along paths which had not been used by a car before, and sleeping hardly at all. Everywhere Duncan and his companions went they left posters, and talked to opposition groups, though in Pondoland they met men so frightened they would not help distribute posters. Driving up to the north, near the Basutoland borders, Duncan and his companion lost their way, and in the end found themselves on a forest track, on top of a mountain high above their destination, and 'between us nothing but a fearfully-eroded slope, occasional sledge and cattle tracks, but nothing resembling a road. By the grace of God we took the car down, sticking twice, and being helped by the local people, and traversing roads such as I have never in all my experience seen cars traverse before.'[100] At a trading store they were given a loaf of bread and a bottle of Communion wine, left some posters and then drove on through the night to Matatiele, and – after an hour's sleep in the car – on to Kokstad and East Pondoland. Soon afterwards the car broke down, and they missed various of the people they wanted to see, though others still took posters. When the car was repaired, they drove on to the companion's home, where they slept; next morning, Duncan went on to East London, where he left the car in readiness for Randolph Vigne's visit the next week, and flew back to Cape Town and the start of his banning order.

In less than five days in the Transkei, Duncan had managed to see no less than twenty sets of people who had taken posters and listened to his views; what is more, there was obviously close political co-operation between the Transkei politicos and the Liberals. It is a good example of the kind of network which Duncan, Vigne and other Liberal Party members had built up in the Transkei; moreover, as Duncan wrote with relish in his diary, 'I am sure the police never knew I'd left, and that they did not catch up that I had been to the Transkei until I got back.'[101] Certainly, the newspaper headlines said, 'MYSTERY POSTERS IN UMTATA': 'Huge, mysterious posters urging the Transkeian Territorial Authority to reject the Transkeian draft constitution have appeared in Umtata.... They are unsigned and no one appears to know where they come from.'[102]

The day after his return from the Transkei the security police came to confiscate the South African passport which had been issued to him six weeks before; to get it Duncan had signed an undertaking that he would not give any interviews, address any meetings, or 'be active in any way publicly outside the Republic'. He had not intended to be public anyway; he had planned to visit his sister.

This was yet another sign of the gathering pressure on him; if he stayed, he would either have to accept his ban or do what he had said he would, defy it. Peter Brown and others took this to mean defying the ban inside South Africa and accepting the consequences, probably a jail sentence. But there was, for Duncan, another way of defying; he would slip over the border into Basutoland. After long discussions with Cynthia, Hjul, Vigne and others, he decided that he would do the latter. A pantechnicon took most of the *Contact* office files and quantities of Duncan's personal possessions to Maseru; the *Contact* staff were in fact told of its safe arrival in a telephone call from the Cape Town security police, who seemed to have known of Duncan's plans. On the evening of 3 May, while Cynthia went to hear their son Patrick singing at the City Hall in a performance of *Belshazzar's Feast*, Hjul and Vigne left Cape Town in one car, Duncan in another. A hundred and twenty miles outside Cape Town, they swapped cars; Hjul and Vigne drove back to Cape Town, and Duncan drove on, crossing the border into Basutoland quietly at nine-thirty the next morning. It was his last political act inside South Africa.

The day he arrived in Basutoland, he wrote to Cynthia: 'Today was fearfully clear-cut. If I have been wrong to come there's no going back. If it is a serious fault then I am finished ... politically.'[103] Paton, Brown, and others who believed that a prime duty was to stay, no matter what the cost, thought he had been mistaken; what was needed were Liberals inside South Africa, to say that racialism was wrong, to fight it as best they could, but to stay there to show their commitment to a particular idea of South Africa. Others had no choice but to stay, either because they were locked up or because they were too poor to choose to leave home and job, or because they could not think of starting new lives in other countries. Duncan had a choice, and he chose to leave; one may argue that he was in a sense forced to leave, that the government had made it intolerable for him to stay. If it is true that the security police knew of his plans, they chose to let him leave, presumably because they thought he would be powerless outside South Africa. But he could still have stayed, as others stayed – Luthuli himself, even though banned and gagged; Peter Brown, who was banned and gagged for years; Sobukwe, Mandela, Fischer and others, who went to jail, some for life. Peter Hjul, who at the time advised Duncan to leave, was afterwards to feel that he should have stayed to face the consequences. But Duncan chose to leave not simply for the negative reasons of the banning order and the likelihood of even tougher action against him, but because he though he could do more from relative freedom in Basutoland than from confinement in the Cape; he had after all already investigated the possibility of having *Contact* printed at the Morija printing works, and he had already thought of implementing the scheme he had first suggested for the Bechuanaland–South-West Africa borders, but this time on the Basutoland border near the Transkei, where he had already a network of contacts and colleagues. Moreover, he had a head-start in Basutoland; he knew hundreds of Basotho and he knew the country and its ways. He was an honoured man already. In his terms, he was not running away; he was making a fresh assault from a new position; and if he ever regretted the decision himself, he never said so, privately or publicly. Looking back was not permitted.

BOOK FOUR

Exile

25 Kubung, Basutoland, 1962

26   Pat Duncan arriving at London Airport from Brussels with his two sons, Patrick (left) and Alexander (right). They were met by Cynthia Duncan and daughter, Ann, April 1963

27   Pat and Cynthia Duncan camping in the Algerian desert, January 1966

CHAPTER 10

May 1962–March 1964
'I know I shouldn't be here, but I am'

In the long term, Duncan's plan in Basutoland was to set up what he had originally conceived of for Bechuanaland, some kind of staging-post-cum-refugee-centre near the borders with South Africa; initially, it would probably be simply a place for refugees from South Africa, but later it might serve as a training-camp and a place from which people could move back into South Africa. He wanted, too, to find a way of having *Contact* printed in Basutoland, because he was sure that when the Sabotage Bill became law *Contact* would be banned; the Minister of Justice, Vorster, had made it quite clear that he would use the provisions of the Act which allowed the banning of newspapers and demanded a deposit of R20 000 (£10 000) before a new newspaper could be set up (the second clause to ensure that *New Age* did not continue its old practice of starting under a new name each time it was banned). As early as 20 May 1962 the *Sunday Times* carried a story based on well-founded rumours that *New Age* and *Contact* would be banned as soon as the Sabotage Bill, then being discussed in the House of Assembly, became law.

In the short term, he had to get himself accepted as a resident in Basutoland. As an ordinary visitor, he was allowed to stay a month; if he were applying for permanent residence he was allowed three months; but if his application for permanent residence were to have any chance of succeeding he had to set himself up as a trader, because only born Basotho, officials, missionaries, doctors, teachers and a few traders were ever allowed to become permanent residents. Even when he had found a trading post, he would have to get the permission of the administration and of the Paramount Chief.

When he first arrived, he would say only that he was there for a visit; meeting Gordon Hector, the Government Secretary, in the street on his first morning in Maseru, he asked for and was given an appointment a few days ahead to discuss his stay. Immediately, he left for Teyateyaneng and the hotel that had been established there, in a vain attempt to avoid the South African press, already in pursuit of a statement: all he would say was that he was 'on holiday', and 'I know I shouldn't be here, but I am'.[1] Still pursued, he left the hotel, saying that he was going into the hills for a rest, but in fact taking refuge on the mission-station with friends. He met Leabua Jonathan by accident and arranged a date to see him, then drove to the Paramount Chief's place at Matsieng to pay his respects, then to the ex-Regent, Mantsebo, then to Morija, to talk about the possibility of printing *Contact* there, then to a trading station that was for sale, then re-engaged one of the servants from Riverside days, Tokelo, to be his driver (Tokelo had been out of work for four months, so Duncan bought him new clothes and gave him an advance on his wages), then to see old friends (including one who had a house to sell), then to see Elias Ntloedibe and Joe Molefi, two PAC exiles in Basutoland, and Julius Malie, a Liberal exile, then to Archdeacon 'Forty' Makhetha, then to tea with Leabua; after tea he and Tokelo drove back to Teyateyaneng, where the Paramount Chief had left a message for Duncan to telephone him. To Cynthia he wrote: 'Today has been a *wonderful* experience. It's been a welcome beyond anything I could have hoped for.'[2]

Next day (a Sunday) he bought a house in Maseru, mainly to have an address from which to register *Contact*, called on the new Resident Commissioner, borrowed a house from friends who were going on holiday, called on the Anglican Bishop, went to church to hear 'Forty' Makhetha preach, telephoned home, and called on the Lebonas (the Liberals from the Orange Free State who had joined the party at the same time as he had). Next day was his appointment with Gordon Hector, where he talked of his plan to set up as a trader (but presumably not the more secret parts of the plan), and in the afternoon he called on the Paramount Chief; Duncan quoted him as saying, 'My people all know you, and always blame you for having left your home in 1958': 'My people were angry when they heard what the SA Government had done to you. Now they say that they are glad that you have come home.'[3]

If the welcome from the Basotho was as warm as it could possibly have been, the welcome from the British administration was as cold as the Basutoland winter; he had offended many with his rough handling of the police and administration over the Ganyile affair, and they were worried, too, that his unpopularity with the South African authorities would create difficulties for them. His popularity among the Basotho meant that the British administrators had to handle him gently, even if not always very politely; he was interviewed by the Immigration Control Officer, who doubled up as Police Superintendent, and was cross-questioned rigorously about his plans, before being allowed to proceed with his application for residence. Yet the welcome from old friends – like Gordon Driver, who had both preceded and succeeded him as Judicial Commissioner; Dr Makotoko, who, when he heard Duncan had returned permanently, clapped his hands and said, 'When you were confined you could have gone abroad anywhere. I was delighted when I heard you had come here: it was just like you';[4] and dozens of others – more than made up for the stony disregard of some of the British officials.

Almost immediately he was involved in Basotho politics again. To both the Paramount Chief and Leabua Jonathan he talked about the threat of communism in Basutoland; rumours that both SACTU and *New Age* were planning to set up offices in Basutoland as a prelude to their expected bannings in South Africa were rife, and he was glad to hear that a Suppression of Communism Act was being discussed by the Legislative Council, despite his own experience of the South African version of the Act; he actually drafted an amendment to the Basutoland Obscene Publications

Act to ensure that the government was able to refuse a licence to a newspaper (this was to prevent *New Age* moving into Basutoland; he wanted no competition for his Basutoland *Contact*). He met Mokhehle and talked with him of ways and means of keeping the communists and particularly *New Age* out of Basutoland, and went on meeting him to discuss the questions of independence and the needs of Basutoland. To his sister Deborah Cowen, then with her husband in Chicago, he wrote:

> ... tell Denis that the Basuto problem is easy to state, and extremely hard to solve ... the new constitution ... will have to solve the clash between what the PC [Paramount Chief] and what Mokhehle wants. Mokhehle wants what the others, the Nyereres etc., have got. The PC, it is said on unimpeachable authority, wants what the Shah of Persia has got, General de Gaulle, and President Kennedy. I am not taking sides on this one. All I can say is that both PC and Mokhehle have devastating aces in their hands. If the PC thought of holding a referendum on the type of government ... it is probable that he would romp home.... Yet Mokhehle remains the outstanding popular leader.[5]

In view of the crisis of 1970, when Prime Minister Leabua Jonathan sent the King into exile, it was a prescient view. In June, Duncan made to Leabua Jonathan a suggestion which Leabua calls, simply, the turning-point of his political career.[6] Leabua and Duncan had been discussing the problem of unemployment in Basutoland and in Maseru, at that time extremely serious (so much so that Duncan had sought out his old servants from Riverside to help them with money for the winter); Duncan suggested to him 'that he offer all the 600 Maseru unemployed work at 10c the day on the local contour banks, and that I would pay for five days. At the outside 400 would turn out. That means £100. I have a cheque from D..... and will add my own. I have told Leabua to get government to lend the shovels and picks and to point out the banks that need mending, and to ask the traders to contribute rations and money for a second week. He is delighted. Ho tsosoa khoma e itekang – God helps those that help themselves.'[7]

Which is exactly what Leabua Jonathan did; even Khaketla in his very critical account of Leabua's activities in *Lesotho 1970* admits the efficacy of the action: 'Chief Leabua had achieved his purpose which was to demonstrate to the world and impress upon the electorate that he was the only political leader in Lesotho who was greatly concerned with the plight of the underdog.'[8] (By an odd irony, Khaketla gives credit for the original idea to Joe Matthews of the ANC.)

The incident could have done little to improve Duncan's standing with the British administrators; he had, it is true, been invited to the Queen's Birthday Reception at the Residency earlier in June, but even that had not been altogether a success, since many officials continued to cold-shoulder and even to cut him. As he told the friends whose house he was staying in, 'The anti-Duncan campaign flourishes, with officials ticked off for having had me to their houses. In addition, you will be interested to know, I betrayed government secrets when I left the service, I did the riots, and the strike [both incidents of the 1960 elections, which he had condemned in *Contact*], and I am a communist.'[9] But Duncan was never one to play things coolly; he tackled one of those who was being most cold, saw him in his office, and accused *him* of being soft on communism. He heard a rumour from friends in Cape Town that he was not to be given an unconditional residence permit, but rather one conditional on his not being active in politics, and that if he were nevertheless active against *apartheid* (which was after all his purpose in going to Basutoland) either, if he were to leave Basutoland, say to go to Europe, would not be allowed back, or – worse still – would be expelled from the country. He wrote immediately to the Resident Commissioner:

> My belief ... is that close relations with apartheid are no help to anyone in international questions, and that opposition to apartheid is no less in the long-term interests of the United Kingdom than it is of the Basuto. For this reason among others I intend to fight against these proposals with all the honourable weapons available to me, and to fight for the issue of an unconditional permit.[10]

Diplomatically, he then tones down his letter: '... as I wish you personally well, and British Policy in general, I would wish there to be no fight, and no need for anyone to have to climb down in the end'. But he cannot resist going on to specify what weapons he has at his disposal: pressure on governments other than the British, and 'a small committee set up in London, broadly representative of the three parties, so that the question may be brought to the attention of various influential bodies and persons'. He does not mention the obvious, which is his personal position in Basutoland and his friendships with all but one party; but renewing his Basotho friendships was politic as well as pleasant, and he continued to see the Paramount Chief, Leabua Jonathan, and especially Mokhehle.

All the same, he did nothing to hide his more public political intentions. He went to the University College at Roma and talked to a large meeting of staff, students and visitors on the role of the Liberal Party in South Africa. He saw a great deal of the PAC men in Maseru; with one of them he went on a tour of the southern areas, looking for a suitable trading store but seeing, too, other PAC men who were living in more remote areas. He wrote editorials for *Contact* and telegraphed them to Cape Town, and sent down reports on Basotho politics. He wrote articles for South African newspapers, knowing that, under the terms of the Sabotage Act, once a list of banned people was published he would never be heard of in South Africa again, for the Act made it an offence to publish, print or even repeat any statement by any banned person. He wrote to the Africa Bureau in London, and to Astor and the *Observer*. He bought the only registered printing company in Basutoland for £70, since he thought that it might otherwise be bought by *New Age*. If he was making life difficult for the communists, the South African authorities did their bit to make life difficult for him; for instance, the five hundred copies of *Contact* sent from Cape Town to Maseru in mid-June disappeared *en route*, and his letters to and from Cynthia were often delayed in the post.

In mid-May Cynthia had come up to see him for a few days, and in late June she and the three elder children came for the school holidays. Together, they moved to the house of the Jacques, who were on leave; they were very happy, despite an unpleasant row with officialdom because the Jacques's house was an 'official' one and both the Jacques were criticized for having lent it to an 'undesirable' and the Duncans were actually asked to 'remove from the house forthwith' by the Chairman of the Housing Committee in Maseru;[11] the Duncans did not do so, of course. With Cynthia there, it was much easier for Duncan to make decisions about trading stores, money, a new family home, and together they looked at various possibilities. Eventually, soon after Cynthia's and the children's return to Cape Town, he settled on two stores, though he had only seen them from the air, in the Quthing district right in the southern bulge of Basutoland, one at Kubung, the other Mohlakoana's; both were very isolated, across the Orange river, and in the southern Drakensberg. Neither was accessible by road; Kubung, the least accessible of the two, was thirty miles on horseback from the nearest road-head.

Duncan was beginning to run short of money, since *Contact* had eaten up a great deal of the capital he had handed over to Cynthia earlier; though he had been promised, some time earlier, a large donation towards his political purposes by Bill Lloyd, son of one of Sir Abe Bailey's daughters, the money had not yet come through, and to raise the money to buy the stores he was forced to borrow against Cynthia's investments. After some negotiation, he got Kubung for £1010, and Mohlakoana's for £510, pending government approval, which he thought could hardly be refused, since not having trading stores in those places was very hard on the local population; the stores not only sold supplies but bought up local produce, skins, hides, wool, mohair, beans, wheat and craftwork. At the end of July, he, Adam Hochschild (who had come up to stay with him), and Joe Molefi of the PAC drove to Quthing and then on as far as the car would go; borrowing horses, they rode two hours to Mohlakoana's across the Quthing river, to find it 'far far nicer than it seemed from the air'. It was, Duncan told Cynthia, a 'simple mountain station', 'with quite a nice house with 3 bedrooms and in the passage wall-to-wall carpeting. It is completely furnished.... The worst thing is the absence of a proper water supply. There was a pipeline from a fountain, but it has broken down. The shop is compact and in moderately good order ... about 10 outbuildings.'[12] Flowering baileyanas in full bloom and two white stinkwoods made the place less bleak than the scenery, and soon after they arrived the local chief, Mahlomola Nking Letsie, called to greet them.

After lunch, they rode on to Kubung, arriving there after sunset, in the bitter cold, to find no caretakers and not enough blankets. For tea they ate bread, peanut butter and sardines and drank water; as always, Duncan enjoyed being a spartan. Kubung was, he said, '... a lonely dwelling, with stone paths, water supply that works, but oddly only two bedrooms and a dining room that has no door to the rest of the house, only a hatch! Beautiful trees, a staggering view up the Maletsunyane valley, and about a mile above the Orange river.'[13] Built on the mountainside out of the local pinkish-tinged sandstone, with wooden beams, and all the woodwork painted dark red, some of the roofs thatched, the rest of corrugated iron also painted dark red, Kubung with its seven acres of land, some stony, some arable, an orchard of a hundred fruit-trees and vines, a rose-garden, and with the Orange river six hundred feet below was a spectacularly beautiful place. The other advantage was that it was 'discreet ... not near any official place'.[14]

Friends continued to visit him both while he waited in Maseru for the licences to start trading and when he moved to Kubung: Robin Farquharson, the brilliant and eccentric young university teacher (later to write *Drop-Out* and then to die tragically in a fire in London), Dennis Brutus, of the South African Sports Association and the South African Non-Racial Olympic Committee, Tim Holmes, Randolph Vigne, Peter Hjul and others. He continued to see a great deal of Mokhehle. He saw the Paramount Chief to give him a letter of introduction to David Astor, and was pleased to be invited to the Paramount Chief's wedding. He arranged supplies for the stores, and found that the Government Secretariat was now more helpful, apparently anxious to have the trading stores reopen in the Quthing district. At the beginning of August Cynthia came again for a few days and, on the 13 August, having taken on an assistant, who was to start by helping at Kubung and eventually to take over Mohlakoana's, he moved up to Kubung.

His first reactions were of delight. The villagers came out to greet him, the headman was charming, the local chief friendly and helpful, and the whole atmosphere one 'of peace and joy': 'I am more in love with this place than ever,'[15] he told Cynthia. Tokelo, his driver and i/c transport, worked long hours with him, and he employed various helpers, including the Chief's brother and three of the servants from Riverside. Since its previous owner's death, Kubung had been neglected. He had to get a gang of workers in to clear the undergrowth from the site, to reclaim the garden and rebuild the cattle-kraal, to fix the house and install new plumbing. He had to arrange the transport of stock from Maseru and then by donkey-train up to the store. He had to buy horses. He had to arrange to buy goods, to store them, to transport them, to resell them. The boats for crossing the Orange had to be repaired and repainted. Though his assistant was an experienced trader who could cope with book-keeping well enough to look through the old books to establish local patterns of trading, Duncan was starting an entirely new career, aged forty-four – his fifth career, in fact. Whatever the secret purposes of the stores, their ostensible purpose had to be made effective; there was not as much money left as there had been before *Contact*, and anyway if he wanted to stay in Basutoland he would have to be a real trader, not a gentleman-trader.

The delight wore off quickly; Duncan felt that the villagers were trying to take advantage of him, and was very angry to discover pilfering from his goods. He was missing his wife and children very badly (almost every letter he wrote home contained some plan to bring Cynthia and one or other of the children up to Kubung). He was not eating properly, nor sleeping well. He found – he told Cynthia – 'the position of arbitrary power here is a continual temptation to bullying, and I have taken a terrifically tight rein on myself'.[16] The Licensing Board was so slow in giving him a licence that he began to worry; and, when his assistant rode down to where the car had been left, taking R1400 (£700) with him to buy stock, and then did not come back (in fact because the car had broken down), Duncan decided the assistant must have run off with the car and the money, so got in touch with the police and his lawyer, telegraphed his brother John for help, and – quite simply – panicked. When the assistant discovered what Duncan thought of him, he at once resigned.

Duncan's misjudgements, haste and panic were a sign both of the strain he was under and the extent to which he was missing Cynthia's usual calm advice. 'How much I need your advice,' he wrote to her. 'I have come to lean very heavily on you and to discuss everything with you ... without you I am too impulsive.'[17] Randolph Vigne remembers being very disturbed to find the state Duncan was in, nervous, over-talkative, living on Nutron (a kind of powdered soup used to supplement the food-supplies of the malnourished) and milk, for the only time that he ever knew him drinking more than was good for him, making wild plans which he would change a few moments later. He was desperately lonely, for local people were peasants whose lives he found dreary, desperate, abject from poverty and isolation. Norman Bromberger, a friend in the Liberal Party who visited him at the time, remembers what he thought of as an extraordinary outburst in which Duncan said how badly human beings compared with nature. When horses and other animals sweated they did not stink like humans; rotting or decaying vegetation lacked the offensiveness of human refuse and excrement; and more of the same. Duncan took Vigne out to see the beehives he was so proud of, and discovered that someone had broken into them and not only taken the honeycombs but smashed the hives: '... he stood there and said, "Absolutely typical, you know, not content with taking the combs they wreck the hives."'[18] It was a remark so untypical of the Duncan he knew that it worried Vigne almost more than anything else. 'I am no less non-racial,' he wrote to Julius Lewin, 'but I realize more fully the enormous gap between life and the middle-class way of thought I have been brought up in.'[19]

Fortunately, in mid-December Cynthia arrived permanently in Kubung with all the children, though Patrick and Alex were to return after the holidays to board at Bishop's. This made all well again; the children were old enough to enjoy the wildness of Kubung, and the sheer adventure of going to their new home in the mountains. Duncan arranged for them to be flown to Nkau's, to the north-east of Kubung; Cynthia, Alex and Ann rode five hours on horseback over the mountains to get to Kubung, while Patrick, Emma and Duncan himself went down the Orange in a canoe. By March he could write to his sister: 'Cynthia and I revel in the utter peace and silence of this place. Especially on moonlight nights it is something never to be forgotten, with no smells, noises or lights that are disagreeable.'[20]

The stores were beginning to be profitable, too, the local people were selling to the stores, and he was transporting out of Kubung a great deal of local produce for sale in Maseru; the problems over the licences and residence permit seemed solved when the local chiefs and Paramount Chief signed the forms (in quadruplicate) which made the stores officially his and his permanent stay in Basutoland permissible. The government was still, however, being a little petty in its dealing with him – in February Duncan was fined in the Quthing court for not providing the quarterly accounts for the stores, even though he did not know he had to provide them, had had no reminders about them, and had hardly started trading. But early in 1963 Joe Nkatlo, whose banning in 1962 had left him in great need, was secretly driven up to take over the running of Mohlakoana's, and that, too, was a great help.

So confident did Duncan feel about his position in Basutoland that, in March 1963, he began to make plans to leave the country temporarily to go overseas; to cover his absence from the store he arranged for one of his *Contact* assistants, Ebrahim Abraham, to come up to Kubung to take over the trading side of it. Cynthia would fly out normally with the two girls, going via

Bloemfontein and Johannesburg, and Duncan and the two boys would fly out in a small chartered aeroplane, straight across South Africa and into Bechuanaland, from where they would make their way up Africa and across to England; of course Duncan could not land in South Africa without being arrested.

When Duncan arrived in Basutoland in 1962 he was still a member of the Liberal Party; by the time he left in April 1963 he had resigned from the Liberal Party and was a paid-up member of the PAC. In effect, it was another of Duncan's 'giddy traverses', yet in the context of his personal history and temperament it was completely consistent.

First, there was the matter of violence. By the time of his arrival in Basutoland Duncan was convinced that one should no longer be afraid to use violent means of opposition. At about this time Duncan wrote an apologia for his views, probably as a supplement to the autobiography which he had begun in detention in 1960:

> I think that at this stage I ought to define my attitude to Gandhian non-violence. I am very nearly a Gandhian, yet not quite. In the same way I am very nearly a pacifist, yet not quite. It seems to me that there comes a stage in personal and national affairs, when force is right.
> I think, for instance, that it was right for the Allies to have attacked Hitler. I think that *satyagraha* offered by or on behalf of the Jews would have been quite useless.
> What I feel passionately is that there is a spectrum all the way from extreme violence to extreme non-violence. Our duty is to pull whatever situation we are involved in as far towards the non-violence side as lies within our powers. But there do come times when it [is] right that revolutions be made. . . .
> I feel about Gandhi's *satyagraha* in much the way as I feel about democracy: they are ideals. We lose sight of them at our peril. But it is often necessary to work towards them by methods less perfect. . . . Often the path to democracy lies through autocracy. . . . In the same way the path to true non-violence may at times run through violence. But let us never forget the spectrum, and our duty to press through a whole lifetime, for the nearest approximately to the non-violent end as is consonant with action in this world.[21]

Though some Liberals like Vigne, Neville Rubin and Adrian Leftwich (both former Presidents of the National Union of South African Students), and Eddie Daniels were in fact at the time organizing the African Resistance Movement, it was clear that the Liberal Party itself would never follow Duncan in this change of mind. The PAC had already made the move.

Secondly, the Sabotage Act of 1962 had made any kind of non-violent opposition even more difficult. It had, for instance, removed Duncan from the pages of *Contact*, for when in July 1962 the government published the 102 names of those banned under the Suppression of Communism Act – Luthuli, Abram Fischer the lawyer, Segal of *Africa South*, Cachalia, Dennis Brutus, Mandela, Kotane, Alex la Guma the writer, and the rest, Duncan among them – it became an offence for a newspaper to publish, print or repeat any statement made by any of these. Removed by his own choice from South Africa, now removed by government edict from saying publicly what he thought, where else had he to turn but violence?

Thirdly, from the Emergency onwards Duncan felt himself closer and closer to the PAC in more and more of its attitudes. He admired it for its opposition to communists in the ANC and to the Freedom Charter. He admired it for its ability to draw to itself a mass of the African people, what he had always wanted from the Liberal Party and had not got. Nor did he feel it was as racialist as some of his fellow-Liberals did, and even when it was he thought he understood why; for instance, after *Contact* had published an article by Elias Ntloedibe,[22] which Paton felt so strongly was racialist that he for a time considered dissociating himself from *Contact*, Duncan wrote to Brown: 'I think the article (which I saw this morning for the first time) is pretentious rubbish. . . . I disagree with him [Ntloedibe] in much but I regard his mind as having been crippled by the experience of apartheid and I *understand* why he feels as he does.'[23]

Fourthly, if his secret plan for the trading stores was ever to come to fruition, he would need the support of the PAC.

Personally, his relations with the PAC were good, and had been since long before his arrival in Basutoland. For instance, in January 1961 Philip Kgosana, having been released on bail, slipped over the border into Swaziland and wrote immediately to Duncan for financial help and to let him know his alias: 'Treat this correspondence as secret. *No one* but you should know. No publicity, until I give the green light PLEASE. I will give you my immediate plans soon.'[24] In August 1961 a group of six PAC men who had taken refuge in Maseru wrote to Duncan for help and again he sent it. He continued to publish articles and statements by PAC men in *Contact*. Through Vigne in particular he continued to keep in touch with those PAC men in Cape Town who had survived the Emergency. As soon as he arrived in Maseru he got in touch with PAC men there, and let them use the house he had bought as offices for *Contact*. When P. K. Leballo was released from prison and sent into exile in Zululand, Duncan immediately went to some trouble to get in touch with him, and was partly responsible for Leballo's leaving Zululand and coming to Maseru in July 1962.

Initially, Duncan planned to stay a member of the Liberal Party, and had opposed from Kubung a suggestion, then gathering ground in the party, that it should rename itself the Socialist Party and change its policies to those of democratic socialism: Duncan told Brown that he had stopped being a socialist when he was nineteen, and wouldn't stay as a member in a socialist party.[25] But the problem really lay elsewhere. Through a friend he had written to Astor, both explaining his new attitudes and asking Astor to arrange to have a 'trained saboteur' sent out to Basutoland; quite how he thought Astor would manage this is not clear.[26]

In December he wrote to Peter Brown in veiled terms about his new attitudes, and said, 'I want to tell you that I have joined an organization which shares much of this point of view'.[27] Brown replied at once, saying that Duncan's new attitudes were so out of tune with Liberal Party policy that he thought Duncan 'should now slip quietly out of the Party'.[28] On 10 February 1963, Duncan wrote again:

Well, I've thought it all over, and feel that in the circumstances I should leave the party. The circumstances are that I understand that the party has set its face against any of its members playing any part in a forceful attack on apartheid. I think that it might have been better not to present our members now with the need to choose – i.e. that a wiser path might have been to have let it ride, knowing that many of our best members have in fact joined other organizations whose sole aim is a violent assault on apartheid.

But there it is, Peter. And here is my resignation. But I do not think I can just slide out without saying anything. I should like it said, in these terms, that I have left: 'Patrick Duncan has resigned from the Liberal Party because he is no longer able to accept the party's policy of non-violence.' You, I think, should be the one to say this. Please do not say it *yet*, but let me know if you are willing to say it. If you are not willing to say this, then I shall have to try to get someone else to say it.

Cynthia feels as I do and also wishes to leave.

Duncan was referring to the African Resistance Movement, about which he had learned definitely late in 1962, when Robert Watson, an enigmatic Britisher who was the technical expert on sabotage in the ARM, came to visit him. In the circumstances of South Africa of 1963, it was an extraordinarily indiscreet letter for Duncan to write, and Peter Brown was understandably angry and disturbed. He replied that he was not prepared to make a statement about Duncan's reason for leaving the party, especially since he thought it would endanger both Duncan's position in Basutoland and his family in South Africa, and then said:

I think it is a safe assumption that a photostat copy of your letter is filed away by people who will be glad to make use of it at a time suitable to themselves. It will confirm in writing accusations which have been made these past months. If there are, as you say, people here who share your views, I think you should warn them at once of this fact. I do not myself know of people who do share these views. However, if I did know of them, I would have to ask them to make up their minds between continuing to work within the limits of our policy and leaving us. Apart from anything else this is an obligation to those people who have joined us believing that our policies say what they mean.[29]

Duncan was stung by this, and wrote back furiously to say that 'after eight years, and after all we have done together for the cause your valedictory letter . . . contained not one generous word . . . no reference whatsoever to Cynthia's resignation'.[30] Early in March 1963 Brown issued a statement to say that since Duncan had said he was 'no longer able to subscribe to the Party's policies . . . his membership . . . has therefore terminated'.[31]

Duncan and Peter Brown never resumed their friendship, and only when he was dying did Duncan repair the friendship with Paton, broken as an inevitable result of his resignation, the manner of it, and his joining the PAC. To other old friends, too, the resignation was not only a mistake but also a disloyalty; since Duncan himself was quite willing to be friends with people whose views he disagreed with violently, it hurt and bewildered him that they should not understand why he had done what he had. In his own mind he was not inconsistent; the Liberal Party had not become his long-since-dreamed mass party, so naturally he should join a movement closer to his own views. Even in his friendship with Jordan Ngubane, who had shared so much of his thinking for nearly ten years, there was a shift, and his review of Ngubane's book, *An African Explains Apartheid*, reveals an impatience with Ngubane's gentleness and idealism.[32]

At about the same time as his resignation, Duncan decided that he could no longer maintain *Contact*, though he told Brown his resignation from the party and the ending of funds for *Contact* were not connected. (The money from Astor had come to an end the year before, and the Duncans had already contributed a great deal to *Contact*.) *Contact* struggled on without the Duncans' help, under various editors and with cheaper formats, for a few years, but eventually went under.

In April 1963 Duncan signed a 'Declaration of membership' of the PAC, and it was countersigned by Z. B. Molete, Percy Gqobosa, and John Pokela of the National Executive of the PAC. Among his papers is his membership card, showing him to have been a fully paid-up member of the PAC for the years 1963–7, a member of Western Cape Region, Retreat Branch. The card is countersigned by P. K. Leballo, National Secretary.

Duncan had first met Leballo early in 1952, after Cyprian Thorpe had written for advice on whether or not Leballo should resign from his post as a teacher in an Anglican-run school after being named by the 'liquidator' as a member of the Communist Party. It was nearly as nonsensical a naming as Duncan's 'suppression' as a communist, for Leballo was one of the original Africanists of the ANC Youth League, and always opposed to communists in the ANC, so much so that in 1954, as Chairman of the Orlando ANC Youth League branch, he had been expelled from the ANC, though his branch immediately confirmed his position. In 1952 he had been jailed for his part in the Defiance Campaign. In 1959 he had been one of the driving forces in setting up the new PAC and during the build-up to the Campaign had been Sobukwe's right-hand man, almost Aaron to Sobukwe's Moses, since he was a gifted demagogue, who used many of the traditional techniques of the Zulu, Xhosa and Sotho praise-poems to reach an audience which more intellectual speakers in the Congress movement often failed to reach: for instance, in Cape Town in February 1960, he had started his speech in Sesotho (for he was a Mosotho by birth): 'Ke Potlako oa bo Leballo u gu thweng oa bona lefatse ea glno le thopilwe ka badichabo.' ('This is Potlako of the Leballos, of whom it is said "hold your shield lightly, your father's land has been looted by foreigners".')[33] (Duncan himself had a streak of the demagogue in him; for instance, in a speech in Guguletu in the Cape after his return from the All-African People's Conference, he had begun by raising his right hand in the air and saying, 'This is the hand that shook the hand of Nkrumah.'[34]) To his opponents, Leballo was simply an extremist, power-hungry, spendthrift, divisive in politics, a womanizer, disloyal to his subordinates; to those who, like Duncan, respected him, he was brave, intelligent, and a charismatic leader of ordinary people. Throughout his time in the PAC Duncan was to give him unstinting loyalty; even after Leballo had sacked him from his post as representative of the PAC in Algeria Duncan was prepared to defend him, though privately he expressed some disillusion with the man.[35]

Although three other members of the National Executive of the PAC signed Duncan's 'Declaration of membership', it is fairly certain that it was essentially Leballo's decision. For Duncan, the fact that he was allowed to join was clear evidence that the PAC was non-racialist; it had accepted him as an African, one 'who owes his only allegiance to Africa and is prepared to accept the democratic rule of an African majority'.[36] Other members of the PAC were angered by the decision, which they felt was too serious to be made simply at the top; though Duncan might feel himself to be an African, he had never suffered entirely as an African. Others thought it a tactical mistake: Duncan, although brave, outspoken, and a man who had already demonstrated his willingness to help the PAC, was more useful to them as a supporter and ally than as an actual member. Some thought that Leballo's reasons for accepting Duncan were mainly opportunist: here was an easy way to deny that the PAC was against whites as whites; here was a man with links in Africa, America and England, who could raise funds for the PAC; here was a man of considerable reputation in Basutoland, who could be useful in keeping pressure off the PAC when it became more active; here was a man who owned stores which would be useful for those who went into the Transkei and Natal.

Joining a movement like the PAC was of course utterly unlike joining a political party, for by 1963 the PAC was entirely underground inside South Africa (except when its members were on trial) and, though vociferous, mainly disorganized outside. In 1963, it was meant to be based on self-sufficient cells, with only the leader in touch with other cells; Leballo in 1963 claimed 150 cells, though the size of each cell varied. Technically, it was ten members per cell; Leballo claimed that one cell had in fact got more than a thousand members. Those cells were preparing for a great uprising in 1963. Whether Duncan knew what the plans for 1963 were cannot be known for certain; he had told Peter Brown in December 1962 that he was 'doing something about it, too' and, although a gnomic statement, the context makes it clear that he meant 'violence'; but he may have been referring to the ARM. Another Liberal who saw Duncan at Kubung remembers that he was then talking of making raids down into the Transkei; yet another who visited him in 1962 remembers what he thought at the time a crazy scheme to provoke an incident on the Basutoland borders which would result in South Africa invading Basutoland, and the British, possibly assisted by the United Nations, stepping in to restore peace, and, he hoped, taking over South Africa. Given that kind of planning, it seems likely Duncan knew the plans for an uprising by *Poqo* in South Africa in 1963; it is certain that he was privy to a number of PAC secrets – for instance, he was told in January 1963 of a plan to rescue Sobukwe from prison, and that the rescue would be followed by violence throughout the country. He had been told of trained fighters who were being brought back into the country, and of secret movements across the border, both of the Free State and of the Transkei (it was reported openly in *Contact* in late 1962 that Leballo had left Basutoland to go to the United Nations in New York and had then returned to Basutoland, so people were crossing illegally); he had also been told of a plan to assassinate Chief Matanzima of the Transkei.[37]

In the regrouping of the PAC after Sharpeville and Langa, and the decision to abandon non-violence, the plan had always been to take until 1963 to reorganize. On 27 March Leballo gave a press conference in Maseru in which he claimed that the PAC had a membership of 155 000 organized in their cells poised to deliver the 'blow' when he gave the word; at the same press conference, he said that the Paarl riots (where a large group of PAC men attacked the white town and killed a young man and a girl) and Bashee Bridge killings (where a family of whites were murdered in their sleep) were premature actions by *Poqo* groups who had 'jumped the gun'.[38] On 1 April the Basutoland police raided the PAC office in Maseru and questioned PAC members, though Leballo himself evaded their attentions; most important of all, the police confiscated a list said to have ten thousand names on it, mostly of PAC members inside South Africa. Shortly afterwards, the South African police began another series of raids in South Africa, and arrested hundreds of PAC men throughout the country; in South Africa at the time, it was commonly assumed that the Basutoland police had passed the list to the South Africans, and the arrest in South Africa of two of Leballo's couriers, Cynthia Lichaba and Patricia Lethalo, soon afterwards seemed to confirm the collaboration.[39] The taking of the lists, the arrest of the couriers, the arrests of April 1963, and subsequent trials, were crippling to the PAC and, subsequently, Leballo's reputation among many of his fellow-members of the PAC stood much lower than before; Duncan, however, continued to believe in him, and in June 1964 told Cyprian Thorpe that he very much admired him, and that he was the 'only PAC man out of jail worth anything'.[40] To Philip Mason he wrote that Leballo was 'the most interesting figure in the South African resistance. He will almost certainly dominate the scene in the near future.... The South African press has tried to make him out a braggart and a liar. He is a general urging on terrified troops, telling that victory is certain' – 'troops', he added in a postscript, 'does not refer to the movement but to the terrorized population'.[41]

Did Duncan ever understand what was meant by violence? Philip Mason remembers a conversation with Duncan in 1963 in which he talked of a 'sacrificial rebellion', in which men would attack a police-station with their bare hands as a symbolic gesture to focus world attention on South Africa; Mason says that Duncan clearly saw himself as taking part.[42] Soon after the Bashee Bridge murders, a friend in Basutoland asked him if he had had anything at all to do with them, and remembers his reply as being simply, 'No, thank God, I didn't'.[43] Duncan was capable of anger; he was a man capable, too, of acting as his feelings told him to act – he gave up too many chances of an easy and peaceful life for one not to believe that. Would he have been capable of killing? Was his notion of violence a romantic one, not based on the actuality of the dead and mutilated body of a person whom he had himself killed? Possibly he was romantic in this; he was never faced with the actual choice, only the theoretical one, though when he joined the PAC in 1963 and helped it afterwards he must have understood the implications of his actions. It is easier to see Duncan at the head of a column of men marching unarmed to attack a police-station as a symbolic gesture of sacrifice, or leading a platoon of men up a hillside to attack a machine-gun post, than it is to see him lying in the bushes at a roadside with a grenade in one hand and a panga in the other, waiting for a family on holiday to drive down the road.

On 4 April, soon after the raid on the PAC headquarters, Duncan left the stores in the hands of Ebrahim Abraham and Joe Nkatlo and joined Cynthia and the children in Maseru. After a number of delays, he and the two boys went to Maseru Airport on 12 May and met their pilot, a former mercenary from the Congo. Duncan was nervous about being flown by a man who made it clear that he was a white supremacist, and even when he gave his word that he would fly straight to Bechuanaland and not set Duncan down in South Africa and into the hands of the police, Duncan left the decision to his sons, since he thought they would be better judges than he was. The boys decided the pilot could be trusted, and they left. Duncan flew part of the way himself, keeping to an altitude of 150 feet to avoid their aeroplane's being spotted on radar screens. Cynthia and the girls went to Johannesburg; she had told her husband that she would not leave South Africa until she knew he had arrived in Bechuanaland, but it was in fact only after the flight to London had been called that she got the message that he was safely across South Africa.

From Bechuanaland Duncan and the boys flew to Elisabethville in the Congo, then to Munich, then London, then all came together again for a short holiday at Hexton Manor. At a press conference on 20 April, Nana Mahomo, London representative of the PAC, announced that Duncan had joined the PAC and Duncan gave his reasons. In May he gave his reasons at more length in an article in *The Times*, 'Gathering darkness in South Africa' (copies of *The Times* of 6 May 1963 reached South Africa with the article on page 13 cut out): a 'violent clash' was approaching, 'the major responsibility for which lies squarely on the Government' of South Africa, on the lines of the Algerian War, not in the distant future, since 'revolutionary violence is already occurring, and on an increasing scale'. Sabotage, incidents like those at Paarl and Bashee Bridge, the troubles in the Transkei, all would recur as a result of the 'driving force' of the PAC, which had gone underground 'more effectively' than the ANC and which had '150 "cells" ... it is not uncommon for a "cell" to have 1000 members'. (Exaggerated though Leballo's and Duncan's claims may have been, even the Snyman Commission gave *Poqo* in Paarl between 250 and 300 members.[44]) Three barriers, which had hitherto prevented the 'southward sweep of emancipation' – the Federation, South-West Africa, and the High Commission Territories – were 'being dismantled'.

The article ends with a call for reassessment in 'the following form':

The present rule of white supremacy is evil in the sense that Hitlerism was evil. It is unacceptable to any other state, and anathema to the non-white two-thirds of the human race. It is in any case approaching its end.

Since there is now no possibility of a constitutional solution to the problem of apartheid, support should be given to all who can minimize the danger and suffering of the transition to majority government. In particular, since intervention by the United Nations might well spare our country, Britain should no longer impede the influence of the United Nations in southern Africa.

For once, there was real reaction. Even the *Star* in Johannesburg commented: 'One of the features of the stock exchange this week has been the exceptional weakness of South African gold shares which followed the publication in Monday's London *Times* of an article by Patrick Duncan.'⁴⁵ He was interviewed on the BBC, he attacked the co-operation of the British authorities with the South African police in suppressing the PAC, he spoke at a public meeting with Dingle Foot, Jeremy Thorpe, Humphry Berkeley, Nana Mahomo, Robert Resha of the ANC (who attacked the PAC, calling Leballo an 'agent provocateur'), he appeared on 'Panorama' with Denis Healey, he talked to David Astor, he attended the Amnesty International Conference and talked to Peter Benenson of Amnesty, he dined with Patrick Wall (the Tory MP), he sent a postcard to Vorster, saying 'Having a lovely time – wish you were here'; and on 4 June he was declared a prohibited immigrant in the High Commission Territories.⁴⁶

It was a savage blow; all his plans depended on his living in Basutoland. Nor had he expected it; with the kind of personal backing he had in Basutoland from the Paramount Chief down, and the permission he had already been granted for the stores, he had thought his position secure. Soon, he became convinced that the decision had been the result of pressure by the South African authorities, that they had known about his flight to Bechuanaland, and that they had allowed it only on condition he did not come back.

He did what he could to fight the decision: both Dingle Foot and Jo Grimond asked the Secretary of State for the Colonies, Duncan Sandys, in the House of Commons, for an explanation, and were told that the 'Basutoland Executive Council recommended that (in view of statements made by Mr Duncan in which he associated himself with a policy of organizing violence in the Republic of South Africa) his presence in Basutoland would be an embarrassment to that country'.⁴⁷ Similar reasons applied in the other Territories. A letter from Sandys to Fenner Brockway gave fuller reasons and stressed that the Basotho themselves were involved in the decision;⁴⁸ after reading it, Duncan wrote to Brockway:

> Sandys delights in quoting how many black faces he has on his control boards [of immigration]. These at the moment are willing instruments of government policy. But a new constitution is coming, and it is likely that other influences will assert themselves when it comes. At the moment I think Sandys has me fixed, but I would hope that when I am able to get back to Basutoland to make representations I would not be stopped by London. I am confident that if I do get back I shall be able to enlist support from the Basutoland Congress Party and from the Paramount Chief. . . .⁴⁹

It is odd that he does not mention Leabua's Basutoland National Party; ironically, it was Leabua who was to protest most strongly, speaking out in the Legislative Council.⁵⁰ Although the Paramount Chief made it clear that he had not approved of the prohibition order, he was clearly in a difficult position, both personally and politically, especially with the new constitution under discussion.⁵¹

To add to the difficulties, the Basutoland administration now claimed that the Paramount Chief had not given his consent to the transfer of ownership of the stores to Duncan; even when he managed, by writing to the Paramount Chief personally, to get his confirmation, the administration still decided that the formalities had not been properly fulfilled, and talked of confiscating the stores. Duncan was already in considerable financial difficulty, and there was also Joe Nkatlo and his family to consider. He was too fair-minded not to understand that there was at least a case for keeping someone of his views out of Basutoland, particularly since he had said so openly what they were, for the country was desperately dependent on South Africa; but the 'shabby decision' to try to 'confiscate my home because I have been banned'[52] offended his sense of justice; 'an act of piracy' he called it in a letter to Schmoller.[53] Eventually, after appealing to the Paramount Chief, he managed to get the administration to accept that he had bought the stores properly, and eventually he was able to sell the stock of Kubung to Joe Nkatlo, and then to sell Kubung itself; Mohlakoana's he eventually gave to Nkatlo as a gift. But for all of 1963 and most of 1964 the issue of the stores was unresolved, and a considerable worry; he was still without a job, and short of money to the extent that he was even forced to ask members of the PAC to whom he had lent money to repay it. Though he had plenty to occupy him as an overseas representative of the PAC, he had also to find a job which would pay him a salary of some kind. Yet, as he told Cynthia, 'I know I could be applying for a job in the ordinary line, but I know I have something unique to contribute to the solution of apartheid, and to turn aside now would be to lose that unique opportunity of contributing to one of the most worthwhile causes of history.'[54]

But exactly what to contribute? It was a question he was not to resolve for nearly a year and, though it was to be a year of great activity and some success, it was also a year of doubt and confusion, of hectic activity but often without a central core of meaning.

Most of his battle against the decision to declare him a prohibited immigrant was conducted from the United States, where he had gone on PAC business soon after the announcement was made. His purposes were to canvas support and funds for the PAC, and encourage opposition to *apartheid*, and he set about them as energetically as always. Those were still the high days of the Kennedy administration, and not only was Duncan sure that American policy on South Africa would be changed, but also the style in which change would be sought suited him, for he admired the Kennedys' combination of idealism and hard-headedness.

The first week was spent with his sister Deborah and her daughters in Chicago; her marriage was in the process of breaking up and he had advice and comfort to give. He worked, too, on articles for the *Atlantic Monthly* and the *New York Times*, and was interviewed by Claude Barnett of the Associated Negro Press and for CBS News. Then he went back to New York where he joined up with Nana Mahomo. On the advice of various American friends, they set up 'a strategy' for meeting all those who might help the PAC, then began a round of visits to trade unions, United Nations officials and diplomats, churchmen, businessmen, State Department officials, Senators, the American Committee on Africa, and others. Cynthia and Alex joined Duncan in June, and they travelled to stay with Harold Hochschild, Adam's millionaire father; when Cynthia and Alex returned to England, Cynthia to look for a house, and with Mahomo following soon afterwards, Duncan continued his efforts, talking to diamond merchants to try to get them to boycott South Africa, to Adlai Stevenson about the arms embargo on South Africa, to State Department officials about an oil embargo. He did a great deal of lobbying in Washington, more successfully than on his last visits in 1961, spoke to various meetings and addressed the United Nations Special Committee on Apartheid on behalf of PAC.

There were moments of misery: he learned of Kgosana's attack on him in *Drum*, which saddened him a great deal, since he had respected Kgosana; on 1 August he wrote to Cynthia, 'Yesterday I touched a low point – despair would be too strong a word but I could see its dark aura'.[55] He wrote furiously to Jim Bailey to say that he should have stopped the articles appearing, and did not believe Bailey's reply that he allowed his editors a free hand. When he ran into the ANC representatives by mistake, they treated him with cold hostility. But soon he was working on an article for *Foreign Affairs*, which he was sure was the 'most important thing I have ever written'.[56] 'Toward a world policy for South Africa' was its title, and it tried to show the necessity of the United States taking sides in South Africa – she should, he urged, support United Nations intervention in South-West Africa, should help to impose an oil boycott, should end her investment in South Africa, should make her diplomatic practices and exchange programmes properly non-racial, and should give more scholarships to those opponents of *apartheid* who were forced into exile.[57] Then, on the 15 August, he was called to see Bobby Kennedy, and given his chance to put his plans for attacking South Africa from Basutoland:

> He listened with quietness and intelligence and without any impatience, dressed informally in his shirtsleeves. . . . He impressed me as a man like a steel spring. He is utterly committed on the integration front, yet unlike any other white liberal I've met he is tougher than almost any segregationist one can think of. Thus it is enormously encouraging to meet such a person.
>
> I know that similar ideas for neighbouring territories have been put to him recently, and that the whole concept is no surprise. . . . He took my address and indicated he would be calling back: I can perhaps see myself sitting here till my hair is white, but in more optimistic moments I can see the call coming early in the week.[58]

Six days later he did call back, to tell Duncan that he had thought about the plan, had consulted others, and that he wanted Duncan to get in touch with him again. Duncan was delighted, and wrote at once to Cynthia: 'even if nothing comes of it at this stage the immensely important fact is established that this young man with so much power is prepared to think as audaciously as this on our problem'.[59] The next day Bobby Kennedy's secretary telephoned again: would Duncan commit his ideas to paper? Immediately he sat down to write and rewrite a memo on his plans: 'I do hope it reaches far with the decision-making process,'[60] he wrote to Cynthia. Hearing on the diplomatic grapevine that Duncan had seen Bobby Kennedy, Eric Louw, Foreign Minister of South Africa, launched a characteristically hysterical attack: 'I wish to express my amazement and also my dismay that Mr Robert Kennedy ... has been prepared to receive such a rascal.'[61]

Soon after his meeting with Bobby Kennedy, Duncan met Teddy

Kennedy, too, and they talked about the southern African problem; once again Duncan was impressed by a combination of power, idealism and intelligence. It was also obvious that public knowledge of his meetings with Robert Kennedy had improved his position considerably among local politicians and with the press, all of whom tried hard to pump him for information about the talks. He saw more trade unionists and Senators, and it was apparent that funds for the PAC were beginning to come in. The FBI was very interested in his activities, and after he left the United States an FBI agent went to visit one of the people Duncan had seen most of, and questioned him closely about Duncan's attitudes and activities. Duncan had fortunately gone to some trouble to have himself registered as the agent of a foreign power, as United States law required.

On 28 August he joined the great Civil Rights March in Washington, and the next day flew back to England, stopping over for a day in Canada, quite certain that he had made an impact on American foreign policy towards South Africa, knowing that he had raised funds for the PAC, and having written at least one article which was bound to be noticed, since *Foreign Affairs* was an important source of new ideas in American diplomacy. As long as the Kennedy brothers stayed in power, he thought there was a good chance that both the world and America herself would become better places. It was an optimism he shared with many of his generation.

After a brief holiday, Duncan began work on a book he had been thinking about ever since he had collected evidence of police brutality in Langa and Nyanga; its title was to be *South Africa's Rule of Violence*, its technique to document and comment on a series of cases in which the South African authorities had used violence and torture against the population, and its purpose to justify the use of violence to overthrow an unjust and brutal regime. In October Cynthia and he took a flat in London, and he was able to see more of people like Sampson and Scott, and to talk to Mahomo about PAC plans in Europe and America. There was some talk of jobs; he asked the Institute of Race Relations if there was anything likely to suit him, and he thought for a time of taking up an offer made to him by Conor Cruise O'Brien, then Vice-Chancellor of the University of Ghana, to go there as a visiting lecturer in the Institute of African Studies; in December 1963, after the resignation under pressure from Nkrumah of the Chief Justice, Sir Arku Korsah, he wrote to O'Brien to say he was no longer interested in visiting Ghana. O'Brien replied at length to explain some of the complexities of his own position and of democracy in Ghana, to urge Duncan 'not to adopt a purely negative attitude towards Ghana. You say – and your life has proved – that you want to serve Africa. Ghana is neither the least democratic nor the least important part of Africa and even a regrettable action by her government will not change that fact.'[62] Duncan's reply shows once again how far his political beliefs were from ordinary liberalism:

> I agree with your views on Ghana.... After all, in the last few thousand years there have been few regimes out of the many of which we have records, which have not been autocracies. I remain a believer in democracy, but it seems clear that democracy can only flourish where there is a long tradition of settled rule, and where all parties trust the basic

determination of all others to tolerate opposition, and to treat the constitution fairly. In the nature of things, largely because the independent African states have had so short an innings, it is not surprising that so many have become autocracies. I agree with your admiration for the material progress that Ghana is making, and I shall never join the chorus here of those who as you so rightly say criticize the good things that Ghana is doing. . . .[63]

The same attitude was to become even stronger in the next few years; it was a clear development of that theme of his father's life which had become so significant to him. In just the same way as he had long ago criticized his fellow-Liberals for their ability 'to speak about the nice times when the colour bar has gone', but their inability to 'tackle the really important business of how do we get there',[64] so now he was looking ahead to a time when his country would need what he called an 'interim period of strong autocracy'.[65]

In mid-September he was asked to go to Denmark to talk to a students' union, the Studentersamfundet, and to Danish dockers who had been trying to enforce a blockade on South African goods; his lecture-tour was a great success, so much so that he was at once invited to return the next year. At a meeting of three hundred students in Copenhagen, he read out parts of a letter which had just reached him from Andreas Shipanga, of SWAPO, who had escaped to Bechuanaland from South Africa where he had been in jail, and telling the story of Dennis Brutus, who had just been shot and badly injured while trying to evade the police in South Africa.

On his return to England, he and Cynthia drove Patrick and Alex to Winchester where they were starting school. His only worry was that they should not 'catch the ruling bug of snobbishness, which is in any case much less virulent than it used to be',[66] though he was 'most agreeably surprised' to find that Winchester was less upper-class than in his day; 'one family was very lower middle class', he told Tim Holmes, there were the children of Dutch and Japanese and Canadian families, and 'the place is twice as democratic as it was when I was here'.[67] But, even if it had not been, he would still have been happy to leave them there, where he had been so happy himself, particularly because his children's lives had been disrupted and uncertain since his flight to Basutoland; he had warned both Patrick and Alex that they might find his own views on South Africa made life a little difficult for them there, though he hoped that Winchester would still tolerate his oddities as it had done years before.

In mid-October something happened which once again brought back some of the conviction about the rightness of his actions which the prohibition from Basutoland had shaken for a time. During his visit to America he had stayed very briefly with Freya von Moltke, and in October she wrote to him in England saying that she wanted to give him for his personal or political use the proceeds of the English publication of Helmuth's letters from prison in Germany. For Duncan, without a job, with the threat of the loss of the stores in Basutoland still hanging over him, with his political future unresolved, it was both a help with money (the gift came to about £500 altogether) and, even more importantly, a moral recognition that he was following in the steps of the man he called 'the finest man I have ever known'.[68] But he had to know for certain that Freya von Moltke understood his views on violence before he accepted the gift; he wrote to her to explain, and she replied:

> I have carefully pondered the question of whether Helmuth would approve 'even for weapons' thinking of your peaceful person and the hard decision it must have been for you, it means for you risking the lives of many of your closest friends.... I came to the conclusion that Helmuth's was the view that fights are unavoidable and fight one must if necessary and the weapons must be the adequate ones.... I am convinced you have chosen the right weapons.[69]

In late October he was asked to do a tour of Britain to talk about South Africa, and accepted; he spoke in Rugby, at Sheffield University, to the West Riding Council for African Affairs, in Glasgow, in Aberdeen, in Edinburgh, in Darlington, in Oxford, in Cardiff, in Swansea. It was hectic work, of speech-making, private talks, fund-raising, committees. But it was still not what he called real work, though he often enjoyed it. On his return, he gave a talk at Chatham House about the prospects for South Africa, he talked to schoolchildren, and in December went to Deal to address a meeting organized by Cresswell George, an old soldier who had written to him after the *Times* article. But most of his time went in finishing *South Africa's Rule of Violence*, and late in 1963 he delivered the manuscript to Methuen, who brought it out quickly enough for it to be on sale in March 1964. By the end of July Methuen had sold 1500 copies of the paperback and 750 of the hard-covered edition, though in fact the book never sold well enough even to earn the advance Methuen had paid him. While the book is useful to those who wish to demonstrate that violence in South Africa is endemic in the whole notion and practice of race supremacy, it is really no more than an anthology of press cuttings and a commentary on them, though of course the stories deserve to be told again and again until they are actually heard:

> In his lifetime Andries Sehule worked on the farm Sandspruit, in the Muldersdrif district of the Transvaal. His employer was Stephanus Lodewyk van Zyl. Van Zyl, one Andries Lubbe, and an unnamed white youth, chased Sehule after there had been some trouble. The youth caught him and brought him down. Lubbe hit Sehule on the stomach with a piece of wire rope, while Sehule lay on his back. (Not even dogs are accustomed to continue a fight if one of the combatants lies on its back.) The youth hit Sehule in the face with his fist and also kicked him.
> Van Zyl hit Sehule in the face with the flat of his hand. Lubbe then said: 'Wait, let me show you how a person hits a kaffir'. He then lifted Sehule up to his feet and banged his head on the ground.
> The whites then went away. Sehule remained, lying on the ground. The Africans carried him to his room. He could not speak. He breathed fast. His eyes were open. There was a wound on his head. His lip was cut and was bleeding. The police came in a *'vangwa'* (catch-wagon, meaning a pick-up truck), and took Sehule away, to die.

It was in the uncertainties of these months that Duncan began to think about what was to become *Man and the Earth*, his posthumous book. Part of it grew out of his old interests in the soil and agriculture; then, in December 1963, he took his sons, both of whom had particular interests in biology, to visit the Laboratory of Molecular Biology in Cambridge – this was the laboratory in which the spectacular discoveries on the nature and structure of DNA had been made. After talking to Perutz, Duncan came up with the idea of writing something 'simple [and] popular'[70] on DNA, and put to Methuen the idea of a book called *The Golden Helix*. Methuen put the idea to Dr Perutz, who felt that Duncan was not the man to do the job, since he had no scientific training; Duncan accepted this with good grace, though the kind of questions, both moral and material, raised by the DNA discoveries remained with him and were to become one strand of *Man and the Earth*. The third source was his friendship with Richard Hare, then a Fellow of Balliol, and teaching philosophy at Oxford, particularly moral philosophy. Hare and he had been undergraduates together, and had corresponded occasionally, Hare telling Duncan in 1945 of his war-time experiences as a prisoner of the Japanese (he was one of the survivors of the building of the Thailand railway), then sending him a telegram at the time of the Defiance Campaign, and so on. In May 1963 Hare got in touch with Duncan to broach the possibility of his discussing some problems in moral philosophy on which Hare had been working, in a programme for the BBC. Eventually, after Duncan's return from America, he and Hare had their discussion, and made a tape of it, called 'Blacks, whites and animals in Africa'; the tape was never used by the BBC, but the kind of moral problems which Hare posed to Duncan – for instance, on the uses and abuses of violence, on the differences in status between, say, the white supremacists' argument that blacks were a lower form of life and an agricultural officer's argument that locusts must be controlled – remained in his mind, and indeed became a dominant problem in his thinking. In a sense, Hare was helping Duncan to put together and make sense of all the major concerns of his life – the need to nurture the soil, the need to feed the hungry, the need to overthrow injustice, and the means by which those needs could be met. When was violence justified, when not? Pushed by Hare to see the logic of his own argument, Duncan in the interview came to 'the only answer I can give', that there is an 'arrangement' on this planet 'that is pleasing to the Creator, to God'.

> I can't get past that one. . . . Anything else involves the use of power and force, which is *I*, the dictator, saying that this is just, therefore it's just, and I'll bloody well make it just with guns. And nothing else seems to answer it except . . . there is a creator . . . that in some way it is the organization of good; things which are good are related to it in some way I don't understand.[71]

It was not, as Hare told him and as Duncan knew himself, a satisfactory answer, and seeking out that answer became the underlying urgency of the next years of his life, after a time even more urgent than the concerns which had dominated it for so long.

The PAC in exile from 1961 onwards was – to express a complex situation very simply – a muddle. The movement had, after all, only been in legal existence in South Africa a year, and that year had included what organization and preparation took place for the Anti-Pass Campaign, one of the results of which was the banning of the organization; its constitution laid down that the central power was to be held by an Executive Committee, with a President, National Secretary, and Treasurer-General and its principle of organization was centralism; but many of the Executive members were sent to jail in April 1960 or during the Emergency, and a few left the country. A few having gone to jail then came out, and either stayed in the country (some underground, some inactive) or went into exile; some went back to jail, many after the mass arrests of 1963. P. K. Leballo, acting President because Sobukwe was in jail, set up office in Maseru; others set up offices in Cairo, the Congo, Dar es Salaam, Addis Ababa, Ghana, London; others stayed in Swaziland or Bechuanaland. Even outside the country, PAC representatives were not safe: Southern Rhodesian and Nyasaland authorities had a policy of sending exiled South Africans who entered their territory back to South Africa; South African police were capable of crossing borders to kidnap refugees; once a bomb was exploded in refugee headquarters; and exiled politicians had a habit of getting involved in local politics (they often needed to, to survive) and ending up in jail. After the police raids in Maseru in April 1963, for instance, Ntloedibe was deported to Bechuanaland, and Leballo disappeared, either to the mountains or, some said, to Tanganyika; then he reappeared in Basutoland, it was said with very powerful friends in high places (Leballo's skill in disappearing was such that one of the rumours about him was that he had 'the gift of invisibility'). Later, Pokela, another Executive member of the PAC, was kidnapped from Maseru and put on trial in South Africa. There were also very real problems of informers infiltrating the movement. A young African who arrived, saying he had been active for the PAC in the Transkei and had escaped the police, might in fact be in the pay of the police, or he might be someone inactive in politics but with an eye on the main chance who wanted the PAC to find him a scholarship to America; his need might be real enough, yet what should be done with him?

As well as the material difficulties, there were the ideological ones, though the PAC was not a heavily ideological movement. Some members were anti-communist, some merely against white communists; some were capitalists, many for a kind of African socialism. Sometimes policy was expressed from the new headquarters in Maseru and, when it was transmitted to other centres, was either deliberately misinterpreted or not noted or was misunderstood; occasionally it was understood, but by then the central policy had changed (often for good reason, since the movement was under heavy pressure). Three members, including Kgosana, who tried to set up a government-in-exile in 1961, were expelled by the surviving members of the Executive; others were expelled for deviations of one kind or another, though an acting President in Maseru found it difficult to control a representative in, say, Accra. Occasionally instructions would come from the leaders inside South African jails; but sometimes those instructions conflicted with each other, since two people had brought out different versions of the same instructions. Some of the conflicts were more to do with personal feuds than with ideological differences. Other conflicts were to do with the relationship of the PAC with the ANC; in some centres there were good working relationships between individuals in each organization, and in others outspoken hostility; in some the local government insisted on good relationships – in Dar es Salaam, for instance, the government had insisted on a 'non-aggression pact' between ANC and PAC, though in London there was at least verbal aggression, as Mahomo and Duncan had discovered. When united fronts were set up, were they not in contradiction of the PAC policy to 'go it alone'? And yet those not involved in the disputes were impatient at the lack of unity.

Many of the conflicts within the PAC centred on money. Obviously if, say, the London representative managed to collect money from one source or the other he was not going to send all of it to a central account in Maseru, when he might then find himself with no money to run his office; but – or so the central office in Maseru argued – in a centralized organization the centre should control the funds. But for the London representative it was not only theory involved. He would want to be sure that the money he raised would be spent usefully, not merely squandered; not simply because he might be able to use it himself, but because, if it were improperly used, he would not be able to raise any more.

In late January 1964 Duncan decided to go to Dar es Salaam; in the diary[72] he kept of his visit, he gave as his main reason that he 'suddenly felt an urge to go', though he said, too, he was worried that the Liberation Committee (sometimes called the Committee of Nine), which had been set up by the Organization of African Unity the previous year to assist the liberation of southern Africa, might give aid only to the ANC. Given his own friendship with Nyerere, he thought that he might be able to influence decisions taken in Dar es Salaam. Soon after Mahomo had agreed that Duncan should go, a young PAC man who had been acting as courier between Dar es Salaam, South Africa and Maseru, and whom Duncan had worked with in Maseru, arrived in London, where he told Duncan a series of stories about the situation in Dar es Salaam which convinced him that his hunch had been correct. With a ticket given him by Mahomo, Duncan took off for Dar es Salaam, and almost immediately found himself in a tangle of financial, political and personal squabbles. Although he was himself in a tricky position – the only white man in the movement, an ordinary member and not a full representative, not on the National Executive nor even an acting member of it (there had been no National Conference since the one which set up the Anti-Pass Campaign; only a National Conference could elect an Executive; hence the number of 'acting' posts on the Executive) – he felt he had to sort it out; PAC people were being sent back to Bechuanaland, where they were in danger of being deported, others were destitute, others were deserting to join the ANC, not because they approved of its policies but because it was better organized, and the reputation of the PAC stood very low. The Treasurer-General of the PAC, A. B. Ngcobo, was in Dar es Salaam, but had no control over the funds at all, since Peter Molotsi, the local representative, had banked the £10 000 given him recently by the Liberation Committee in an account to which he was sole signatory. There was also doubt about £2000 which had come from Ghana and £3000 from the United Arab Republic. Some of the money had been sent to Maseru, some was still in the Dar es Salaam account. Molotsi's assistant, Gaur Radebe, was in jail, suspected of having been involved in the mutinies which had nearly toppled Nyerere.

Duncan himself was scrupulous in money matters; wishing to be independent of personal possessions, he had given all his own money away, to his wife, then to *Contact*, and – though this is not certain – a large sum to the PAC before he left Maseru. He had been brought up in a tradition in which corruption was an unforgivable offence against the commonwealth. He was also convinced that Leballo was a fine leader, and he was completely loyal to him; he was certain that if the PAC in exile was to remain a viable organization it had to stick to Leballo's instructions. He was also sure that, somehow, the exiled organization must be centred in one spot; while Maseru had advantages, he and apparently Mahomo favoured the Congo, where they already had a centre and a training camp for their forces, where they had the support of Holden Roberto and the expertise of his forces, and from where they would be able to move down into South-West Africa and the Bechuanaland borders as soon as they were ready and the international situation right. Before a decision of that kind could be reached, the power – and in part that meant the money – had to be back in the control of the centre, which meant the official Treasurer-General and Leballo, and those loyal to the original leadership of the PAC.

With J. D. Nyaose and A. B. Ngcobo, Duncan discussed what was to be done. When they had discovered the extent of the troubles, and had received instructions from Maseru to set themselves up as a commission of inquiry, they enlisted the support of Oscar Kambona, Tanganyikan Foreign Minister and Minister of Defence, and Chairman of the Liberation Committee, and his Permanent Secretary, Sebastian Chale. The bank account controlled by Molotsi was frozen on government orders. Other PAC members in Dar es Salaam rallied round: Lawrence Masimini, the PAC's 'military attaché', Sister Gertrude Mathulta, 'in charge of women's affairs in Africa', and others. Although Ngcobo left halfway through the crisis for the Congo, Duncan managed to persuade J. D. Nyaose not to leave for Nairobi, and later persuaded Ngcobo to return to take charge of the money; he was also able to meet up with Lawrence Mgweba, the PAC representative in Cairo, to try to sort out what had happened to the money given to Molotsi for the PAC by the UAR government.

In the end, after much toing and froing between the PAC and the Committee of Nine, the whole matter was placed in the hands of the Tanganyikan Department of Justice; the PAC office, official car, and files were turned over to the control of Gertrude Maltulta and Lawrence Masimini; the bank account was placed in the control of A. B. Ngcobo; and Peter Molotsi was suspended from office and his travel document revoked. It was altogether an unpleasant business for everyone; Duncan himself behaved with complete propriety, and in one sense enhanced his position in the PAC, since he had demonstrated his loyalty to the Maseru leadership. In another sense he had weakened it, for by involving himself so clearly on the side of one faction in the PAC he was henceforth much more exposed to re-criminations about his role. But it gives some idea of how he was seeing his position in the movement that while in Dar es Salaam he wrote a detailed memo for the PAC to place before the Liberation Committee and the Union of Non-Independent African States (the organization which had replaced and expanded the short-lived United Front of the ANC and PAC, and which included the Southern Rhodesians, the South-West Africans, the Angolans and Mozambiquans, as well as the two main South African movements). The memo, he told Cynthia, was aimed at 'co-ordinating the military efforts now being made by unskilled and unprofessional people into one professional effort'.[73] It was, for Duncan, not enough just to be a member of the PAC.

Sadly, one of the side-effects of his involvement in the crisis in Dar es Salaam was a break in the friendship between himself and Mahomo. As part of his follow-up to sorting out the money problems, Duncan wrote a series of letters to the organizations in America which had been giving money to the PAC, asking them to send money only to the new central bank account in Dar es Salaam, not to any other account; Mahomo, when he heard of this, felt it was an attempt to undermine his position in London, and was so deeply offended that he broke with Duncan. Later he, too, was to be suspended from his position in the PAC.

In between sorting out the financial and personal problems, Duncan did his usual tour of friends and officials; as well as the Tanganyikan officials he met in the course of his work for the PAC – Oscar Kambona, Chale, Otini Kambona younger brother of Oscar, Herbert Chitepo the Director of Public Prosecutions, Roland Brown the Attorney-General, most of whom entertained him in their homes – he got in touch with Joan Wicken, personal assistant to Nyerere, and was invited to see Nyerere, and then to an official reception where he met Lee Kuan Yew. He talked to Jimmy Hadebe, the local ANC representative, whose wife and children he had given a lift from Bechuanaland to Tanganyika in 1961, and went to see the Hadebe family at home. He met officials from various embassies, including the Russian, Chinese and American; one of the Americans, Jack Mower, whom he had known in Cape Town, introduced him to Eduardo Mondlane of FRELIMO, to whom he talked at length, though he wrote in his diary that he was not particularly impressed. He met the local representatives of SWANU and SWAPO. He moved from his hotel to stay with a local architect and old friend, Ax Nelson, and then to other friends. When Cynthia came out to join him for a short holiday, they went off for weekends at the seaside. He met various old journalist friends, including Anthony Sampson and George Clay (who soon afterwards was to be killed by a landmine in the Congo). He talked to various local academics, including Terence Ranger the Africanist, Tom Karis the American scholar and co-worker with Gwendolen Carter of Northwestern University, and South Africans teaching at Kivukoni College. In short, it was a renewal and development of his acquaintance with another of the circles he moved in.

Partly of course it was simply a matter of enjoying the company of old and new friends, but there is another sense in which a map of Duncan's life based on the people he knew and talked to would consist of a series of overlapping circles: there was the 'kindergarten'–Winchester–Oxford circle; there were the Basutoland circles, the officials, the Paramount Chief, chiefs, politicians, teachers, journalists and missionaries; there was the South African left-liberal circle, of the Congress leadership and the Liberal Party; there was (though he was less part of it) the American circle, Mennen Williams, the Kennedys, Irving Brown, Philip Kaiser, Philip Crowe, Elliot Richardson, George Houser and others; there was the English Fabian–anti-colonial circuit, Harold Laski, Fenner Brockway, Scott,-Huddleston, Fox Pitt, Astor, and others; and there was the African circle, Nkrumah, Nyerere, Mboya, the Khama family, Padmore and others. And those circles by no means exhaust all his friendships. Where, for instance, does one fit Anton Rupert or Piet Cillié of Afrikanerdom? Smuts, Reitz, Van der Byl? Or his wife and her family and friends? In these circles he came the closest to power that he ever came, and some of the people he talked to were of course very powerful men – Nkrumah for a time, Nyerere, Bobby Kennedy for a time, Leabua Jonathan in a smaller country; but mainly those Duncan talked to were themselves the men and women who talked to the powerful men, the lobbyists, those with ideas, interests and strategies, not those who controlled armies or international companies or states. Duncan might have abandoned *satyagraha* in 1962, but in another more complicated sense he did not, at least not in an essential sense: he still believed that a man speaking out of passionate principle would be heard, and that the ideas he had would be taken up by those with real power when they heard them, because the ideas were right, were good. Even though he had abandoned the possibility of talking to men like Erasmus, Rademeyer and Vorster in such a way that they would wish to listen, he still believed that most other men would *hear* him, nor just *listen to him*; that was one of the reasons he so enjoyed talking to Bobby Kennedy – this was a man who heard, who then telephoned to say, 'Put these ideas on paper,' and then would get something done. Duncan was not a fool, he knew that not all ideas would be heard, he understood why Macmillan 'went deaf' at a crucial point, because power was a complicated business. Autocracy might be necessary, at least as a stage towards democracy; or else one might need to look to the mass of the common people to bring this power into play; or one might have to bring the armies in, for a time at least. But he lived in a world where ideas still mattered, not one where people only listened and then said afterwards, 'Such a charming man, but what nonsense he talks', but where they heard the ideas and, if they were persuaded by them, did something about them; after all, was that not what he did himself? If he was convinced of the rightness of an idea, did he not follow it wherever it led him, no matter how uncomfortable the journey might be, or the arrival?

In a world where all power is assumed to be material, where power is in the mouth of a gun, and history a purely materialist process, a man like Duncan is bound to seem something of an oddity, though he was by no means the only one of his type in his times. He believed that ideas had to go in search of power, but was sure that, when ideas met up with power, power would follow. It is not enough to label him as an idealist, and so have done with him; not only did he live out his own ideas, but he also took them out into the world, spoke and wrote about them, and expected them to be heard. They were often not listened to, and he regretted that; it did not mean they were wrong, nor that they would not be heard eventually.

In other words, that map of overlapping circles reveals not simply something about Duncan's politics, but about his view of the world; and if his view of the world was entirely wrong, then it is not only a comment on him, but on a world where it is supposed that men do not ever hear each other or each other's ideas, where power and history move on lines so steady and fixed that if one tries to deflect them all that happens is they brush one aside.

During the latter part of their stay in Tanganyika, the Duncans went to visit the Ngurdoto and Ngorongoro craters which had been turned into game reserves; Duncan was deeply moved by the experience of being able 'to see, to hear, and to smell the world as it was before man conquered it':

> From the thickly forested rim we looked down on the open grassland of the floor of the crater and on its shallow pools. We looked down on herds of elephants and rhinoceros, on the strange giraffes, and on the antelopes and the lions. We saw, high above the clouds, the glaciers and snows of Kilimanjaro's 6000-metre peak, an astonishing backdrop....[74]

The sense of wonder was as strong as ever.

Cynthia left for England a few days before he did, since he needed to get in touch with Peter Raboroko, the Secretary for Education on the PAC Executive, who was then teaching up-country in Tanganyika, about the rearrangements of the PAC office; he found Raboroko much in sympathy with his actions. He spoke to the pupils in a secondary school, and got them to sing their National Anthem, which is sung to the same tune as 'Nkosi sikelel' iAfrica' ('God save Africa'); he then talked of the origins of the hymn, and its significance to South Africans as the national anthem of black South Africa. He went to visit Zanzibar. Eventually, on 3 February, he went back to England.

A week later, he left again, this time for Denmark, to speak again to students, longshoremen, the Danish South Africa Committee, to give an interview on the State Radio Service, and to talk in schools. Then, on 28 March, he left England yet again, this time for Algiers, where he was to take over as the official representative of the PAC to the Algerian government.

CHAPTER 11

March 1964–July 1965
'*This unproductive bitterness is not liberation*'

Leballo himself appointed Duncan as the PAC representative to Algeria, though Duncan had asked to be posted there, mainly to get away from the internecine squabble developing in London between Mahomo and Leballo's supporters; the appointment seems to have been partly as a return for what Duncan had done in Dar es Salaam. The only positive reason for the appointment was that Duncan had fluent French, which very few other PAC men had, though Leballo's letter of appointment called Duncan 'a devoted member of our Party', whose 'loyalty and service to the Party are unquestionable', and who 'should acquit himself admirably in all duties entrusted to him'.[1] Several PAC men – for instance, Matthew Nkoana – thought the appointment unwise, though personally they liked and respected Duncan; certainly, given his anti-socialism, it was an odd place to send him to, for post-revolutionary Algeria was hardly anti-socialist, particularly during the time of Ben Bella.

Duncan's first task when he went to Algiers at the end of March was to get accredited to the Algerian government as the new PAC representative. This was not as easy as it seemed, since he arrived just as a meeting of the Afro-Asian Solidarity Committee was ending, and he discovered that the PAC representative to that meeting, Gora Ebrahim, had been instructed to stay on as Algerian representative by Lawrence Mgweba, the Cairo representative. He managed to sort this out amicably with Gora Ebrahim. Then he found that the last PAC representative had lent the flat given to the PAC by the Algerian government to some Angolans, and they were of course reluctant to give it up to a man they did not know, though Duncan found them otherwise very friendly. The Algerian Foreign Ministry, from which he needed to get the accreditation, was overloaded first with the Solidarity Committee meeting, then with a visit by Sekou Toure and Eric Williams (of Trinidad). So he had time to look around Algiers, to visit some of the older parts of the city and an old Roman town nearby, to talk to the Anglican parson Lee-Warner, whom he found shared his interest in old books, to buy up about seventy-five old books on Algerian history for about £10 (some *colon* had left them behind), and to talk to some of the other southern Africans in Algiers. He met Eduardo Mondlane again, and told Cynthia that he was 'beginning to like him more';[2] he had a long talk to an old friend, Nquka, of the Swaziland Progressive Party, and Zwane, his colleague; he met Chakela and Moses Molapo, representing the BCP in Algiers; and he met Robert Resha of the ANC and some of the other ANC men there.

The most pleasant part of his stay was an expedition to plant trees at Arbatache, twenty miles outside Algiers, on the *journée de l'arbre*, 'the day of the tree', set aside for planting trees to help in the fight against soil erosion. He could hardly have found an occupation which pleased him more, and it immediately made his feelings for the new government of Algeria very warm indeed – socialist it might be, but if it planted trees against erosion there was much to be said for it. Moreover, the whole exercise had been efficiently planned, with trains, buses, lorries, saplings, spades, mattocks, pickaxes, all carefully laid on, and plots ploughed and marked. Better still, the saplings were cypresses and pines, and not only eucalyptus, which Duncan disliked because it desiccated the ground; so he planted nine cypresses and pines 'with all the skill I have, and with a murmured wish that it might last a hundred years, that it might itself thrive and give shade and protection to man and wild things for all that time'.[3]

It was a good start to his stay, and he soon fell in love with Algeria; it was, he felt, very like South Africa could be after its revolution. Algiers itself, in climate and situation, with both sea and mountains, seemed like Cape Town without the South-easter. Moreover, Algeria offered Duncan political hope: he was impressed by the way the National Army had turned from fighting to reconstruction, by the way in which the government had tackled the problems left behind by the massive departure of the *colons* to France, and with the lack of bitterness against the French:

> ... the idiot terrorism of the OAS ... might have provoked a counter-folly, that of wanting to clear everything French ... out of the country. In place of so predictable a reaction both the government and the people have shown a forbearance, a lack of vengeance, which is one of the noblest things I have seen.[4]

On 7 April the Algerian government gave him full accreditation, with control of the PAC flat and office, and a telephone, as well as an official 'attestation', much stamped and signed, and with a formal request for all 'autorités civiles et militaires' to offer him 'aide et protection'. With these arrangements made, Duncan flew back to England, to join Cynthia and the children, who were on holiday, and to arrange to move the family to Algiers; the two boys would stay at Winchester, but the girls would join Cynthia and him in Algiers.

What was Duncan doing for money? For instance, between May 1963 and April 1964 he spent, on his PAC activities alone, nearly £1000 – paying part of the PAC office telephone account in London, his air-tickets to America and to Algeria, and giving about £630 to the PAC, either in direct donations to the Maseru office (for example, £300 in June 1963, £100 in October 1963) or in loans to members. What money he had personally was tied up in the stores in Basutoland. Yet, in May 1964, when he listed the money he had spent on behalf of the PAC and sent a copy to the headquarters in Maseru, he was not asking for it to be repaid, since he wrote at the bottom: 'I renounce all claims. PD 15.5.64.'

In 1962 one of Abe Bailey's grandchildren, Bill Lloyd, had apparently promised Duncan a gift, for his personal use in politics, of £10 000; he told Duncan, too, that he would leave him £25 000 in his will, for the same purpose. Exactly how much of this Lloyd gave Duncan is uncertain, or when; but sometime in 1963 Lloyd gave him about £4000 (in one letter Duncan says £8000⁵). Some of this money Duncan may have given to the PAC before he left Maseru; certainly he sent at least £400 to Maseru in 1963–4, and helped other PAC men with money in 1963–4, paying for an air-ticket for Mahomo, and giving money to J. D. Nyaose. By March 1964 he was again running perilously low on money, and in several letters talks of a 'financial crisis'.

Tragically, mainly for his family but for Duncan, too, who had liked and admired him, Bill Lloyd was drowned in the Mediterranean in August 1963, when the motor-boat carrying him and Bill Willoughby, Lord Ancaster's son, was caught in a storm. Duncan, who had been relying on getting the rest of Lloyd's promised gift, was in a quandary; he did not know whether Lloyd had already made arrangements to give him the rest of the money, nor did he know if Lloyd had made him a legacy of £25 000. He had been fond of Lloyd, and Lloyd's uncles Jim and Sir Derrick Bailey were two of his oldest friends, though they often disagreed in politics; yet a legacy from Lloyd would give him the freedom to commit himself totally to the PAC, and enable him to do much more than simply talk on its behalf. He wrote tentatively to Jim Bailey to find out what was being done to have Lloyd's death presumed, and to lawyers to find out about the rest of the donation Lloyd had begun to give him; but, eventually, knowing the kind of pain that pressing his claim on the estate would cause Lloyd's family (who were apparently convinced that he was still alive somewhere), he resolved to forget the whole business, and simply be grateful for what Lloyd had done before his death.

Fortunately, the PAC office in Algeria was supported by the Algerian government, which gave it a subvention of DA2500 a month (then worth about £185). This enabled Duncan both to run the office and to pay his personal expenses and for the running of his home, though he was by no means a rich man on that amount; fortunately, Cynthia was able to pay for most of their other expenses, and the children's school fees were paid out of the trust their grandfather Ashley Cooper had established for them. He continued to keep meticulous accounts, and regularly submitted them to Maseru for scrutiny – copies are among his personal papers. Since one of the accusations regularly made against Duncan while he worked for the PAC was that he was in the pay of the American CIA, it is worth noting these details.

Soon after his return to London in April, Duncan was told that the South African government intended to deprive him of citizenship. The Secretary for the Interior had written to him on 14 January saying that he would be 'glad to learn why it is impossible for you to use a South African passport'; since the government had confiscated his passport in April 1962, Duncan thought it such a nonsense he did not reply. Hence, in April, he was asked if he wished to say anything about the impending deprivation of citizenship; he replied:

I am interested in my South African citizenship. South Africa is the only country that will ever be my home. To the true South Africa I am inflexibly loyal. If there are new laws which lead you to wish to submit my name to the minister for deprivation of citizenship, that is an affair between you and the minister, an affair into which I do not seek to intrude myself.

If you take away my citizenship I shall continue to feel myself a South African, because I know that any decision of this kind made by today's authorities cannot represent the wishes of more than a tiny minority of the population, and because I know that such a decision will not last very long.[6]

It was a brave reply, but losing his citizenship hurt him nonetheless, for it was confirmation of the irrevocable choice he had made; still, even if he were excluded from both South Africa and Basutoland, at least he was going back to Africa, and to a country on which his own might one day model its future.

In late May he, Cynthia and the two girls moved to Algiers, first into various flats and then into a beautiful old French colonial house, 'La Consulaire', with thick whitewashed walls, Arab carpets scattered on the tiled floors, old furniture, a terrace on which they took their meals, and a view over the bay of Algiers and the Casbah to the west of them. To Peter Benenson of Amnesty he wrote: 'It is in a way coming home, to come here.'[7] However, almost as soon as his new role began, he discovered that life as the PAC representative in Ben Bella's Algeria was not going to be easy. In London, a commission of inquiry set up by Leballo was investigating Mahomo's handling of the office there, and Duncan was dragged in because of the role he had played in Dar es Salaam. That would not have mattered, since Duncan had left London mainly to remove himself from squabbles; but some of the PAC dissidents approached the Algerian Embassy in London, and Duncan found that the ground he had so carefully prepared in early April was swept away. Moreover, the ANC in Algeria, then under the leadership of Robert Resha, was antipathetic both to the PAC and to Duncan personally, and even his predecessor as the PAC representative, Ndibongo (known as Machema abroad), spoke against him. Machema had also, Duncan thought, offended the Algerian authorities by some of his actions as representative, and so Duncan lost out every way: those sympathetic to the PAC had been offended by Machema, and those antipathetic to the PAC listened to the scurrilous stories about Duncan which some ANC men spread. Even the PAC flat, office and files were not after all available to him, and it took him until early August to persuade the government to insist that as representative he should control them.

By the end of the year, Duncan could report to headquarters that, despite the difficulties, he had 'good friends in the Algerian Government, in the Ministry of Foreign Affairs, the Presidency, and the Political Bureau'.[8] The visit of Leballo, Raboroko and others in November 1964 for the Independence Anniversary celebrations helped, and persuaded Duncan once again that Leballo was in control of the PAC, despite the dissidents. (All the same, after Leballo's visit, he wrote to Anthony Steel, the PAC legal adviser in London, to say to him: '... *PLEASE*, urgently, get someone trustworthy in UK to advise PK on the rudiments of cipher. He thinks (*a*) that a letter glued up is proof against Verwoerd. I am writing to say that he must know that any such letter can be unglued and read. And (*b*) that a simple replacement code (A equals Z, etc.) is proof against decoding. With frequency rules anyone can break such a code in a matter of minutes.'[9]

Duncan arranged a public lecture for Leballo at the time of his visit, though unfortunately hardly anyone came to listen. He began a newsletter, 'Pan-Africa', in French. He visited Ministries to press the case of the PAC. He spent much time talking to other liberation movements, and in December reported to Leballo that

> Excellent relations exist with: SWAPO, GRAE (Holden Roberto's movement) ... National and Popular Front for Equatorial Guinea; Ethiopian People's Movement Council; Canaries' Liberation Movement (MPAIAC); the Delgado wing of the Portuguese Revolutionary Movement; the UPC (Cameroons Liberation Movement). Good relations exist with: ANC.[10]

He called on Embassies and was invited to their functions: China, the United States, the Soviet Union, the United Kingdom, Morocco, Albania, Brazil, Bulgaria, Chile, Cuba, Czechoslovakia, Denmark and twenty-four more. He had not, he told Leballo, contacted the other thirteen represented in Algiers, but would do so when he could. He had attended dozens of official receptions and, whenever there was an official welcome or seeing-off at the airport, he went out. When PAC 'students' (usually a euphemism for guerilla-trainees) arrived, he used to go to meet them at the airport and arrange their transport to the training camp; he was deeply impressed by the quality of the men who came for training, though he had little to do with them, except for providing them with books on warfare and, once, getting two out of an Algerian jail after some unspecified trouble. The PAC decided that it was necessary to have a new name for South Africa, and settled on 'Azania'. It was a name Evelyn Waugh had used in *Black Mischief* and one of the PAC members wrote to Waugh to ask where he got the name from; the reply came: 'As you should know it is the name of an ancient East African kingdom.'[11] All the same, Raboroko, Duncan and Ntantala went on a delegation to the offices of *Le Peuple Algier* to urge the adoption of the new name,[12] and henceforth the PAC talked of Azania.

In short, he was a kind of mini-Ambassador, a *chargé d'affaires*, for the PAC, and it was often a thankless task, however well he got on with local officials and some of the Embassies. Mainly the trouble was the PAC itself, at least in its exiled form: 'Our reps are too damn lazy and disloyal to write letters to each other, and to work for the movement instead of each trying to run a racket, using PAC money for their own glorification.'[13] Intrigues, embezzlement, dismissals, commissions of inquiry, expulsions, suspensions, threats, counter-threats and international tours were not his idea of the struggle against *apartheid* in South Africa and, though he still believed that Leballo was the main leader of quality, and though he held out for a 'regrouping round Maseru' as the best solution, he was beginning to question some of Leballo's decisions: for instance, Lawrence Mgweba, the PAC representative in the United Arab Republic, whom he knew to be loyal to the Maseru leadership, was suddenly dismissed from his post, and on learning this Duncan at once wrote to Leballo to say, as gently as he could, that it was a mistake. Something had gone temporarily wrong with his relationship with A. B. Ngcobo, who wrote to him angrily to mind his own business, though by August 1964 they were on better terms again, since Ngcobo sent money to help in the running of the office. Even Elias Ntloedibe, once his Basutoland editor of *Contact*, seemed to have lost sympathy with him, for reasons Duncan was not sure existed, though again relationships were soon restored. Though Leballo, J. B. Nyaose, Gertrude Mathulta and others remained his confidants, he knew that he was not unthreatened, despite all his hard work in Algeria.

Fortunately, he and Cynthia and the girls were very happy there; the climate and the style of life suited them, the girls were happily installed in a *lycée*, and the family saw something of the countryside. The boys came out for Christmas, and Hermione Hichens came to stay, too (she and Duncan stayed up until the small hours having a furious argument about Nkrumah, Duncan defending him, Hermione Hichens attacking; eventually, Cynthia ordered both of them to leave off arguing and go to bed). Duncan and .Cynthia made close friends with Claude Wauthier, a French journalist and writer. In late November, the girls, Cynthia and he joined in another mass tree-planting exercise at Arbatache, though this time it poured with rain. In January, they visited the Sahara, and Duncan wrote to Astor afterwards that 'it was like walking on the moon, a strange, man-free, utterly clean, dazzling world'.[14] He began, indeed, to develop intense feelings of personal loyalty and commitment to the country very soon after arriving there. In August 1964 he wrote to Astor to urge him to get the *Observer* to do something to counteract the critical press which Algeria was getting: 'Patrick Wall is able to quote it as a top human failure. It is, on the contrary, full of remarkable success (as well as failures). . . .'[15] As a result Astor arranged for Patrick Seale to go out to write a report, though what he wrote angered Duncan enough for him to write a furious letter to Astor to say that the 'dispatch . . . made me feel quite sick. I had hoped the *Observer* would do something in depth on this fascinating and increasingly important country, showing the real achievements . . . as well as the weaknesses and failures.'[16] Instead, Seale had written of appalling unemployment, a near-revolutionary situation in eastern Algeria (which Duncan did not believe existed), and the oppression of the press. Astor replied gently, and – after the overthrow of Ben Bella, and another article by Seale – Duncan wrote 'to eat my angry words to you about his last article . . . his guess was closer to the truth than mine'.[17] It was characteristic both of Astor's gentle fairmindedness and Duncan's passionate reversals; but it reveals, too, how much he had adopted Algeria as his latest home. Though he retained what Randolph Vigne called his 'quaint views on the virtues of Western capitalism',[18] which Duncan said meant only that Western capitalism 'is a good deal better than the absurd social experiments that claim to abolish exploitation at untold cost in suffering',[19] he did also see virtues in Algerian socialism; he told Hochschild:

It is a continuing pleasure to be here, and each day carries something of interest. This is specially true for a South African, as so many of the apparently insoluble South African problems have been solved here. One of the most interesting subjects here is the taking over of empty factories, houses, and farms by 'Comités de gestion', or workers' control committees, a form of organization that probably has a big future in the industrial field in all countries, especially in the less complex industries.[20]

To another young friend who had recently left South Africa, he wrote: 'You could not live one day in Algeria without realizing the joy that the victory of the FLN has created, without realizing that with all the present problems, that victory over racism has cured the human race in Algeria of a dangerous disease.'[21] So strongly did he feel about Algeria that when, in August 1964, he was asked by Amnesty to investigate political arrests which were taking place in Algeria he refused, arguing that strict control was an inevitable consequence of the revolution.[22]

In fact, during his time in Algeria – and particularly because his job was not so demanding that he did not have time to think – his political ideas were beginning to change and develop considerably. In the first place, he had lost many of his illusions about the saving role of the United Nations because of 'the mess' it had made in Cyprus and the Congo;[23] like many of his generation, the assassination of President Kennedy had been a shattering blow to his hopes of a more equitable foreign policy from the United States and, although he was delighted that Bobby Kennedy continued to take an active interest in South African affairs, by May 1965 he was so disillusioned with American foreign policy that he wrote to Houser of the American Committee on Africa to dissuade him from visiting Algeria: 'You probably don't understand how unpopular your government is here, and rightly, after Stanleyville, Viet Nam, and the Dominican Republic.'[24]

American behaviour over Katanga, United Nations' inability to settle the civil war in the Congo, what he thought British cowardice in the High Commission Territories led him to believe less and less in intervention, and more and more that the struggle in South Africa depended on black Africans being prepared to fight; this is one of the most consistent strands of his letters between 1964 and 1967. In December 1964 he wrote to Randolph Vigne that only one thing could reverse the way the international 'balances' had been thrown against the South African liberation movement: 'a hard hit into Verwoerd's solar plexus by the African people of SA'.[25]

To Astor in July 1966 he wrote:

For perhaps 18 years it has been reasonable to hope that the UK and the US, as the big powers that were able to do something in that area, might be persuaded to act against apartheid. At one stage, in 1960, it was touch-and-go, and I think that there was nearly then launched a 'world-wide move to strip the southern whites of power'.... Such hopes are not, in my view, any longer reasonable. The power of the UK has been exposed in Rhodesia for the worthless thing that it is. Kennedy is dead; and the UN and OAU have never been so unable to move. Free Africa has greatly overplayed its hand. Fascinated by UN voting power some of them seem actually to have believed that the Gambia was the equal of the US and USSR. Verwoerd has strengthened his hold over both blacks and whites in the south, has built a strong economy and army, and could not now be tackled without a major military effort. This was not true in 1960. Even as a psychological effort it now seems tinkering with the problem to ask a housewife not to buy South African sherry.

Put somewhat differently, each state, while mainly motivated by selfishness in its foreign policy, does possess a fringe around this central selfishness in which it can afford to be unselfish and moral. In the past, the South African problem was small enough to lie within this fringe in the policies of the UK and US. This is no longer true. The appalling performance of Mr Wilson over Rhodesia is surely attributable to the fact that he discovered this truth *in mid course*, and tried then to change horses. That governments cannot be more unselfish may be deplorable, but that they cannot has been a political fact of millennia.... The southern end of the continent is sliding into a war of liberation in which, eventually, black men from the Union will face white men with guns, a situation in which the possibilities for violence are unlimited.... The lessons of SWA and Rhodesia seem quite clear for the Africans of South Africa; until they learn to fight as the Algerians fought they will have to remain slaves....[26]

He had moved a long way from the man who had seen United Nations intervention as the only way of saving South Africa from itself.

As a concomitant to his disillusion with the idea of intervention was his view that the mass emigration of French *colons* from Algeria was what would happen to white South Africans, though this, too, may be traced to before his going to Algeria (and perhaps explains one of his reasons for going there, rather than being simply explained by his going there). For instance, to Harold Hochschild he wrote in August 1963: '... even if we were able to magically transform the country into a democracy with no suffering or loss of life, a large part of the white minority would choose to leave'.[27]

These attitudes were very closely related to the kind of theory of Africanism which had lain behind the foundation of the PAC. It is commonly assumed that the foundation of the PAC was simply a matter of black chauvinism, of rejection of communists in the ANC and in the Congress Alliance, or of personal grudges; while it is true that the PAC was never a heavily ideological movement, there are ideas in Africanism which cannot simply be dismissed. During the first part of 1965 Duncan worked hard on a paper (which he never published, though he did deliver an earlier version of it to a meeting of the PAC in London in May 1965, and did in fact consider publishing it at his own expense as a pamphlet) which was in effect an attempt to turn his and others' ideas into an ideology for the PAC.

The paper starts by rejecting both of the usual versions of the South African struggle, the liberal version which sees it as a 'civil rights struggle', the Marxist as 'basically a class struggle'. Duncan puts forward a thesis that, in fact, it is a 'struggle between two nations'.

I have come to hold this nationalist view with some difficulty. I used to think that the apartheid problem consisted in this: that one limb of a multi-racial nation was oppressing another limb. This may possibly once have been true. But whether or not it ever was true, events have overtaken it, and the possibility no longer exists of welding the black and white South Africans into one nation.[28]

He goes on to develop his argument of two nations 'struggling for the control of this territory now and for the centuries ahead'. The 'probable eventual victory of the African nation' will result in the other nation, the 'Afrikaner-led white or European nation', mainly wishing to leave the country.

Acknowledging both the sadness with which he has reached that view, and the misery an exodus will entail, he says that nevertheless the struggle will henceforth be a 'military' one.

However, 'victory for the African nation is far from certain'; the failure of the OAU, and of the United Nations in Africa, the strength of the South African economy and military, the defeat of the 'revolutionary "Poqo" movement', the collapse of sanctions, the fact that independence in the High Commission Territories, to which he and others had once looked for practical hostility to *apartheid*, had led to better relations between themselves and the Republic, all made the task of the African nation harder. Yet it *was* a nation, 'physically homogeneous, with common ancestors, speaking closely allied languages . . .', and with common elements in a traditional culture, and had now been made even more of a nation by oppression. The white nation, faced with a common enemy, too, was less and less prone to think of itself as two groups, but as one. Just as the white nation had once conquered the black nation, so now the black nation would have to conquer the whites.

Taking the Algerian revolution as model, he argues that the revolution started as a struggle for rights, and became a nationalist struggle, 'the idea of Algerian nationalism against the idea that Algeria was French'. In South Africa, too, the struggle would become more and more nationalist. 'Seen in its most fundamental aspect', the South African struggle was not a class one:

> In SA to a certain degree, admittedly, the conquering nation has succeeded in reducing the conquered nation to the status of proletariat, and to this extent it is true to say that the struggle for the rights of the black nation is a class struggle. But the events of the last thirty years have shown that it is not possible for political organizations among Africans to be built on a basis merely of class cohesiveness, whereas it is possible . . . to build political organizations on a basis of a common nationalism. The only successes achieved in South Africa since 1920 by marxists have been successes achieved by a manipulation of the power of African nationalism. And as the years pass, so does the power of African nationalism grow.

Furthermore, the struggle in South Africa had to be seen as 'an incident in the expansion and contraction of Europe', in other words as part of colonialism, which was an aspect of European nationalism, the 'contemporary name' of which was 'christianity':

> Even today, though the progress of christianity is no longer seen as being related to the success of Europe's arms, there remains an unspoken worldwide freemasonry of those who stem from Europe, of those with white skins. This freemasonry has done and still does much to preserve in European and white hands a quasi-monopoly of power, wealth and status.

Duncan then looks at South Africa's military strength, notes the annual expenditure on defence had increased from £17 million in 1960 to £115 million in 1964, mentions its nuclear potential, and its ability to produce poison gas, notes that the 'geography of South Africa is being reshaped in a manner that will facilitate the use of such weapons against the African population', and argues that the Bantustan scheme foreshadows partition – Bantustans are not meant to work as Bantustans, but they would make partition easier in the end; eventually, Africans could be forced out of 'white areas', and into black areas – they would once again be subjected to a form of conquest. If that plan failed, at least the white nation would have the chance of partition. All those resolutions to the problem were possible: genocide, balkanization, partition, or a race war in southern Africa which would affect first all Africa and then the world.

There were no more 'comfortable illusions'; this was going to be 'a life and death struggle between two nations, both of which cannot win, and neither of which can assimilate the other'. From that position of profound pessimism (or perhaps realism, though he did not notice the ambiguity of his phrase, 'both of which cannot win', which may mean either that one must win, or that neither can win), he jumps, without explaining why, to the 'one decent solution' – a victory for the African nation:

> One must hope that victorious African nationalism would continue to be non-racial ... that a good percentage of the present white population ... will opt ... to stay on under an African government. But the disadvantages of the status quo are so great that, even if a future African government were to oppress the whites, one would have to prefer such a system, for the quantity of oppression would be less than that suffered today....
> This nationalist view ... is like an arc-lamp: its harsh light shows things in high contrast. But its harsh brilliance reveals the truth.... There have in the past been too many comfortable and inaccurate analyses. If anyone finds the nationalist view uncomfortable, let him disprove its validity....

Harsh his view certainly is, yet it is a clear development of his other ideas of the time, and the pessimism, hardly ameliorated by the phrase 'one must hope' (one *may* hope, but one must not deceive oneself in hoping), cannot be ignored without falsifying his views. If, until 1964 or 1965, he had been a romantic revolutionary, in this paper he was not; perhaps he still did not envisage the act of violence itself, the bomb thrown into a crowded cinema, the off-duty policeman shot down while watching television with his children, but this was no soft version of revolutionary violence. After all, he was living amid the material evidence of what had been a long and vicious revolution.

Oddly enough, the only time the ideas in the paper were argued in public, at a meeting of PAC supporters in London in May 1965 when he delivered an early draft of the paper, some PAC supporters walked out because Duncan made a remark about Tibet and its subjugation by China.[29] The PAC at the time was doing its best to get Chinese aid, as a counterbalance to Russian and Comintern aid to the ANC, and anything at all a man of Duncan's views said about China might have provoked a protest. At all events, it diverted his audience from the substance of his speech, one of the most clear cases for Africanism ever made. Ironically, he was considerably more sympathetic to the Chinese version of communism than he ever was to Russian communism, and he got on well with the Chinese Embassy staff in Algeria; he told Leballo:

> I happen to have good relations with the Chinese here, whom I admire very much. I have said and written things that they do not like, and I do not conceal from them that I am a believer in the bourgeois, parliamentary, liberal system, though being a member of a socialist

movement. My feeling is that they respect frankness of this kind more than they do the usual bootlicking flattery and 'me-tooism'. My instinct also is that marxism really is quite a small constituent in new China, and that the secret of People's China is that they are doing in the twentieth century what the Japanese did in the nineteenth, that is to say, keeping the European steamroller off something infinitely valuable, the inherited values and culture of the east.[30]

There had been talk for some time of his being transferred from Algiers, first to London, then to Scandinavia. In both cases he had written to Leballo asking not to be transferred; he liked Algeria, he said, and his work there was beginning to be effective. In London he would be even more exposed to the smears and innuendoes of the ANC and its supporters. Nor did he have any desire to live in Scandinavia, though in fact he was always a great success in Denmark, so much so that in April 1965 he was asked to join forces with Mazisi Kunene of the ANC (with whom he got on very well personally) to help launch a Danish Anti-Apartheid Committee.

Then in July 1965 a letter came from Leballo dismissing him from his post as PAC representative in Algiers.[31] The reasons given were, first, that he had 'engaged in a one-man crusade against the People's Republic of China', for instance in *South Africa's Rule of Violence*, his article in *Foreign Affairs*, the May speech in London. The first two had been written before he became a representative of the PAC (and indeed before the PAC began to develop its links with China), and had in fact been approved, so Duncan said, by his then superior in London, Mahomo. In his reply to Leballo's charges, Duncan said:

> I deeply respect the Chinese people. In most ways I have a great respect, too, for their government. I much admire their sincerity in their correct policy towards African Liberation. I admire, too, the pioneer work done by Chairman Mao in developing the necessary techniques of guerilla war. I have distributed over the months since January many dozens of Mao's books to our students in this country, and have bought from my own booksellers in the UK several copies of his Yu Chi Chan for our students. I am on good and friendly terms with the Chinese embassy here, and they always invite me to represent PAC at their receptions....[32]

The second charge was that he had 'on many occasions closed the office for weeks on end without prior approval'. This was nonsense, and Duncan said so; when he was away on PAC business, he always arranged a substitute.

The third charge was that he had written an 'infamous letter to Chief Leabua'. Duncan had indeed written to him, with a copy to Leballo, asking him to treat sympathetically two PAC men who had been arrested in Maseru. (Duncan did not realize, however, that a personal letter he had written to Leabua to congratulate him on his election as the first prime minister of independent Lesotho had been shown by Leabua to the Basotho press.)

The fourth charge was that he had 'clashed often with other PAC representatives', only 'for you to report later that they were right and that they had not told you'. Duncan said, 'I do not know what you are talking about', although he had in fact had rows with other PAC men, usually over their casual inefficiency; but rows of that kind, in his world, were soon enough forgotten. Another charge quoted him, out of context, as criticizing the Algerian government for its attitude to the PAC generally, when the context was the situation when he arrived in Algiers in 1964, when the PAC had been very unpopular.

Later Duncan was to discover that the real reasons for his dismissal were, first, his personal letter of congratulations to Leabua (it was useless for him to explain that, although he disliked some of Leabua's policies, he was an old friend, whom he had influenced a great deal and whose party he had helped found; it was not a distinction the PAC would accept) and, secondly, that, after getting no reply to a cable to Maseru about the attitude he should take to the new Algerian government after the coup against Ben Bella on 19 June, he had gone ahead on his own to welcome the government, congratulating it on the 19 June coup, then on the formation of the new Cabinet, and then on 5 July, National Day. It was useless for Duncan to explain that his action had done the PAC a great deal of good with the government, and that the coup, which removed many of the more pro-Moscow elements in the Algerian establishment from power, had done the ANC a great deal of bad.

Instead, he fought back on the question of efficiency, listing the thirty-two letters he had written to headquarters since December which had not been answered, on the way the leadership of the PAC was ignoring its own constitution, on the injustice of the way he had been treated. Of course this time a reply to his accusations came promptly enough, and at huge length; the concluding sentences were:

> Some sons of the soil do not understand that the Pan Africanist Congress, of which they are members, is an instrument for carrying out the tasks of revolution. They do not realize that they themselves are the makers of the revolution, but think that their responsibility is merely to their individual superiors and not to the revolution. This passive mentality of 'an employee' is a manifestation of individualism. This mentality explains why there are not very many *activists who work unconditionally for the revolution*. Unless this mentality is eliminated, the number of activists will not grow and the heavy burden ... will remain on the shoulders of a small number of people....[33]

In some instances of his political career, the accusation of 'individualism' against Duncan might have had considerable point – he was 'a bad combiner', after all; but the irony was that dismissal should come to him when he had tried so hard to keep in line, had tried so hard to stay with the PAC despite all its splits and counter-splits. For instance, though he knew Randolph Vigne was a supporter of the PAC, he was not sure he was actually a member; before he felt free to write openly to the man who was now his closest friend, or to invite the Vignes to use the PAC flat in Algiers when they came on holiday, he had to know 'Have you taken the oath? Have you a card? Have you paid your dues? If I am not given this detailed information it makes my position quite impossible, as I have taken the oath etc.'[34] 'You know it is an article of faith, justified or not, of the nefarious effect whites have on African Nationalist movements. If I should be believed to be discussing party matters with a non-member ... my colleagues ... would feel that I had betrayed a trust.'[35] 'You of all people know how careful any non-African must be to be worthy of the trust put in him by our movement. I simply cannot go on doing things in politics with anyone, especially an old comrade, white, from the LP days who is not a member of the PAC in the fullest sense.'[36]

At first, Duncan was very bitter at his dismissal, not least that the letter should come from Leballo, to whom he had been so loyal despite the criticisms he might have made, and from Raboroko, who had stayed a month with him in March–April 1965; he told Vigne: 'I was knocked sideways on Monday, but began to breathe more freely on Tuesday. And now I wouldn't take it back if it were offered in any form.'[37] In fact, the work had been becoming more and more tedious, as his letters of the time show; he knew the weakness of his own position, and suspected the fruitlessness of being a mini-Ambassador. In March, when it was suggested that George Mbele come from Ethiopia to assist him as representative, Duncan replied that, while he would be glad to have Mbele there, the truth was that the 'work in Algeria does not keep one man busy let alone two'.[38] The sheer inefficiency of the PAC annoyed him again and again: 'My life has been lived for years now in a welter of inefficiency':[39]

> there is a seemingly infinite quantity of irresponsibility and inefficiency.... I am beginning to think that unless African Nationalists in SA and democrats in the world do something and stop talking big the white nation is going to expel the black nation.[40]

> more and more I know there is a limit to the amount of inefficiency, discourtesy, laziness, pointlessness that I can put up with.... I feel that our great continent is in danger of making itself a laughing stock with its imaginary battles and that what we need above all is The Truth and a bit of understatement.[41]

Even the letter of dismissal, which terminated his appointment as from 30 June, was dated 20 July.

Despite his dismissal as representative Duncan was allowed to remain a member of the PAC; for all his disillusion with 'the extraordinary world of exile politics', he still valued 'very highly the finer elements in the PAC, and ... wish[ed] them all the success possible',[42] and remained on fairly friendly terms with Leballo and most of the leadership, though by 1967 he was to begin to accept criticism made of Leballo by other PAC leaders. His successor in Algiers was Elias Ntloedibe, and he did all he could to help him settle into the post; soon he was able to write to Vigne that his 'removal from the office in Algiers has been a good thing for the PAC'. 'Elias Ntloedibe is doing much better than I ever did. He gets tickets out of the Alg. Govt – general support – gets our chaps out of gaol – fixes the poor old battered ANC.'[43] So, despite the temptation to reveal publicly why he had been dismissed, and how unjust the reasons given had been, he kept his peace. After seeing Leballo in Algiers in late July, he had begun to realize that the reasons given had not been the true ones: '... the manner of it [the dismissal], and the ridiculous reasons given, were unjust: the decision itself justified, except that since my removal PAC has accepted the benefits of my message! But that's politics isn't it!'[44] To Anthony Steel, who wrote of his shock at the news of the dismissal, Duncan added that he had succeeded 'in building a middle-class way of life that was perhaps out of line with the movement's ideas',[45] and certainly there is something a little incongruous in the image of Duncan's going out to the airport to greet a squad of young PAC recruits on their way to a camp in the desert for training, or his handing out Mao's thoughts on guerilla warfare to them. All the same, it was a comfort to him to know that others in the PAC thought his dismissal unjust, and when he heard from Mimmie Tsele, a PAC member in London, of her disgust at the way he had been treated by 'PK and Co.', and her own disillusion at the difference between the PAC on paper and the PAC in action,[46] he replied to say how much he appreciated her letter, but ended:

> So, Mimmie, don't be too sorry for me. I am still willing to give everything up for the victory for Africa in South Africa, but at the moment it is impossible to make such sacrifices, and so I must wait. I remain convinced of the rightness of our PAC stand, and confident that in the end it will triumph.[47]

But, with exile politics in general, and the squabbles among the PAC leaders in particular, he had increasingly less patience. To Randolph Vigne he wrote:

> I confess I have developed an acute allergy to political rhetoric. By definition, the basic constituent of the form of 20th C activity seems to be The Lie. I imagine there is somewhere a 'Lloyds register of Politicians' in which meticulous men count speeches, particularly in Africa, for any trace of truth – the punishment for which is instant removal from the register.[48]

To Peter Hjul he wrote of South African exile politicians: 'They are not only stupid and noisy and boring: they represent little if anything. In my view none of them (including perhaps myself) has much further to contribute to our solution.'[49] To Mary Benson, because she had called him in *Struggle for a Birthright*[50] an 'acrimonious anti-communist', and 'acrimonious' in the *Oxford Dictionary* meant 'bitter and irritating', he wrote angrily of 'the swamp that many SA exiles call the "liberation fight". For this unproductive bitterness is not liberation....'[51] Though he remained committed to his loathing of *apartheid*, to his belief in the necessary means for destroying *apartheid*, and to the idea of the PAC and Africanism, he saw the timescale now as much longer, the struggle as much harder and the exiled leadership as much less important.

For the *Contact* Liberals, as well as for their old central figure of the more exciting years of 1958–62, 1964 and 1965 were bad years. Although *Contact* kept going under various editors, it gradually got thinner and thinner, moving from newsprint to offset litho to cyclostyling; one after the other its editors were banned. There was a serious of court-cases against Randolph Vigne for reports he wrote on the Transkei and for breaking the banning order he had received in 1963. Kaiser Matanzima, the new Prime Minister of the Transkei, blamed the Bashee Bridge murders on 'incitement by Patrick Duncan'.[52] In the House of Assembly in Cape Town, De Wet Nel, Minister of Bantu Administration and Development, was reported as saying that 'it was a fact that at one stage wherever Patrick Duncan slept in the Transkei, a murder was committed that morning'.[53] Patrick Duncan and Randolph

Vigne had (so the Commissioner-General of the Transkei, Hans Abraham, maintained at the funeral of Chief Zwelihle Mtirara, his mother, and a lay preacher, murdered in February 1965) 'lathered' the people of the Engcobo district into a 'fury of murder', and then left them in the lurch.[54] Zwelihle was the same man whom the Liberals had entertained in the Cape in 1960, and he and Duncan got on well together, which made even more nonsense of Abraham's charge.

Worse than all these were the 'July raids' of 1964 in which dozens of Liberals were rounded up and detained under the '90 Day Detention' Act; many broke down in detention and told the security police what they knew; some broke quicker than others, and two in particular turned State Evidence, including one man to whom Duncan had once offered the editorship of *Contact*. Most of those detained were asked about their association with Duncan; one detainee, who said that Duncan was a friend whom he admired and that he had eaten a meal with him in New York the year before, was told by Captain Rousseau of the security police that he would not sit down at the same table as Duncan.[55] (Told this story afterwards, Duncan remembered Rousseau as the man who had 'insinuated' himself into his home in Maseru by posing as a travelling salesman.) Some escaped from the country, including Robert Watson, who had recruited Duncan into the ARM for the brief period before he joined the PAC. Randolph Vigne managed to get away in a Norwegian cargo-ship to Canada. He was smuggled aboard at the Duncan Dock in Cape Town by colleagues and friends, chief of whom was James Currey. Currey used his passport, name and persona for the exercise, only to find himself confronted at the departure gangway by the shipping agent, who, somewhat suspiciously, had sold him the sailing-ticket. With great resource he ducked away and jumped for the quay, but nearly missed, only just catching the side of the dock and scrambling up. The captain and the pilot watched all this from the bridge but, unaware of the manhunt going on for Vigne, blamed Currey's leap on the effects of a farewell party. Meanwhile the police waited for Vigne on the borders of Basutoland and distributed thousands of 'Wanted' notices.

Some were released from detention, and most of these left the country as soon as they could. Neville Rubin, arrested by the PIDE in Mozambique on his way from Swaziland, where he was doing research, managed to get the British authorities to insist on his release, since he had by then a British passport. John Harris, a by then banned member of the Liberal Party who had written for *Contact* when Duncan was Editor, filled a suitcase with explosives and a detonator and left it in the main concourse of the Johannesburg station before telephoning a warning to the police; either the police ignored his warning or it was too late, for the bomb went off, killing an old woman and maiming a child, as well as injuring others. He was arrested and brought to trial, and then executed. Others in the ARM were sentenced to imprisonment, the longest sentence going to Eddie Daniels, a Liberal Party member, who got fifteen years.

About Vigne's escape Duncan was delighted, and wrote that 'the entire Duncan family was overjoyed yesterday to learn you had reached England . . . we have been holding thumbs since mid-July when we first learned you had launched out'.[56] He was one of the few of his circle to attempt forgiveness of those who gave evidence for the State, although he also told Vigne 'the moment I heard A—— had been detained I *knew* intuitively that he would talk'.[57] To A—— himself he wrote, 'Don't be depressed by it all ... nothing was to be gained by continuing to resist. The only thing to be gained was clemency.... I send you all my sympathy for what you must have gone through';[58] and, when Vigne protested at Duncan's letter, he wrote, 'What I was trying to put across is that as the years pass the positive achievements of all of you in ARM will not fade whereas the mistakes will fade'.[59] As for John Harris, Duncan thought his action 'showed supreme courage and sanity', not the insanity which was pleaded at his trial, and he wrote a letter to *Contact*, after it had condemned Harris's action, to say that not only would silence have been 'more decorous', but that condemnation was wrong: '... in fact, his one little bomb did shake the morale of *apartheid* as many hundreds of tons of literature have failed to shake it ... in court he, perhaps the sanest white man in South Africa, was persuaded to plead insanity.... Yet his death streng-thened all that *Contact* stands for, in the eyes of those who really suffer under *apartheid*....' The letter could not of course be published, since Duncan was banned; but he signed himself 'Your Founder'.[60]

Duncan felt much the same when he heard that the Liberal Party, as well as disavowing violence, had expelled all those convicted or self-confessed members of the ARM; to Vigne he wrote in anger about 'sanctimonious speeches' and 'an aura of incense' for he believed that the actions of the ARM were something no one 'need ever be ashamed of'.[61] 'All atrocities are appalling', he wrote in response to stories in *The Times* and elsewhere about atrocities in the Congo, '[but] isn't it astonishing that people who thought nothing of bombing the open city of Dresden and killing 140 000–160 000 civilians in one series of attacks, are today pacifists who deny the right of any nation or group to use force in achieving political aims.'[62]

But it was not only the Liberals of the ARM who had bad years; many who had had nothing to do with the ARM were banned, left the country, or were deported. Hjul, Cape Chairman, banned in 1963, went into exile in Britain; Jordan Ngubane, banned in 1963, went into exile in Swaziland; Barney Zackon, Cape Chairman after Hjul, was banned in 1965 and went into exile in Britain; John Blundell, of *Defence and Aid* and the Liberal Party, was deported from South Africa; of the Liberals in Natal, Peter Brown, E. V. Mahomed of Stanger, H. J. Benghu and others were banned. Eddie Roux, banned in 1963, was forced to resign from the Liberal Party. Ann Tobias and Harold Head, for a time the Editors of *Contact*, were banned and went into exile. Others were detained or jailed or lost their passports or were deported. Peter Hjul wrote to Duncan from London: 'The way I feel at present ... I never want to see the country again and will be quite happy to spend the rest of my days in Europe.... Over the past year I have seen the collapse of almost everything we worked for, and the worst of it was that I could be little more than a silent witness. The opposition has not collapsed: it has simply been ground down.'[63] Many shared his feelings, though some stayed in South Africa, working in the Liberal Party until its dissolution in 1968, when it became illegal for blacks and whites to be members of the same organization.

CHAPTER 12

July 1965–June 1967
'*We are all under sentence of death ...*'

Both Cynthia and Patrick Duncan wanted, if possible, not to leave Algiers; they had uprooted themselves or been uprooted eight times, from Teyateyaneng to London to Maseru to Riverside to Cape Town to Basutoland to London to Algiers, in a married life of eighteen years. For the boys, settled as they were at Winchester, another change would not have altered their lives much; but the girls were happily settled in their new home, they enjoyed their school, they were becoming fluent in French, and they had their own friends. The Duncans had been very uncomfortable their first few months in Algiers, moving from flat to flat; now they had a lovely home, and wanted to leave neither it nor Algeria, for the country appealed more and more to them. It seemed non-racial; it was independent; it had a feeling of historical continuity stretching right back to Roman times and before, yet it was post-revolutionary; things were happening there; changes were being made; there were beaches to swim from, places to visit, the solitude of the desert to explore, friends to talk to; and yet they were not isolated from Europe (in July 1965, just before the news of the dismissal came through, they had spent a holiday in Italy with Duncan's old friend from Winchester, Jeremy Pemberton). And where else could he have gone, after all?

So he looked for a job; he told Anthony Steel, 'I am looking for *anything*, preferably here, as we love this country, this town, and this house, and preferably something I believe in, such as work for the Alg. govt, or for wild life conservation, etc. Rather hard-to-please! I feel I have something to give and want to give it.'[1] But it was difficult; he tried the government radio services, the Ministries, teaching, the University, the press – both local and English, for he wrote to Ryan of *The Times* – the Fauna Preservation Society, a Japanese importing firm, he advertised for translations, and he asked Amnesty International if it might perhaps have work for him. But nothing happened. He gave a few lessons in English, to keep himself busy and to earn a little money. He claimed in a letter to one of his friends that 'I have seldom been happier. The relief of not having to represent an HQ that has not written to me since March. . . . And the bliss of being in this house, this town, and this country, all of which I increasingly love.'[2] But looking back he was more honest: to Hans Schmoller he said, 'the transition has been such a strain that for some time private letters have been impossible', and he called the experience of being out of work and job-hunting 'like walking on the top of a very high cliff with a very steep drop'.[3] So high a cliff it was, in fact, that his son Alex, who was then back from Winchester on holiday, remembers that his father told him and his mother that he had been considering suicide. He was learning lessons which he had tried to teach to Denis Cowen two years before when the Cowens' marriage was breaking up:

> We two are nearing 50 and we must learn that there are limits beyond which the will cannot act. If it attempts to act beyond, action becomes self-defeating, sometimes self-destructive. There are limits set by the strength of the body and there are limits already laid down in the record.[4]

He had given up much for the PAC; even those who understood his politics – and there were not many – thought he might have been wiser to have been an influence in the background, not to insist on a public commitment. He had tried hard to adapt himself to the PAC, to control his dislike of socialism, not to make efficiency a god, to understand and accept the tensions created by the fact that he was a white man in a black organization, and to accept the leadership of men often less able than he was – in short, to control his individuality as he had never been able to do before. Yet they had dismissed him. He claimed to be relieved, but the rejection was deeper than that; Alex calls it 'a deadly blow at his identity as a committed opponent of *apartheid* and ally of black Africans'.[5] It was deeper even than that, because on the one hand his individuality had made him what he was, had made him reject the society and the ideas he was born into, had driven him to follow his ideas and feelings to their logical end; yet that end required him to curb his individuality, which he tried to do and – to an extent at least – succeeded in doing. It was not enough; though he could remain a member of the PAC, he could not represent it. Both his individuality *and* his commitment had been rejected. Of course it was a relief to go back to being himself, but it was self-destruction, too. He had given himself utterly to his great aim, and yet there was nothing more that his great aim wanted of him. He had to learn to sit still and wait, and it was not easy if one had never been able to wait. That was one of 'the limits ... of the body'; and the limit 'of the record' meant there was nothing more to do for the time being.

Two things (besides home and family) saved him: first, in September he got a job – initially for a year, though in June 1966 it was extended to September 1967 – as Director of Operations in Constantine for the Comité Chrétien de Service en Algérie (CCSA), and, secondly, he began work on the book which was to become *Man and the Earth*. To Peter Hjul's despairing letter after his leaving South Africa, in 1965, he replied:

> I myself want one day to get back into the fight.... I now see clearly that there are two major things that I want to do.... One, in the realm of ideas, is to launch a book with my *weltanschauung* in it ... the race question will form a very minor part of this book, which deals rather with Man in the World in space and time.... The other is to wield real blows at the evil SA system. For the moment I can do a little with the book, and nothing for the second. It is in a way humiliating, as I had hoped to give the rest of my life to SA, but there is no choice, and I must accept the necessity.[6]

To recognize that he had no choices left was the hardest thing of all; so he must have, almost in the nature of things, faced that last choice: to live or not. He chose to go on living, until even that choice ran out.

The CCSA had been set up by the Church World Service and other Christian organizations to organize the relief operations mainly in the eastern part of Algeria in the aftermath of the War of Independence. Its two main functions were to distribute food (mainly surpluses from America) and clothing (collected by the Mennonite Churches, the World Council of Churches, the Church World Service and other groups) and to organize and finance self-help projects. Duncan's immediate superior was a young American called Jim Paton, and his boss was Jan van Hoogstraten, Director of Service of the Africa Department of the National Council of the Churches of Christ (NCCC) in the United States, which provided much of the finance of the CCSA. After four months in the CCSA, Duncan actually became officially an employee of the NCCC; though his religious views remained agnostic, his colleagues did not seem to mind his not being a churchgoer. Under Duncan were about fifteen helpers, some from abroad, some Algerian. He was paid DA42 000 a year (about £3500), tax-free, and was given a car and apartment, as well as having his gas, electricity and water bills paid for him; he was also required to join an American medical insurance scheme.[7]

His work involved 'directing' a number of 'operations', which ranged from self-help schemes to school-feeding to supervising the distribution of clothing from two warehouses to feeding the poor and old; he had to talk to Algerian officials about the integration of CCSA and government pro- grammes, inspect warehouses, supervise the small factory where American surplus flour was turned into noodles, show visitors such as the Executive Committee of CCSA around (it turned out that the Chairman of the Executive Committee was Vernon Littlewood, whom he had met twenty years before in Maseru; Littlewood had helped build a rockery for Lady Duncan). 'The job', Duncan told Alex, 'stretches such capabilities as I have to the limit,'[8] and he found he again needed to organize his time as rigorously as he had done in Cape Town, particularly if he wanted any time for his book. But it was work he enjoyed, and after the squabbles and inflated rhetoric of the PAC it was a delight to be among hard-working, understating, quick and enthusiastic people.

The main disadvantage of the job was its being in Constantine, 460 kilometres to the east of Algiers; since their house, 'La Consulaire', the girls' school and Algiers itself were among their reasons for staying in Algeria, he had therefore to become a 'temporary migrant worker'.[9] He was usually able to get back to Algiers at least once a fortnight, either flying or taking an overnight sleeper, and occasionally Cynthia, or Cynthia and the girls, too, would come to spend a weekend with him; but, though he hated being away from them, and was sometimes lonely in Constantine, it was a job he could believe in, and both Algerians in the town and the people he worked with and met were hospitable and friendly.

Working for the CCSA meant he could take no part in active politics, but in the aftermath of the PAC débâcle that became a refuge; though he continued to see PAC people when he was in Algiers, particularly Elias

Ntloedibe, his practical concern with politics was more passive than it had ever been since his time as Judicial Commissioner. 'I am utterly happy in this new job,' he wrote, 'and am thrilled to be out of the extraordinary world of exile politics.'[10]

Three of the 'operations' he directed gave him particular pleasure. The first was a reforestation scheme, started by the CCSA as one of its self-help projects and recently taken over by the Algerian government as the Chantiers Populaires de Reboisement. During the War of Independence, Colonel Tahar Zbiri had had his headquarters in the magnificent cedar-forest of the Aures, and the French had destroyed most of it with napalm; until 1964, the mountains had been a graveyard of giant cedar-wood trunks. In order to do something about unemployment in the area, CCSA had built a saw-mill at Ben-Hmama in June 1964, and then organized a work-force both to run the saw-mill and to replant the mountain with young cedars, paying the men in food (wheat, oil and milk) which the American government shipped in. 'I have rarely seen so many ills healed in one action,' Duncan wrote, though he accepted that the CCSA had 'not been able to do more than touch the problem'[11] and therefore welcomed the fact that the government had taken the scheme over.

The second 'operation' – and the one he felt most personally involved in – was looking after thirteen old and ailing Jews, all who remained of the Jewish community of twenty-seven thousand which, Duncan thought, must date back to the Diaspora, since he had found a record of a tombstone of the 2nd–4th centuries AD erected by a young woman to her father 'Pompeius Judeus'. When the Jewish community left Constantine, only thirty stayed behind, some blind, some weak, all too old to wish to leave. The thirteen who were still alive in 1965 lived together in one of the thirteen synagogues they had once owned, and the CCSA helped them with flour, oil, cheese, tea, crushed wheat and milk; occasionally Duncan would lunch with them, and he found their peaceful acceptance of what had happened to them deeply moving: 'their radiant and loving faces', he told Schmoller, 'showed not only their weakness but their pleasure in supporting each other'.[12]

The third was the work with children, both officially and privately; for, as well as the school-feeding schemes which he oversaw, the street in which he lived became a playground in the day time. Duncan would meet the children going between his house and office and, when some of them tried to talk English to him, he arranged an evening class for about ten or eleven of the boys, where he taught them a little English and much history. He told his son Patrick, 'I ... thoroughly enjoy it, and am continually amazed at their immense energy and enthusiasm and intelligence. I am beginning to see that this outpouring of joie-de-vivre is perhaps part of the process of liberation that this country so courageously began on 1 November 1954. Anyway, for the first time I have some good friends among this class of the nation, and I must say that for me it is a rewarding friendship. The [y] couldn't be nicer or more courteous.'[13]

What mattered to him in Constantine besides his work for the CCSA was the continual presence of history; almost all his letters of the time contain at least a reference to the Roman or pre-Roman past. So he wrote to his son Alex of the history of Constantine,[14] and to his son Patrick of a visit to Timgad, a

Roman provincial town which once held twenty-five thousand people, now a marble and sandstone ruin though still with mosaics and tesselated pavements 'that equal oriental carpets in richness and colour but that are essentially European in spirit'.[15] Or he wrote of his awe at the Roman Empire which held together 'well over 100 000 people over thousands of miles with nothing but horses and small sailing boats ... and the grave tread of their legionnaires down their geometrically-straight, paved roads. They built to last, which is more than we do today.'[16]

For, however he had changed, one of the things which he had not lost was his capacity for wonder:

> I must ... describe something that happened 35 minutes ago. ... It is now 5 past 5 in the morning. I woke at about 4.25 GMT to see a strange sight in the sky, somewhat to the north of the first light of the sun in the east. It seemed to be three glowing stars, nebulous, brighter than the stars and planets in that part of the sky. These glowing stars were linked by a thinner line of the same kind of light. This light was an eery green, somewhat like the green of the luminous parts of a luminous watch. The line was somewhat bent. I got out of bed, and watched. I realized I must be looking at some sort of space experiment. As I watched another of these 'stars' appeared, to the west of the existing line, of the same colour. It was clearly some sort of explosion, as it grew rapidly in size to a round shape larger than the diameter of the sun, but of the same order of size. I was suddenly afraid: I thought I might have seen a nuclear explosion in space and that its light might be dangerous to one's eyes. I watched this extraordinary sight, all in the darkness of the pre-dawn, all among the stars. The line between the points of light began to twist slowly until it assumed an S form. As I went on watching it became bigger slowly in size and twisted more. After ten minutes it had clearly faded a bit. Now, at 5.15 a.m., with the brightening of the sky, it has completely disappeared.
>
> There was no sound of any plane at the time, and I am sure that I saw something either in space or at an immensely high atmospheric altitude. I think the former, for if it had been merely at say 100 000 feet it must have been located over Tunisia, and who is going to do such things in Tunisia? Writing to you now I feel I have seen an atomic explosion in space, probably over eastern Europe.[17]

This intensity of experience comes through his letters again and again – for instance, as the postscript to another letter, 'At this moment the most beautiful rainbow I have ever seen is glowing outside. There are three bands of green and violet below the violet i.e. on the ultra-violet bands.'[18] The combination of the superlative, the instantaneous and the scientific is typical.

Sometimes his sense of curiosity and his wide-ranging knowledge were too much for his children; 'he constantly forced us to be curious', Patrick remembers, and 'sometimes this was maddening, because I felt that I could never have a fraction of what he knew in my head, but a life like this made us taste everything'.[19] When Duncan was home with his children, there were much-enjoyed general-knowledge tests at meal-times, and he spent what time he could teaching them – 'French, Maths ... geography, astronomy, history, driving, chess, snorkelling etc.', Ann recalls, though she was often a little afraid of him: 'I remember him teaching me about the Earth revolving around the Sun, when I was about 11, and when Mum asked me what we'd been doing, Dad told me to explain it to her. I hadn't understood, and so started crying, and he told me I should have said that I hadn't understood etc.'[20] For he was always a strict, if a loving and generous, father; disobedience was punished, usually physically. His love was, Patrick writes, 'never very overt, effusive, but it was the cement of our lives'.[21] Even Emma, who was only seven in 1966, remembers that when she listened to his conversations, 'if he was discussing something he cared about, he seemed almost to descend on the subject, and devour it'.[22] And, to leaven the passionate curiosity and the strictness, there was the boisterous laughter at the incongruous, the funny joke, the silly remark, the near-accident. They may have been uprooted more than is good for children, but it was turned into a richness and an adventure: climbing a mountain, going down the Orange river in a canoe, being caught in a flood at the bottom of a *donga*, exploring a ruined Roman city, going on camels for a camping expedition into the desert, or going out on a boar-hunting expedition with the Mayor of Constantine. Looking back, the children do not regret their young lives.

Duncan continued to keep in touch with Basotho affairs, mainly through his correspondence with the Rev. Victor Phoofolo, who had been a leading member of the BAC in its early days, and who now ran the Sebuku English Church Mission at Butha Buthe. Phoofolo and Duncan had started a scheme they called the 'boiler suit movement', which proselytized the idea that people worked better in boiler suits than in Basotho blankets, and both Duncan and Phoofolo themselves wore them for rough work; Phoofolo told Duncan in early 1964, 'the boiler suit movement has succeeded amazingly.... I am sure it is producing its desired results in increased work and multiplied production'.[23] They shared ideas about the necessity of 'self-help' and the undesirability of all new projects – roads, agricultural schemes – coming from the government; the Sebuku mission ran a two-acre communal garden, half of which was truly communal – that is, the gardeners grew things in bulk for selling, and put the proceeds in a common fund – the other individual and numbered plots, in which gardeners grew vegetables for their own houses, and in 1964 there were forty-three other communal gardens. Of all of this Duncan thoroughly approved, so much so that Phoofolo used to remind Duncan he was a priest, and not in the least inclined to become a farmer or a public works department. Phoofolo was also able to give Duncan news of the progress of the two main political parties, of Leabua Jonathan and Ntsu Mokhehle, and of why the people of Basutoland, against all the odds, elected Leabua and the BNP into power in 1965 and not Mokhehle and the BAC, while Duncan in due course was able to tell Phoofolo about his work in Constantine and the CCSA self-help projects. When the South Africans made a gift of grain to Lesotho in 1965, as a sign of how pleased they were with Leabua's policy of co-operation, Phoofolo described the reaction thus:

We are unusually entertained in the last few months by the distribution of grain gift from the Republic to Leabua. There was the usual campaign of defilement and falsehood by those aiming at utter destruction of Leabua. The Basuto are sensible people: they went to the protest meetings, listened with polite interest, went back, inspanned their oxen and donkeys and went to 'phaka' (collect their share of) the grain. Many of the slanderers also sent their wives and aunties to receive their shares for them, and there are those even who spoke against the grain by day and went to steal it at night. Such are the Basuto and their political manoeuvres! You must possess the highest intelligence and sense of humour to be able to get along with them without wanting to commit suicide sooner or later.[24]

When the Paramount Chieftainess 'Mamohato came to open a new road made by the community and school at 'Muela, Phoofolo wrote of his delight: '... it has been an unqualified success; but remember it started in a conversation between you and me in this house here!'[25] The work Duncan was doing in Constantine for the CCSA was not, after all, such a new departure, except that he was now doing himself what he had long encouraged others to do.

During his time at Constantine Duncan made friends with one of the very few other English-speakers there, a young man called Christopher Powell who taught at the Lycée Hihi el Mekki from September 1965 to June 1967. They shared antiquarian interests, and in Duncan's first year with CCSA usually had a meal together once or twice a week, when they would talk Africa, discrimination, ecology; together they did trips into the desert and to archaeological sites like Timgad, or visited the Quaker community at Skikda on the coast, and Powell camped in the desert with the Duncans over the New Year of 1966, and remembers Duncan giving them all an impromptu lecture on the stars. Powell remembers, too, that Duncan told him all about quasars, matter and anti-matter; like Duncan's own children, he remembers a man of wide-ranging knowledge and intense curiosity.

Duncan talked very little to Powell about the years before he had started work for CCSA, and it was only on his visits to Algiers that Powell learned of Duncan's history; knowing that, he began to understand a little better why Duncan was so devoted to the small but practical work he was doing in Constantine. Powell saw, too, the reverse side of Algeria; Duncan had found that one of his workers was pilfering supplies, and despite being warned the man would not stop. So Duncan reported the matter to the police. When he went to the police-station where the man was being questioned, he found that the police were torturing him; when Duncan tried to stop the torture, the police explained it was not for the pilfering, but because they had found he was living with a woman he was not married to. It was the only time Powell saw Duncan visibly distressed.

Duncan himself had other experience of the Algerians' puritanism; once, travelling with an Algerian secretary – pretty and xenophilic – he was forced off the road by some Algerians in a large car and, when he protested, was himself questioned by the police, who told him that to travel alone with a woman not his wife was 'against religion'. Small wonder, then, that Duncan thought Islam obsessive, wasteful of energy, and an obstacle to social progress.

Duncan's religious views in these years were explored more fully in *Man and the Earth* but, although he was working for a Christian organization, he continued to call himself an agnostic, and would argue that agnosticism was part of the 'scientific method', unrigid, undoctrinaire, pragmatic, questing.

Yet he still believed to an extent at least in the efficacy of prayer, perhaps not as communication with God, but as a kind of internal dialogue; from Kubung he had replied to Father Benoit, who had written to encourage him and assured him of his prayers, 'I do pray a bit, though mostly only at the selfish level, but surprisingly they often receive an answer'.[26] From whom? Perhaps from the Unknown God, or perhaps his own conscience, for he told Schmoller in 1965 that 'I find myself worshipping at two main altars, that of The Unknown God whom I do not find in the established churches, and of Human Worth in a World of Beauty'.[27]

So when he was asked to write an article on 'The Churches' role in Africa', what he chose to stress was that the role of the Christian churches could be 'purely disinterested', that 'the day of organized evangelization is over, and that Christians best serve their churches by self-sacrificing service'.[28] In short, this was a Christianity of works, not faith.

Working in Constantine meant he had less time to devote to his book than he had in Algiers, but still he managed to work at it for a few hours each morning before going to his office, and sometimes again in the evenings. In October 1965 he wrote anxiously to Schmoller to ask if he had a copy of *The Enemy*, which Schmoller had printed for him in 1942, and which he needed for his book. By November he had done a first draft of 'the first passage of a projected book – the most important act I think of my life',[29] copies of which he sent to Schmoller and to Peter Scott, to whom he had written about the possibility of a job in the Fauna Preservation Society. The book was to be 'a call for a new ethic, based on the planet rather than on the human race.... It seeks to show that it is now urgently necessary, for political, social and conservation reasons', for men to accept 'an ethic based on the earth as the object of the highest value known to us'.[30] By January 1966 he had completed the first five chapters, though he was still not satisfied with the first, and by August 1966 had a complete draft done.

The central theme of *Man and the Earth* goes back even before *The Enemy*, since as early as 1939 he wrote to his father about his reading of Freud on totemism, and of Bertrand Russell:

I believe that a great deal of rot is talked ... by philosophers about man. They seem to think that man is something absolute, immeasurable. I think that we will soon leave this absurd state and look on man as something meet to be observed, and that just as Galileo and Kopernik took men away from the geometric theory, so we will soon see the anthropocentric philosophy disappear, and something more worthwhile take its place.[31]

As he said to Schmoller, his 'basic *Weltanschauung*' had not changed, for what he was after was 'a new morality based on the totality of the planet', an ethical system which he called Geism, the -ism of the planet Earth.[32]

Yet *Man and the Earth* was in no way a retreat; rather it was a development, a way of putting all his concerns into perspective. Duncan had never been subject to the liberal piety which hoped for an easy change, over not too long a period, from one kind of social system to another, or an easy belief in democracy. He was a democrat, in that he wanted everyone to have the vote and the opportunity to be equal; but he was too much his father's son to hope for change without power – hence his willingness to accept autocracy, his willingness to see those with power lay down rules of conduct. But he was also committed to ideas and to the idea that ideas change people. So *Man and the Earth* could be important. Yet it would not reach everyone; it would reach only a few, and they would make the changes. 'Somehow I doubt if my book will have the great appeal to the ordinary reader that [Rachel Carson's] *Silent Spring* had, and it will be more necessary for mine to be inoffensive to the experts.'[33] But, again, even the experts would not effect change without the power of the *demos*, the 'mass' he had always wanted to recruit to the Liberal Party, the 'mass' he had hoped for in the PAC; and the 'mass' would sometimes need to act in physical force, not only in 'soul-force'.

Writing to Julius Lewin from Kubung in 1963, Duncan had begun to state the problem; reopening the stores had been hard work, he wrote: '... this land is poor.... And what the drought would have spared man has not.... The minds of the people are affected, and inefficiency and unreliability have reached proportions that would stagger you.... One is faced in fact with a serious degree of breakdown in society, and man cannot depend on his fellows for support, or even for affection.'

> I am no less keen on the success of South Africa's revolution, but I now believe that the most urgent task of our generation is the nurturing of a balance between man and the totality of his environment. This nurturing cannot, in my view, happen in SA before we have exorcized the tribal hatreds, i.e. before our revolution has succeeded. I therefore do not hold back from the liberatory struggle, but I see it as only part of a greater whole, that whole being the achievement of a balance between man and man, man and animal, man and soil, man and the universe as a whole.[34]

He made a similar point to Marion Friedmann, a South African Liberal who had gone to live in London, and argued that England

> as the pioneer of the industrial revolution, must now pioneer ... the clearing up of the rubble of that revolution, the repairing of the traumas, the growing of healing grass over the slag heaps, the marrying of the technologically workable with the roots that plunge straight back to the bronze age and earlier, and the re-building of Tonnies' gemeinschaft in place of the San-Francisco-to-Vladivostock gesellschaft. Such material tasks will take a generation to achieve, pending the spiritual re-birth that man hungers for, that must and will come, but only when the time for it has come. How *can* there be unemployment while there are slums to clear? Have the unemployed not hands, and can those hands not clear up the rubble? Of course they can, but only if some teacher has inspired the brains that direct those hands.[35]

There is another side to the complex of feelings which, though uncomfortable, cannot be ignored: his increasing sense of disgust at humanity, the kind that Bromberger noted with such astonishment at Kubung, the kind expressed when he wrote to Astor of his delight in the Sahara because it was so 'clean', so 'man-free'. By 1965 he was writing thus:

> There is a good case ... for the thesis that mankind is now possessed of devils and has taken irrevocably a wrong turning. Certainly man's greed, his dirt, the reckless way he is ruining our gloriously beautiful planet, his

nastiness to his fellows, his unstoppable fertility that is filling our world up with ungovernable, noisy, aggressive and sometimes criminal young people, make me each year more like Swift with his Yahoos.[36]

He went on to qualify his case in two important ways: his love of the 'vast areas of Tellus that man has not yet ruined', and 'man's wonderful drive on towards knowledge'; but the almost irrational disgust remained. In an early draft of *Man and the Earth*, probably the second draft, called still *Geism, An Interim Ethic for the Age of Science*, he wrote:

If in knowledge Man has become godlike, in other ways he has become diabolical. His technical excellence has been bought at the cost of much beauty and much goodness. For Man is perhaps the ugliest and in many ways the cruellest of the mammals. This curious biped, hairless save for a few purposeless tufts of vestigial mammalian hair, with his shuffling gait, cuts a poor figure indeed when compared with the lithe leopard, the leaping, sounding dolphin, the swift antelope or the stooping eagle. Alone of mammals he smells bad. The normal human body smell, when the exudations are not removed with soap and water, is repellent to other humans. Most men live in an environment glittering with broken glass, contaminated by their own garbage and excrements, in conditions of dirt that wild animals do not tolerate....

A little later in the draft he noted that 'Man, the narcissist, disbelieves in the uglier side of his nature.... The most despicable human behaviour is called "animal", "bestial", "brutal" or "beastly"; but loving kindness, strangely, is called "humanity".'

Against the phrase, 'Alone of animals he smells bad', one of Duncan's early readers wrote, 'This really is not true – we don't know how many other animals smell repellent to each other. Probably most....' So that particular remark does not appear in quite the same form in the published version; yet the attitude there is even stronger: Duncan imagines a visitor from Alpha Centauri visiting Earth and taking notes of human progress from birth to age:

Only human babies howl. Why? Why is the entry into human society so painful, so much a matter of despair? Could it be a painful impact with the accumulation of a million years of evil? ... alone of young things, only the human kind seem to have constantly-running noses and to be naturally dirty ... larger children [are] ... instinctively cruel ... to their own kind ... human adolescents ... are subject to acne, rashes of pustules ... Man alone ... is built incapable of excreting cleanly ... it is only men and pigs (who resemble men so closely in anatomy and in habits of feeding) that produce thoroughly unpleasant-smelling excreta ... alone of animals, Man is ravaged by the ageing process.... How few of us are able to age with beauty or serenity.... If anyone should doubt the truth of this, let him look round in a bus at those lack-love apathetic, greedy faces.... And if he should still doubt its truth, let him look, if he is middle-aged in his own mirror. Our visitor would note the extraordinary distribution of human hair, betraying perhaps Man's curious irresolution about his own nature.... He would see, with distaste, that many men grow hair, sometimes mats of it, on parts of their bodies.... Man's bad smell is not limited to the armpits. Alone of animals his general smell is repellent....

And so on, through man's behaviour, his treatment of the countryside, of other forms of life, of the whole planet, his towns and cities, his wars – and the conclusion of the space-visitor, as he leaves Earth, is to name man as ' "bacillus sapiens", the intelligent microbe', agent of 'a world-cancer'.

It would be easy enough to dismiss many of the specific examples, or even the whole argument, with 'nonsense' or 'blimpishness' (which some of it sounds suspiciously like), or to put it down to the ravings of a desperately ill man (and some of the work on *Man and the Earth* was done when he was dying); but the feelings go back farther into his personality and history than his last illness.

Where from, then? While it is tempting to trace the feeling back to his childhood – say, to the time of his osteomyelitis – and to assume it derived from self-disgust, there is no evidence of this. Rather, and provided one assumes that the disgust at humanity was not felt before it was expressed, it seems to be tied to Duncan's flight from South Africa in 1962; this means it is also intimately associated with his realization of the failure of *satyagraha*. One could read the story this way: however hard one tried to convince one's opponents of what was right and good, it seemed that some were incapable of hearing, of feeling; they were men who had lost their souls. To move them one had to kill them. Then, having made that traverse, Duncan went into the spiritual isolation of Kubung, where local people would filch from the store he had opened partly to make their lives easier, where they would not only steal the honey from the hives but smash the hives, too. Again, he learned that one might have to force people to behave decently. Then he left Basutoland and, while he was away, the people he had once worked with declared him a prohibited immigrant; moreover, they tried to confiscate his property. Then America, in which he had placed so much trust, turned out to be as self-interested as any other state. Then, the man he had offered his loyalty to and the organization he had sacrificed so much for both rejected his services, when he knew that they needed him.

Of course, this is only a partial version of what his attitude might have been – and it includes a note of self-pity which Duncan seems never to have felt; similarly, disgust at humanity is only a part of *Man and the Earth*. First, Duncan made it clear in 'Some saving clauses' which preceded his foreword in *Man and the Earth* that he did not except himself from humanity:

> there is much in this book that is critical of, and even hostile to the human race. I do not wish it thought that I am condemning from an imaginary judgement-throne with myself immune from condemnation. No, these criticisms are directed as much against myself as against any fellow-men. I do not feel myself morally superior to my fellow-men, rather the contrary.[37]

Secondly, whatever Duncan might have felt about man as cancer, he wished still to rescue him from himself and from human history; in other words, some men could still hear, could still be drawn to the right path. In just the same way, disliking humanity did not prevent Duncan from loving actual people.

If this is one theme of *Man and the Earth*, the thesis is that 'these two greatest needs, the conservation of the biosphere and the establishment of a generally acceptable ethical system for the human race can both be met by one development: the growth of Man's love for the world'.

It is the thesis of this book that the key to the bewildering problems that beset us lies in our seeing the world from this new angle, and in re-thinking our relationships with the world, so as always to remember its uniqueness and its beauty. This uniqueness and beauty exist quite independently of the existence of Man, and the world has no need of Man for this uniqueness and beauty to exist. Man, of course, depends entirely on the world for his existence.

The final chapter, 'Man and Earth', is the 'interim ethic' for the age of science. Religions have failed to hold the people; not only are they inadequate in that way, but they are also 'foolish and often harmful'. For instance, the central statement of Christianity, 'that God became man', is 'so extraordinary that the onus of proof is unavailable and must surely remain unavailable'. Moreover, Christianity is more than 'the example of Jesus and the dogmas of the church':

> it is also the cult of Jehovah, the God of Abraham and Isaac. The Old Testament is an integral part of Christianity, as much as it is of Judaism. And what a repulsive cult it is! To understand how repulsive one must read the whole Old Testament, and not merely the selected pieces that are read as lessons from the brass lecterns. Jehovah's character was violent. As he has told us himself, he was 'jealous'. . . . He incited his chosen people to commit crimes of genocide on a Nazi scale, apart from the minor crimes of fraud that were committed in his name.

Other religions were equally unpleasant or equally inadequate. Marxism, 'near-religion', was fading. Humanism had failed both because it placed Man at the centre, though this 'most successful murderer . . . is not a fit character to sit at the centre of any ethical system', and because it lacked a teleology.

Yet an ethical system was necessary: the refurbishment of the old religions or of Marxism would not do, and no new Messiah was likely. So he suggests a new system, geism, in which good and bad should come to mean: ' "what is good (or bad) for the Earth and its rocks and waters; for its biosphere, with all its non-human and human life, the human life always being seen as part of the whole" ', and the decision of which was which should always be made 'in the light of the next three generations'. Its mainspring would be love of the Earth, a new and larger form of nationalism or patriotism; it would involve self-renunciation, at least in the short term, but it would not mean the dismembering of the old religions or even be inconsistent with Marxism – it would be 'a stop-gap, an interim ethic, until something better can be found'. Scientific, rational, even traditional, linked to the best in art and music and literature, geism would be a ' "yes" to life, and a focus for love'. It would not necessarily deny God, at least in 'the sense of being the Essence of the Universe', but it would provide a temporary substitute which might eventually make a new pathway to a greater truth.

The failings of *Man and the Earth* are more or less self-evident; in 'Some saving clauses' at the start of the book Duncan admits the most serious:

Human affairs – even on the scale of the individual – are so complex that it is scarcely possible to make any positive statement that is both valuable and completely true. It is even more difficult to make general statements without important saving clauses. On the world-scale the difficulty is still greater. Many of the situations are not quantifiable, nor computable, and can only be illuminated by intuitive flashes of insight.

It is therefore necessary, at the beginning of this book which has a somewhat wide scope in time and space, to utter a caution: all generalizations in this book which are not based on statistics are to be taken as intuitive judgements, statements which in my opinion, are as near to the truth as possible; statements made in the knowledge that in making them one creates many exceptions. They are to be taken as statements which, despite this necessary inaccuracy, I feel to be valuable and true enough to be worth making.

Even some statements based on statistics may be doubted. Duncan knew himself how ambitious the book was: when he was typing the final draft, in April 1967, he told Alan Paton that it was 'horribly ambitious' and 'makes all previous versions look awful as I try to do it all over again'.[38] To combine moral philosophy and conservation, in neither of which he had much training, to argue about genetics when he was not a scientist, to discuss literature, music, the history of creation, the future of the planet, all in eighty thousand words, was a tall order and, like most polymathic books, it looks most thin to the reader where he happens to have particular expertise. Though Duncan knew a great deal about a great many things, he did not know enough. After he had given the manuscript to some of his friends and acquaintances to read, he noted that 'some of the reactions have been immensely encouraging, those from John Wilson, from Wills (who founded the Farmington Research Unit that John Wilson directs), from Morrice James, and from Albert Hourani, Director of the Middle East Institute. The unfavourable, ones are from Fraser Darling the ecologist, and (partly unfavourable, partly very favourable) Richard Hare, the new professor of moral philosophy at Oxford. In general it is the ordinary people who give most encouragement, the experts in these fields who dislike it.'[39]

Yet at the same time, and for all one's reservations, the book has qualities which do make it worth reading. First of all, it is informed with a sense of passionate urgency. In a way this could be called a failing, because, for all that one of the 'saving clauses' claims that the reader 'will find in this book ... judgement as free as can be from considerations of self', it remains a very personal book; as Duncan said himself, 'all generalizations in this book ... are to be taken as intuitive judgements'. Yet the urgency is personal. The problem is here and now; it cannot be safely avoided. If it is, hell will follow soon afterwards. When Schmoller saw the first draft of the first chapter, he wrote gently:

I admire your courage in trying to look at man and the world, and their ills and problems, with so vast a sweep of mind. As the work progresses you may feel the importance of achieving an outward air of detachment, however great your personal involvement. There is perhaps a danger of exhausting yourself and the reader by the sheer intensity of feeling which is reflected in your writing. The more coolly you can set down your facts, and the more you can avoid an appeal to the emotions, the better. But I can see how difficult this must be.[40]

This is good advice from an experienced publisher, and is what the book essentially lacked as a work in moral philosophy and conservation, especially as it praised the scientific method as 'super-event'. But where the book catches fire, where it is most alive, is exactly where it is most personal – where, for instance, Duncan records his particular moments of wonder: when, for instance, he is describing 'some water-memories', the mountain-water of the Cape Peninsula with its 'colour of beer and . . . taste of peat', the chalk-streams of Winton, and the water at Kubung, running 'gently from a fountain, green with watercress and wild mint'. 'I mention these memories, not to write autobiography, but to try to awaken in my readers the same feelings of reverence and delight that pure water seldom fails to awaken in me.' Or again:

> The day before writing this I went on a fishing expedition on a glorious summer morning from a small Algerian port. Three lines, each baited with small pieces of shrimp, were let down to a depth of about eight metres through the clear blue water to the rocky bottom, which was hazily and refractively visible. Within minutes of the first line being let down a fisherman announced that he had caught a *cochon de mer* (hogfish). He began to pull the line in, and, down near the bottom weaving backwards and forwards, there was the hogfish manoeuvring, twisting, turning upside-down, as it tried to free itself from the hook. But the hook was too sharp, and the nylon line too strong, and soon a second fisherman had a landing-net underneath him. Out he came, some 2 kg. in weight, shaped like a gibbous moon, beautifully coloured, something like his cousin the beautiful angel-fish of the coral reefs. The hook was through the prog-nathous jaws, which were well-equipped with strong teeth. He had an expressive eye which dilated and contracted as we watched it. It was a 'sporting' fish, and as its captor bent to cut the hook out of its jaws it snapped at him in a last attempt to defend itself. Then the fish was placed under one of the boat's benches to die a slow death. The hogfish took nearly a half hour to die. Even though it was out of the sea it seemed able, to some extent, to be able to breathe, since it gulped down air in regular paroxysms. A quarter of an hour after it was caught it flapped and twisted its body, and at one moment it danced on its tail under the bench on the hot deck. Then it lay still, and I watched its eye dilating and contracting faster than before. The breathing became feebler, and towards the end it uttered a cry, a cry that was quite comprehensible across the hundreds of millions of years that separated us. This cry earned it a kick from its Muslim captor who remarked 'Le cochon de mer est très méchant. Il est comme le cochon de terre'. He then explained that he had caught so many that he had no interest in eating them. A few minutes later the fish died.

Another quality of the book is that, even when its argument does not persuade, one is always persuaded that Duncan himself is profoundly excited about the ideas he is discussing. For instance, when he is talking of DNA, he suddenly digresses: 'These facts awaken one's numinous feelings, the sense that one is very near to the secret of the universe.'

In March 1967 Duncan was still working on the book; when reactions came in from Peter Scott and Dr MacEwan of the Conservation Society, he wrote to Vigne: 'I want to do a lot of reading round the subject, and during that reading to recast the form of the whole, and then to rewrite what I have written.'[41] Its limitations are partly created by the fact that he never had the chance to do this; he was still working on the final draft of *Man and the Earth* two days before his death. Eventually it was published by a Scottish press for the Conservation Society in 1974, with a 'Message from Peter Scott', and 'Prefatory remarks' by MacEwan; it was dedicated 'To my wife without whose help I should have made many more mistakes'. Sadly enough, it is poorly printed by offset litho on cheap paper, with bad plates and binding; Duncan, who loved fine books, would not have admired it very much. But he had meant what he said, and it was worth saying:

> One trembles to think of the appalling world that we are bequeathing to our children and grandchildren. One can hardly bear to think of the damage that is now unavoidable by the first third of the twenty-first century. One can hardly bear to think of the disturbances that world-hunger is now fated to cause, as vast throngs of ill-educated people swarm over the globe. Unless in our time the parents of these throngs learn to deepen their love of the world, this paradise that we inherited from our parents will have become an irredeemable slag-heap.

In May 1966, soon after doing a tour of mountain villages which had been badly hit by a drought, he and Cynthia went to England for a brief holiday, staying with Deborah Cowen, who had moved to Oxford with her daughters, and seeing Randolph Vigne and his family in London. Hearing while he was there that an old friend, Stephen King-Hall (Lord King-Hall, of *King-Hall's Newsletter*), was dying of lung-cancer, Duncan went to visit him; as Ann, King-Hall's daughter, and he were leaving, both in tears, Duncan turned to her and said, to comfort her, 'We are all under sentence of death: the only difference is the date of the certain execution'.[42] He had himself been suffering from anaemia for some time; in 1964, when he was ill in England, anaemia was diagnosed, and again, in January 1966, in the follow-up to his medical examination for CCSA, the doctors had reported anaemia. A supplement to his medical report notes that 'We have written to candidate concerning the need for further studies of his anaemia which appears refractory to iron medication.'[43] As a result he took so many iron pills for the next few months that his sweat actually turned yellow, but he still seemed anaemic, and in late May flew over to Germany to the Institute of Tropical Diseases in Tubingen. The doctor there reported 'Signs of slight anaemia' but added 'a special treatment is not needed'.[44] Duncan was given some pills to take, and was cleared fit for work in tropical countries. So, after visiting some of his German relations, he went back to Constantine and his work there.

However, despite the drugs that had been recommended to him at Tubingen, Duncan was no better and, in July, developed such bad symptoms – breathlessness, lassitude, blinding headaches and crippling backaches – that he had to go home to Algiers, where a local American doctor treated him with chloromycetin (chloramphenicol); he had been treated with the same drug and with other antibiotics earlier in the year. One night he himself told Cynthia he thought he had some disease of the blood, and actually mentioned leukaemia; he knew that he must be very short of haemoglobin because even the mildest exertion would make his heart beat as if he had done something really strenuous. Afterwards, he wrote, 'I felt [then] I might be fatally ill, and the image that presented itself to me was a wall – an impossibly high wall that was unscalable – lying right across my path. I soon became too ill to worry much about it, and did not, at that time, care whether I lived or died. I told my wife that it did not matter because for the moment there was nothing I could do about the South African mess'.[45] Gradually he got worse, then picked up an infection of the chest which sent his temperature up to $102°$; the combination of this, his anaemia, and his feeling that doctors in Algeria were not able to diagnose his illness properly made him decide to go to England to consult doctors there.

Duncan, Cynthia and young Patrick flew to England, together with Dr Moyniham and his wife, who had been on holiday in Algeria. At Orly airport, where they changed planes, Duncan could hardly manage the stairs on his own; 'my heart seemed to be trying to blow my head clean off my neck!'[46] he wrote afterwards, and called the stairs 'the low point of my trouble'. With the help of a specialist, his doctor soon diagnosed aplastic anaemia, a disease in which the marrow stops producing various of the components of blood, and Duncan was found a bed at the Westminster Hospital. He had already asked his doctor and the specialist if he were fatally ill but, although they told Cynthia how dangerous it was, they did not tell him; instead, 'it took me some weeks to know how small my chances were. I was given an encouraging peptalk as if remissions were fairly common.'[47]

Duncan had believed for years that doctors should tell the truth to their patients, without covering up. Hearing from Naomi Mitchison about the death of her brother J. B. S. Haldane from rectal cancer, and that Haldane had not been told how slim his chances were, Duncan replied:

> What you tell me of your brother's death confirms me in the view I have strongly held for many years: that a doctor or a hospital has no right whatsoever to conceal from anyone, least of all someone like JBSH, such knowledge as they may have gained about serious illness.[48]

In a long letter which Duncan wrote to Frances Baker (now Dr Frances Dower), Sir Herbert Baker's grand-daughter, then a medical student at the Westminster, in early December, when he knew more exactly what his chances were, he explained:

> Doctors say that often the patient does not want to know if he is fatally ill. This is no doubt often true, but a desire to avoid a subject often produces constraint, and I wonder how many patients do not ask the central question because they feel that would upset the doctor. I feel that an understanding doctor would let the patient see clearly that to him the subject is not taboo ... when I first got into hospital I felt terribly in the dark about myself. I realized that it was pretty serious: looks in eyes and inconsistencies in answers had shown me that. I was anxious....
> Some people never realize that they are dying: one instances some children, some trusting patients under sedation, and victims of, say, an air crash.... But many do know they are on their way out and that their time and their life are very limited. Such patients need great understanding and

care. Their task is to die well, and to do so they have to steer a serene course, balanced between too much optimism and too much pessimism. Most of such patients need to know the truth as the doctor sees it, because most people's lives contain loose ends which need tying up, and which they will tie up if they know that they will not (in all likelihood) recover. I am not preaching for doctors to terrify their patients with pessimism which the patient will exaggerate and read the worst into, but I am preaching for the maintaining of a link of trust and affection between doctor and patient, and I am saying that this link is broken in more cases than many doctors will concede by an absence of candour on the doctor's side. If this link is broken, and it may just as easily be broken by glib optimism as by unwise pessimism then the patient will suffer periods of the blackest pessimism and of overwhelming self-pity, and he will not tell the doctor about them.[49]

He knew himself that he was an exacting patient, but he had to know what was happening to him; and when he was not told he found out for himself.

Since the transfusions seemed to have helped, the doctors allowed him to return to Algeria in late July. Cynthia stayed with him a few days in Constantine, then returned to Algiers, while he stayed to work both for CCSA and on the book, finishing the first draft of 120 000 words by early August. By mid-August he was so ill again that he returned to Algiers, and once again he, Cynthia and the girls flew to England. Back in the Westminster, he was given more transfusions – four pints – and a new drug, an extract, developed by Dr Humble, from the ordinary runner bean, phytohaemagglutinin, usually called just 'the bean', which it was hoped would get the marrow working again. On 19 September he wrote to Randolph Vigne: 'The treatment seems to be going well. I am feeling better than for 2 months.' Released from hospital on the 20th, with a haemoglobin count of 63%, he decided to stay in England with Cynthia and the children at Hexton Manor. A week later, another doctor – not one of the Westminster staff – took a sample of blood, told Duncan the count was 68–9%, and predicted it would be up to 75% in a week. This was marvellous news, because it meant that production of blood had started again, and he told his family and friends he was very hopeful that a cure had started.

> In fact, the next week it was down to 48% and I had to go in for further transfusions, and my hopes crumbled. They had been hopes I had shared with my family and with many others who were anxious. I now realize that the 68–9% reading was quite inaccurate. Was it done as a genuine mistake? Or was it done to encourage me? I sense the latter. If so, he misread the situation hopelessly. When I had to disabuse my friends and family I felt I had been made a fool of, and the disappointment broke my morale. I felt I could see Death looking in at the door.[50]

A second set of tests showed that in fact production had not restarted, and on 8 October he went back into the Westminster for more transfusions, this time into the femoral artery:

> To get the catheter in is less pleasant than putting one into an arm, and I was taken down to the radiology department so that the successful entry might be viewed on a screen. There were two doctors: the expert ... whose name is S—— and another. I was anxious, never having had this done to

me before. S—— was excellent. He spoke quietly and calmly about what he was doing, even when it didn't go well. The other whispered. S——'s calm openness was right, because no one likes being whispered about at the best of times. I feel that on an occasion like this it is better to speak out so that the patient can hear or not to speak. A seriously-ill patient feels isolated. All round him are doctors and nurses who are well. He needs allies and counsellors, perhaps even a hand to hold. If in his presence people whisper about him he feels doubly isolated. When one's back is to the wall it is better to face known dangers with counsellors whose reports on these dangers are truthful....[51]

Cynthia had had to return to Algiers on the 8th, when he went into hospital again, to get the girls back to school and to look after their home. Duncan wrote to her: 'This is as difficult a parting as the first day at prep boarding school. I shall fight this with all I have, so that we can have many years together.'[52] He now knew what he was up against; he had had a long talk with his sister-in-law Patricia Serocold, a physician, who 'concealed nothing of the mortal nature of this disease, and replied to my many questions as fully as she could. I felt that she had shared a great load which up till then had been on my shoulders alone....'[53] Now, too, he persuaded Dr Humble to tell him exactly what was going on, and he set himself to finding out everything he could about aplastic anaemia; he had already discovered that one of the antibiotics he had been given in Algiers, chloramphenicol, could conceivably have caused the disease, and he read everything he could lay hands on. He still did not have the complete truth, for he was suspicious of the conflicting answers of the doctors; when he asked two of them separately what the chances of a cure were, one said 30%, one said 55%. But at least he now had an idea of the odds.

Seeing Vigne, too, had encouraged him to begin to speak out on politics again. In June he had been to a meeting of the Institute of Race Relations at Chatham House to hear Harry Oppenheimer speak and, stung by something Oppenheimer said, he asked an aggressive question. In October, he wrote a letter to *The Times* to spur on the controversy about whether overseas academics should go to teach in South African universities; Duncan thought not, since 'English South Africa capitulated long ago (except for ineffectual and half-hearted protests) to Afrikaner South Africa on the question of rights for the Africans'.[54] Replies came from Professor Sir Keith Hancock, Lady Beit, Robert Birley (ex-headmaster of Eton, then teaching in a South African university) and others. Duncan's counterblast was not published, but he wrote to the Association of Commonwealth Universities arguing that they were, by advertising jobs in South African universities and handling applications, in fact 'handling recruitment for South African universities'.[55] Though he disapproved strongly of Birley's breaking the boycott of South African universities, he did also write to him to wish him well in his work there. He wrote an article on Lenin's *The Development of Capitalism in Russia* which he called 'A myth of 1917' and submitted it to *Encounter*, though it was not published. After a visit from Randolph Vigne he wrote to say how much he had enjoyed their talk: 'what was best was that you recalled me to a sense of duty'.[56] One of the PAC men in Maseru, Pokela, had been kidnapped, taken across the border, and put on trial in South Africa, and Duncan promised that he would do what lobbying he could on his behalf. Almost immediately he talked to Morrice James about the problem, later talked to Joe Kotsokoane, the Lesotho High Commissioner in London, and wrote personally to Leabua Jonathan. He had dozens of visitors – Vigne, Hjul, Henry Baker, Morrice James, Astor, Ann Tobias, Barney Zackon, and more, so many that visits had to be staggered to fit them in. He saw a great deal of Elizabeth James, Morrice's wife, who was then an outpatient at the Westminster for cobalt treatment for cancer. 'I realized that her chances were slim. The image that presented itself was of both of us going down to the Styx together,' he wrote in December, a month after she had died;[57] but he wrote to Cynthia about a South African Liberal then in London who twenty years before had been given six months to live because of the same disease.

The next day he had a row with a doctor who suggested as an antibiotic to control Duncan's reaction to the transfusion one which he recognized as thought to be a cause of aplastic anaemia. As a result, he told Cynthia he was going to America to search out a cure there: 'the time before which I must find a cure is not unlimited', he told her.[58] Transfusions could not go on for ever; sooner or later his body would reject the stranger's blood, and if his own body had not itself by then started to produce the proper components of blood he would die. But by 16 October the blood-count was good enough for him to leave the Westminster, and he joined his sons at Hexton; by the 18th his reaction to the new blood was entirely gone, the wound in his groin from the transfusion was healing, and he took his sons over to Cambridge for a visit. Returning to the Hichens in North Aston, he told Cynthia he was 'longing to be active' again[59] and, four days later, wrote to her to say 'I have felt very well today and woke feeling that I might be getting better'.[60]

The same day he went into the Radcliffe Science Library at Oxford, to do some work on the book. Instead, he consulted a medical encyclopaedia; it was 'the worst moment':

> I saw all my symptoms in the section on aplastic anaemia. At the end the article said that although some patients had been kept going with trans-fusions for 3–4 years, 'this disease is always fatal'. I could read no more, and walked out into the wet and cold of an October evening. My mind was full of coldness, of the hardness of iron, and the moisture of sweat. For some days after that I calmly weighed the pros and cons of suicide. Was my life worth all the expense in blood, time and money? Would a quick end not be easier than a long-drawn-out affair? I often felt the urge to steer my car into an immovable obstacle at speed....[61]

Again, his sister-in-law helped by pointing out that since the book had been written cures and remissions had been recorded; so he returned to his battle, and did not tell Cynthia what he had read, though he told her everything else, one day that he was 'strong, well and optimistic' and the next 'miserable – nothing that a good night's rest won't cure'.[62] He saw the Schmollers and the Hares, his sister, his old schoolmaster Walter Oakeshott, who was then Warden of Lincoln College, and he went to talk to John Wilson of the Farmington Research Unit about his book. He went to see his sons at Winchester, staying with friends on the way, and was delighted with their progress: Patrick was head of house, and Alex was much happier than he had been when he first left Bishop's and South Africa.

By 1 November the old symptoms were back, so much so that Cynthia flew over from Algiers to join him. A blood test showed that the haemoglobin-count was declining less fast than before, though Duncan was still making very few red cells and his blood was beginning to lose even more of its clotting power than at the time of the tests in July. In mid-November he went into hospital for another transfusion and another dose of 'the bean', which seemed to cause less reaction than before, and he began to talk of going back to Algeria – he was feeling very guilty at having done so little work for the CCSA since mid-August. Both Jan van Hoogstraten and Jim Paton, however, insisted that they could manage without him, and that his first priority was to find a cure. Duncan was also worried about money; although he had taken out medical insurance when he joined the CCSA and then the NCCC, the policy did not cover all his expenses and, while the British National Health Service paid for much, there were air-fares to and from Algiers, and other expenses. He began, with the help and encouragement of Sir Michael Cary, to try to get a fellowship for a year in the United States, writing to Professor Neustadt at the John F. Kennedy Institute of Government at Harvard University, and getting help from Philip Kaiser, then in the American Embassy in London. Although he was in the end offered everything but the money to get him there, it came to nothing, and his plan of having a year's unpaid leave of absence from the CCSA in order to work more on *Man and the Earth*, to try American doctors for a cure, and to do what he called 'some forward thinking' on the South African question[63] had to be laid aside. He was now convinced, too, that the treatment he was getting at the Westminster was as good as he would get anywhere. In November he heard, with relief, that a temporary replacement was being sent to Constantine, and in early December Jim Paton wrote to say he was going to leave the replacement in Constantine and transfer Duncan to the Algiers office: 'Your working here in this office', Paton wrote to him, 'instead of C[onstantine] should *under no circumstances* be regarded as a demotion. Certainly you know my esteem of your work and my confidence in you.'[64] Duncan replied: 'About Paul's taking Constantine, *I am so pleased*. Jim, I didn't join the CCSA with any personal ambitions. In any case I don't regard being in Algiers as demotion. And I am thrilled at the prospect of once again being able to live en famille. So no problem exists in persuading me to accept gladly and *thankfully* any work the CCSA has for me in Algiers.'[65]

The exchange is characteristic of both the generous and indeed loving way in which the CCSA and its directors treated Duncan, both before and during his illness, and the serenity which Duncan had achieved in his illness; as he told Vigne, 'With the continuation of my anaemia I am anxious to reach reconciliation everywhere it is possible to'.[66] Family, English friends, South African visitors and exiles, visitors from America, all used to come to see him. There were also visitors from the hospital itself – a young houseman, Dr Simon Joseph, to whom Duncan lent a draft of *Man and the Earth* to read, Frances Baker, other doctors off duty, other patients; in short, he was once again holding the kind of court he had once held, at Riverside and then in Cape Town. He knew a great deal of what was happening in the hospital, and would talk medicine to the doctors and students, international affairs with Morrice James, newspapers with Astor, South African politics with the exiles, ecology and ethics with anyone. As Simon Joseph told Cynthia after his death: 'He was more demanding than the average patient, but then he gave so much more as well.'[67]

He was learning a new kind of happiness and, though on occasions he did break down, it was never for long and never in public:

> A fruit seller in Basingstoke spoke unusually kindly to me, and I had to take refuge in the car to avoid public tears. Another loss of serenity was the sight of the fall of autumnal leaves. . . . Again I was in the car, and the swirl of falling leaves was carried along by the slipstream. . . . Vergil's line hit my mind with irresistible sadness: 'As are the generations of leaves, so are the generations of man.' This line renewed my self-pity, and I felt that I was the lost beech-leaf that the car's tyres crushed. . . .[68]

A more common mood of the time, both in his letters and in the memories of people who visited him in hospital, is different; he was still alive, and once again living to his limit:

> Because I felt that this autumn might be the last I should see, its colours regained the brilliance that they had had in childhood. The joys of working in the Oxford libraries were multiplied many times; the sights and sounds and smells of that precious academic life printed themselves on my mind with unprecedented clarity.[69]

A particular happiness was to hear that Patrick had got a scholarship to Wadham College, Oxford; perhaps best of all, he was planning to read for a degree in biology. As Duncan told his wife, 'I am immensely proud of him'.[70] But it was more than that, too, for he was trying to put his affairs in order; when he went to see Maurice Bowra, Warden of Wadham, about Patrick's going up there in 1967 and about his plans in the meantime – he was going off to work in the Serengeti National Park for the nine months between school and university – he said, as he was leaving, 'Take care of my boy, because I'll be dead in six weeks'.[71]

Yet he had not given up hope. In mid-December he had another transfusion, and it went better than the others had done; there were still no signs of the reaction which would mean that his body was rejecting the foreign blood. Reading an article in the *New Scientist*[72] on the effect of antibiotics on the nucleic acids, especially of chloromycin on DNA in the presence of metal ions, he wondered if the antibiotics he had taken in early 1966 had worked with the iron pills to produce aplastic anaemia; he sent his question to various doctors, who assured him that his theory was unlikely. He was intensely curious to know exactly what had happened and what was happening, and he talked at length to his doctors, his sister-in-law, and any scientists he could persuade to listen.

Christmas he spent with the Ashley Coopers at Hexton, for Cynthia was not able to come over until the beginning of January, when the girls went back to school. Duncan continued work on his book, writing to MacEwan, talking to Richard Hare, ecologists, anyone who might be able to help him strengthen his arguments. He went to talk to Dingle Foot and the Attorney-General, Elwyn Jones, about his ideas for Rhodesia. Given that Britain had not intervened militarily when she should have done, the other priority was for Britain to align herself firmly with the black majority in Rhodesia, and not climb down whatever happened – for instance, in the guerilla war which seemed inevitable to him. He entered a *Punch* competition to 'compose a newspaper apology to make the offended party wish he had never raised his complaint' and was delighted when his entry, with six others, won a one-guinea book-token.[73] Much to Duncan's delight, Henry Baker organized his election to the Athenaeum, and in February he became a member.

On 20 January he went into the Westminster for another transfusion, and now at last Cynthia persuaded his doctors to agree that, although no remission was in sight, he could return to Algiers and either have his transfusions there or, if they could afford it, fly back each time he needed new blood. So, on 26 January he flew to Algiers. There, he worked in the CCSA office, read and lazed in the sun on the terraces of 'La Consulaire', wrote letters to friends, made plans to buy a plot of land on the coast at Tabarka with Patrick Seale the journalist to use for holidays, and revised his book. Although he did not feel as well as he had done after the last two transfusions, he did not, he told Vigne, feel 'positively ill'.[74] Thanking Vigne for all he and his wife Gillian had done for him in the last three months, he wrote wryly, 'Unfortunately I think it is likely I shall be in England again soon'.[75] Ten days later he wrote again to Vigne:

> no proof of a cure is yet forthcoming, but I have not had a test for 3 weeks. Nor, however, is there any proof that haemolysis has begun – the attack by the body on the immigrant transfused blood. So, as far as I know there is no change. No change except the relentless tick of the clock.
>
> Because of the above I am living as if I were in love: hypersensitive to the sun and blue sky; to the violets Cynthia has taken out of our garden for my desk – and I send you one; to the loud games Ann and Emma are playing in the playroom; to the kindly folk I work for; and above all to the noble side of the Algerian people. I don't know when I have savoured more intensely the beauty of this world.
>
> All this is not to say I've given up hope. Far from it. Yet the fact is that I have exactly 5 months' less time to resume production – haematopoeia – than the day you came to lunch in Daisy Spickett's flat. I expect to return to the UK, perhaps next week.[76]

He read a report of a lecture by Dr Ahmed Taleb, Algerian Minister of Education, on Camus's attitudes to Algeria and Arabs, and wrote in great excitement to Vigne about the similarities between Camus and white South Africans.[77] A few days later, he was back in England for three days for another transfusion, then immediately back to Algiers. Now there began what he had known was bound to happen sooner or later; his blood had so little clotting power left that he started to bleed badly from the mouth and the nose. Dr Taylor at the Westminster gave him a drug, Predmisone, to help the blood clot, but while it helped the bleeding it brought, too, an allergic reaction. On 13 March he wrote to Taylor: 'I'm not complaining, but itching spots now cover 90% of my body. The itch is not unbearable, and is not even severe. Do I go on with Predmisone? I imagine that it has caused the spots.' Otherwise, he said, he was feeling 'wonderfully well in comparison to the earlier "runs"' and was even 'permitting myself the delicious luxury of optimism'.

I am getting a good deal of sun. Two days ago I took a racing skiff (solo) out on the waters of the port. Yesterday I did my first hard physical work in months, 2½ hours cutting inaccessible branches of a figtree and a jacaranda tree. Sometimes I got extremely breathless, but a lot of this breathlessness must be put down to general laziness and bad condition over 8 months. I keep a cheerful colour, not all of it due to my nightly scotch and soda.

For these reasons I shan't be coming over for some time.[78]

'Some time' was a fortnight later; there had been talk of his having the transfusions done in Algiers, despite the difficulties of matching the blood-type exactly – the quantity and number of the transfusions Duncan was getting made exact matching very important. Now, however, the Church World Service offered to pay for his flights whenever necessary.

The eighth transfusion done, Duncan returned again to Algiers. Soon afterwards, he wrote to Alan Paton, one of those with whom reconciliation had been made:

My health is worse and better. Worse physically as the rate at which blood corpuscles are formed is worse than before. I am now feeling the effects of much too few platelets and white blood corpuscles, and for most of the last 30 days I have bled from the mouth and nose. The amount I have lost is not important: perhaps 2 pints at the outside, but losing 20–30 cc in a night through the gums can be extremely unpleasant to the loser, and offensive to those near him.

So much for the way in which I am worse: I am better in this, that I have learnt to cope with life lived on transfusions, and to take it all as a matter of course. Most important of all I have learnt to live as Pascal (I think it was) who said life was best lived as if one were under a sentence of death. Last year the thought of the tenuousness of life worried me a good deal. It still does, but one learns to live with almost anything, and the sharp edge is off this one for me. It is almost counterbalanced by the acute enjoyment that ordinary things give, for one has removed the dark glasses, the 'take-it-for-granted' glasses, that we nearly all wear throughout our lives.

Do not from the above assume that I have abandoned hope. I haven't, and I do not believe that there are no cures and remissions.... But I know from the look in the doctors' eyes that it isn't a big hope. I keep on asking them for actual figures, and always they find some way of evading!! Still they are very good doctors, and are astonishingly kind to me, so I have no real objections.[79]

Then, in April, happened one of the most extraordinary events of these last months. Immediately after it happened he wrote it down:

I am writing this to record one of the most remarkable happenings in my life.

Yesterday morning I lay in a bed in a hotel at Timimoun, deep in the Sahara, and over 1200 km away from home, prostrated by a terrible headache. I had only once before had such a headache – in September 1966 when my haemoglobin count had fallen into the thirties due to an aplastic anaemia which I had and still have.

The earlier headache and weakness had almost immobilized me during a trip to London to get medical help.

This headache of yesterday was almost certainly due to a night spent out in the Sahara desert between El Golea and Gharda'i'a – a night when I froze – but which I don't regret. Now, too, my haemoglobin is very low.

Within 12 hours of this exposure I produced boils and the headache. I was, then, in bed and with me were Cynthia and our girls aged 7 and 12. We were booked to fly to Gharda'i'a yesterday on our return and to pick up our car at Gharda'i'a. Somehow from there I had to bring family and car back home to Algiers, a distance of 620 km. Yet I could not sit up in bed, let alone walk to the bathroom without great pain.

There is only one plane a week out of Timimoun.

In Algeria it is not possible for a lone woman to drive on the main roads. Yesterday morning I did not know what to do. My thoughts had for about 12 hours been a bit delirious – curious ideas and images passing through my mind, and I had a temperature. I found myself saying these words in silence. (I recorded them $1\frac{3}{4}$ hours later.)

PD: God, I need your help. But I suppose if you are Jehovah I can't expect you to do anything for me.

R: I am Jehovah (the reply came instantaneously). How can you expect me to do anything for you after the rude things you said about me in your book?

Another person: In any case you should not ask for selfish things in prayer. You should ask for general benefits, that God's will be done etc.

PD: Maybe, but if prayer can't help in cases like this it can't be much use.

Within ten minutes the pain had gone, my temperature had returned to normal and since then I have felt well, except when I climbed the steps into the aircraft. The healing concerned only these symptoms. There has as yet been no miraculous healing of the anaemia.

We found the car at Gharda'i'a and I drove about 500 of the 620 km home, arriving at 10 p.m., without a twinge of pain. Looking back on this story I feel it is one of the most remarkable things I have ever experienced.[80]

Duncan was in no ordinary sense a visionary, even though he had called his earlier insights into the nonsense of racialism and the possible use of even a 'bent tool' 'visions'. He was what Cynthia calls 'a practical man', a doer, an active agent who wished to live the way he thought; and although there was in him a sense of asceticism, of self-renunciation in the service of a cause other than himself, it was only a part of him. He was always capable of intense perceptions, grabbing and holding *this* moment *now*; but though the quality sometimes makes poets (which Duncan was not) it is not enough to make a visionary. Of course he was an ill man then, less than two months from death; but even that does not explain why he should have had this particular vision. Part of the explanation lies in the Christian Science which he had, without desiring to do so, brought with him from childhood; certainly, there are many ways in which this vision is like the visions which Christian Scientists record at moments of healing. Of course it was only a very temporary healing, for shortly afterwards he had to go back to London for his ninth transfusion, but it was a healing of a kind; and the vision confirms the extent to which he remained, all his life, whether he liked it or not, a Christian Scientist.

One knows, too, that the vision mattered to him, though he did not talk about it to many outside his immediate circle of family and closest friends. Dr Otto Spohr, who had once managed Africa Books for the Duncans, saw Duncan briefly in hospital in early May 1967 while on a visit to England:

There he was, on the one side of him the blood-container dripping blood into his arm, on the other side the telephone. He looked well and cheerful.... We talked a lot about our families, mutual friends, very little politics. In between Patrick would regulate his blood supply, summoning and instructing this nurse who was less experienced than he, alas. Once he 'phoned the doctor and asked him how long he would be likely to live still. As far as I could gather, the doctor stalled. Pat later told me one episode which had made a deep impression on him. Apparently when last he had been in Algiers he had gone on safari! It was most strenuous and suddenly his strength left him and he felt the end had come. Suddenly, after prayer or some similar sort of spiritual contemplation, he had a mystical experience and was flooded by a tremendous feeling of well-being and strength and could finish the safari in a fit state.... [Leaving him] was not like leaving a sick patient who was getting tired, not at all. Pat was lively, and, as usual, stimulating and positive. You could not feel depressed in his company – only afterwards![81]

It was a reaction many visitors had: Walter Oakeshott wrote after one of his visits, 'I was so excited by my few minutes with you: I could not forget; do not want to forget it; and never shall forget it'.[82]

Duncan was to need his serenity, for the new transfusion, the ninth, at the end of April and beginning of May, went very badly, and he had such a heavy reaction to the new blood that his doctors insisted that he stay in England; there were also fears that the bleeding from mouth and nose would get worse. He went to his sister in Oxford and, while working on the book, looked up more information on aplastic anaemia; this time he did tell Cynthia:

I am writing in the Radcliffe – having done my reading up of aplastic anaemia – I have found the answer. It is certainly not a 50% chance, but for someone my age it is 10%–20%, as far as I can see. I feel so *encouraged*. Henceforth I shall just calmly remember the 10%–20%, and give up worrying, living each day as well as possible.[83]

He saw various old friends in Oxford, drove with Alex to Winchester, went punting on the Cher, went to hear the May Morning Carol and bell-ringing at Magdalen, proudly stayed at the Athenaeum and had the Vignes to dinner there, stayed with the Vignes, then with Morrice James and then with George and Betty Sachs, and at the request of Vernon Littlewood spoke on Algeria to a group of collectors for Christian Aid. On the 10th he wrote to Cynthia that he was still feeling very well, with no bleeding, and he was able to persuade the doctors to let him go back to Algiers.

He went to work again in the CCSA office: he wrote to Jan van Hoogstraten on 22 May, just after he had been appointed to a new post as PRO for CCSA, to say how much he was enjoying the work and how well he was: '... the bleeding is almost completely under control. Not quite but I've had nothing in the month of May to compare with the difficulties of April.... I've had 1½ glorious weeks here but already I can see my next visit to London coming closer.'[84]

He was still working at *Man and the Earth*, checking details, tidying up the style, trying to make it as good as he could, though he was still hoping for time to rewrite it completely. In April he had written to Colonel Jack Vincent of the International Council for Bird Preservation about the *Red Data Book*, the list of threatened animal species: the Barbary hyaena was not, Duncan thought, extinct, though the Barbary leopard was; there were Barbary stags at Sera'i'di, and possibly small herds at A'i'n-Essel and Cheffia. He ended his letter: 'Two possible misprints: the Kashmir Stag's scientific name is surely hangul, not hanglu, and the spelling of 2/17 should surely be Siphonor*N*is.' Vincent replied, thanking Duncan, then arguing that 'Siphonorhis' was correct, since it was so spelt by Slater in *Proceedings of the Zoological Society*, 1961, page 77. The spelling of the Kashmir subspecies of the Kashmir stag or hangul as 'C.e. hanglu' was also correct, since Wagner in 1844 spelt it thus in the 'Schreb. Saengelt. Supplement'.

On the 22 May, Duncan answered:

I think that though these spellings seem to have acquired a certain venerable age, they must be misspellings that, over the years, must lead to confusions.

My knowledge of Urdu or whatever the language is is nil, yet I am willing to bet my shirt that the forms *hangul* and *hanglu* cannot both be right: if they are they have no right to be! I feel science ought to put them in a hat and pick one out and stick to it.

As to siphonor*h*is, it simply cannot be right. The last five letters are clearly ornis, the Greek for bird. Probably someone misread a florid Victorian N for an H. I should have thought there was a good case for straightening this out, too, if for no other reason than that small mistakes like this can clutter your correspondence table and cost postage in replying to correspondents like me. And so, again thanking you for the courtesy of your letter, I end by saying that it is unnecessary to reply to this one.[85]

Vincent replied on 24 May, saying that Duncan was unlikely to lose his shirt, since they would never know exactly what the authors had in mind; but, he said, 'Siphonorhis' need not be from 'ornis', but from '*Siphon*, hollow and *rhis*, nose'.

Duncan did not have time to reply. But he was still very alive, and enjoying himself so much.

Christopher Powell, his young friend from Constantine, had visited him in hospital in England soon after Christmas; while they were lunching together, he showed Duncan an eighteenth-century silver watch he had bought and was going to have repaired. Duncan offered to collect it from the watchmaker's and bring it out to Algiers, then told Powell of an old Dutch watch he had in South Africa, which was engraved with Father Time and his scythe, and a Latin inscription; one of the words in the inscription was 'Aether', and together they decided it should have been written 'Aeter', short for 'Aeternitas', since 'eternity' would make better sense in that context than 'ether'.

At Eastertide 1967, Powell went to Algiers from Constantine for a few days, partly to see Duncan; he had assumed from Duncan's nonchalance that he was not seriously ill, but was horrified now to see how badly his condition had deteriorated. To make conversation and to cover his shock, he asked if Duncan could remember the exact wording of the inscription on his Dutch watch. Duncan could not, but promised to let Powell know if he did remember. They said goodbye for the last time, but in May Powell had a brief postcard from Duncan in hospital, the message on which ended: 'The inscription on my watch was "mihi destinet Aether". Ever, P.'[86] *I am bound eternity* – or for the 'ether', the air, if that is what the engraver meant.

On 29 May, Duncan flew to London for the tenth transfusion; Cynthia did not go with him partly because of the two girls, partly because, as she told David Astor afterwards, 'people do recover from that disease and I never believed that he would be one of those who wouldn't recover – I suppose it was mainly because I didn't want to believe it. He had got over so many crises in his life that I believed that the ordinary rules didn't apply to him.'[87] When he got to the Westminster, his doctor was not there, as it was a public holiday, so he had to wait. Morrice James came to see him, and they talked international politics, especially Nigeria and the Middle East. There was more delay, since the doctors wanted to try 'the bean' again, and had to test his blood first. On the 31st the transfusion began, and Duncan wrote to Cynthia that having 'the bean' would mean an extra five days. He had had a lot of visitors, he said; he was feeling very well and looking forward to being home.

By the 2nd, the Friday, he had a bad reaction both to blood and the 'bean', but wrote to Cynthia to say that he would probably be back on Sunday. There were more visitors. He was still very cheerful, reading *The Pilgrim's Progress* again for the first time since 1942, and looking forward to getting out of hospital and on a plane to Algiers.

On Saturday a heavy reaction started, and by the evening he was so ill that his sister Deborah was summoned from Oxford. She came and sat the night by his bedside; occasionally, he talked a little to her. Next morning Alex, too, was summoned from Hexton Manor, where he was spending the weekend; there seemed no urgency in the call, so his uncle drove him up after lunch. By the time they arrived, at three o'clock, Duncan was unconscious; Deborah told Alex that he had whispered to her, just before he went under: 'It's just like an El Greco painting.' The doctor and nurses put an oxygen-tent up, and a pump to keep his lungs clear, but he did not regain consciousness. At about five o'clock the doctor said that he was dead.

BOOK FIVE

Judgements

CHAPTER 13

'I think a summing-up after the death is needed'[1]

When Duncan was writing his autobiography in detention in 1960, he made his sub-title, 'My defence: examination of personal success or failure'. In true Gandhian spirit, he was examing his spiritual worthiness for the task he had set himself. As epigraphs he took two quotations from Ortega y Gasset's *Revolt of the Masses*:

> All life is the struggle, the effort to be itself.

and

> Really to live is to be directed towards something, to progress towards a goal. . . . The apparent egoism of great men is the inevitable sternness with which anyone who has his life fixed on some undertaking must bear himself.

His opening sentences were:

> For eight years now I have been living a directed life: every book I read (with few exceptions), every person I meet, my very holidays, all I try to do, has been done with a purpose: to do what I can to put an end to the colour-bar, and to bring political equality to South Africa.
>
> I firmly believe that this goal is being realized day by day; and that it is South Africa's destiny that it is realized, in these times of ours. My destiny is thus intertwined with my country's, as I should wish it to be.

Judged in those sole terms, his life was a failure: he did not succeed in what he set out to do, and his destiny was not intertwined with his country's, though it would be a savage judgement which depended only on where he got to and not how he got there. Yet it *was* part of his failure that he took so much upon himself, that for so long he saw himself in the role of great man, of leader. Once, he said to Alan Paton, 'I've decided who our Gandhi should be'.

'Who?'

'You.'

But it was himself really, for all his acknowledgement of his own inadequacies. It is that attitude (for the story is serious as well as funny) which makes so many people judge him still as 'totally and dangerously *simpliste*' (the phrase is Ronald Segal's) or, if they are kinder, as a 'lovable ass'. In the context of part of his life, and part of his political thinking, such judgements have some validity; yet they ignore (or, more properly, are ignorant of) what he experienced in the last few years of his life: his later vision of politics ran much deeper than seeing only the wickedness of racialism. While there is much that is magnificent in the passionate simplicity of Duncan's initial loathing of the *apartheid*-state, simplicity became at times a form of blindness. In 1953 he wrote to an African friend: 'To me the whole South African situation is so simple. We are saddled with an incubus of wrong thinking with all its hates and fears. We have to get rid of it.'[2] The activity of the desire – 'we have to get rid of it' – is of course preferable to the kind of reaction which sees so much complexity it is left totally passive: 'with so much complexity where do we dare to begin?' Even if he was mistaken in thinking the South African problem only 'an incubus of wrong thinking', at least he was prepared to get rid of it. Part of the necessary tragedy of his life was that, as he recognized more and more that the wrong was not so simple, so the possibilities of action became more and more curtailed. As the vision of a complex politics was shaped, so it, too, became more and more tragic: even if he never completely understood the ambiguity of his own judgement, 'Both cannot win', he did see that 'our country is clearly fated to be the scene of vast population movements, vast suffering, and tremendous casualties'.[3] Whether he was right or wrong in this may not be known for a generation at least, though in one small sense it does not matter to the making of judgements whether he is proved right or wrong; what matters is that he learned the inadequacy of his own creed of individualism. He learned to see the stage as larger than that on which he was protagonist. Yet, though the action available to him grew more and more limited, until indeed he reached a place where there was nothing more for him to do but write his book, he was not trapped into passive negations. Even if he himself could not act, somebody had to act; the old urgency never disappeared. However, he had learned, during the last years of his life, to accept the limitations which his body, his mind, his record, his time and history had placed and were in the process of placing on the choices he had: he was not an isolated free chooser, monarch of all he surveyed; he was a being infinitely more complicated.

He was a man both before and after his time. He was after it in that for years he believed in an individualism which neither suited the times nor even all his own political perceptions. For most of his political life there was a conflict between his individualism (defined so that it contains the notions of leadership, of *soul-force*, of personal sacrifice) and his recognition that the creative force in southern African politics was the 'latent power' of the blacks. He wanted not 'the Iron of Doctrine', but 'the greatest freedom of the finest minds to range at will, and for the executive to be obedient to the desires of the mass',[4] but was never able to resolve the relationship of executive and mass except in the word 'obedient', nor could he explain how that obedience of the 'finest minds' was to be achieved, except in notions of selfless public service for the undefined commonwealth – notions which suited the thinking of his father's generation better than his own. Even if one accepts – like Duncan – that revolutions are not made in the 'Iron law of history',[5] how does one judge some revolutions as good, some bad? Some necessary, some unnecessary, some inevitable? Even those who believe in the forward process of history distinguish revolutions and counter-revolutions, and make judgements of prematurity. But, in Duncan's world, when could the 'desires of the mass' be mistaken, or inadequate, or short-sighted? Could the 'finest minds' (or call it the party if one wishes) then ignore the masses, or at any rate decide to lead them, not be obedient to them directly but to some idea of their longer-term interests? It is possible, if not always easy, to do so if one has a law of history to help one make the judgements; but if one has no dialectic of history, no moral order in the universe, no theology, such judgements are much more difficult, perhaps even impossible, except in the plainly Protestant ethic of the individual conscience. As long as Patrick Duncan continued to be a Gandhian, to believe that his conscience was working on the consciences of the white rulers of South Africa, it was possible to resolve the conflict; when he lost that belief, when he realized that the intransigence of the rulers was stronger than any appeal to conscience, he had inevitably to lose some of his belief in individualism. The collective became much more important and he tried to find a place for himself in a collective force; but the collective soon enough rejected him and what he had to offer in the way of influence, intelligence and moral force.

Jan Kott says that, for tragedy,

> History is the only framework of reference, the final authority to accept or reject the validity of human actions.... History contains both the past and the future. Actors from previous scenes keep coming back, repeating old conflicts, and want to play parts that are long since over. They needlessly prolong the performance and have to be removed from the stage. They arrived too late....
>
> Those who came too early, striving in vain to speed up the course of history, are also history's tragic heroes. Their reasons, too, are one-sided; they will become valid only in the next historical phase, in the succeeding act. They failed to understand that freedom is only the conscious recognition of necessity. Consequently they were annihilated by historical necessity, which solves only those problems that are capable of solution....[6]

One may disagree that history is the 'only' framework of reference; for many, there are other perspectives – for the Christian the love of God, for the existentialist personal authenticity – but history is one framework of reference into which an individual's acts may be fitted. Validity was a concept which mattered to Duncan; discussing the contradictions of his upbringing, he wrote:

> Christian Science, European democracy, and South African herrenvolkism: it was a strange mixture to have to sort out in one's own young life. The best way to understand it all is to go back to the beginning, and to follow me as I did finally sort out the truth from the untruth, as it was to be valid in my own life and my own time.[7]

But even here he looked for validity in the context of his *own* life, his *own* time; in this he was still the complete individualist.

Yet, later in his life, he did begin to see himself as before his time; when Vigne said as much to him in 1966, he replied: 'You flatterer ... and yet it isn't flattering to be told that one is years before one's time. It is a mistake in timing nearly as serious as to be behind one's time. Yet, I do have this feeling that I can look about 20 years ahead on quite a lot of things.'[8] For his own example he cites what he wrote about overpopulation in the early 1940s; with at least a little hindsight, one may add now the extraordinary letter he wrote to the *Observer* in January 1963 pleading for a massive rise in the international price of oil as a way of redistributing the wealth and power of the world.[9] One may cite, too, letters he wrote in 1963 saying that he was 'certain that the time is coming when international brigades of the Spanish model will be in action in Africa';[10] in the knowledge of the significance of Cuban brigades and Russian advisers in Angola, one does not nowadays easily dismiss this as 'sentimental politics' or a 'lunatic idea'. One of the fascinations of the future will be to see if any of his other ideas turn out to be right after all.

The fact is that he had an extraordinary political imagination, not only in that he had original ideas, but also in that he saw some things early and very clearly. He saw, for instance, exactly why it was so many blacks distrusted and feared liberals. While it was true that liberals wanted non-racialism and democratic rights extended to everyone, Duncan saw why this was not enough: he knew that Africans wanted to rule their own country, and he hoped they would extend rights even to those who had so long deprived them of theirs. He recognized what Trollope had seen years before: 'South Africa is a country of black men and not of white men. It has been so; it is so; and it will be so.'[11] Liberals had failed in 'their readiness to plead for integration of the African in a European way of life, but not for integration of the whites in an African way of Life'.[12] Hence the importance of his public commitment to the PAC, and the importance of the fact that when he was sacked by Leballo he made no public protest; he had accepted African leadership and, even when he fell foul of that leadership, he continued to accept it. Hence, too, the importance of his later belief that one day there would be as massive an emigration proportionally of whites from South Africa as there had been of the French from Algeria. Again, it does not matter entirely whether history does prove him right or wrong in this; what matters is his public recognition that South Africa was a black country, into which whites who wished to stay would have to integrate. The real problem in South Africa was not the 'native question', nor even the 'race question', but the 'white question' or – as the PAC would put it – the 'settler question'.

Similarly, after the years in which his opposition to Marxist versions of South African history made him treat the country always as a 'special case', a unique aberration, not as an aspect of the history of European imperialism, he began, in his last years, to talk of the 'free-masonry of white skin',[13] of the long history of European racialism, and to see southern Africa as part of a complex process of world history. Even his implacable opposition to communism underwent changes in those years, for he began to understand why socialism mattered. In 1965 he wrote:

> The more I see of the world the less enchanted I am with socialism, and the more impressed I am with the liberal bourgeois system, with all its faults. But there is no doubt that the world, particularly the third world, is filled with extremely important people who believe in socialism the way the early Christians believed in Christianity. And to see them actually working on these theories is a sight of interest and importance.[14]

It would, in some ways, be convenient to make out that this represented a shift towards socialism in his political thinking (just as it is convenient for those who disliked his anti-communism to brand it as obsessive or pathological, not reasoned, or for those who disliked his anti-racialism to find the source of his rebellion in his lameness, or his relationship with his parents, or jealousy of his brother Andrew); yet, though he admired much of what he saw in Algeria, and was not simply a capitalist, to see either as a movement towards socialism would be to falsify him. Paradoxically, once he had given up the Liberal Party, he became more properly liberal. This again he understood himself. He told Schmoller of 'another change in my thinking':

> I turned away from totalitarianism thirty years ago. That was a final decision, and I shall never go back to it. But it was a decision based more on the revolting notion of the European tyrants than on the strength of liberal-bourgeois-capitalism. The change is that I am becoming more and more impressed with the latter....[15]

In a sense he was merely restating his fundamental conservatism, his desire to hold on to traditional values of the kind of world he grew up in. But he was right to see it as a change, rather than a return to past belief: since he was a man who followed the impulses of his own imagination, he was not retreating to an old set of values, but making a new set. Admiring Algeria as he did, he could easily have pretended a *rapprochement* with socialism; it would certainly have made his life easier as a South African politician 'of the left'. yet he was incapable of that kind of easy adjustment; part of the reason for his being both before and after his time was that he would never serve his time.

In just the same way, though he became more properly liberal in those last years, he continued to see that liberalism had not solved the crucial issues of authority. Recognizing the problem was of course not the same as solving it; it would take a greater political thinker than he ever was to suggest proper relations of the 'finest minds' and the 'masses'. Failing to solve the problem of authority was probably the crucial failing in his political thought; yet it is one he shared with many others and, though he may have been sometimes 'totally and dangerously *simpliste*', at least he did not fall for an easy and sentimental version of mass politics, where 'the people' are 'always right' (those who believe the people are always right inevitably define 'the people' in such a way as to exclude some people from *the* people).

Part of the same paradoxical process was that he began to understand the ways in which he had both overestimated and underestimated Marxism. Though he continued to think of it in religious terms (to compare Marxism to Christianity may say something about the fervour of some Marxists, but is hardly a satisfactory way of treating it as a method of historical and intellectual analysis), he began to see, too, that it was more flexible than he had realized – that, in so far as it is a method of analysis, it may be applied to different situations in different ways, and that international communism is therefore a less cohesive force than he had at one time feared. He began to realize that the search for human freedom would continue even in states under that 'Iron Law of History' which 'Marx tried to discover, and thought he had'.[16] Realizing this, he was at last able to see that the choices were not only between capitalism and communism, nor between collectivism and individualism; the world was a more complicated place than its theorists allowed.

It is tempting to apply to Duncan himself a comment he made to Alan Paton about Hofmeyr: Hofmeyr's life, he wrote, 'was a magnificent one, but it has political relevance only under the stars, only seen in the longest of views'.[17] Yet, for all that Duncan's place in some future history of South Africa may be only in a footnote, or in a bibliography as the compiler of a remarkable set of documents and letters, he has a more profound relevance than that. What one observes in his life is close to a process Camus recognized in 1955, the 'visible transformation of individualism, and ... the slow recognition by the individual, under the pressure of history, that he does have limits': 'Today, man is proclaiming his revolt while knowing this revolt has limits, is demanding liberty and undergoing necessity, and this contradictory man, torn apart, conscious henceforth of human and historical ambiguity, is the essentially tragic man.'[18] That he was in many ways a contradictory man is obvious: the non-racialist who joined an exclusively Africanist movement; the agnostic who postulated a new ethic for 'an age of science', but who heard Jehovah in the desert; the lame man who had a super-abundance of physical and intellectual energy; the politician with his creed of individualism who thought he had found his final place in a mass movement; the liberal who accepted authoritarianism as necessary, and the revolutionary who turned back to liberalism; the Gandhian who turned to violence; the warm and loving man who was increasingly disgusted by humanity; the man who looked for a 'great aim' to direct his life, but who found most delight in the immediate, in 'spots of time' which he wished to record and hold. The list goes on and on, and all the explanations in the world, all the tracing of growth and of changes of mind, will never entirely resolve all the contradictions.

It is easy enough to demonstrate that Duncan's own dealing with the contradictions was heroic; as Camus explained,

> There is not one human being who, above a certain elementary level of consciousness, does not exhaust himself in trying to find formulae or attitudes, that will give his existence the unity it lacks.... It is not sufficient to live, there must be a destiny that does not wait on death.... This passion which lifts the mind above the commonplace of a dispersed world, from which it nevertheless detaches itself, is the passion for unity....[19]

Not only Duncan's preparedness to sacrifice himself for his political ends, but also his passionate search for resolutions to his own contradictions (some of which, like his class and race, he had little or no control over) made him heroic.

One may well regard some of his political decisions as mistaken. Some will think that he would have been better employed in keeping himself a little aloof from party politics, rather than in committing himself first to the Liberal Party and then to the PAC. Might he have been more influential in South African politics if he had, for instance, kept his links with the Congress Alliance intact after the Defiance Campaign, rather than committing himself to the Liberal Party? Should he, for instance, have taken Eddie Roux's advice and joined the Congress of Democrats, despite the communists in its ranks? Might *Contact* have been politically more significant if it had been even less closely tied to the Liberal Party? After all, it was in pre-independent Basutoland that he was most directly influential, and it was then he fitted most closely this view of the proper role of the white man in anti-*apartheid* politics: the adviser, the 'guest of honour'. Even some members of the PAC feel that he would have been more useful to them as a figure in the background, not as a publicly committed member.[20]

Yet all those questions miss the point of the kind of man he was; he had to commit himself publicly, he had to be an activist, not simply an influence. The only reason he was able to stay in the background in Basutoland was that he had his primary commitment outside; it was the necessary corollary of his fanatic individualism.

One finds a similar answer to the question 'Was he wrong to leave South Africa after his second banning order?' Peter Brown and many other Liberals who have stayed in or returned to South Africa feel that he was wrong; so, too, does Peter Hjul, who had originally advised him to leave, and who was eventually to leave himself. Should he have stayed in South Africa and faced out his ban? Accepted the imposed silence and all the concomitant frust-rations? Accepted the possible house-arrest? Gone to jail for years if necessary, for life if necessary, as others have done? He knew himself that it was a crucial decision, for he told Cynthia soon after he had left that it might mean the end of his political influence; and perhaps in the long run it did. Perhaps it would have been better for him to have stayed to 'bear witness' to his commitment to non-racialism inside South Africa.

Yet that answer, too, misses the point: first, he was always insistent that politics was power, not just principles, and he could not see himself as having any power under a banning order or in jail. Secondly, he had grown beyond non-racialism; it was not the whites who were going to decide the future of South Africa, but the blacks. It was their country, not his; the only way he could demonstrate that conclusion was by an active commitment, and he could not see how such a commitment would be possible if he stayed inside South Africa.

It does not matter very much – now, at least – whether his commitments were wrong or not; they were made, and it is too late to regret any of them, even if one wishes to. What matters far more is that the commitments were heroic: in his search for resolutions to his own contradictions he was always prepared to make difficult and dangerous choices. It is less easy to explain why the contradictory and heroic man was the 'essentially tragic man', too. Of course one does not mean 'tragic' in the sense of sad or unhappy; one could not call his life either of those. 'In all the great tragedies, tragedy is a joy to the man who dies';[21] it is 'the sense of life as potentially glorious that gives the catastrophies of tragedy their special poignancy'.[22] Where it becomes valid (and valuable) to talk of Patrick Duncan as a tragic figure is exactly in those contradictions which he could not resolve, because they could not be resolved without falsifying their force: he *was* the son of his father, he *was* a white man and the son of a settler, he *was* made by Europe as well as Africa, so he could never be entirely an African, however much he desired to be. He wanted to give everything, but was permitted to give only something (more than most, but less than he was capable of). If he had been a lesser man, he might have contrived some arrangement, found some comfortable shelter from the contradictions of his personal history and the larger history, the contradiction of his own self and the purpose he desired. He wanted more than history would allow him.

In the end, he learned to accept necessity.

> At the centre of liberal tragedy is a single situation; that of a man at the height of his powers and the limits of his strength, at once aspiring and being defeated, releasing and destroyed by his own energies. The structure is liberal in its recognition of defeat or the limits of victory....[23]

Yet, splendidly though that image fits Duncan in many ways, still one wishes to complicate it, for he had moved beyond liberalism in two crucial ways: first, in his recognition that liberalism again and again ducked the crucial issues of authority and, secondly, in the fact that he was all passion and no guilt; only once in his life did he seem to feel any contradiction between the way he lived and what he thought and felt, and that was after his sacking as PAC representative in Algiers, when he recognized a certain incongruity between the life he lived with his wife and children in 'La Consulaire' and the work he was doing for the PAC. Yet he was never guilty about who he was; it had just happened like that. It was other people who found something incongruous in the Governor-General's son who went to jail as a symbolic defiance of unjust laws, the Wykehamist who wanted to make a revolution, the anti-communist who handed out Mao's thoughts on revolution to trainee guerillas, the liberal who was prepared to accept autocratic centralism. When he became a revolutionary, it was not so much that he was choosing a particular course of action (and so accepting a further load of guilt) but almost that he was allowing himself to be chosen. What else was there to do? It is the classic cry of the tragic hero when he has only one way left to choose. Revolution in South Africa was not only necessary but also inevitable; it would mean suffering, probably even more suffering than presently existed, but that could not be helped. It was not a matter of individual choice any more. Yet all the time, and for all the contradictions and 'giddy traverses', he remained a single, complicated, a-typical person – an individual, not a representative.

No biography can ever catch the whole of a man; all it can do is to offer moments, details, images, a few patterns through the infinitely complicated process of a life. No doubt there are other patterns other biographers would trace; yet, as I write these last sentences, it is in the certainty that Patrick Duncan's life was, in the end, both heroic and tragic. He set out to do something which no man could do; not only was he the wrong man, but it was also the wrong time. The overthrow of the *apartheid*-state will take more time than he had, and more lives (and deaths) than his alone. Eventually, he realized this himself and, when he did, came close to despair; but then there was another great aim, much more private, much more individual: to die well. That, certainly, he achieved; the curiosity, serenity and gaiety with which he experienced his own dying were his great victory. One may curse history that it allowed him to do so little of what he could have done; one is nevertheless thankful that he did not die in a car on the wrong side of a road.

NOTES

1 Most of these notes refer to the Patrick Duncan Papers now on indefinite loan to the University of York. These are referred to as UYPD. Each of these references is followed by a set of three numbers: the first number refers to the section, the second to a set of papers in that section and the third to a numbered letter or paper in that set. For example:

UYPD 2–4–149 refers to
Section 2 (family correspondence)
Letters from Patrick Duncan to Cynthia Duncan
Letter dated 4 July 1953, no. 149 in the file.

2 The Patrick Duncan Papers are described in more detail in a catalogue in the J. B. Morrell Library at the University of York, available on application to the Librarian. The catalogue includes summaries of the more significant documents and letters, only some of which have been relevant to this biography. The Patrick Duncan Papers represent a very important source of often first-hand information on modern South African history and politics.

3 We have given as full citations as possible in the notes which follow. However, on occasion we have cited an 'unattributable source', either because we were asked to, or because citation might endanger either the freedom or the reputations of the living.

CHAPTER 1

1 Alice Duncan's diary, Nov 1921. Jagger Library, Cape Town, BC 294. E5–3–1.
2 Patrick Duncan interviewed by Cyril Dunn, Maseru, 1955. Transcript. UYPD 5–29–21.
3 ibid.
4 Alice Duncan's diary, 10 March 1921, Jagger Library, Cape Town, BC 294. E5–3–2.
5 ibid., Nov 1923. Jagger Library, Cape Town, BC 294. E5–3–1.
6 Patrick Duncan's unpublished autobiography, ch. 1, f. 8. UYPD 9–1.
7 ibid. ch. 1, f. 12.
8 ibid. ch. 2, f. 16.
9 ibid. ch. 2, ff. 18–19.
10 ibid. ch. 2, f. 20.
11 ibid. ch. 1, f. 3.
12 Patrick Duncan (Snr), *Suggestions for a Native Policy*, 2nd edn (Johannesburg: Central News Agency, 1927).
13 Patrick Duncan's unpublished autobiography, ch. 1, f. 4. UYPD 9–1.

14   John Duncan interviewed by Tom Lodge, Plettenberg Bay, 1976.
15   Patrick Duncan's unpublished autobiography, ch. 2, f. 20*c*. UYPD 9–1.
16   ibid.
17   Patrick Duncan (Snr) to his son Patrick, 28 Feb 1939. UYPD 2–1–115.
18   ibid. UYPD 2–1–200.
19   Alan Paton, *Hofmeyr* (Cape Town: Oxford University Press, 1964), p. 170.
20   Patrick Duncan (Snr) to his son Patrick. UYPD 2–1–50.
21   Patrick Duncan's unpublished autobiography, ch. 2, f. 26*a*. UYPD 9–1.
22   Patrick Duncan to his mother, 28 March 1927. UYPD 2–3–9.
23   ibid.
24   ibid. 21 June 1927. UYPD 2–3–21.
25   ibid. 11 March 1927. UYPD 2–3–5.
26   Ridge Preparatory School report, 1928. UYPD 4–1.
27   Ronald Currey interviewed by Tom Lodge, Grahamstown, 1976.
28   Patrick Duncan to his mother, 1 Oct 1937. UYPD 2–3–146.
29   Patrick Duncan's unpublished autobiography, ch. 2, f. 21. UYPD 9–1.
30   Ronald Currey interviewed by Tom Lodge, Grahamstown, 1976.
31   Patrick Duncan's unpublished autobiography, ch. 2, f. 22. UYPD 9–1.
32   ibid. ch. 2, f. 3.
33   Patrick Duncan to his mother, 1 Oct 1937. UYPD 2–3–146.
34   From the title of Cyprian Thorpe's obituary of Patrick Duncan in *South African Outlook*. UYPD 5–96.
35   Patrick Duncan's unpublished autobiography, ch. 2, f. 29. UYPD 9–1.
36   Hubert Kidd to Patrick Duncan (Snr), 21 March 1934. UYPD 4–1–3.
37   Lady Bryan interviewed by the author, Sawdon, 1975.

CHAPTER 2

1   Patrick Duncan to his father, 23 Aug 1934. UYPD 2–3–25.
2   Patrick Duncan interviewed by Cyril Dunn, Maseru, 1955. UYPD 5–29–21.
3   Patrick Duncan to his father. UYPD 2–3–27.
4   Winchester College school report, Nov 1935. UYPD 4–1–2–6.
5   Winchester College school report, Dec 1935. UYPD 4–1–2–7.
6   Winchester College school report, March 1935. UYPD 4–1–2–2.
7   Malcolm Robertson to Patrick Duncan (Snr), 26 June 1936. UYPD 4–1–2–3.
8   ibid.
9   ibid.
10   Patrick Duncan to his parents, 5 Oct 1935. UYPD 2–3–70.
11   ibid. 16 Nov 1935. UYPD 2–3–75.
12   Patrick Duncan interviewed by Cyril Dunn, Maseru, 1955. UYPD 5–29–21.
13   Patrick Duncan to his parents, 22 June 1935. UYPD 2–3–56.
14   Patrick Duncan's unpublished autobiography, ch. 2, f. 35. UYPD 9–1.
15   Patrick Duncan to his father, 14 March 1936. UYPD 2–3–102.
16   Patrick Duncan to his mother, 21 Nov 1936. UYPD 2–3–140.
17   Patrick Duncan to his father, 12 Nov 1936. UYPD 2–3.
18   ibid. 3 March 1936. UYPD 2–3–100.
19   ibid. UYPD 2–3–100.
20   ibid. UYPD 2–3–131.
21   ibid. UYPD 2–3–132.
22   Rudyard Kipling, *Many Inventions* (London and New York, 1893), p. 212.
23   Patrick Duncan's unpublished autobiography, ch. 2, f. 44*b*. UYPD 9–1.
24   ibid.
25   Patrick Duncan to his mother, 1 Oct 1937. UYPD 2–3–146.

26 Patrick Duncan to his parents, 13 Jan 1935. UYPD 2–3–43.
27 Patrick Duncan to his father, 21 April 1936. UYPD 2–3–107.
28 ibid.
29 Patrick Duncan (Snr) to his son Patrick, 9 Aug 1935. UYPD 2–1–35.
30 ibid. 20 Aug 1935. UYPD 2–1–37.
31 ibid. 23 Aug 1936. UYPD 2–1–87.
32 ibid. 20 Sept 1939. UYPD 2–1–112.
33 ibid. 20 Feb 1936. UYPD 2–1–61.
34 ibid. 27 Feb 1936. UYPD 2–1–62.
35 ibid. 19 March 1936. UYPD 2–1–65.
36 ibid. 9 April 1936. UYPD 2–1–68.
37 ibid. 13 March 1943. UYPD 2–1–196.
38 ibid. 17 June 1935. UYPD 2–1–29.
39 Patrick Duncan to Lionel Hichens, 13 Sept 1939. Original in possession of Mrs Deborah Cowen.
40 ibid.
41 Patrick Duncan (Snr) to his son Patrick, 23 Jan 1940. UYPD 2–1–128.
42 ibid. 9 April 1943. UYPD 2–1–198.
43 Winchester College school report, March 1937. UYPD 4–1–2–8.
44 Patrick Duncan to his father, 19 Feb 1938. UYPD 2–3–179.
45 ibid. 3 Dec 1937. UYPD 2–3–157.
46 ibid. 26 May 1938. UYPD 2–3–204.
47 ibid. 27 Aug 1938. UYPD 2–3–222.
48 Patrick Duncan to his mother, 22 April 1938. UYPD 2–3–190.
49 Patrick Duncan to Jeremy Pemberton, 18 March 1938. UYPD 5–76.
50 Patrick Duncan interviewed by Cyril Dunn, Maseru, 1955. UYPD 5–29–21.
51 Patrick Duncan to his mother, 5 July 1938. UYPD 2–3–215.
52 Patrick Duncan to his father, 26 April 1939. UYPD 2–3–272.
53 Duncan's diary of a visit to the Canary Islands, 1937–8. UYPD 3–2–1.
54 Patrick Duncan to his parents, 23 Dec 1937. UYPD 2–3–163.
55 Patrick Duncan to his mother, 9 April 1938. UYPD 2–3–189.
56 Patrick Duncan's unpublished autobiography, ch. 2, f. 54. UYPD 9–1.
57 Patrick Duncan to Jeremy Pemberton, 16 Aug 1938. UYPD 5–76–10.
58 Patrick Duncan's first draft of a report on the German *Arbeitsdienst*, 1938. UYPD 3–5–12.
59 ibid.
60 Public Record Office, London. FO 371/21677/01247.
61 Patrick Duncan to his father, 27 Aug 1939. UYPD 2–3–222.
62 Letter from Freya von Moltke to Tom Lodge, 22 April 1976.
63 Duncan's diary of a visit to Germany, 8 Aug 1938, f. 80. UYPD 3–5–1.
64 Terrence Prittie, *Germans against Hitler* (London: Hutchinson, 1964), p. 226.
65 Duncan's diary of a visit to Germany, 17 Aug 1938, f. 100. UYPD 3–5–1.
66 ibid. f. 100.
67 ibid. f. 93.
68 Patrick Duncan to his mother, 8 Sept 1938. UYPD 2–3–224.
69 Letter from Richard Hare to Tom Lodge, 24 Nov 1975.
70 Patrick Duncan to his parents, 13 Oct 1938. UYPD 2–3–229.
71 Patrick Duncan's unpublished autobiography, ch. 2, f. 53. UYPD 9–1.
72 Patrick Duncan to his mother, 5 Oct 1938. UYPD 2–3–227.
73 Patrick Duncan interviewed by Cyril Dunn, Maseru, 1955. UYPD 5–29–21.
74 Patrick Duncan to his father, 23 May 1938. UYPD 2–3–199.
75 Patrick Duncan to his mother, 20 Nov 1938. UYPD 2–3–236.
76 Patrick Duncan to his father, 24 March 1939. UYPD 2–3–265.
77 ibid. 4 April 1939. UYPD 2–3–267.

78 Patrick Duncan's unpublished autobiography, ch. 2, f. 60. UYPD 9–1.
79 Patrick Duncan to his parents, 15 Oct 1939. UYPD 2–3–293.
80 ibid, 21 Oct 1939. UYPD 2–3–297.
81 Patrick Duncan to his father, 18 Dec 1939. UYPD 2–3–306.
82 Patrick Duncan to his mother, 6 Dec 1939. UYPD 2–3–304.
83 Patrick Duncan's unpublished autobiography, ch. 2, f. 63. UYPD 9–1.
84 Patrick Duncan to his father, 11 Sept 1940. UYPD 2–3–352.

CHAPTER 3

1   Patrick Duncan to Jeremy Pemberton, 7 April 1941. UYPD 5–76–19.
2   ibid. 9 April 1943. UYPD 5–76–23.
3   Patrick Duncan to his mother, 8 Feb 1941. UYPD 2–3–370.
4   Patrick Duncan's unpublished autobiography, ch. 3, f. 4. UYPD 9–1.
5   Patrick Duncan to his mother, 9 March 1941. UYPD 2–3–379.
6   Patrick Duncan's diary, 7 Oct 1943. UYPD 3–9.
7   Patrick Duncan's unpublished autobiography, ch. 3, f. 8*b*. UYPD 9–1.
8   Patrick Duncan interviewed by Cyril Dunn, Maseru, 1955. UYPD 5–29–21.
9   *Star* (Johannesburg), 22 July 1943.
10 ibid.
11 Patrick Duncan's unpublished autobiography, ch. 3, f. 8*c*. UYPD 9–1.
12 Patrick Duncan (Snr) to Hilda Grenfell, 17 March 1943. UYPD 5–41–32.
13 Patrick Duncan's diary, 7 Oct 1943. UYPD 3–9.
14 Patrick Duncan's unpublished autobiography, ch. 3, f. 9*e*. UYPD 9–1.
15 Patrick Duncan interviewed by Cyril Dunn, Maseru, 1955. UYPD 5–29–21.
16 Hans Schmoller interviewed by Tom Lodge, London, 1975.
17 Patrick Duncan's unpublished autobiography, ch. 3, f. 9*f*. UYPD 9–1.
18 Patrick Duncan to his father, 5 March 1941. UYPD 2–3–378.
19 'Melanchthon', *The Enemy* (Morija, 1943), p. 18.
20 Patrick Duncan's unpublished autobiography, ch. 3, f. 9*c*. UYPD 9–1.
21 ibid. ch. 3, f. 9.
22 *The Times*, 10 June 1967.
23 Patrick Duncan to his mother, 28 March 1943. UYPD 2–3–559.
24 Michael Cassidy interviewed by Tom Lodge, Hilton, Natal, 1976.
25 Letter from Basil Whitworth to Tom Lodge, 25 March 1976.
26 Patrick Duncan to his parents, 6 April 1943. UYPD 2–3–562.
27 Letter from Gideon Pott to C. J. Driver, 22 May 1976.
28 Patrick Duncan to Jeremy Pemberton, 24 Jan 1945. UYPD 5–76–26.
29 Patrick Duncan's diary, 18 Sept 1944. UYPD 3–9.
30 ibid. 6 March 1945. UYPD 3–9.
31 Patrick Duncan to his mother, 17 Feb 1945. UYPD 2–3–592.

CHAPTER 4

1   Patrick Duncan's diary, 24 July 1948 (referring to an earlier period). UYPD 3–9.
2   Patrick Duncan's unpublished autobiography, ch. 3, f. 13. UYPD 9–1.
3   Patrick Duncan's diary, 24 July 1948. UYPD 3–9.
4   ibid.
5   Patrick Duncan's unpublished autobiography, ch. 3, f. 12. UYPD 9–1.
6   Patrick Duncan's diary, 25 July 1948. UYPD 3–9.
7   Letter from Cyril Dunn to Tom Lodge, 24 Feb 1976.

8 Patrick Duncan to Alan Paton, 24 April 1967. UYPD 5–75–54.
9 Patrick Duncan to his wife, 11 May 1949. UYPD 2–4–48.
10 Patrick Duncan's diary, 24 July 1948. UYPD 3–9.
11 ibid. 25 July 1948.
12 See Brian Bunting, *Moses Kotane: South African Revolutionary* (London: Inkululeko, 1975), p. 153.
13 Monica Wilson and Leonard Thompson (eds), *The Oxford History of South Africa*, Vol. 2 (Oxford: Clarendon Press, 1971), p. 417.
14 Patrick Duncan to his mother, 19 June 1947. Jagger Library, Cape Town, E–11–5–20.
15 L. J. Du Plessis to Patrick Duncan, 21 Aug 1947. UYPD 5–30–7.
16 Patrick Duncan to L. J. Du Plessis, 18 Aug 1947. UYPD 5–30–2.
17 Patrick Duncan to his wife, 22 Aug 1948. UYPD 2–4–38.
18 Patrick Duncan to Edgar Brookes, 30 Dec 1948. UYPD 5–13–1.
19 ibid. 2 Aug 1949. UYPD 5–13–8.
20 Patrick Duncan to his wife, 21 Aug 1948. UYPD 2–4–37.
21 Patrick Duncan to Cyprian Thorpe, 12 Oct 1949. UYPD 5–95–2.
22 Patrick Duncan to his mother, 7 March 1943. UYPD 2–3–552.
23 Patrick Duncan to his father, 29 Nov 1942. UYPD 2–3–529.
24 ibid. 20 March 1943. UYPD 2–3–557.
25 Patrick Duncan to his mother, 12 July 1943. UYPD 2–3–582.
26 ibid. 8 Feb 1941. UYPD 2–3–371.
27 ibid. 9 June 1942. UYPD 2–3–489.
28 Patrick Duncan to his father, 8 June 1942. UYPD 2–3–488.
29 Patrick Duncan's unpublished autobiography, ch. 3, f. 23. UYPD 9–1.
30 Patrick Duncan to his mother, 28 March 1943. UYPD 2–3–559.
31 Patrick Duncan to his mother, 21 May 1945. Jagger Library, Cape Town, E–11–3–22.
32 ibid. E–11–3–22.
33 ibid. 28 May 1945. E–11–3–23.
34 ibid. 5 June 1945. E–11–3–24.
35 Patrick Duncan's unpublished autobiography, ch. 3, f. 23. UYPD 9–1.
36 ibid. ch. 3, ff. 23–4. UYPD 9–1.
37 Letter from Ezekiel Mphahlele to C. J. Driver, 3 June 1976.
38 Patrick Duncan's unpublished autobiography, ch. 3, f. 4. UYPD 9–1.
39 Freya von Moltke to Patrick Duncan, 24 Jan 1947. UYPD 5–98–2.

CHAPTER 5

1 Patrick Duncan's unpublished autobiography, ch. 3, f. 28. UYPD 9–1.
2 Patrick Duncan interviewed by Cyril Dunn, Maseru, 1955. UYPD 5–29–21.
3 Patrick Duncan to his mother, 30 April 1946. Jagger Library, Cape Town, E–11–4–19.
4 Patrick Duncan to François Junod, 14 Jan 1950. UYPD 6–3–27.
5 Patrick Duncan to his wife, 17 Feb 1950. UYPD 2–4–68.
6 ibid. 20 Feb 1950. UYPD 2–4–69.
7 Patrick Duncan's unpublished autobiography, ch. 3, f. 29. UYPD 9–1.
8 Draft review of Hunt's *Theory and Practice of Communism* by Patrick Duncan, 29 Dec 1949. UYPD 8–9–5.
9 Patrick Duncan to Cyprian Thorpe, 8 Dec 1949. UYPD 5–95–1.
10 Patrick Duncan's memoir of Laski. UYPD 5–59–10.
11 Patrick Duncan to François Junod, 14 Jan 1950. UYPD 6–3–27.
12 Undated memo attached to a letter by Patrick Duncan to his wife, 8 Nov 1949. UYPD 2–4–59.

13   *The Times*, 13 April 1949.
14   Patrick Duncan to Alistair Buchan, 14 April 1950. UYPD 5–15–1.
15   Patrick Duncan's unpublished autobiography, ch. 3, f. 39*e*. UYPD 9–1.
16   ibid. ch. 3, f. 38. UYPD 9–1.
17   Patrick Duncan to his wife, 8 Feb 1951. UYPD 2–4–81.
18   Patrick Duncan to Edgar Brookes, 14 Aug 1950. UYPD 5–13–11.
19   Patrick Duncan to his wife, 24 Aug 1951. UYPD 2–4–102.
20   See Patrick Duncan to Hans Schmoller, 29 June 1952. UYPD 5–86–13.
21   Patrick Duncan to his wife, 20 Aug 1951. UYPD 2–4–100.
22   Patrick Duncan to Hans Schmoller, 29 June 1952. UYPD 5–86–13.
23   Letter from Sir Brian Marwick to Tom Lodge, 12 April 1976.
24   Letter from Leonard Thompson to C. J. Driver, 5 Oct 1975.
25   Patrick Duncan's unpublished autobiography, ch. 3, f. 40. UYPD 9–1.
26   ibid. ch. 3, f. 41. UYPD 9–1.
27   ibid.
28   Patrick Duncan to Edgar Brookes, 2 Aug 1949. UYPD 5–13–8.
29   Patrick Duncan to Lord Hailey, 'Memorandum on native administration in Basutoland', 10 Dec 1950. UYPD 7–1–1.
30   Patrick Duncan's unpublished autobiography, ch. 3, f. 43. UYPD 9–1.
31   Patrick Duncan to Basil Davidson, 28 May 1953. UYPD 5–26–13.
32   'Melanchthon', *Three Centuries of Wrong*, no place of publication, 6 April 1952.
33   Printed letter announcing Patrick Duncan's resignation, May 1952. UYPD 8–53–9.
34   Lady Bryan interviewed by C. J. Driver, Sawdon, 1976.

CHAPTER 6

1   Patrick Duncan interviewed by Cyril Dunn, Maseru, 1955. UYPD 5–29–21.
2   Anthony Sampson to Patrick Duncan, 1 Jan 1953. UYPD 5–85–8.
3   Patrick Duncan to Nelson Mandela, 3 Dec 1953. UYPD 6–19–38.
4   Philip Motseta to Patrick Duncan, undated. UYPD 6–19–122.
5   Patrick Duncan to Cecil Williams, 12 Feb 1953. UYPD 8–9–8.
6   Patrick Duncan to Albert Luthuli, 9 March 1954. UYPD 6–20–74.
7   Patrick Duncan to Eddie Roux, 3 Feb 1954. UYPD 6–24–34.
8   Eddie Roux to Patrick Duncan, 21 Feb 1954. UYPD 6–24–36.
9   Patrick Duncan to Manilal Gandhi, 5 Aug 1952. UYPD 5–33–11.
10   Patrick Duncan to Cyprian Thorpe, 22 July 1954. UYPD 5–49.
11   Patrick Duncan to Patrick Cullinan, 12 July 1954. UYPD 5–23–6.
12   Patrick Duncan to Julius Lewin, 21 Sept 1952. UYPD 5–61–22.
13   Patrick Duncan to Sir de Villiers Graaf, 30 Oct 1952. UYPD 6–5–38.
14   Christopher Gell to Patrick Duncan, 13 Aug 1952. UYPD 5–34–2.
15   ibid. 27 Oct 1952. UYPD 5–34–7.
16   Letter from Cyril Dunn to Tom Lodge, 24 Feb 1976.
17   *Advance* (Cape Town), 4 Dec 1952.
18   Patrick Duncan's unpublished autobiography, ch. 4, f. 6. UYPD 9–1.
19   *Rand Daily Mail*, 8 Dec 1952.
20   Letter from Cyril Dunn to Tom Lodge, 24 Feb 1976.
21   *Star* (Johannesburg), 10 Dec 1952.
22   *Rand Daily Mail*, 5 Feb 1953.
23   ibid.
24   *Observer* (London), 28 June 1953. *Friend* (Bloemfontein), 29 June 1953.
25   Patrick Duncan to David Astor, 11 Dec 1953. UYPD 5–5–10.
26   *Bantu World* (Johannesburg), 7 Nov 1953.

27 Patrick Duncan to Julius Lewin, 8 Jan 1953. UYPD 5–61–32.
28 Various conversations between Tom Lodge and former Congress members in South Africa and Lesotho, May–June 1976.
29 *Advance*, 18 Dec 1952.
30 Patrick Duncan to his wife, 12 May 1953. UYPD 2–4–124.
31 Quoted in an article about Duncan, published twelve years later, *The Times*, 29 Sept 1964.
32 Patrick Duncan to Betty Taylor, 28 June 1953. UYPD 6–27–2.
33 *Advance*, 25 June 1953.
34 Patrick Duncan's unpublished autobiography, ch. 3, f. 30. UYPD 9–1.
35 *Indian Opinion*, 24 July 1953.
36 ibid.
37 *New Republic*, 19 Oct 1953.
38 Patrick Duncan to Philip Motseta, 29 June 1954. UYPD 8–12–28.
39 Patrick Duncan to Radford Jordan, 7 June 1954. UYPD 5–50–28.
40 Printed newsletter by Patrick Duncan, no. 1, 'To the voters of the Transvaal – OFS Senate seat', July 1954. UYPD 8–53–115.
41 *Guardian* (Cape Town), 22 Aug 1946.
42 Printed newsletter by Patrick Duncan, no. 1, July 1954. UYPD 8–53–115.
43 Patrick Duncan's unpublished autobiography, ch. 4, f. 28. UYPD 9–1.
44 Patrick Duncan to Radford Jordan, 7 June 1954. UYPD 5–50–28.
45 Patrick Duncan to Arthur Blaxall, 28 Jan 1954. UYPD 5–10–22.
46 Patrick Duncan to Christopher Gell, 29 March 1954. UYPD 5–34–49.
47 Patrick Duncan to Arthur Blaxall, 28 Jan 1954. UYPD 5–10–22.
48 Patrick Duncan to Oscar Bull, 28 Aug 1952. UYPD 6–5–14.
49 Patrick Duncan to Archbishop Clayton, 25 April 1952. UYPD 6–5–22.
50 Archbishop Clayton to Patrick Duncan, 22 Oct 1952. UYPD 6–5–23.
51 Patrick Duncan to Archbishop Clayton, 25 April 1952. UYPD 6–5–22.
52 Patrick Duncan, *The Road through the Wilderness*, Johannesburg, May 1963.
53 Bishop's charge to the first session of the Diocesan Synod, 30 Nov 1952. UYPD 7–9–16.
54 Patrick Duncan's speech to Diocesan Synod, Dec 1954. UYPD 7–9–18.
55 Circular from Bishop of Basutoland to all clergy and lay officials of the diocese, 1 June 1955. UYPD 6–19–56.
56 'He supports "Mohlabani"', *Mohlabani*, Oct 1955, p. 11.
57 Draft manifesto of BAC with handwritten comments by Patrick Duncan. UYPD 7–21–1.
58 J. Dickie and A. Rake, *Who's Who in Africa* (London: African Developments), p. 222.
59 Patrick Duncan to Hugh Ashton, 20 Oct 1965. UYPD 6–36–4.
60 ibid.
61 *Contact*, 9 Aug 1958.
62 Patrick Duncan to Cyril Dunn, 12 April 1955. UYPD 5–29–7.
63 Patrick Duncan to Deborah Cowen, 15 June 1962. UYPD 2–8–65.
64 Dickie and Rake, *Who's Who in Africa*, op. cit., p. 222.
65 Memorandum written by Leabua Jonathan, Maseru, June 1976. UYPD 5–49–2.
66 Patrick Duncan to Hugh Ashton, 20 Oct 1965. UYPD 6–36–4.
67 Draft manifesto for a Christian Democratic Party. UYPD 5–48–14.
68 Draft manifesto for a Basuto National Party. UYPD 5–48–15.
69 Patrick Duncan to Leabua Jonathan, 10 Jan 1958. UYPD 5–48–16.
70 Leabua Jonathan to Patrick Duncan, 12 April 1958. UYPD 5–48.
71 Patrick Duncan to Hugh Ashton, 20 Oct 1965. UYPD 6–36–4.
72 B. M. Khaketla to Patrick Duncan, 27 Oct 1952. UYPD 5–55.

73 Patrick Duncan to B. M. Khaketla, 20 Nov 1952. UYPD 5–55.
74 *Potchefstroom Herald*, 1 June 1954.
75 Patrick Duncan's unpublished autobiography, ch. 4, f. 33. UYPD 9–1.
76 Patrick Duncan to Mrs Snell, 17 Oct 1952. UYPD 6–5–200.
77 Patrick Duncan to his wife, 4 July 1953. UYPD 2–4–149.
78 Patrick Duncan to Jordan Ngubane, 12 Feb 1955. UYPD 5–73–3.
79 Reprinted in *Friend* (Bloemfontein), 9 July 1955.
80 *Star* (Johannesburg), 4 Oct 1955.

CHAPTER 7

1   *Observer* (London), 27 Dec 1953.
2   Patrick Duncan to Christopher Gell, 20 Oct 1953. UYPD 5–34–31.
3   Patrick Duncan to Colin Legum, 23 Nov 1953. UYPD 5–60–10.
4   Patrick Duncan to Christopher Gell, 25 May 1953. UYPD 5–34–29.
5   Patrick Duncan to Julius Lewin, 8 July 1955. UYPD 5–61–57.
6   Patrick Duncan to Oden Meeker, 25 June 1954. UYPD 6–19–67.
7   Patrick Duncan to Christopher Gell, 21 Dec 1954. UYPD 5–34–43.
8   ibid. UYPD 6–19–67.
9   Patrick Duncan to Oden Meeker, 25 June 1954. UYPD 6–19–67.
10 ibid. UYPD 6–19–67.
11 *Golden City Post* (Johannesburg), 6 Nov 1955.
12 ibid. 23 Nov 1965.
13 *Sunday Tribune*, undated press cutting. UYPD 8–54.
14 Patrick Duncan to Julius Lewin, 28 May 1956. UYPD 5–61.
15 Patrick Duncan to Radford Jordan, 7 June 1954. UYPD 5–50–28.
16 Patrick Duncan to George Sachs, 11 Feb 1965. UYPD 6–35–294.
17 *Star* (Johannesburg), 29 June 1953.
18 Patrick Duncan to Alan Paton, 22 July 1956. UYPD 5–75–1.
19 Patrick Duncan to Oliver Tambo, 8 Feb 1955. UYPD 6–27–18.
20 *Montreal Star*, 9 Feb 1955.
21 Patrick Duncan to Jordan Ngubane, 12 Feb 1955. UYPD 5–73–4.
22 Patrick Duncan to Alan Paton, 23 March 1955. UYPD 5–75–7.
23 ibid. 7 March 1955. UYPD 5–75–5.
24 Patrick Duncan's unpublished autobiography, ch. 4, f. 38*a*. UYPD 9–1.
25 ibid.
26 *Contact* (Pietermaritzberg), Nov 1955.
27 Jock Isacowitz to Patrick Duncan, 4 Aug 1955. UYPD 6–15–9.
28 Todd Matshikiza to Patrick Duncan, undated. UYPD 6–19.
29 Brian Bunting, 'Multi-racial conference', *Liberation*, Nov 1957, p. 18.
30 Janet Robertson, *Liberalism in South Africa* (Oxford: Clarendon Press, 1971), p. 217.
31 Alan Paton to Patrick Duncan, 18 March 1955. UYPD 5–75–6.
32 Patrick Duncan to Julius Lewin, 16 Feb 1956. UYPD 5–61–62.
33 Patrick Duncan to his wife, 29 July 1960. UYPD 2–4–237.
34 Albie Sachs interviewed by Tom Lodge, London, 1976.
35 Patrick Duncan to Anthony Sampson, 18 Feb 1957. UYPD 5–85–36.
36 Patrick Duncan to Alan Paton, 11 Nov 1957. UYPD 8–17–30.
37 J. Nehru, *Toward Freedom: The Autobiography of Jawaharlal Nehru* (New York: The John Day Co., 1941), p. 46.
38 *Contact*, 9 Aug 1958.
39 Patrick Duncan to his wife, 20 Aug 1957. UYPD 2–4–219.

40 Patrick Duncan's unpublished autobiography, ch. 4, f. 30. UYPD 9–1.
41 Patrick Duncan's diary, 7 March 1956. UYPD 3–9.
42 Patrick Duncan to Alan Paton, 7 May 1956. UYPD 5–75.
43 Peter Brown to Patrick Duncan, 24 May 1956. UYPD 8–16–29.
44 Patrick Duncan to Alan Paton, 8 June 1956. UYPD 8–17–7.
45 Patrick Duncan to Dr A. B. Xuma, 27 Jan 1956. UYPD 6–30–3.
46 *Africa Today*, May–June 1956.
47 *Fighting Talk* (Johannesburg), June 1956.
48 Mary Benson interviewed by Tom Lodge, London, 1975.
49 *House of Assembly Debates*, 30 April 1956, p. 4593.
50 Patrick Duncan to Jordan Ngubane, 10 April 1956. UYPD 73–11.
51 *Advance*, 12 March 1953, quoted in Bunting, *Kotane*, pp. 194–5.
52 *Contact* (Pietermaritzberg), April 1956.
53 Hugh Ashton, *The Basuto* (London: Oxford University Press, 1952).
54 Patrick Duncan's unpublished autobiography, ch. 4, f. 52. UYPD 9–1.
55 ibid. ch. 4, f. 56.
56 *Morning News* (Khartoum), 20 July 1956.
57 Peggy Rutherfoord (ed.), *Darkness and Light* (London: Faith Press, 1958).
58 Patrick Duncan's unpublished autobiography, ch. 4, f. 60. UYPD 9–1.
59 Patrick Duncan, 'The break-down of white domination in South Africa', 23 July 1956. Text of talk at the Royal Institute of International Affairs. UYPD 9–5–15.
60 Patrick Duncan to Jordan Ngubane, 15 June 1956. UYPD 5–73.
61 Patrick Duncan's unpublished autobiography, ch. 4, ff. 62–3. UYPD 9–1.
62 ibid. ch. 4, f. 64.
63 ibid. ch. 4, f. 41.
64 Peter Brown to Patrick Duncan, 26 Aug 1957. UYPD 8–16–84.
65 Patrick Duncan to Peter Brown, 4 May 1956. UYPD 8–16–24.
66 ibid. 1 June 1956. UYPD 8–16–32.
67 *The Policies of the Liberal Party of South Africa* (Cape Town, 1955), p. 9.
68 ibid. p. 21.
69 Undated memo by Patrick Duncan entitled 'Constitutional means'. UYPD 8–20–8.
70 Patrick Duncan to Alan Paton, 18 April 1957. UYPD 8–17–16.
71 ibid. 17 April 1958. UYPD 8–17–36.
72 Patrick Duncan to Jordan Ngubane, 2 May 1957. UYPD 5–73–19.
73 See UYPD 8–30–1.
74 Ronald Segal, *African Profiles* (Harmondsworth: Penguin, 1962).
75 Patrick Duncan's unpublished autobiography, ch. 4, f. 43. UYPD 9–1.
76 ibid. ch. 4. f. 44.
77 *New Age* (Cape Town), 22 Nov 1956.
78 Peter Brown to Patrick Duncan, 4 Dec 1956. UYPD 8–16–55.
79 Patrick Duncan's unpublished autobiography, ch. 4, f. 75. UYPD 9–1.
80 Liberal Party National Organizer's report, 19 Dec 1956. UYPD 8–28–3.
81 Liberal Party National Organizer's report on visit to ANC Conference at Queenstown. UYPD 8–28–3.
82 Alan Paton to Patrick Duncan, 29 Dec 1956. UYPD 8–17–12.
83 Statement by Alan Paton (enclosed with letter of 29 Dec 1956). UYPD 8–17–12.
84 Patrick Duncan to Alan Paton, 3 Feb 1957. UYPD 8–17–14.
85 Alan Paton to Patrick Duncan, 30 May 1957. UYPD 8–17–20.
86 *Liberation*, no. 28 (1957).
87 Alan Paton to Patrick Duncan, 27 Nov 1957. UYPD 8–17–31.
88 Patrick Duncan to B. H. P. Curran, 3 Feb 1958. UYPD 8–29–28.
89 Patrick Duncan to Yusuf Cachalia, 3 Feb 1958. UYPD 8–41–8.

90 Bunting, *Kotane*, op. cit., p. 237.
91 Patrick Duncan to Alan Paton, 11 Nov 1957. UYPD 8–17–30.
92 Patrick Duncan to Peter Brown, 11 Feb 1958. UYPD 8–16–97.
93 Patrick Duncan to Alan Paton, 3 Feb 1958. UYPD 8–17–33.

CHAPTER 8

1 Patrick Duncan to Alan Paton, 11 June 1957. UYPD 11–1–2.
2 ibid.
3 Patrick Duncan's notes from a conversation, 20 July 1957. UYPD 11–1–81.
4 George Clay, 'Memo to correspondents', 27 Dec 1957. UYPD 11–1–84.
5 ibid.
6 Patrick Duncan to George Clay, 3 Feb 1958. UYPD 11–1–53.
7 Patrick Duncan to his wife, 12 March 1958. UYPD 2–4–229.
8 Alan Paton to Patrick Duncan, 11 April 1958. UYPD 8–17–35.
9 Patrick Duncan to Alan Paton, 17 April 1958. UYPD 8–17–36.
10 Patrick Duncan's diary, 19 March 1958. UYPD 3–9.
11 Patrick Duncan to Peter Brown, 3 Feb 1958. UYPD 11–1–48.
12 Notes on a telephone conversation with Bertrand Russell, 20 April 1958. UYPD 6–24–49.
13 Patrick Duncan's diary, 19 March 1958. UYPD 3–9.
14 *Contact*, 13 July 1959.
15 Patrick Duncan to Julius Lewin, 29 Dec 1959. UYPD 11–5–106.
16 Patrick Duncan's notes on a conversation with Anthony Clarke, 12 Aug 1958. UYPD 11–16–36.
17 Undated, unsigned memo, *c*.Aug 1958. UYPD 11–16–54.
18 Patrick Duncan to Julius Lewin, 14 April 1949. UYPD 11–5–80.
19 Colin Legum to Patrick Duncan, 18 Feb 1959. UYPD 11–5–48.
20 All-African Peoples' Conference, Provisional Agenda. UYPD 8–14–2.
21 *Sunday Express* (Johannesburg), 14 Dec 1958.
22 *Cape Times*, 15 Dec 1958.
23 ANCYL circular signed by Tennyson Makiwane, 19 Dec 1958. UYPD 8–54–60.
24 Chinua Achebe, *Man of the People* (London: Heinemann, 1966), p. 60.
25 Christopher Gell to Patrick Duncan, 6 May 1958. UYPD 5–34–90.
26 Patrick Duncan to Christopher Gell, 8 May 1958. UYPD 5–34–92.
27 *Counter Attack* (Johannesburg), Nov/Dec 1958.
28 Patrick Duncan to *Counter Attack*, 23 Dec 1958. UYPD 8–54–56.
29 Patrick Duncan to Alan Paton, 24 Nov 1958. UYPD 5–75–23.
30 ibid.
31 Alan Paton to Patrick Duncan, 25 Nov 1958. UYPD 5–75–24.
32 *Contact*, 2 May 1959.
33 E. Roux, 'Open letter to the Editor', *Contact*, 16 May 1959.
34 *Contact*, 16 May 1959.
35 Alan Paton to Patrick Duncan, 25 May 1959. UYPD 5–75–30.
36 Alan Paton interviewed by C. J. Driver, Cambridge, 1975.
37 *Contact*, 31 Oct 1959.
38 Alan Paton to Patrick Duncan, 4 Aug 1959. UYPD 5–75–35.
39 P. Raboroko, 'The Africanist case , *Africa South*, June 1960.
40 ibid.
41 Randolph Vigne interviewed by Tom Lodge, London, 1975. See also *Contact* 2 May, 30 May, 25 July 1959.

42 Patrick Duncan to Jordan Ngubane, 23 Jan 1958. UYPD 11–1.
43 ibid.
44 Robert Sobukwe to Patrick Duncan, 27 March 1958. UYPD 6–26–29.
45 *Contact*, 31 Oct 1959.
46 Matthew Nkoana interviewed by Tom Lodge, London, 1975.
47 *Contact*, 3 Oct 1959.
48 ibid. 21 Feb 1959.
49 ibid. 19 March 1960.
50 ibid. 31 March 1960.
51 ibid. 8 March 1958.
52 Patrick Duncan, 'Some thoughts on the 1957 Multi-Racial Conference', typed MS, f. 7, undated. UYPD 8–40–1.
53 Patrick Duncan to Alan Paton, 18 Nov 1959. UYPD 5–75–39.
54 *Liberal Party Cape Divisional News*, no. 56, July 1959.
55 *Cape Times*, 13 Oct 1959.
56 Patrick Duncan to Julius Lewin, 14 April 1959. UYPD 11–5–80.
57 Patrick Duncan to Peter Hjul, 14 Oct 1966. UYPD 5–42–12.

CHAPTER 9

1 Patrick Duncan, 'The two thousand', *Contact*, 16 April 1960.
2 *Friend* (Bloemfontein), 28 Jan 1960.
3 Patrick Duncan to Peter Brown, 10 Feb 1960. UYPD 5–14–97.
4 *Contact*, 20 Feb 1960.
5 Quoted in ibid.
6 Quoted in ibid.
7 Text in ibid.
8 Complete text in Marion Friedmann (ed.), *I Shall Still Be Moved* (London, 1963), p. 92.
9 Collingwood August's diary, 21 March 1960. UYPD 8–71–6.
10 Philip Kgosana, 'How I organized the Pass Campaign', pt II, *Drum*, March 1961.
11 Patrick Duncan's diary, 21 March 1960. UYPD 3–9.
12 *Contact*, 2 April 1960.
13 Patrick Duncan's diary, 23 March 1960. UYPD 3–9.
14 ibid. 24 March 1960.
15 Typed MS by Philip Kgosana on events of March–April 1960, dated Nov 1975. UYPD 5–53–4.
16 Patrick Duncan's diary, 25 March 1960. UYPD 3–9.
17 Kgosana's press statement to the Chicago Associated Negro Press, 19 July 1963. UYPD 5–53–3.
18 Peter Hjul interviewed by Tom Lodge, London, 1976.
19 Collingwood August's diary, 25 March 1960. UYPD 8–71–6.
20 Patrick Duncan's diary, 28 March 1960. UYPD 8–71–5.
21 Anthony Delius interviewed by Tom Lodge, London, 1975.
22 Patrick Duncan's diary, 30 March 1960. UYPD 8–71–5.
23 Kgosana typescript, 1975. UYPD 5–53–4.
24 Eulalie Stott interviewed by Tom Lodge, Cape Town, 1976.
25 R. W. Johnston, *How Long Can South Africa Survive?* (London: Macmillan, 1977).
26 Peter Hjul interviewed by Tom Lodge, London, 1976.
27 *Cape Times*, 1 April 1960.
28 Patrick Duncan's diary, 25 March 1960. UYPD 8–71–5.

29 ibid. 31 March 1960. UYPD 8–71–5.
30 *Contact*, 16 April 1960.
31 Patrick Duncan's diary, 29 Dec 1961, f. 43. UYPD 3–9.
32 Figures extrapolated from *Contact* files. UYPD 11–58–11–85.
33 Colin Legum to David Astor, 7 May 1960. UYPD 5–5–25.
34 *Cape Argus*, 31 May 1960.
35 ibid. 30 June 1960.
36 ibid. 29 July 1960.
37 John Duncan interviewed by C. J. Driver, York, 1976.
38 Patrick Duncan to his wife, 1 Aug 1960. UYPD 2–4–238.
39 ibid. 9 Aug 1960. UYPD 2–4–245.
40 *Cape Argus*, 25 Aug 1960.
41 Patrick Duncan, 'Report on a journey around South Africa', 27 July–30 Aug 1960. UYPD 8–39–1.
42 *Contact*, 2 July 1960.
43 Patrick Duncan, 'Report on a journey around South Africa'. UYPD 8–39–1.
44 ibid.
45 ibid.
46 *Contact*, 30 July 1960.
47 ibid. 27 Aug 1960.
48 *Friend* (Bloemfontein), 12 Oct 1960.
49 *Star* (Johannesburg), 18 Oct 1960.
50 *Cape Argus*, 25 March 1960.
51 Patrick Duncan's diary, 29 Dec 1961, f. 43. UYPD 3–9.
52 ibid.
53 Patrick Duncan to his wife, 20 Oct 1960. UYPD 2–4–250.
54 Patrick Duncan's diary, 29 Dec 1961, f. 43. UYPD 3–9.
55 Patrick Duncan's unpublished autobiography, ch. 1, f. 2. UYPD 9–1.
56 L. Blom-Cooper, *The Law as Literature* (London: Bodley Head, 1961).
57 'The *Contact* case', *Contact*, 3 Dec 1960.
58 *Cape Times*, 30 Nov 1960.
59 *Indian Opinion*, 9 Oct 1960.
60 Patrick Duncan in ibid. 13 Jan 1960.
61 Patrick Duncan to David Astor, 12 Nov 1960. UYPD 5–5–33.
62 ibid. 17 July 1962. UYPD 5–5–47.
63 *Contact*, 4 June 1960.
64 Patrick Duncan's diary, 29 Dec 1961, f. 44. UYPD 3–9.
65 *Contact*, 31 Dec 1960.
66 Matthew Nkoana interviewed by Tom Lodge, London, 1975.
67 Peter Hjul interviewed by Tom Lodge, London, 1976.
68 Matthew Nkoana interviewed by Tom Lodge, London, 1975.
69 *Contact*, 1 June 1961.
70 Nelson Mandela, *No Easy Walk to Freedom* (London: Heinemann, 1965), p. 105.
71 *Contact*, 28 Dec 1961.
72 Randolph Vigne interviewed by Tom Lodge, London, 1975.
73 Patrick Duncan to his wife, 12 Jan 1961. UYPD 2–4–252.
74 ibid. Jan 1961. UYPD 2–4–254.
75 *Contact*, 16 June 1961.
76 Patrick Duncan to David Astor, 27 March 1961. UYPD 5–5–39.
77 ibid. 8 Sept 1961. UYPD 5–5–4.
78 ibid. 28 Nov 1961. UYPD 5–5–52.
79 Letter from Cyril Dunn to Tom Lodge, 24 Feb 1976.
80 *Cape Times*, 12 April 1961.

81 Unattributable source.
82 *Cape Argus*, 7 Sept 1960.
83 *Contact*, 3 Dec 1960.
84 *New Age*, 22 Dec 1960.
85 ibid. 23 Feb 1961.
86 *Contact*, 25 Feb 1961.
87 *New Age*, 2 March 1961.
88 *Contact*, 9 March 1961, or his letter to *New Age*, 9 March 1961.
89 ibid. 2 Nov 1961.
90 *Cape Argus*, 28 Feb 1961.
91 Patrick Duncan's diary, 29 Dec 1961, f. 42. UYPD 3–9.
92 *Fighting Talk*, June 1961.
93 Patrick Duncan's diary, 29 Dec 1961, f. 46. UYPD 3–9.
94 ibid.
95 *Contact*, 25 Jan 1962.
96 See 'Bechuanaland betrayed' in *Contact*, 13 July 1961.
97 *Contact*, 19 Nov 1960.
98 Patrick Duncan's diary, entry for 29 Dec 1961, f. 47. UYPD 3–9.
99 ibid.
100 Patrick Duncan's diary of a journey to the Transkei, April 1962, f. 5. UYPD 8–39–6.
101 ibid. f. 6.
102 *Cape Times*, 30 April 1962.
103 Patrick Duncan to his wife, 4 May 1962. UYPD 2–4–271.

CHAPTER 10

1 *Sunday Times* (Johannesburg), 5 May 1962.
2 Patrick Duncan to his wife, 5 May 1962. UYPD 2–4–272.
3 Patrick Duncan to Jane Symonds, 7 May 1962. UYPD 5–1–17.
4 Patrick Duncan to his wife, 16 May 1962. UYPD 2–4–281.
5 Patrick Duncan to Deborah Cowen, 15 June 1962. UYPD 2–8–65.
6 Memorandum written by Leabua Jonathan, June 1976. UYPD 5–49–2.
7 Patrick Duncan to his wife, 16 May 1962. UYPD 2–4–281.
8 B. K. Khaketla, *Lesotho, 1970* (London: Hurst, 1971), p. 28.
9 Patrick Duncan to Horace Coaker, 20 June 1962. UYPD 6–31–104.
10 Patrick Duncan to A. F. Giles, 13 June 1962. UYPD 6–31.
11 Chairman of Housing Committee to Patrick Duncan, 16 July 1962. UYPD 6–31.
12 Patrick Duncan to his wife, 30 July 1962. UYPD 2–4–310.
13 ibid. 30 July 1962.
14 ibid. 30 July 1962.
15 ibid. 15 Aug 1962. UYPD 2–4–319.
16 ibid. 15 Aug 1962. UYPD 2–4–310.
17 ibid. 9 Sept 1962. UYPD 2–4–326.
18 Randolph Vigne interviewed by Tom Lodge, London, 1975.
19 Patrick Duncan to Julius Lewin, 21 Feb 1963. UYPD 5–61.
20 Patrick Duncan to Deborah Cowen, March 1963. UYPD 2.
21 Untitled typescript. UYPD 9–2–8.
22 Paton seems to have been referring to E. L. Ntloedibe's 'Race and nationhood', in *New African*, vol. 1, no. 9, Sept 1962, not to any article in *Contact*.
23 Patrick Duncan to Peter Brown, 22 Oct 1962. UYPD 5–14–114.
24 Philip Kgosana to Patrick Duncan, Jan 1962. UYPD 8–42–2.
25 Patrick Duncan to Peter Brown, 21 July 1962. UYPD 5–14–112.

26 Letter from unattributable source to Tom Lodge, 4 July 1976.
27 Patrick Duncan to Peter Brown, 13 Dec 1962. UYPD 5–14–117.
28 Peter Brown to Patrick Duncan, 14 Dec 1962. UYPD 5–14–118.
29 ibid. 25 Feb 1963. UYPD 5–14–120.
30 Patrick Duncan to Peter Brown, 16 March 1963. UYPD 5–14–122.
31 Statement dated 11 March 1963. UYPD 5–14–121.
32 *Institute of Race Relations Newsletter* (London), July 1964.
33 Philip Kgosana, 'How I organized the Pass Campaign', pt 1, *Drum*, Feb 1961.
34 Unattributable source.
35 For a favourable description of P. K. Leballo see Jordan Ngubane, *An African Explains Apartheid* (London and Dunmow: Pall Mall Press, 1961), p. 101.
36 Pan-Africanist Congress, Declaration of Membership. UYPD 8–44–2.
37 Unattributable source to Patrick Duncan, Jan 1963. UYPD 8–43–6.
38 *Contact*, 5 April 1963.
39 *Cape Times*, 28 May 1963; *Contact*, 19 April 1963; *The Times*, 20 April 1963.
40 Patrick Duncan to Cyprian Thorpe, 6 June 1964. UYPD 5–95–49.
41 Patrick Duncan to Philip Mason, 5 Nov 1964. UYPD 5–46–30.
42 Philip Mason interviewed by Tom Lodge, London, 1975.
43 Unattributable source.
44 Government of South Africa, *Report of the Commission Appointed to Inquire into the Events on the 20th to 22nd November, 1962, at Paarl* (Cape Town, 1963), p. 9.
45 *Star* (Johannesburg), 10 April 1963.
46 *The Times*, 5 June 1963.
47 *Hansard*, 20 June 1963, p. 88.
48 Duncan Sandys to Fenner Brockway, 17 March 1963. UYPD 8–52–6.
49 Patrick Duncan to Fenner Brockway, 15 Aug 1963. UYPD 8–52–7.
50 'Basuto reject speech from the throne', *Basutoland News*, 3 Sept 1963, p. 4.
51 Paramount Chief Moshoeshoe II to Patrick Duncan, 10 July 1963. UYPD 7–32.
52 Patrick Duncan to Paramount Chief Moshoeshoe II, 25 July 1963. UYPD 7–32.
53 Patrick Duncan to Hans Schmoller, 27 July 1963. UYPD 5–86–3.
54 Patrick Duncan to his wife, 15 Aug 1963. UYPD 2–4–385.
55 ibid. 1 Aug 1963. UYPD 2–4–313.
56 ibid. 10 Aug 1963. UYPD 2–4–382.
57 *Foreign Affairs*, Oct 1963.
58 Patrick Duncan to his wife, 16 Aug 1963. UYPD 2–4–385.
59 ibid. 22 Aug 1963. UYPD 2–4–389.
60 ibid. 23 Aug 1963. UYPD 2–4–390.
61 *New York Times*, 11 Sept 1963.
62 Conor Cruise O'Brien to Patrick Duncan, 23 Dec 1963. UYPD 6–34–222.
63 Patrick Duncan to Conor Cruise O'Brien, 8 Jan 1964. UYPD 6–34–223.
64 Patrick Duncan's diary, entry for 10 June 1957. UYPD 3–9.
65 Patrick Duncan to Julius Lewin, 21 Feb 1963. UYPD 5–61–71.
66 Patrick Duncan to Deborah Cowen, 21 Sept 1963. UYPD 2–8–94.
67 Patrick Duncan to Tim Holmes, 21 Sept 1963. UYPD 5–44–5.
68 Patrick Duncan to Freya von Moltke, 31 Aug 1964. UYPD 5–98–16.
69 Freya von Moltke to Patrick Duncan, 26 Oct 1963. UYPD 5–98–14.
70 Patrick Duncan, *South Africa's Rule of Violence* (London: Methuen, 1964), pp. 98–9.
71 Transcript of a recorded conversation between Richard Hare and Patrick Duncan, 'Blacks, whites, and animals in Africa'. UYPD 9–5.
72 Patrick Duncan's diary of his visit to Tanzania, 1964. UYPD 8–46–1.
73 Patrick Duncan to his wife, 2 Feb 1964. UYPD 2–4–406.
74 Patrick Duncan's diary of his visit to Tanzania, 1964. UYPD 8–46–1.

CHAPTER 11

1   P. K. Leballo's letter of introduction for Patrick Duncan. UYPD 8–44–3.
2   Patrick Duncan to his wife, 28 May 1964. UYPD 2–4–413.
3   'Promise for nine small trees in Algeria', *The Times*, 23 April 1965.
4   Patrick Duncan 'Day of the tree', unpublished typescript, 5 April 1964. UYPD 9–6.
5   Patrick Duncan to John Blundell, 11 Dec 1965. UYPD 6–36–14.
6   Patrick Duncan to the South African Ministry of Interior, 11 April 1964. UYPD 8–52–18.
7   Patrick Duncan to Peter Benenson, 2 June 1964. UYPD 5–3.
8   Patrick Duncan's report on work at PAC office, Algiers, May–Dec 1964. UYPD 8–44–6.
9   Patrick Duncan to Anthony Steel, 4 Nov 1964. UYPD 8–48–56.
10 Report on work at PAC office, Algiers, May–Dec 1964. UYPD 8–44–6.
11 Patrick Duncan to Randolph Vigne, 22 March 1965. UYPD 5–97–61.
12 *Le Peuple Algier*, 20 March 1965.
13 Patrick Duncan to Anthony Steel, 5 June 1964. UYPD 8–48–46.
14 Patrick Duncan to David Astor, 19 Feb 1965. UYPD 5–5–73.
15 ibid. 10 Aug 1965. UYPD 5–5.
16 ibid. 10 Oct 1964. UYPD 5–5–69.
17 ibid. 18 July 1965. UYPD 5–5–77.
18 Randolph Vigne to Patrick Duncan, 12 June 1966. UYPD 5–97–101.
19 Patrick Duncan to Randolph Vigne, 22 June 1966. UYPD 5–97–102.
20 Patrick Duncan to Adam Hochschild, 30 Oct 1964. UYPD 5–43–23.
21 Patrick Duncan to C. J. Driver, 11 Dec 1964. UYPD 6–35–86.
22 Patrick Duncan to Amnesty International, 27 Aug 1964. UYPD 5–3–22.
23 Patrick Duncan to Walter Lamont, 19 June 1964. UYPD.
24 Patrick Duncan to George Houser, 14 May 1965. UYPD 5–2–107.
25 Patrick Duncan to Randolph Vigne, 21 Dec 1964. UYPD 5–97–54.
26 Patrick Duncan to David Astor, 27 July 1966. UYPD 5–5–79.
27 Patrick Duncan to Harold Hochschild, 18 Aug 1965. UYPD 5–43–3.
28 Patrick Duncan, unpublished article, 'Two nations are struggling for the land of South Africa'. UYPD 9–6–2.
29 Matthew Nkoana interviewed by Tom Lodge, London, 1975.
30 Patrick Duncan to Randolph Vigne, 20 Aug 1965. UYPD 5–97–84.
31 The letter of dismissal is missing from Duncan's papers. It is described in a letter by Duncan to Randolph Vigne, July 1965. UYPD 5–97–82.
32 Patrick Duncan to P. K. Leballo, 31 Aug 1965. UYPD 8–48–12.
33 P. K. Leballo and P. Raboroko to Patrick Duncan, 9 Sept 1965. UYPD 8–48–13.
34 Patrick Duncan to Randolph Vigne, 2 April 1965. UYPD 5–97–64.
35 ibid. 21 March 1965. UYPD 5–97–59.
36 ibid. 2 April 1965. UYPD 5–97–64.
37 ibid. July 1965. UYPD 5–97–82.
38 Patrick Duncan to George Mbele, 2 April 1965. UYPD 6–35–227.
39 Patrick Duncan to Randolph Vigne, 14 May 1965. UYPD 5–97–69.
40 ibid. 20 May 1965. UYPD 5–97–71.
41 ibid. 2 July 1965. UYPD 5–97–80.
42 Patrick Duncan to John Blundell, 11 Dec 1965. UYPD 6–36–14.
43 Patrick Duncan to Randolph Vigne, 9 Nov 1965. UYPD 5–97–87.
44 ibid. 26 Jan 1966. UYPD 5–97–92.
45 Patrick Duncan to Anthony Steel, 3 Sept 1965. UYPD 8–48–67.

46 Mimmie Tsele to Patrick Duncan, 21 Oct 1965. UYPD 8–48–68.
47 Patrick Duncan to Mimmie Tsele, 12 Nov 1965. UYPD 8–48–69.
48 Patrick Duncan to Randolph Vigne, 9 Nov 1965. UYPD 5–97–87.
49 Patrick Duncan to Peter Hjul, 18 March 1966. UYPD 5–42.
50 Mary Benson, *Struggle for a Birthright* (Harmondsworth: Penguin, 1966), p. 266.
51 Patrick Duncan to Mary Benson, 19 Dec 1966. UYPD 5–9–61.
52 *Star* (Johannesburg), 19 May 1964.
53 *Cape Argus*, 7 May 1965.
54 *Rand Daily Mail*, 1 March 1965.
55 Author's recollection.
56 Patrick Duncan to Randolph Vigne, 18 Aug 1964. UYPD 5–97–50.
57 ibid. 9 Nov 1964. UYPD 5–97–47.
58 Patrick Duncan to A———, 29 Jan 1967. UYPD 5–97–112.
59 Patrick Duncan to Randolph Vigne, 8 Feb 1967. UYPD 5–97–115.
60 Patrick Duncan to *Contact*, 7 June 1965. UYPD 5–97–77.
61 Patrick Duncan to Randolph Vigne, 9 Nov 1964. UYPD 5–97–47. For Alan Paton's statement disassociating Liberals from ARM saboteurs see Robertson, *Liberalism in South Africa*, op. cit., p. 225.
62 Patrick Duncan to Randolph Vigne, 21 Dec 1964. UYPD 5–97–54.
63 Peter Hjul to Patrick Duncan, 9 Nov 1965. UYPD 5–42–7.

CHAPTER 12

1 Patrick Duncan to Anthony Steel, 3 Sept 1965. UYPD 8–48–67.
2 Patrick Duncan to Randolph Vigne, 20 Aug 1965. UYPD 5–97–84.
3 Patrick Duncan to Hans Schmoller, 29 Oct 1965. UYPD 5–86–51.
4 Patrick Duncan to Denis Cowen, 13 Aug 1963. UYPD 2–8.
5 Alex Duncan to C. J. Driver, 10 Oct 1975.
6 Patrick Duncan to Peter Hjul, 17 Nov 1965. UYPD 5–42–8.
7 See UYPD 5–19.
8 Patrick Duncan to Alex Duncan, 30 Sept 1965. UYPD 2–10.
9 Patrick Duncan to John Blundell, 11 Dec 1965. UYPD 6–36–14.
10 ibid.
11 Patrick Duncan to his son Alex, 30 Sept 1965. UYPD 2–10.
12 Patrick Duncan to Hans Schmoller, 29 Oct 1965. UYPD 5–86–51.
13 Patrick Duncan to his son Patrick, 30 Sept 1965. UYPD 2–10.
14 Patrick Duncan to his son Alex, 30 Sept 1965. UYPD 2–10.
15 Patrick Duncan to his son Patrick, 30 Sept 1965. UYPD 2–10.
16 ibid.
17 Patrick Duncan to his son Alex, 30 Sept 1965. UYPD 2–10.
18 Patrick Duncan to Father Benoit, 15 March 1963. UYPD 6–31–30.
19 Patrick Duncan (jnr) to C. J. Driver, 20 Aug 1976.
20 Ann Duncan to C. J. Driver, 7 July 1976.
21 Patrick Duncan (jnr) to C. J. Driver, 20 Aug 1976.
22 Emma Duncan to C. J. Driver, July 1976.
23 Vincent Phoofolo to Patrick Duncan, 30 Jan 1964. UYPD 5–77–3.
24 ibid. 29 Nov 1965. UYPD 5–77–14.
25 ibid.
26 Patrick Duncan to Father Benoit, 15 March 1963. UYPD 6–31–30.
27 Patrick Duncan to Hans Schmoller, 22 March 1965. UYPD 5–86–47.
28 Undated MS, 'The churches' role in Africa'. UYPD 9–5.
29 Patrick Duncan to Hans Schmoller, 12 NOv 1965. UYPD 5–86–52.

30 Patrick Duncan to John Blundell, 11 Dec 1965. UYPD 6–36–14.
31 Patrick Duncan to his father, 27 Nov 1939. UYPD 2–3–302.
32 Patrick Duncan to Hans Schmoller, 29 Oct 1965. UYPD 5–86–51.
33 Patrick Duncan to Randolph Vigne, 3 March 1967. UYPD 5–97–117.
34 Patrick Duncan to Julius Lewin, 21 Feb 1963. UYPD 5–61–71.
35 Patrick Duncan to Marion Friedmann, 11 Feb 1963. UYPD 6–31–212.
36 Patrick Duncan to Hans Schmoller, 22 March 1963. UYPD 5–86–47.
37 Patrick Duncan, *Man and the Earth* (Peterhead: Volturna Press, 1974), p. 13.
38 Patrick Duncan to Alan Paton, 24 April 1967. UYPD 5–75–54.
39 Patrick Duncan to Randolph Vigne, 3 March 1967. UYPD 5–97–117.
40 Hans Schmoller to Patrick Duncan, 20 Nov 1965. UYPD 5–86–53.
41 Patrick Duncan to Randolph Vigne, 3 March 1967. UYPD 5–97–117.
42 Patrick Duncan to Frances Baker, 7 Dec 1966. UYPD 5–6–34.
43 Eva J. Weddigen, Associated Mission Medical Office, Supplement to Health Report, 1 June 1966. UYPD 13–3.
44 Dr Röllinghoff to Eva J. Weddigen, 25 May 1966. UYPD 13–3.
45 Patrick Duncan to Frances Baker, 7 Dec 1966. UYPD 5–6–34.
46 ibid.
47 ibid.
48 Patrick Duncan to Naomi Mitchison, 22 Jan 1965. UYPD 5–70–13.
49 Patrick Duncan to Frances Baker, 7 Dec 1966. UYPD 5–6–34.
50 ibid.
51 ibid.
52 Patrick Duncan to his wife, 8 Oct 1966. UYPD 2–4–483.
53 Patrick Duncan to Frances Baker, 7 Dec 1966. UYPD 5–6–34.
54 *The Times*, 6 Oct 1966.
55 Patrick Duncan to Association of Commonwealth Universities, 17 Oct 1966. UYPD 6–37.
56 Patrick Duncan to Randolph Vigne, 10 Oct 1966. UYPD 5–97–108.
57 Patrick Duncan to Frances Baker, 7 Dec 1966. UYPD 5–6–34.
58 Patrick Duncan to his wife, 14 Oct 1966. UYPD 2–4–491.
59 ibid. 18 Oct 1966. UYPD 2–4–495.
60 ibid. 22 Oct 1966. UYPD 2–4–499.
61 Patrick Duncan to Frances Baker, 7 Dec 1966. UYPD 5–6–34.
62 Patrick Duncan to his wife, 23 Oct 1966. UYPD 2–4–500.
63 Patrick Duncan to Alan Paton, 22 Dec 1966. UYPD 5–75–53.
64 Jim Paton to Patrick Duncan, 2 Dec 1966. UYPD 5–19.
65 Patrick Duncan to Jim Paton, 28 Dec 1966. UYPD 5–19.
66 Patrick Duncan to Randolph Vigne, 8 Feb 1967. UYPD 5–97–115.
67 Simon Joseph to Cynthia Duncan, 17 June 1967.
68 Patrick Duncan to Frances Baker, 7 Dec 1966. UYPD 5–6–34.
69 ibid.
70 Patrick Duncan to his wife, 23 Dec 1966. UYPD 2–4–527.
71 Adam Hochschild to Tom Lodge, 27 March 1976.
72 *New Scientist*, 8 Dec 1966.
73 *Punch*, 4 Jan 1967.
74 Patrick Duncan to Randolph Vigne, 29 Jan 1967. UYPD 5–97–112.
75 ibid. 29 Jan 1967. UYPD 5–97–112.
76 ibid. 8 Feb 1967. UYPD 5–97–115.
77 ibid. 13 Feb 1967. UYPD 5–97–116.
78 Patrick Duncan to Dr Taylor, 13 March 1967. UYPD 6–37.
79 Patrick Duncan to Alan Paton, 24 April 1967. UYPD 5–75–54.
80 Patrick Duncan's notes on his vision in the desert, April 1967. UYPD 9–8.
81 Otto Spohr to Degenhardt, 5 March 1975. UYPD 5–92–4.

82   Walter Oakeshott to Patrick Duncan, 7 March 1967. UYPD 6–37.
83   Patrick Duncan to his wife, 1 May 1967. UYPD 2–4–539.
84   ibid. 22 May 1967. UYPD 2–4–543.
85   Patrick Duncan to Jack Vincent, 22 May 1967. UYPD 6–37.
86   Christopher Powell to Tom Lodge, 8 Nov 1975.
87   Cynthia Duncan to David Astor, 16 June 1966. UYPD 5–5–84.

CHAPTER 13

1   Patrick Duncan to Alan Paton, 22 Dec 1966. UYPD 5–75–53.
2   Patrick Duncan to K. Ntsane, 4 May 1953. UYPD 6–20–27.
3   Patrick Duncan to Christopher Hill, 14 Dec 1964. UYPD 5–46–34.
4   Patrick Duncan to Hans Schmoller, 22 March 1965. UYPD 5–86–47.
5   ibid.
6   Jan Kott, 'King Lear, or Endgame' in *Shakespeare Our Contemporary* (London: Methuen, 1964), pp. 111–12.
7   Patrick Duncan's unpublished autobiography, ch. 1, f. 11. UYPD 9–1.
8   Patrick Duncan to Randolph Vigne, 22 June 1966. UYPD 5–97–102.
9   Patrick Duncan to Editor, *Observer*, 16 Jan 1963. UYPD 5–5–49.
10   Patrick Duncan to Rev. Trevor Bush, 21 Sept 1964. UYPD 5–17–6.
11   Anthony Trollope, *South Africa* (London, 1878).
12   Patrick Duncan to Randolph Vigne, 13 Feb 1967. UYPD 5–97–116.
13   Author's recollection of visiting Patrick Duncan in hospital, 1967.
14   Patrick Duncan to Hans Schmoller, 15 March 1965. UYPD 5–86–45.
15   ibid. 22 March 1965. UYPD 5–86–47.
16   ibid.
17   Patrick Duncan to Alan Paton, 22 Dec 1966. UYPD 5–75–53.
18   Albert Camus, 'The future of tragedy', lecture given in Athens in 1955, trans. Philip Thody (London, 1970).
19   Albert Camus, *The Rebel* (London: Hamilton, 1953), p. 228.
20   A. B. Ngcobo interviewed by Tom Lodge, London, 1975.
21   W. B. Yeats, introduction, *The Oxford Book of Modern Verse* (London: OUP, 1936), p. xxxiv.
22   Helen Gardner, *Religion and Literature* (London: Faber & Faber, 1971), p. 93.
23   Raymond Williams, *Modern Tragedy* (London: Chatto & Windus, 1966), p. 87.

BIBLIOGRAPHY OF BOOKS, PAMPHLETS AND ARTICLES BY PATRICK DUNCAN

This list has five sections: books, pamphlets, articles, shorter newspaper articles, and book reviews. In each, titles are listed in order of date of publication.

BOOKS

Patrick Duncan, *Sotho Laws and Customs*. Cape Town: Oxford University Press, 1960.
Patrick Duncan, *South Africa's Rule of Violence*. London: Methuen, 1964.
Patrick Duncan, *Man and the Earth*. Peterhead, Aberdeenshire: Volturna Press, 1975.

PAMPHLETS

'Melanchthon', *The Enemy*. Morija, 1943.
'Melanchthon', *Three Centuries of Wrong*. Johannesburg: White Ltd, 6 April 1952.
Patrick Duncan, *The Road through the Wilderness*. Johannesburg: Hygrade Printers, May 1953.

ARTICLES

Patrick Duncan, 'The Hex River crash', in *The Ridge Preparatory School Magazine*, Johannesburg, April 1928.
Patrick Duncan, 'Moral elements in South African politics', in *Forum*, Johannesburg, December 1952.
Patrick Duncan, 'English in South Africa a subordinate minority', in *Forum*, Johannesburg, June 1953.
Patrick Duncan, '*Satyagraha* in South Africa', in *Round Table*, London, March 1953.
Patrick Duncan, 'Africa can be saved', in *New Republic*, Washington, DC, 19 October 1953.
Patrick Duncan, 'Dr Malan and Basutoland', in *Forum*, Johannesburg, May 1954.
Patrick Duncan, 'Basutoland, land of promise', in *Black Sash*, Johannesburg, April 1956.
Patrick Duncan, 'Inside Strijdom's South Africa', in *Africa Today*, New York, May–June 1956.
Patrick Duncan, 'Passive resistance', in *Africa South*, Cape Town, October–December 1956.
Patrick Duncan, 'Liberal Party analysed: a reply', in *Forum*, Johannesburg, February 1957.
Patrick Duncan, 'South Africa after the Nationalists', in *Liberation*, Johannesburg, November 1957.

Patrick Duncan, 'Britain's Protectorates threatened by South Africa', in *United Nations News*, New York, 1957.

Patrick Duncan, 'Non-violence at Accra', in *Africa Today*, January–February 1959.

Patrick Duncan, 'Violence or non-violence', in *Africa Special Report*, February 1959.

Patrick Duncan, 'The world takes up the challenge: some thoughts on the economic boycott', in *Tsopano*, Blantyre, January 1960.

Patrick Duncan, 'A statement in answer to the charge of seditious libel', in L. Blom Cooper, *The Law as Literature*. London: Bodley Head, 1961.

Patrick Duncan, 'Notes on my education', in *The New Era*, Cape Town, February 1961.

Patrick Duncan, 'South Africa: America could help', in *New Republic*, Washington, DC, 3 July 1961.

Patrick Duncan, 'South Africa's knife-edge', in *New African*, Cape Town, March 1962.

Patrick Duncan, 'Now the Great Debate is over', in *Southern Africa*, London, 5 April 1963.

Patrick Duncan, 'The overthrow of *apartheid*', in *New Republic*, Washington, DC, 3 September 1963.

Patrick Duncan, 'Should the West intervene with force?', in *Current* (United States), June 1963.

Patrick Duncan, 'The conflict ahead', in *Rally* (United States), September 1963.

Patrick Duncan, 'Towards a world policy for South Africa', in *Foreign Affairs*, Washington, DC, October 1963.

Patrick Duncan, 'End of the Colonial Era', in *Forum* (United Nations), New York, Autumn 1963.

Patrick Duncan, 'Comment je vois la fin de l'apartheid', in *Jeune Afrique*, Paris, 4 November 1963.

Patrick Duncan, 'South Africa: other views', in *Encounter*, London and New York, December 1963.

Patrick Duncan, 'South-West Africa: a timetable for freedom', in *The Nation*, New York, 16 March 1964.

Patrick Duncan, 'Une lettre du PAC', in *Revolution Africaine*, Algiers, 30 May 1964.

Patrick Duncan, 'Mort a l'apartheid', in *Revolution Africaine*, Algiers, 12 September 1964.

Patrick Duncan, 'The principles and policy of the PAC', in *Mainstream* (India), 6 February 1965.

'Sebaretlane', 'The price of withdrawal', in *New African*, London, March 1965.

Patrick Duncan, 'Is *apartheid* an insoluble problem?', in *Race*, London, April 1965.

SHORTER NEWSPAPER ARTICLES

Efforts have been made to trace and locate as much of Duncan's work as possible. However, the list below is incomplete: references in Duncan's papers to published material were sometimes very vague and in any case the more ephemeral *Contact* items have been deliberately omitted.

Patrick Duncan, 'Memo on *apartheid* to UN Committee on South Africa', in *Indian Opinion*, Phoenix (Natal), 24 July 1953.

Patrick Duncan, 'The certainty of victory', in *Indian Opinion*, Phoenix (Natal), 7 August 1953.

Patrick Duncan, 'Wanted – goodwill and justice', in *Indian Opinion*, Phoenix (Natal), 18 September 1953.

Patrick Duncan, 'Battle for soil being won by co-operation', in *The Friend*, Bloemfontein, 28 September 1953.

Patrick Duncan, 'My two weeks in gaol', in *The Observer*, London, 27 December 1953.

Patrick Duncan, 'Africa: what can one do?', in *International Fellowship of Reconciliation Newsletter*, London, March 1954.

Patrick Duncan, 'The traditional South African way of life', in *Indian Opinion*, Phoenix (Natal), 18 December 1954.

Patrick Duncan, 'The future of Basutoland (1): Recommendations to end dualism in Basutoland government', in *The Friend*, Bloemfontein, 12 January 1955.

Patrick Duncan, 'The future of Basutoland (2): Why Moore Report is being opposed by Chiefs', in *The Friend*, Bloemfontein, 13 January 1955.

Patrick Duncan, 'Why the Protectorates should stay British', in *Golden City Post*, Johannesburg, 6 January 1955.

Patrick Duncan, 'Now Malan has gone', in *Indian Opinion*, Phoenix (Natal), 28 January 1955.

Patrick Duncan, 'On organization and organizations', in *Indian Opinion*, Phoenix (Natal), 4 March 1955.

Patrick Duncan, 'Our racial disease', in *Indian Opinion*, Phoenix (Natal), 29 April 1955.

Patrick Duncan, 'The situation in the Union', in *Mohlabani*, Maseru, July 1955.

Patrick Duncan, 'Stephen Ramosodi', in *Indian Opinion*, Phoenix (Natal), 5 August 1955.

Patrick Duncan, 'African opinion', in *Indian Opinion*, Phoenix (Natal), 7 October 1955.

Patrick Duncan, 'After *apartheid* ... what?', in *Indian Opinion*, Phoenix (Natal), 3 February 1956.

Patrick Duncan, 'A plea for neutrality', in *Fighting Talk*, Johannesburg, April 1956.

Patrick Duncan, 'Manilal Gandhi' (obituary) in *Contact*, Pietermaritzberg, April 1956.

Patrick Duncan, 'Why Tomlinson won't work', in *Indian Opinion*, Phoenix (Natal), 4 May 1956.

Patrick Duncan, editorials in *Contact*, Cape Town, from 14 June 1958 to 31 May 1962. (Only the longer and more important ones will be mentioned in this list.)

Patrick Duncan, 'I say', in *Contact*, Cape Town, 14 June 1958.

Patrick Duncan, 'Fair comment', in each issue of *Contact*, Cape Town, from 28 June 1958 to 20 February 1960 and 7 May 1960 to 30 July 1960 and 10 September 1960 to 24 September 1960.

Patrick Duncan, 'Freedom to trade', in *Indian Opinion*, Phoenix (Natal), 7 September 1960.

Patrick Duncan, 'South Africa is no write off' (editorial), in *Contact*, Cape Town, 8 February 1960.

Patrick Duncan, 'Against the SABRA talks', in *Golden City Post*, Johannesburg, 6 July 1958.

Patrick Duncan, 'A door is opened for the Basuto people', in *Golden City Post*, Johannesburg, 3 August 1958.

Patrick Duncan, 'Basutoland report alarms and annoys Nats', in *Contact*, Cape Town, 9 August 1958.

Patrick Duncan, 'Who's Who among Basutoland leaders', in *Contact*, Cape Town, 9 August 1958.

Patrick Duncan, 'Julius K. Nyerere – Tanganyika's new leader', in *Contact*, Cape Town, 4 October 1958.

Patrick Duncan, 'Significance of Accra Conference for South Africa', in *Cape Times*, Cape Town, 16 December 1958.

Patrick Duncan, 'Pan-Africanism or communism', in *Contact*, Cape Town, 13 December 1958.

Patrick Duncan, 'Liberal delegates played their part at Accra', in *Contact*, Cape Town, 27 December 1958.

Patrick Duncan, 'Pan-African movement', in *Contact*, Cape Town, 27 December 1958.

Patrick Duncan, 'Profile: top Soviet Africanist', in *Contact*, Cape Town, 10 January 1959.

Patrick Duncan, 'Accra Conference in perspective', in *Contact*, Cape Town, 24 January 1959.

Patrick Duncan, 'Open letter to Chief Lutuli', in *Contact*, Cape Town, 2 May 1959.

Patrick Duncan, 'Let's take Kruschev's proposals seriously' (editorial), in *Contact*, Cape Town, 3 October 1959.

Patrick Duncan, 'Lionel Forman' (obituary), in *Contact*, Cape Town, 31 October 1959.

Patrick Duncan, 'The South Africa Foundation', in *Contact*, Cape Town, 29 December 1959.

Patrick Duncan, 'To the Basotho freedom comes with poverty', in *Contact*, Cape Town, 9 January 1960.

Patrick Duncan, 'Basutoland – parties and politics' in *Contact*, Cape Town, 23 January 1960.

Patrick Duncan, 'Ntsu Mokhehle, man of power', in *Contact*, Cape Town, 6 February 1960.

Patrick Duncan, 'Implications of landslide victory for Congress party', in *Contact*, Cape Town, 6 February 1960.

Patrick Duncan, 'United Nations must intervene' (editorial), in *Contact*, Cape Town, 2 April 1960.

Patrick Duncan, 'Fortune favours the brave' (special editorial), in *Contact*, Cape Town, 2 April 1960.

Patrick Duncan, 'The Monday beatings', in *Contact*, Cape Town, 16 April 1960.

Patrick Duncan, 'The two thousand', in *Contact*, Cape Town, 16 April 1960.

Patrick Duncan, 'The power of non-violence' (editorial), in *Contact*, Cape Town, 16 April 1960.

Patrick Duncan, 'Now the Tembus resist', in *Contact*, Cape Town, 24 September 1960.

Patrick Duncan, 'The Congo' (editorial), in *Contact*, Cape Town, 24 September 1960.

Patrick Duncan, 'Nat. poultry farmer has his own farm gaol', in *Contact*, Cape Town, 5 November 1960.

Patrick Duncan, 'Assaults in Roeland Street prison', in *Contact*, Cape Town, 19 November 1960.

Patrick Duncan, 'Anglicans endorse de Blank's line', in *Contact*, Cape Town, 3 December 1960.

Patrick Duncan, 'Progressives try to stifle powers of oppressed', in *Contact*, Cape Town, 17 December 1960.

Patrick Duncan, 'How Progressives weaken struggle for democracy' (special four-page feature on Molteno report), in *Contact*, Cape Town, 17 December 1960.

Patrick Duncan, 'Why *New Age* attacked *Contact*', in *Contact*, Cape Town, 9 March 1961.

Patrick Duncan, 'Liberalism is a revolutionary idea in South Africa', in *Liberal News*, London, 9 March 1961.

Patrick Duncan, 'The 'Maritzburg Conference', in *Contact*, Cape Town, 6 April 1961.

Patrick Duncan, 'The *apartheid* battle may be won very soon', in *Liberal News*, London, 16 April 1961.

Patrick Duncan, 'Stay at home!' (editorial), in *Contact*, Cape Town, 4 May 1961.

Patrick Duncan, 'More blood will flow', in *Liberal News*, London, 25 May 1961.

Patrick Duncan, 'Angola war effects all of southern Africa', in *Contact*, Cape Town, 29 June 1961.

Patrick Duncan, 'Government hides the truth', in *Contact*, Cape Town, 10 August 1961.

Patrick Duncan, 'Is Britain planning to supply arms for *apartheid*?', in *Liberal News*, London, 17 August 1961.

Patrick Duncan, 'Swaziland, Basutoland face big decision', in *Contact*, Cape Town, 7 September 1961.

Patrick Duncan, 'Britain avoids her obligations as a protecting power' (on Ganyile kidnapping), in *Contact*, Cape Town, 19 October 1961.

Patrick Duncan, 'Capitalism – potent instrument to abolish backwardness. Lenin's views examined' (editorial), in *Contact*, Cape Town, 16 November 1961.

Patrick Duncan, 'Stop the bombs!' (editorial), in *Contact*, Cape Town, 28 December 1961.

Patrick Duncan, 'A warning out of Africa', in *Liberal News*, London, 4 January 1962.

Patrick Duncan, 'Why Ganyile was freed', in *Contact*, Cape Town, 25 January 1962.

Patrick Duncan, 'Let's call them backvelders', in *Liberal News*, London, 10 February 1962.

Patrick Duncan, 'Verwoerd bends under pressure', in *Liberal News*, London, 21 April 1962.

Patrick Duncan, 'Questions to British businessmen', in *Liberal News*, London, 19 May 1962.

Patrick Duncan, 'Basutoland – sacrifice for *apartheid*', in *Liberal News*, London, 9 June 1962.

Patrick Duncan, 'How Britain helped Verwoerd's police', in *Tribune*, London, 26 April 1963.

Patrick Duncan, 'Gathering darkness in South Africa', in *The Times*, London, 6 May 1963.

Patrick Duncan, 'Questions and answers on South Africa', in *Peace News*, London, 14 June 1963.

Patrick Duncan, 'Should Britain break with South Africa?' in *Yorkshire Post*, Leeds, 28 October 1963.

Patrick Duncan, 'Last acts of *apartheid*', in *Spectator*, London, 22 November 1963.

Patrick Duncan, 'Flashpoint South Africa', in *Aberdeen Clarion*, December 1963.

Patrick Duncan, 'En losing pa Apartheidproblemat', in *Een Verden*, Copenhagen, December 1963.

Patrick Duncan, 'Promise for nine small trees in Algeria', in *The Times*, London, 23 April 1965.

BOOK REVIEWS

Patrick Duncan, review of R. C. Hunt's *Theory and Practice of Communism*, in *The Economist*, London, 1953.

Patrick Duncan, review of Shaddick's *Land Tenure in Basutoland*, in *Man*, London, January 1957.

Patrick Duncan, review of Filesi's *Communism and Nationalism in Africa*, in *Contact*, Cape Town, 10 January 1959.

Patrick Duncan, review of Henry Pelling's *British Communist Party*, in *Contact*, Cape Town, 21 February 1959.

Patrick Duncan, review of Jordan Ngubane's *An African Explains Apartheid*, in *Institute of Race Relations Newsletter*, London, July 1964.

Patrick Duncan, review of Gordon's *The Passing of French Algeria* in *New African*, London, July 1966.

INDEX OF NAMES

GENERAL INDEX

www.ingramcontent.com/pod-product-compliance
Lightning Source LLC
Chambersburg PA
CBHW060225100726
47907CB00003B/511